Lecture Notes in Business Information Processing 570

Series Editors

LNBIP reports state-of-the-art results in areas related to business information systems and industrial application software development – timely, at a high level, and in both printed and electronic form.

The type of material published includes

- Proceedings (published in time for the respective event)
- Postproceedings (consisting of thoroughly revised and/or extended final papers)
- Other edited monographs (such as, for example, project reports or invited volumes)
- Tutorials (coherently integrated collections of lectures given at advanced courses, seminars, schools, etc.)
- Award-winning or exceptional theses

LNBIP is abstracted/indexed in DBLP, EI and Scopus. LNBIP volumes are also submitted for the inclusion in ISI Proceedings.

Hans-Georg Fill · Yves Wautelet · Jolita Ralyté ·
Jelena Zdravkovic
Editors

The Practice of Enterprise Modeling

18th IFIP Working Conference, PoEM 2025
Geneva, Switzerland, December 3–5, 2025
Proceedings

Springer

Editors
Hans-Georg Fill
University of Fribourg
Fribourg, Switzerland

Jolita Ralyté
CUI
University of Geneva
Carouge, Switzerland

Yves Wautelet
KU Leuven
Brussels, Belgium

Jelena Zdravkovic
Stockholm University
Kista, Sweden

ISSN 1865-1348 ISSN 1865-1356 (electronic)
Lecture Notes in Business Information Processing
ISBN 978-3-032-12062-5 ISBN 978-3-032-12063-2 (eBook)
https://doi.org/10.1007/978-3-032-12063-2

This Springer imprint is published by the registered company Springer Nature Switzerland AG
The registered company address is: Gewerbestrasse 11, 6330 Cham, Switzerland

Preface

This volume of the Lecture Notes in Business Information Processing series contains the proceedings of the 18th IFIP WG 8.1 Working Conference on the Practice of Enterprise Modeling (PoEM), held in Geneva, Switzerland, from December 3 to 5, 2025. The PoEM conference aims to improve the understanding of the practice of topics related to enterprise modeling and architectures by offering a forum for sharing knowledge and future challenges between the academic community and practitioners from industry and the public sector.

This year, the theme of the conference was *Enterprise Modeling for Sustainable Reindustrialization.* The conference attendees got the opportunity to explore novel EM methods, techniques, and tools enabling enterprises to support the reindustrialization of society through the sustainable integration of advanced technologies such as digital twins, robotics, artificial intelligence, and cyber-physical systems. All of these challenges require support to ensure alignment between business and information technology. This congruence is essential for driving innovation, improving operational efficiency, and enabling businesses to adapt to evolving technological demands while maintaining competitiveness.

The discipline *Enterprise Modeling* with its related topics spanning Enterprise Architecture, Requirements, Process and Enterprise Engineering, Driven Approaches, and Ontologies, is well positioned to support scientific advances by providing methods and tools for system development, as well as investigating and reporting on both the current state of research and state of practice.

PoEM 2025 received 44 full paper submissions, with all submissions being in the scope of the conference and reviewed independently by at least three Program Committee (PC) members, in the single-blind form. The recommendations were discussed further by the program co-chairs, before final decisions were made. Following this process, 15 papers were accepted resulting in a 34% acceptance rate. In addition, 4 submissions were accepted as short papers, leading to a total acceptance rate of 43%. Finally, 11 submissions were invited for acceptance to the PoEM Forum.

As a tradition at PoEM, the conference program started with the Workshops, PoEM Forum, Business Case and Tool Demonstrations, and Doctoral Consortium. We would like to thank all the Chairs of these events for their great effort and enrichment of the overall conference program. The main conference included sessions on research papers, keynotes, and a panel.

The accepted papers were grouped into the following topical sessions: *Enterprise Modeling for Sustainable Reindustrialization, AI and Model-Driven Approaches for the Next-Generation Enterprise, Human and Cognitive Dimensions of Enterprise Modeling, Contextual and Process-Oriented Modeling*, and *Intelligent and Secure Digital Transformation.*

The three invited keynote presentations were: (1) *"Green AI in Enterprise Modeling: Challenges and Roadmap"* by Xavier Franch, from the Service and Information System

Engineering department (ESSI) at the Universitat Politècnica de Catalunya, Spain; (2) *"Enterprise Modeling Needs to Integrate Nature as a Stakeholder"* by Birgit Penzenstadler, from the Department of Computer Science and Engineering at Chalmers University of Technology and Gothenburg University, Sweden; and (3) *"Design the business. Architect its future. Enterprise models are key"* by Christian Lichka, from BOC Group, an international leader in Enterprise Management Systems, Switzerland. Speaking on behalf of our community, we are grateful to the keynote speakers for showcasing the significant impact of enterprise modeling research on our society yesterday, today, and tomorrow.

As the editors of this volume, we want to express our heartfelt thanks to all authors submitting their novel research results to the conference, and to the members of the Program Committee for their dedication and expertise in reviewing and discussing paper submissions. We are grateful to the Organizing Committee for arranging all aspects of preparing and running the conference, including its promotion, attracting submissions, administering conference information, designing the portal, communicating, and actioning any progress towards and throughout the conference. Finally, we warmly thank the University of Geneva for hosting PoEM 2025.

December 2025

Hans-Georg Fill
Yves Wautelet
Jolita Ralyté
Jelena Zdravkovic

Organization

General Chairs

Jolita Ralyté	University of Geneva, Switzerland
Jelena Zdravkovic	Stockholm University, Sweden

Program Committee Chairs

Hans-Georg Fill	University of Fribourg, Switzerland
Yves Wautelet	KU Leuven, Belgium

Forum Chairs

Marcela Ruiz	ZHAW, Zurich, Switzerland
Estefanía Serral Asensio	KU Leuven, Belgium

Doctoral Consortium Chairs

Anne Gutschmidt	University of Rostock, Germany
Irina Rychkova	Université Paris 1 Panthéon-Sorbonne, France
Janis Stirna	Stockholm University, Sweden

Business Case and Tool Forum Chairs

Felix Härer	FHNW University of Applied Sciences and Arts, Switzerland
Eva Polini	IIBA Geneva, Switzerland

Workshop Chairs

Saïd Assar	Institut Mines-Télécom Business School, France
Georgios Koutsopoulos	Stockholm University, Sweden

Steering Committee Chairs

Jolita Ralyté	University of Geneva, Switzerland
Kurt Sandkuhl	University of Rostock, Germany
Janis Stirna	Stockholm University, Sweden

Program Committee

João Paulo Almeida	Federal University of Espírito Santo, Brazil
Souvik Barat	Tata Consultancy Services Research, India
Judith Barrios Albornoz	University of Los Andes, Colombia
Dominik Bork	TU Wien, Austria
Robert Andrei Buchmann	Babeş-Bolyai University of Cluj Napoca, Romania
Evellin Cardoso	Free University of Bozen-Bolzano, Italy
Simon Curty	University of Fribourg, Switzerland
Sybren De Kinderen	Eindhoven University of Technology, Netherlands
Peter Fettke	German Research Center for Artificial Intelligence (DFKI) and Saarland University, Germany
Xavier Franch	Universitat Politècnica de Catalunya, Spain
Ulrich Frank	Universität Duisburg-Essen, Germany
Mohamad Gharib	University of Tartu, Estonia
Ana-Maria Ghiran	Babeş-Bolyai University of Cluj-Napoca, Romania
Jaap Gordijn	Vrije Universiteit Amsterdam, Netherlands
Jānis Grabis	Riga Technical University, Latvia
Giancarlo Guizzardi	University of Twente, Netherlands
Simon Hacks	Stockholm University, Sweden
Martin Henkel	Stockholm University, Sweden
Stijn Hoppenbrouwers	HAN University of Applied Sciences, Netherlands
Jennifer Horkoff	University of Gothenburg and Chalmers University of Technology, Sweden
Felix Härer	FHNW University of Applied Sciences and Arts, Switzerland
Christos Kalloniatis	University of the Aegean, Greece
Evangelia Kavakli	University of the Aegean, Greece
Georgios Koutsopoulos	Stockholm University, Sweden
John Krogstie	Norwegian University of Science and Technology, Norway
Julius Köpke	Universität Klagenfurt, Austria

Ulrike Lechner	Universität der Bundeswehr München, Germany
Beatriz Marín	Universitat Politècnica de València, Spain
Raimundas Matulevicius	University of Tartu, Estonia
Andreas L. Opdahl	University of Bergen, Norway
Elda Paja	IT University of Copenhagen, Denmark
Jose Ignacio Panach Navarrete	Universitat de València, Spain
Oscar Pastor	Universidad Politécnica de Valencia, Spain
Geert Poels	Ghent University, Belgium
Henderik A. Proper	TU Wien, Austria
Ben Roelens	Open Universiteit, Ghent University, Belgium
Irina Rychkova	Université Paris 1 Panthéon-Sorbonne, France
Mattia Salnitri	University of Bergamo, Italy
Kurt Sandkuhl	University of Rostock, Germany
Maribel Yasmina Santos	University of Minho, Portugal
Estefanía Serral	KU Leuven, Belgium
Monique Snoeck	KU Leuven, Belgium
Pnina Soffer	University of Haifa, Israel
Janis Stirna	Stockholm University, Sweden
Stefan Strecker	University of Hagen, Germany
Hans Weigand	Tilburg University, Netherlands
Robert Woitsch	BOC Asset Management, Austria

Additional Reviewers

Sven Christ
Alberto Gaspar
George Georgiou
Bastian Kres
Charlotte Verbruggen
Philip Winkler
Paraskevi-Chrysovalantou Zangogianni

Green AI in Enterprise Modeling: Challenges and Roadmap

Xavier Franch

Universitat Politècnica de Catalunya (UPC-BarcelonaTech), Spain
xavier.franch@upc.edu

Abstract. While AI is often framed as a driver of efficiency, its ecological footprint remains largely invisible in current enterprise modeling practices. Green AI proposes a shift in this approach, leveraging environmental sustainability as a key factor for sustainable reindustrialization. This keynote will reflect on the current challenges to incorporate Green AI concepts into enterprise modeling practices, and will propose a roadmap enumerating a number of research actions to overcome these challenges.

Keywords: Environmental Sustainability · Enterprise Modeling · Green AI

The increased adoption of Artificial Intelligence (AI) within Enterprise Information Systems is reshaping the industrial landscape. In the context of Sustainable Reindustrialization, AI is widely promoted as a driver of efficiency and resource-aware optimization. However, this change does not come without a cost: it often overlooks the environmental sustainability demands posed by AI methods and infrastructures, such as the energy consumption of large-scale model training and the carbon footprint of massive inference processes. These considerations align with the emerging trend of **Green AI**, which advocates for shifting attention from performance-centric AI development towards approaches that consider energy efficiency, carbon reduction, and environmental transparency, and promote adequate trade-offs among all these conflicting forces.

This keynote proposes to add environmental sustainability in enterprise modeling as a way to consider Green AI. It will reflect on possible methodological extensions that systematically integrate sustainability concepts, metrics, lifecycle assessment, and architectural decisions into enterprise modeling. By embedding Green AI principles into modeling practices, organizations can move beyond optimizing information systems for accuracy alone and begin to assess their environmental implications as integral design parameters.

The contribution of this keynote is twofold: first, to identify the conceptual and methodological gaps that inhibit the incorporation of Green AI principles into enterprise modeling within AI-intensive industrial settings; and second, to outline a research and practice agenda for modeling environmentally accountable information systems. In doing so, it repositions enterprise modeling as a strategic instrument for aligning AI-enabled transformation processes with current societal environmental demands.

Acknowledgments. This work has been partially supported by the Grant PID2024-156019OB-I00 funded by MICIU/AEI/10.13039/501100011033 and by ERDF, EU.

Enterprise Modeling Needs to Integrate Nature as a Stakeholder

Birgit Penzenstadler[1,2]

[1] Chalmers Technical University and University of Gothenburg, Göteborg, Sweden
birgitp@chalmers.se
[2] Lappeenranta-Lahti University, Lappeenranta, Finland

Abstract. With the Sustainable Development Goals as central pillar informing many government policies and legislation, we get to think about what it means to include our natural environment as more than a passive backdrop in our operational and business environments. What are the foundations from sustainability science, what are the legal aspects, and what are requirements engineering approaches to deal with this? I give an overview of the work I have done in the area of software-intensive systems and connect to new ideas on an agroecology case to widen our understanding of how nature is a relevant stakeholder.

Keywords: sustainability · stakeholder · requirements engineering · software-intensive systems · agroecology · regenerative agriculture

In Spring 2025, the Dagstuhl Perspectives Workshop 25122 on "Climate Change: What is Computing's Responsibility?" [1] brought together global experts from computing, environmental science, and policy to explore the detrimental impacts of computing technologies on the environment, particularly with respect to climate change. There was agreement that technological development must operate within environmental boundaries while also meeting basic societal needs. As for environmental boundaries, participants stressed that the Manifesto should draw attention to the issue of electronic waste, discouraging planned obsolescence and encouraging the development of repairable and reusable technologies [1]. That workshop further emphasized the need for explicitly integrating nature as a stakeholder in software-intensive systems development, both in software engineering as well as in enterprise modeling.

The foundation of this keynote relies on real stakeholder involvement in sustainability awareness within requirements engineering [3, 5] and the Karlskrona Manifesto on Sustainability Design [9]. We build on that foundation by presenting opportunities for discovering stakeholders and impacts by using systems thinking in terms of analyzing leverage points [6] based on the seminal book by Meadows [2]. We argue that systems thinking concepts must be integrated into the body of knowledge in both SE and RE [4].

Finally, we introduce an exemplary application domain, regenerative agriculture [7], with a system idea to illustrate the instantiation of a reference taxonomy for Nature as a Stakeholder [8]. The taxonomy (Fig. 1) guides further exploration of potential modeling representations, e.g. in the form of ecosystemas [10].

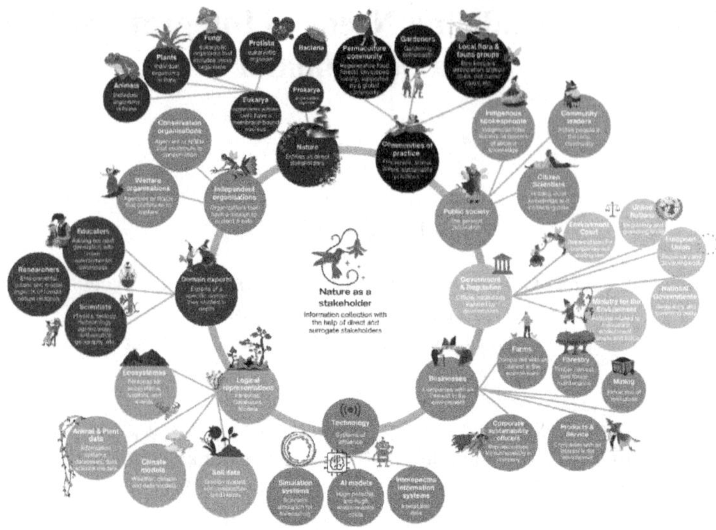

Fig. 1. Reference taxonomy for Nature as a Stakeholder

References

1. Hanson, V., Knowles, B.: Climate Change: What is Computing's Responsibility? (Dagstuhl Perspectives Workshop 25122). Dagstuhl Reports (2025). https://www.dagstuhl.de/25122, https://doi.org/10.4230/DagRep.15.3.113
2. Meadows, D.H., Randers, J., Meadows, D.L.: The limits to growth (1972). In: The Future of Nature, pp. 101–116. Yale University Press (2013)
3. Penzenstadler, B., Mahaux, M., Heymans, P.: University meets industry: calling in real stakeholders. In: 26th International Conference on Software Engineering Education and Training (CSEE&T) (2013)
4. Penzenstadler, B., Fernández, D., Richardson, D., Callele, D., Wnuk, K.: The requirements engineering body of knowledge (REBoK). In: 21st IEEE International Requirements Engineering Conference (RE) (2013)
5. Penzenstadler, B. et al.: Everything is INTERRELATED: teaching software engineering for sustainability. In: Proceedings of the 40th International Conference on Software Engineering: Software Engineering Education and Training (2018)
6. Penzenstadler, B. et al.: Software engineering for sustainability: find the leverage points! IEEE Softw. **35**(4) (2018)
7. Penzenstadler, B.: Sharing a yield: RE for regenerative agriculture research vision. In: 2025 IEEE 33rd International Requirements Engineering Conference (RE). IEEE (2025)
8. Penzenstadler, B.: Growing deeper roots: nature as a stakeholder in software-intensive systems. In: 2025 IEEE 33rd International Requirements Engineering Conference (RE). IEEE (2025)

9. Becker, C. et al.: The Karlskrona Manifesto for Sustainability Design (2014). http://sustainabilitydesign.org
10. Tomlinson, B., Nardi, B., Stokols, D., Raturi, A.: Ecosystemas: representing ecosystem impacts in design. In:Extended Abstracts of the 2021 CHI Conference on Human Factors in Computing Systems, pp. 1–10. (2021)

Design the Business. Architect its Future. Enterprise Models are Key

Christian Lichka

BOC Products & Services AG, Operngasse 20b, A-1040 Vienna
Christian.Lichka@BOC-Group.com

Enterprise models have a long track record — and an even brighter future. As markets stay volatile, regulations tighten, and Gen-AI accelerates change, models become the shared operating language of Business and IT. They turn scattered data into reliable information, cut through complexity, and ground decisions in evidence rather than instinct.

This keynote explores how leading organizations apply enterprise models in business transformation, IT management, and compliance. With model-based Digital Twins of the Organization (DTOs), modelling evolves from documentation to simulation and, ultimately, prediction. That lets teams estimate business and EBIT impact before change goes live, reduce documentation effort through Gen-AI assistance, and use context-rich insights to steer architecture decisions with confidence.

Contents

Human and Cognitive Dimensions of Enterprise Modeling

Contextual and Process-Oriented Modeling

Intelligent and Secure Digital Transformation

Enterprise Modeling for Sustainable Reindustrialization

Measuring Social Sustainability in Business Processes

Mary Jian Falcon(✉), Irene Vanderfeesten, Mathis Wyffels, and Estefanía Serral(✉)

KU Leuven, Warmoesberg 26, 1000 Brussels, Belgium
mjtfalcon@gmail.com, {irene.vanderfeesten,mathis.wyffels, estefania.serralasensio}@kuleuven.be

Abstract. Social sustainability has often been overlooked in business process evaluation compared to the environmental and economic dimensions. However, the concept of social sustainability, which emphasizes fair and just practices towards stakeholders and society, is gaining prominence in business, yet its definition remains ambiguous, obstructing its integration into business process management. This paper investigates social sustainability indicators in current literature related to business processes. A systematic literature review reveals a diverse set of 254 indicators used to assess social sustainability, ranging from standard indicators to context-specific ones, and finds the most common indicators in the realm of employee well-being and development and human rights and labor practices. Our research highlights the need for further studies to address the challenges of defining and measuring social sustainability in the context of business processes.

Keywords: social sustainability · indicators · metrics · business processes

1 Introduction

With the growing pressures of climate change, quickly depleting natural resources, increasing social inequality and evolving global standards, society is increasing its demands for businesses to be transparent and to publish reports about their impacts on the economy, environment, and society [A2, A3, A10, A25, A26]. While the economic/financial and environmental dimensions have been more researched, there is growing attention to the social dimension. Labor practice processes related to personal development and career training opportunities are being given specific attention [A28]. There is also growing interest in diversity, equity, and inclusion in the context of human rights and social sustainability [A6]. Additionally, workers, their working conditions, and aspects such as gender equality are becoming increasingly important [A7]. Managers are noticing cultural and organizational dimensions as important qualitative factors to consider in business strategy integration [A13].

Sustainability in business processes requires incorporating environmental, social, and economic considerations into a company's operations and activity assessment. This

Published by Springer Nature Switzerland AG 2026
H.-G. Fill et al. (Eds.): PoEM 2025, LNBIP 570, pp. 3–19, 2026.
https://doi.org/10.1007/978-3-032-12063-2_1

approach prioritizes sustainable practices instead of only focusing on efficiency and cost-effectiveness [A13, 11]. Evaluating an organization's social contribution requires looking past traditional business process metrics. Business processes are commonly defined as sets of activities that accomplish a specific goal and are assessed using parameters and metrics such as output quality, speed, cost, and added value, and form the base for achieving competitive advantage [5]. Process-oriented performance indicators are typically the key drivers of performance [13] and are used to measure the performance of organizational processes. Using indicators allows for continuous monitoring and process improvement, resulting in a more sustainable organization [7]. Recent research also emphasizes that when creating business processes, companies should consider all stakeholders, not just shareholders [9], further highlighting the importance of the social dimension. Including elements such as stakeholder engagement, governance and leadership, and communication strategies allows businesses to react more quickly to stakeholder expectations and sustainable development goals [A8].

Companies have yet to fully achieve social sustainability because they have not integrated corporate social responsibility (CSR) into their business processes [A20]. Without including CSR in business processes, companies may be unable to align their operations with broader social sustainability goals, reducing their long-term effectiveness [A3, A12]. The objective of this paper is to identify social sustainability indicators that are already used, or could be used, to measure business processes. For the context of this paper, business refers to commercial, industrial, or professional activities that generate economic outcomes and organizational efficiency [A4] and processes are granular, operational activities of a company. We will specifically carry out a systematic literature review (SLR) to identify relevant indicators already published in the literature. In doing so, we seek to answer the following research question: What indicators have been proposed in the literature to evaluate social sustainability in business processes?

This study looks to contribute to the growing body of research on sustainability in business processes by providing insights into the social indicators that can be used. In addition, we propose a framework to categorize such indicators as an aid for their further development and adoption by researchers and practitioners. The rest of the paper is organized as follows: Sect. 2 describes the background and related work, Sect. 3 describes the SLR methodology, Sect. 4 presents the results of the SLR, Sect. 5 discusses our findings, and finally, Sect. 6 concludes the study.

2 Background and Related Work

This section explores key concepts relevant to our study, looking at previous research findings and identifying areas for further investigation in the existing literature. This will provide a solid foundation and context for our research.

2.1 Social Sustainability

In 2015, 17 Sustainable Development Goals (SDGs) on the 2030 Agenda for Sustainable Development were agreed upon and adopted by all United Nations (UN) Member States. These goals aim to set up the people and planet for a more prosperous and equitable future, improve health and education outcomes for all, reduce inequality, and create economic growth [12]. These goals share some similarities with the business concept of the triple bottom line (TBL), which states that firms should commit to focusing on social and environmental issues as well as profits. The concept of the TBL was defined by John Elkington [3], who explained that all three sustainability dimensions (financial, social, and environmental) need to be treated with equal importance; the social dimension refers to all the actions that make it possible to better preserve and develop human resources management [A7].

In recent years, corporate social responsibility (CSR) has grown in popularity among managers, government officials, and academics [A26]. Like the TBL, CSR urges businesses to think beyond financial performance and consider their impact on society and the environment [4]. Companies are expected to behave ethically and responsibly towards different stakeholders, including employees, customers, suppliers and partners, communities, and the environment [4, A26]. Social sustainability focuses on promoting fair and just working conditions, engaging with the community, and safeguarding basic human rights, all of which are essential to achieving long-term sustainable value.

Traditionally, organizations' operational management of business processes have mainly focused on environmental and financial aspects, rarely considering social and organizational aspects [A6, A7, A12, A17, A20]. While the social dimension of sustainability has received increased attention over the past decade, a clear understanding of its scope is still ambiguous [A6, A16]. The concept of "social sustainability" is multifaceted, with scholars offering various interpretations for this dimension. For some authors, the definition is linked to the workforce, covering labor practices, human rights, society, and product responsibility [A3, 6, A21]. Kruger et al. and Peças et al. further highlight the importance of a comfortable and safe working environment [A15, A22], and Contini and Peruzzini frame social sustainability as the preservation and development of human resources management [A7]. Other authors give a broader perspective, defining social sustainability as the equitable distribution of welfare to meet the needs of all citizens [A13, A12], or interpret it as a principle that aligns individual actions with collective well-being and future generations' needs [A6, A10, A28]. This variance, along with a lack of a clear and consistent definition [4], makes implementing social sustainability challenging for companies. Although specific definitions of 'social' differ, general agreement and a consistent theme link it to the impact on individuals in multiple contexts and on society, suggesting a shared understanding of its meaning.

Businesses also often prioritize self-interest and short-term gains over long-term social responsibility, rarely incorporating this into operational management objectives [A20]. This leads to a conflict between corporate and societal goals. However, incorporating social sustainability indicators into business processes provides a more balanced and practical method for evaluating and tracking social impacts at a more detailed and operational level. These indicators enable businesses to identify areas for improvement, monitor performance, and integrate long-term social goals into their daily operations [A5, A6, A17, A25].

2.2 Process Indicator Frameworks

The complexity of organizational processes requires an approach structured to performance measurement. Although isolated metrics and indicators can be used in different domains, their organization within a framework helps to classify and define these indicators in a given process context, giving businesses a consolidated and insightful evaluation of their operations. Several studies discuss frameworks about process indicators in the broader context of sustainability assessment or performance management. Van Looy and Shafagatova propose a framework centered around 140 process-related performance indicators across the four dimensions of the Balanced Scorecard (BSC): financial customer, internal business process, and learning and growth. They offer this to organizations in defining specific indicators [13]. Žižek et al. outline a methodology for calculating process performance indicators (pPIs) for Industry 4.0 implementation. The pPIs were organized into five groups: safety and the environment, production efficiency, production quality, staffing, and plan implementation [A27]. Other authors present frameworks within less human-centric industries such as the automotive and electronics industry [A25], manufacturing [A7, A17], the agricultural food sector [A6], electricity [A9], and swine supply chain [A15]. However, these studies do not focus on the social sustainability aspect.

2.3 Related Systematic Literature Reviews

Previous systematic literature review (SLR) studies related to our topic have found that key performance indicators (KPIs) play a vital role in helping firms align their operations with sustainability goals. Four studies clearly mention business processes in the context of indicators or KPIs [A4, 14, A25, A27]. Al-Shaiba et al. stated that indicators monitor the progress of operational processes such as measuring throughput and the process cycle time to deliver the output along with the quality of the output [A4]. Schöggl et al. found that indicator data can be used in business processes [A25]. Van Looy and Shafagatova extensively addressed business processes in the context of performance indicators, linking business process performance and organizational performance, and finding 140 performance indicators in the literature in accordance with the BSC [13]. Žižek et al. [A27] identified a research gap in how Industry 4.0, which represents the current trend of automation technologies in manufacturing, can collect real-time data on social factors such as labor practices, community impact, and employee satisfaction. They found that business performance can be measured from indicators such as market share, customer satisfaction, and client profitability [A27]. The use of Industry 4.0 technologies could substantially improve the integration of social sustainability metrics into business process measurement systems.

Other SLRs did not explicitly relate business processes with indicators or did not focus on the social dimension of sustainability. Hristov et al. state that KPIs are indicators that monitor the performance of specific business processes, which allow management to plan for medium-term and long-term goals but did not provide examples of how this was done [A13]. Hristov and Chirico did not mention business processes in relation to indicators or KPIs [A12]. Jasiński et al. [A14] emphasize that sustainability-driven innovation should go beyond the transformation of a company's internal business processes, practices, and policies. They advocate for the integration of sustainability into everyday decision-making through tools like algorithms, indicators, or financial mechanisms and acknowledge the challenge of integrating social sustainability metrics effectively. However, this SLR does not mention business processes in the context of social sustainability indicators. Sanchez-Planelles et al. focused their study on environmental sustainability and assessed how business processes were designed from an operational viewpoint [10]. Saeed and Kersten conducted a SLR on sustainability supply chain management and identified performance indicators as tools for monitoring activities and evaluating performance [A24]. However, they stated that assessing social sustainability remains a significant challenge, with a lack of effective tools for measuring sustainability performance, particularly in the context of social sustainability at the process level [A24]. Moreover, while various organizations have developed their own methods to measure social sustainability, the lack of standardized indicators make cross-industry comparisons difficult [A14, A24].

The SLR presented in this paper aims at addressing these gaps by consolidating existing research on social sustainability indicators that can be used in the context of business processes.

3 Methodology

The SLR follows a systematic approach using the Preferred Reporting Items for Systematic Reviews and Meta-analyses (PRISMA) guidelines [8]. This study uses the methodology proposed by Kitchenham and Charters [6] and followed by Van Looy and Shafagatova [13] to identify and classify relevant papers on process performance measurement. The objective of this is to identify existing literature related to the RQ, identify gaps, and critically review previous findings.

The review was performed in three phases: 1.) Planning – formulating the research questions and search strategy. 2.) Conducting – filtering and extracting data based on inclusion and exclusion criteria. 3.) Reporting and Synthesis – synthesizing the findings, which will be presented in the Results and Discussion sections.

3.1 Planning the SLR

In the planning phase, we defined the objective of the SLR by stating the research questions and key concepts, defining the search terms and queries, and outlined the inclusion/exclusion criteria.

Search Termsand Strategy. To improve the clarity of our search strategy and yield quality results, we established the key terms and related search terms as shown in Table 1. From the topic, the key concepts of 'evaluate', 'business process', and 'social sustainability' were identified, along with related search terms like 'measure', 'indicate', and 'metric', which link processes to an organization's strategy [7]. The terms 'corporate social responsibility' (CSR) and 'social responsibility' were included because they overlap with frameworks like the triple bottom line (TBL) [8, A26] and Environmental, Social, and Governance (ESG) [A21]. Although 'triple bottom line (TBL)' includes social aspects, it was excluded to focus on studies specifically related to social sustainability in the context of process evaluation. Similarly, the broader term 'social impact' was removed to maintain focus on sustainability within business processes.

The final search query used was "evaluat*" OR "measur*" OR "indicat*" OR "metric*" AND "business process" AND "social sustainab*" OR "social performance" OR "CSR" OR corporate social responsibility".

Table 1. Starting point for identifying search terms used in database search

TOPIC	EVALUATING SOCIAL SUSTAINABILITY IN BUSINESS PROCESSES		
KEY CONCEPTS	EVALUATE	SOCIAL SUSTAINABILITY	BUSINESS PROCESS
RELATED SEARCH TERMS	MEASURE, INDICATE, METRIC	SOCIAL PERFORMANCE, CORPORATE SOCIAL RESPONSIBILITY, CSR, TBL, SOCIAL IMPACT	

Databases. After Identifying the Key Concepts and Related Search Terms, we Utilized LIMO, the Online Research Database of KU Leuven, to Search and Retrieve Relevant Research Works. LIMO Includes 1,150 Databases Including EBSCO, Elsevier, IEEE, Springer, Web of Science, Etc.

Inclusion and Exclusion Criteria. The Following Three Inclusion Criteria Were Defined:

IC1. Only papers written in English will be reviewed.

IC2. Only papers designated as peer-reviewed will be considered.

IC3. Only papers published from 2015 to present (October 2024) will be considered.

This date range was chosen as the appropriate time frame for published studies, since the 2030 Agenda's SDGs were adopted by the UN in September 2015 [12].

The exclusion criteria included:

EC1. Unrelated papers that do not mention social sustainability or related social components of sustainability.

EC2. Unrelated papers that do not use any indicators or metrics related to the social dimension of sustainability. A vague mention of a social indicator is allowed as long as it is identified as an indicator.

EC3. Unrelated papers that lack context of a business process or of a business organization. Papers must contain discussion of social sustainability indicators within the operations of a business process, company, or industry.

The SLR protocol [2] is shown in Table 2.

3.2 Conducting the SLR

After defining the search strategy and the research protocol, the review used a search approach where the 'AND' operator linked the six key topics, and 'OR' combined keywords within each topic. The field 'Any field' was used to find all related studies and avoid missing any relevant results. The final search query used was: Any field contains "evaluat*" OR "measur*" OR "indicat*" OR "metric*" AND Any field contains "business process" AND Any field contains "social sustainab*" OR "social performance" OR "CSR" OR "corporate social responsibility".

Table 2. The structured literature review protocol

Protocol elements	Application to this study
1/ Research question	What indicators have been proposed in the literature to evaluate the social sustainability of business processes?
2/ Sources searched	LIMO (KU Leuven database)
3/ Search terms	"evaluat*" OR "measur*" OR "indicat*" OR "metric*", "business process", "social sustainab*" OR "social performance" OR "CSR" OR "Corporate social responsibility"
4/ Search strategy	Used combinations of relevant search keywords with the Boolean operator (OR) to refine the search and linked domains with AND
5/ Inclusion criteria	Include only papers written in English Include only peer-reviewed papers Include only papers published from 2015 to the present (October 2024)
6/ Exclusion criteria	Exclude papers that do not mention social sustainability or related social aspects within the context of sustainability Exclude papers that do not include indicators related to the social dimension of sustainability Exclude papers that lack context of a business process or organization
7/ Quality criteria	Only peer-reviewed papers

3.3 Data Collection and Screening

Papers were reviewed first by title, then by abstract, and then in full, each time applying the inclusion and exclusion criteria.

All indicators and categories presented in the final selected paper were extracted for further analysis. Studies were first read in full, then we looked at the categories, isolating the social dimension category of each paper. The indicators from these categories were all then retrieved and entered into a spreadsheet, along with any descriptions and category titles, as well as any applicable subcategory titles. The Excel file provides a breakdown of the methodology steps and dynamic visualization for the successive phases of the research (see https://zenodo.org/records/17226399). The indicators were then filtered for any duplicates, then each indicator name, description, and category and subcategory (if applicable) from the literature were thoroughly examined and assigned an initial measurement category based on its core meaning. To develop a robust framework, the measurement categories were then systematically combined and similar measurements were grouped (e.g., the initial measurement categories of charity, community, CSR, social initiative, and stakeholders were all consolidated under "Corporate Social Responsibility (CSR)" because these categories relate to a company's commitment and actions toward societal well-being.) This grouping minimized redundancy.

4 Results

The keyword search yielded 971 total results. Before the title and abstract screening steps, 19 duplicate studies were removed, along with 3 papers that fell outside the specified date range and 8 papers that were not published in English. After screening 941 results for titles and applying EC1 at this step, 671 papers were eliminated. This left 270 papers to be screened for abstracts. During the abstract screening, papers were categorized as either relevant or irrelevant (EC1). Studies categorized as irrelevant (206) were excluded after reading the abstract and classified under EC1, omitting them from the next step. The remaining relevant studies (64) had abstracts referring to a combination of research ideas of sustainability, social aspect(s), business process performance, and included key performance indicators (KPIs) or indicators, social sustainability, business and firm performance in the title and/or the abstract. Four studies were unable to be retrieved, leaving 60 studies to be read in full and assess eligibility.

These 60 papers were read completely to determine relevance and select pertinent works to the research questions and topic. EC2 and EC3 were applied at this step, excluding 32 papers from the review since they met the defined exclusion criteria. Fig. 1 depicts the identification, screening, and inclusion process via a PRISMA Flow Diagram [8]. Note that only 8 studies included social indicators that were explicitly used in the context of business processes; in the rest of papers, the presented indicators had a broader organizational focus. Since they are still relevant to measure business process social sustainability, we extract all indicators out of the final 28 selected papers (see Table 3). Out of these papers, we retrieved all the indicators related to social sustainability, and the possible categories that were used to group them.

Records removed *before screening*:

- Duplicate records removed (n = 19)
- Out of date range (n = 3)
- Non-English records (n = 8)

From 28 studies, we identified and recorded a total of sixty unique categories and 430 distinct indicators, KPIs, or metrics used to assess various business processes in the 'social' dimension in different industries. Although most studies had typical social indicators, such as customer satisfaction, employee satisfaction, gender equality rate, and number of training hours, some indicators were more context-specific or more granular, namely "transparency of product information and promotion of healthy lifestyles" [A6], "labor contract signing rate" [A9], and "freedom of association and collective bargaining" [A25]. Twenty-six indicators were then removed from the dataset because these

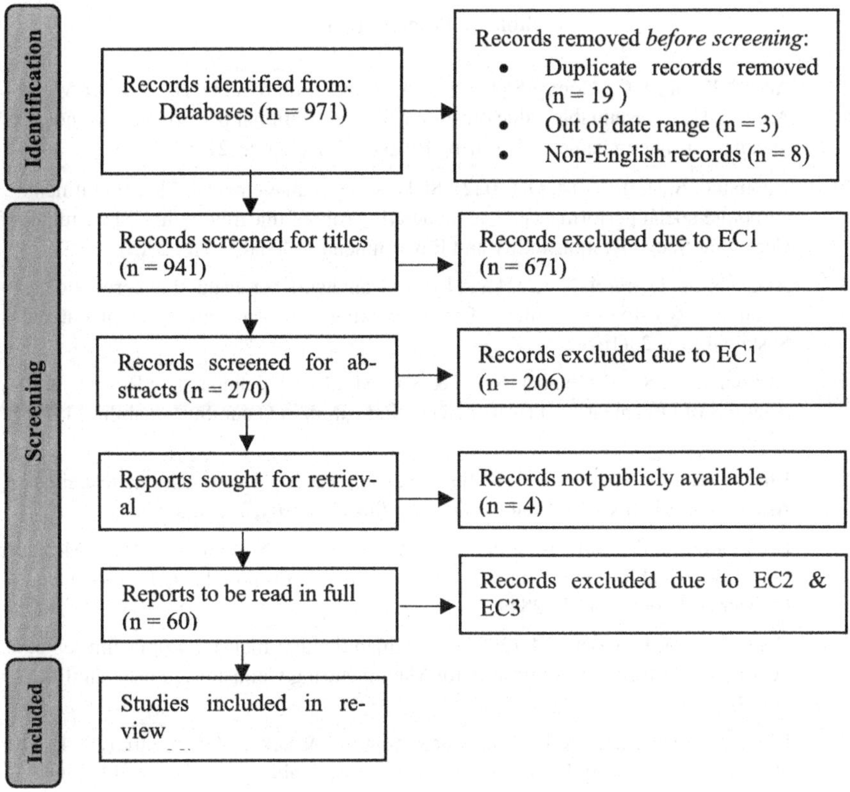

Fig. 1. PRISMA Flow Diagram [8]

were too niche (e.g., "percentage of Qatari nationals employed concerning the total number of employees" [A4], "level of satisfaction with the rural environment" [A15]), unrelated to social sustainability (e.g., "on-grid tariff", "unit cost of electricity generation" [A9]), or too broad and lacking specificity (e.g., "certification" [A22], "R&D & innovation" [A11]) for analysis. This left us with 404 indicators.

We then proceeded to consolidate the categories into core distinct ones through a systematic process grounded in how social sustainability indicators were already grouped in the literature, while refining and consolidating them to enhance clarity and analytical focus. For instance, several studies classified indicators related to employee training, diversity, and welfare under separate themes. However, given their common emphasis on employee well-being and development, we grouped them into a single category—human resources. This consolidation reflects the interdependence between workforce support and professional growth. Similarly, categories addressing health and safety, as well as the physical and psychosocial workplace environment, were merged into workplace health & safety, due to their close conceptual relationship. This reduction of categories allowed for a more streamlined and focused analysis of the literature results. Where studies used broader categories—such as CSR—we preserved the original measurement categories as subcategories to maintain granularity. This allowed us to capture distinctions between

Table 3. Primary studies

A1	Acosta-Prado, J. C., Gómez Sánchez, J. A., López-Montoya, O. H., & Tafur-Mendoza, A. A. (2022). Sustainable value creation and organizational performance in industrial manufacturing companies. Measuring Business Excellence, 27(1).
A2	Adomako, S., & Tran, M. D. (2022). Stakeholder management, CSR commitment, corporate social performance: The moderating role of uncertainty in CSR regulation. Corporate Social Responsibility and Environmental Management, 29(5).
A3	Aktaş, N., & Demirel, N. (2021). A hybrid framework for evaluating corporate sustainability using multicriteria decision making. Environment, Development and Sustainability, 23(10).
A4	Al-Shaiba, A. S., Al-Ghamdi, S. G., & Koc, M. (2019). Comparative Review and Analysis of Organizational (In)Efficiency Indicators in Qatar. Sustainability, 11(23), 6566.
A5	Blinova, E., Ponomarenko, T., & Tesovskaya, S. (2023). Key Corporate Sustainability Assessment Methods for Coal Companies. Sustainability, 15(7), 5763.
A6	Briamonte, L., Pergamo, R., Salerno, C., Uliano, A., & Nazzaro, C. (2024). Measuring Social Sustainability in the Italian Agri-Food Sector: Proposed Key Performance Indicators. Foods, 13(17), 2849.
A7	Contini, G., & Peruzzini, M. (2022). Sustainability and Industry 4.0: Definition of a Set of Key Performance Indicators for Manufacturing Companies. Sustainability, 14(17), 11004.
A8	Dhyanasaridewi, I. G. A. D., Etty Murwaningsari, & Sekar Mayangsari. (2024). The effect of Sustainability Innovation, Proactive Sustainability Strategy, and Digital Transformation on Corporate Sustainability Performance. RGSA: Revista de Gestão Social E Ambiental, 18(6), e05866–e05866.
A9	Dong, R., Shao, C., Xin, S., & Lu, Z. (2023). A Sustainable Development Evaluation Framework for Chinese Electricity Enterprises Based on SDG and ESG Coupling. Sustainability, 15(11), 8960–8960.
A10	Eifert, A., & Julmi, C. (2022). Challenges and How to Overcome Them in the Formulation and Implementation Process of a Sustainability Balanced Scorecard (SBSC). Sustainability, 14(22), 14816.
A11	García-Muiña, F., Medina-Salgado, M. S., González-Sánchez, R., Huertas-Valdivia, I., Ferrari, A. M., & Settembre-Blundo, D. (2022). Social Organizational Life Cycle Assessment (SO-LCA) and Organization 4.0: An easy-to-implement method. MethodsX, 9, 101692.
A12	Hristov, I., & Chirico, A. (2019). The Role of Sustainability Key Performance Indicators (KPIs) in Implementing Sustainable Strategies. Sustainability, 11(20), 5742.
A13	Hristov, I., Appolloni, A., & Chirico, A. (2022). The adoption of the key performance indicators to integrate sustainability in the business strategy: A novel five-dimensional framework. Business Strategy and the Environment, 31(7).

(*continued*)

Table 3. (*continued*)

A1	Acosta-Prado, J. C., Gómez Sánchez, J. A., López-Montoya, O. H., & Tafur-Mendoza, A. A. (2022). Sustainable value creation and organizational performance in industrial manufacturing companies. Measuring Business Excellence, 27(1).
A14	Jasiński, D., Meredith, J., & Kirwan, K. (2021). Sustainable development model for measuring and managing sustainability in the automotive sector. Sustainable Development, 29(6).
A15	Kruger, S. D., Zanin, A., Durán, O., & Afonso, P. (2022). Performance Measurement Model for Sustainability Assessment of the Swine Supply Chain. Sustainability, 14(16), 9926.
A16	Kumar, D., & Garg, C. P. (2016). Evaluating sustainable supply chain indicators using fuzzy AHP. Benchmarking: An International Journal, 24(6), 1742–1766.
A17	Lenort, R., Wicher, P., Samolejova, A., Zsifkovits, H., Raith, C., Miklautsch, P., & Pelikanova, J. (2022). SELECTING SUSTAINABILITY KEY PERFORMANCE INDICATORS FOR SMART LOGISTICS ASSESSMENT. Acta Logistica, 09(04), 467–478.
A18	Liao, P.-C., Xue, J., Liu, B., & Fang, D. (2015). Selection of the approach for producing a weighting scheme for the CSR evaluation framework. KSCE Journal of Civil Engineering, 19(6), 1549–1559.
A19	Lin, C. J., Efranto, R. Y., & Santoso, M. A. (2021). Identification of Workplace Social Sustainability Indicators Related to Employee Ergonomics Perception in Indonesian Industry. Sustainability, 13(19), 11069.
A20	Liu, J.-Y. (2018). An Internal Control System that Includes Corporate Social Responsibility for Social Sustainability in the New Era. Sustainability, 10(10), 3382.
A21	Machado, M. C., & Carvalho, T. C. M. de B. (2021). Maturity Models and Sustainable Indicators—A New Relationship. Sustainability, 13(23), 13247.
A22	Peças, P., John, L., Ribeiro, I., Baptista, A., Pinto, S. M., Dias, R., Henriques, J., Estrela, M., Pilastri, A., & Cunha, F. (2023). Holistic Framework to Data-Driven Sustainability Assessment. Sustainability, 15(4), 3562–3562.
A23	Rajnoha, R., Lesníková, P., & Krajčík, V. (2017). Influence of business performance measurement systems and corporate sustainability concept to overal business performance: "save the planet and keep your performance." E + M Ekonomie a Management, 20(1), 111–128.
A24	Saeed, M. & Kersten, W. (2020). Supply chain sustainability performance indicators - A systematic literature review. Logistics Research. 13.
A25	Schöggl, J.-P., Fritz, M., & Baumgartner, R. (2016). Sustainability Assessment in Automotive and Electronics Supply Chains—A Set of Indicators Defined in a Multi-Stakeholder Approach. Sustainability, 8(11), 1185.
A26	Sledge, S. (2015). An Examination of Corporate Social Responsibility Practices and Firm Performance in U.S. Corporations. Academy of Strategic Management Journal, 14(2), 171.

(*continued*)

Table 3. (*continued*)

A1	Acosta-Prado, J. C., Gómez Sánchez, J. A., López-Montoya, O. H., & Tafur-Mendoza, A. A. (2022). Sustainable value creation and organizational performance in industrial manufacturing companies. Measuring Business Excellence, 27(1).
A27	Žižek, S. Š., Nedelko, Z., Mulej, M., & Čič, Ž. V. (2020). Key Performance Indicators and Industry 4.0 – A Socially Responsible Perspective. Naše Gospodarstvo/Our Economy, 66(3), 22–35.
A28	Zompras, A., Siakas, K. (2015). An Investigation of ISO 26000 and Social Responsibility Practices Applied in IT Companies. 6(2)

specific issues (e.g., community engagement, philanthropy, and ethical behavior) while still aligning with the broader category under which they were grouped.

Although we relied on existing categorizations, we also undertook a review to refine, clarify, and occasionally reassign indicators when their original classification was vague or inconsistent. For example, indicators like "female employees in the company" [A25], initially categorized under broad or ambiguous labels such as "gender awareness," were reassigned to "human resources" under a DEI subcategory.

Some indicator labels required standardization—terms like "employee" and "employees," or "labour practices" and "labor practices" were harmonized—to avoid redundant categories. In total, this process enabled us to consolidate the 60 original categories into eight overarching ones derived from the literature: compliance, CSR, consumer, data & privacy, governance, human resources, job aid, and workplace health & safety, while also creating an "Other" category. Indicators within this "Other" category either lacked measurement clarification in its existing study or did not clearly align with any of the other eight categories. Table 4 shows the indicators classified in these final categories, along with applicable subcategories. The highlighted indicators in the table were used within business processes. For the full list of indicators, including a distinction between concrete and abstract indicators, see https://zenodo.org/records/17226399.

A total of 60 indicators posed challenges due to their ambiguity in categorization or potential overlap across categories. For example, "consumer data protection and privacy" [A28] was relevant to both the consumer and data & privacy categories, and "product responsibility" [A7] could be interpreted under either CSR or consumer. These indicators were carefully analyzed and, where appropriate, assigned to multiple relevant categories to reflect their multifaceted nature.

The indicator sample spanned a wide range of social sustainability dimensions—primarily related to human rights, labor practices, and employee well-being—and came from studies conducted across fourteen industries, with the highest representation in the industrial, management, and automotive sectors. Some indicators were explicitly connected to business process performance. For example, "number of hours of training provided to employees in the last two years" measured professional development [A6]; "measurement of safety hazard correction rate" reflected workplace safety [A9]; and "expenses for local community projects and donations" captured aspects of community engagement [A25]. Other indicators assessed organizational goals more directly, such

Table 4. Social Indicators Framework

New Category (# of indicators in the category): Subcategories	Representative Indicators
Compliance (7)	Awareness of Regulations, B2B Non-compliance, Compliance controls (assurance), Product societal impact regulations, Regulatory Authorities Engagement, Risk, Transparency of operations
Consumer (12)	B2C Social Media Engagement, Consumer data protection and privacy, Convey vital safety information to consumers using symbols, Customer satisfaction, Product safety and health impact
CSR (43): Charity, Community, Social Initiative, Stakeholders	Expenses for local community projects and donations, Local Workforce, % participants in social initiatives, Maintaining contact with corresponding stakeholders, stakeholder perception score (SPS)
Data & Privacy (6)	Confidentiality of data, Cycle time data, Data of workers working alone or with others, Data privacy and security, Substantiated complaints concern-ing breaches of customer privacy and losses of customer data, Security and demographic risks
Governance (5)	Anti-corruption, Effectiveness, Efficiency, Realization of goals, Responsible investment
Human Resources (137): DEI, Labor force, Labor practice, Salary, Training	Employee turnover rate, Female employees in the company, Labor contract signing rate, Number of training sessions per employee, Overtime working hours, occupational health and safety policies and practices
Job aid (16)	Digital equipment, Facilities to help workers during the work (e.g., printer, AC, snacks, and drinks), Lifting aids, power tools, and other job aids in the workplace (e.g., crane, forklift, lift), Personal Protective Equipments (PPEs), Support from peers and supervisor
Workplace Health & Safety (24): Health & Safety, Workplace environment	Consumer, supplier and employees' safety rate, Lost work days due to injuries and/or illnesses, number of general equipment accidents, OSHA citations, Safety hazard correction rate
Other (4)	Conflict minerals used, Justice, Mobility, Protection of private life

as "labor-contract signing rate" and "employee turnover rate" [A9], or human rights compliance via "child labor rate," "equality rate," and "number of disciplinary actions" [A10].

Although some indicators lacked sufficient context to be directly tied to business processes, each was ultimately assigned to one or more categories based on its primary focus and relevance as they may be useful. This classification process, guided by the logic and structure of the literature itself, enabled a consistent and comprehensive mapping of social sustainability indicators across the diverse categories.

5 Discussion

By thoroughly analyzing the literature, we identified 254 distinct social indicators and classified them into 8 social sustainability categories and 11 subcategories according to its business process measurement.

Of the 28 papers that included social indicators or measures, 13 had quantifiable metrics. The remaining 15 presented measures that were ambiguous or open to diverse interpretations. For instance, measuring the quality of life in the community might involve analyzing data on employee participation in the community (e.g. church, mothers' club, community service, etc.) [A15]. Others had various definitions for performance indicators. For example, the term "performance indicators" was used to describe a process, and the term "equation" as a unit of measurement, e.g., "total training hours/total number of employees" to measure training per employee per year [A25]. Due to the lack of explicit business process links in the literature, the varying definitions required us to interpret and discern which or how business processes were being measured by social indicators. Although previous studies widely acknowledged the importance of incorporating all aspects of CSR, within the context of business processes, there remains a gap in existing studies effectively measuring social sustainability practices. This study sought to address this issue by focusing exclusively on social indicators that may be related to business processes and systematically categorizing these indicators to strengthen cohesion.

Some authors had different focuses, making it difficult to classify and isolate indicators. For example, Adomako and Tran had twelve indicators related to stakeholders (e.g., "The company is willing to change its objectives in line with stakeholders' demands", "The company's policies and priorities are adapted to stakeholders' demands") [A2]. Lin et al. had plenty of indicators related to the workspace and work environment of employees (e.g., "Hot or cold surfaces in the workplace (on equipment, tools, desk, etc.)", "Visual and any ergonomic requirements appropriate for the work surface") [A19]. In these cases, we looked at the categories in both studies to guide and reorganize the indicators into the new categories. Many indicators were confusing or difficult to categorize since they contained context that appeared interrelated. However, by doing multiple iterations of categorizations, we were able to classify indicators into new categories more precisely, keeping the initial measurement as a subcategory if the final category was too broad. This is seen with the category of "human resources", with 133 indicators belonging to this term, each with a subcategory. Since our classification includes subcategories that better explain the indicator (e.g., "charity" within the category of "CSR" for the indicator related to charitable contributions and donations), this makes it easier to assign the social indicator's measurement.

The diversity of indicators aligns with the observations of Blinova et al. [A5] and Contini and Peruzzini [A7], who found that indicators for social components are more diverse than environmental and economic components. Social indicators require more intensive work to define specific metrics, mainly due to companies' limited experience in this area and the relatively recent implementation of social and organizational sustainability concepts within corporate operations [A7]. This is reflected in the social indicators in the existing literature, which ranged from process-focused to operational or strategic in nature, along with the diverse categories in which these indicators were assigned.

The evolving nature of social sustainability presents a challenge for businesses. Multiple definitions from various authors and varying industry and context-specific indicators emphasize the need for further research and standardization in this domain. However, despite the diversity of social sustainability indicators and frameworks across businesses, incorporating a set of social metrics assessing business processes strengthens the scope of any sustainability assessment. Effective social sustainability measurements should be clear, purposeful, easy to use, reflect the business process, and incorporate stakeholder needs [11]. For instance, the strategic indicator of data privacy and security can be linked to specific processes. In HR, this could be the percentage of employees who completed mandatory data privacy training or average training quiz scores, while in IT, it could include average detection and response times. By prioritizing a comprehensive approach to measuring and tracking social sustainability indicators within business processes, organizations can achieve long-term benefits. These include improved financial performance, enhanced stakeholder satisfaction, optimized operational efficiency, compliance with relevant regulations, and greater alignment with strategic goals [A9, A19]. In the long run, this approach shows a genuine commitment to corporate social responsibility and contributes to a more sustainable and resilient future.

Even though there are numerous sets of indicators in the literature, a generic set of indicators can be a useful foundation [A7]. Businesses can tailor these indicators and use existing tools and frameworks to align with their specific strategy and business context [8, 14, A27]. For example, tracking the number of likes and followers on corporate and commercial profile posts can measure the effect of social networks on the reputation of the organization [A11] or measuring non-discrimination initiatives via the ratio of female employees [A6]. Furthermore, identifying and linking strategic social indicators, such as customer satisfaction (CSAT), with other metrics assessing business processes could be beneficial for the organization. For example, low CSAT scores may correlate with specific process metrics such as response and resolution times and delivery time accuracy. By targeting improvements at the process level, companies can enhance overall strategic social outcomes. Additionally, the UN's SDGs can also serve as a valuable guideline for measuring sustainability impact, aligning with global standards. Companies can use these tools to evaluate their processes, identify opportunities for growth, and ensure long-term success. Incorporating social sustainability considerations into KPIs that can be measured within business processes could allow companies to incentivize and reward employees for achieving social sustainability goals. This can drive positive social impact while also boosting overall business performance.

Finally, although numerous studies explore sustainability in the context of business process measurement, there remains a gap in research dedicated to social sustainability.

This supports existing findings about the lack of insight and limitations regarding this dimension and highlights the need for further research on social sustainability and the indicators related to it.

5.1 Limitations

Limitations to the literature review search include the exclusion of publications from years prior to 2015 and the exclusion of non-English research studies. A more comprehensive literature review could also include backward and forward snowballing, however, we believe the studies analyzed already provides a comprehensive view on existing social indicators. This review acknowledges potential internal validity threats, particularly researcher bias in study selection and synthesis. To ensure a comprehensive and unbiased search, this review used pre-defined criteria and a systematic search strategy. One researcher led the analysis of the articles, while a second researcher was involved when doubts arose and reviewed the finding. Moreover, data extraction focused on social sustainability indicators for business process measures for consistency, and to reduce bias during the data synthesis, results were quantitatively combined to reduce the influence of individual study interpretations.

6 Conclusion

Social sustainability lacks a universally accepted definition and a standardized set of indicators to be used in industry settings. This systematic literature review (SLR) investigated current social sustainability indicators used to evaluate and inform business processes. The results offer valuable insights into current practices and the challenges organizations face with integrating social sustainability into their operations.

This study revealed a wide variety of social sustainability indicators, primarily focused on employee and labor practices in areas such as diversity, equity, and inclusion (DEI), employee well-being, and employee training and development. These indicators have been proposed as measures for evaluating social sustainability, with many studies emphasizing their role in driving organizational change and improving social outcomes. While most of the studies looked at social indicators and their connection to processes and performance, only eight papers made this explicit link. Furthermore, although studies included indicators pertaining to the social dimension of sustainability, the specific metrics differed depending on the business context, ranging from strategic to operational and process-oriented measures. The variability in definitions across the literature, along with the early stage of social sustainability, may account for the limited depth and process focus of existing indicators.

These findings suggest that the concept of social sustainability is still evolving, and that some industries may prioritize it less due to competing concerns like financial pressures, operating challenges, or regulatory compliance. To advance the understanding of social sustainability within organizations, future studies could develop frameworks that test how effective identified indicators are within business processes. This could be through case studies to research applicability and how effective frameworks are in different sectors. Research could also explore the application of existing and newly proposed indicators in less employee-centric industries, such as manufacturing, logistics, and finance, to understand the nuances in specific sectors. Further investigation of indicators in the context of business processes will help to strengthen and define social sustainability for organizations. Future research could also benefit from making the description of indicators more concrete [1] and determining how these indicators can be practically integrated within the assessment of business processes.

References

1. del-Río-Ortega, A., Resinas, M., Cabanillas, C., Ruiz-Cortés, A.: On the definition and design-time analysis of process performance indicators. Inform. Syst. **38**(4), 470–490 (2013)
2. Boell, S.K., Cecez-Kecmanovic, D.: On being 'systematic' in literature reviews in IS. J. Inform. Technol. **30**(2), 161–173 (2015)
3. Elkington, J.: Partnerships from cannibals with forks: the triple bottom line of 21st-century business. Environ. Qual. Manag. **8**(1), 37–51 (1998)
4. Eyasu, A.M., Endale, M.: Corporate social responsibility in agro-processing and garment industry: evidence from Ethiopia. Cogent Business Manage. **7**(1), 1720945 (2020)
5. Kaniški, I., Vincek, I.: Business processes as business systems. Tehnički Glasnik. **12**(1), 55–61 (2018)
6. Kitchenham, B., Charters, S.M.: Guidelines for Performing Systematic Literature Reviews in Software Engineering (Version 2.3). Keele University and University of Durham (2007)
7. Medne, A., Lapina, I.: Sustainability and continuous improvement of organization: review of process-oriented performance indicators. J. Open Innov.: Technol., Market, Complex. **5**(3), 49 (2019)
8. Page, M.J., et al.: The PRISMA 2020 statement: an updated guideline for reporting systematic reviews. BMJ. **n71** (2021)
9. Rosemann, M., Ostern, N., Voss, M., Bandara, W.: Benevolent business processes—design guidelines beyond transactional value. In: Di Francescomarino, C., Burattin, A., Janiesch, C., Sadiq, S. (eds.) Business Process Management, vol. 14159, pp. 447–464. Springer Nature Switzerland (2023)
10. Sanchez-Planelles, J., Segarra-Oña, M., & Peiro-Signes, A.: Building a theoretical framework for corporate sustainability. Sustainability, 13(1), 273 (2020)
11. Stojkic, Z., Bosnjak, I.: An overview of performance measurement methods in SMEs. In: B. Katalinic (Ed.), DAAAM Proceedings (1st ed., Vol. 1, pp. 0518–0524). DAAAM International Vienna (2019)
12. United Nations: The 17 Sustainable Development Goals. United Nations; United Nations (2015)
13. Van Looy, A., Shafagatova, A.: Business process performance measurement: a structured literature review of indicators, measures and metrics. Springer Plus. **5**(1), 1797 (2016)

Blockchain and Industry 5.0: A Scoping Review of Adoption Across Human-Centricity, Sustainability, and Resilience in Enterprise Systems

Workneh Y Ayele(✉), Shengnan Han, and Rahim Rahmani

Department of Computer and Systems Sciences, Stockholm University, Stockholm, Sweden
{workneh,shengnan,rahim}@dsv.su.se

Abstract. Industry 5.0 places human-centricity, sustainability, and resilience at the core of next-generation enterprise systems. Blockchain has been increasingly recognized as a potential enabler of this transition due to its decentralized architecture, transparency, and trust-enhancing capabilities. Yet, existing literature on enterprise systems remains fragmented in positioning blockchain's role in enabling these foundational pillars. To address this knowledge gap, we screened and examined 11 peer-reviewed journal articles published between 2019 and 2024 using a scoping review methodology. We adopted the three pillars as our analytical lens. Results showed that blockchain, to some extent, can enable enterprise systems transitions to fulfill the core values of Industry 5.0. Two exemplar success stories, one in maritime logistics and one in healthcare, demonstrate feasibility but underscore unresolved scalability limits. Also, the results reveal issues needing further research and development, such as energylatency trade-offs that hinder green transitions, underdeveloped governance models for human-in-the-loop decision-making, and fragile cross-chain interoperability that threatens operational resilience. Future research on the adoption of blockchain in enterprise systems must consider energy-efficient consensus protocols, standardized blockchain-IoT interfaces, and ethically grounded governance frameworks. Also, future research should include the development of ethical frameworks to ensure transparency, fairness, and explainability. Drawing on these insights, we outline a research agenda to move the discourse from conceptual promise to industrial practice.

Keywords: Enterprise Software Systems · Blockchain Adoption · Industry 5.0 · Blockchain and Industry 5.0 · Enterprise Software Implementation

1 Introduction

The evolution from Industry 4.0 to 5.0 is characterized by a paradigm shift from automation and cyber-physical systems to a more human-centric focus. Also,

Published by Springer Nature Switzerland AG 2026
H.-G. Fill et al. (Eds.): PoEM 2025, LNBIP 570, pp. 20–35, 2026.
https://doi.org/10.1007/978-3-032-12063-2_2

this paradigm shift toward human-centric focus emphasizes human-machine collaboration, sustainability, and resilient value chains [1]. Unlike its predecessor, Industry 5.0 prioritizes human-centricity, sustainability, and resilience– the three pillars. It is essential to adopt technologies that enable the fulfilment of the three pillars of Industry 5.0 while developing enterprise systems. One of the enablers of the three pillars is blockchain. Blockchain has emerged as one of the enablers for these three pillars, particularly in enterprise systems, such as supply chains, decentralized finance, and IoT ecosystems [2,3].

However, despite its promises, blockchain adoption in enterprise systems has drawbacks that affect its alignment with the three pillars of Industry 5.0. For example, in 2023, blockchain network vulnerabilities contributed to financial losses of more than $3.2 billion [4]. According to Belchior et al. [4], these vulnerabilities indicate a trade-off between security and scalability. In addition, there is a trade-off, energy consumption vs. transaction throughput, caused by the drawbacks of blockchain's resource-intensive consensus mechanisms [5,6]. Such trade-offs directly conflict with Industry 5.0's sustainability pillar, necessitating energy-efficient protocols and lightweight architectures. Previous research shows that there have been efforts to deal with existing trade-offs, yet the applicability and effectiveness of existing solutions can be debatable. For example, efforts to address the trade-offs that blockchains pose focused on optimizing wireless communication, reducing mining energy consumption, and integrating blockchain with edge computing for IoT devices [7,8].

On the other hand, blockchain provides stronger security for enterprise systems [2,3]. Thus, it aligns well with regulatory frameworks (such as GDPR) [9] and privacy and security standards (ISO 27001) [10], which further emphasize the need for ethical integration of Artificial Intelligence, distributed ledger and smart contracts (blockchain), robotization, and the like to ensure sustainable economic growth [9]. However, existing research remains fragmented. Most studies narrowly examine the role of blockchain in payment systems or logistics [11,12], overlooking its potential to advance human-centric design (e.g., democratizing data access) or resilience (e.g., disaster recovery in smart factories).

Research has acknowledged that blockchain's value for Industry 5.0 lies in its technical capabilities, such as decentralization, transparency, and cryptographic trust [2,3]. However, existing research remains limited and fragmented in understanding blockchain's holistic role in enabling Industry 5.0 for enterprise systems. Most studies narrowly focus on its applications in, for example, payment and financial systems or logistics [11] [12], often overlooking its potential to enable human-centric design (e.g., democratizing data access), sustainability (e.g., energy-efficient consensus protocols), or resilience (e.g., disaster recovery in smart factories).

We conducted a scoping review guided by the focus on foundational pillars of Industry 5.0 and the capabilities of blockchain to address this knowledge gap. A scoping review is particularly suited for emerging and interdisciplinary topics like blockchain, where the literature is dispersed across domains and lacks conceptual cohesion. The scoping review enabled us to map the breadth of existing research, identify thematic patterns, and surface gaps without the constraints of meta-analytic saturation. In this initial phase, we focus exclusively on peer-reviewed journal articles to ensure methodological rigor and scholarly credibility. Therefore, the paper aims to answer the research question:

> *How is blockchain adoption positioned within enterprise systems in relation to the foundational pillars of Industry 5.0?*

Analyzing 11 peer-reviewed journal articles through thematic analysis, we identified three critical gaps: (1) **Energy-latency trade-offs**–Current protocols prioritize security over sustainability, hindering green transitions; (2) **Human-machine governance**–Ethical frameworks for blockchain-augmented decision-making in humanrobot teams are underdeveloped; and (3) **Interoperabilityresilience nexus**–Cross-chain systems lack standardized protocols for fail-safe operations in dynamic environments.

Our findings indicate the need for adaptive and energy-efficient consensus mechanisms, regulatory-compliant blockchain hybrids, and human-in-the-loop architectures. This review contributes by setting a research agenda for conducting a thorough systematic review and investigations for fulfilling Industry 5.0's pillars into blockchain adoption in enterprise systems, offering actionable insights for enterprises advancing to Industry 5.0.

This paper is structured into six sections: background, methodology, results, discussions, and conclusions.

2 Research Background

This section presents the three pillars of Industry 5.0, blockchain for enterprise applications, and previous research on the adoption of blockchain, aligning with the three pillars of Industry 5.0. Blockchain plays a role in developing secure enterprise applications and meeting the three pillars of Industry 5.0. This section also contextualizes the Industry 5.0's human-centric vision, aligning with European policy and innovation frameworks [9,13].

2.1 Industry 5.0 Foundational Pillars

Industry 5.0 is a forward-looking and evolving concept built upon three pillars: human-centricity, resilience, and sustainability [1]. These pillars aim to embed ethical and adaptive design within industrial processes to meet social and environmental goals.

Human-Centric Design. A human-centric design emphasizes that it is essential to focus on the core human needs when we develop technologies, which includes enterprise systems [1]. Rapid digitization under Industry 4.0 led to increased automation and reduced human involvement, prompting scholarly inquiry into the rehumanization of industry [13]. Industry 5.0 addresses human-centricity, for example, it reshapes skills, education, and labor dynamics toward socially inclusive innovation [9].

Key concepts related to human-centricity include:

- **Responsible AI (RA)** Issues like algorithmic bias and pervasive surveillance call for ethical AI systems and enforceable digital rights [1].
- **Worker Equality (WE)** Concerns include exploitation and erosion of autonomy, necessitating frameworks that protect privacy, dignity, and fair access to opportunities [1].
- **Governance** (guarding privacy of individuals and rule of law)**, Regulation** (regulated sustainable production)**, and Standards** (international human rights compliance) **(GRS)** Emphasis on standards that align with UN Sustainable Development Goal 8 to prevent inequality induced by technological disruption [14].

Resilience. Resilience refers to robust and flexible production systems capable of coping with crises and cyber risks [1]. It emphasizes:

- **Cybersecurity (CS)** Multi-level protection from factory floor to digital networks, including AI-driven risk mitigation [1].
- **Flexibility (FX)** The ability to adapt production and supply chains dynamically, which includes the use of AI, big data, and automation [1].
- **Decentralization (DC)** Promotes distributed technologies, such as Distributed Ledger Technologies (DLTs) and smart contracts for transparent, autonomous systems [9].

Sustainability. Sustainability aims to optimize resource use and reduce greenhouse gas emissions for the equity of current and future generations [1]. Key terms include:

- **Green Digitalization (GD)** Supporting carbon-neutral, circular production, which is also possible through the adoption of AI and renewable energy systems [1].
- **Circular Economy (CE)** Reusing and repurposing natural resources to minimize environmental degradation [1].
- **Energy-efficient Technology (EE)** Developing systems that reduce carbon emissions despite increased industrial output [1].

2.2 Blockchain for Enterprise Applications

Blockchain enables decentralization, security, and transparency for enterprise systems, which align with the pillars of Industry 5.0. Also, smart contracts and immutable ledgers, which are supported by blockchain, ensure automation, data integrity, and accountability in supply chains and enterprise platforms [2,3].

- For **human-centricity**, blockchain supports transparent data ownership and privacy through decentralized control.
- For **resilience**, it mitigates single points of failure and enhances security via cryptographic consensus [3].
- For **sustainability**, blockchain helps track emissions, ethical sourcing, and material flows [2].

Blockchain supports a distributed architecture in a system, which facilitates interoperability, secure, platform-agnostic data sharing [15]. It aligns well with Industry 5.0's governance ideals by decentralizing control and fostering localized decision-making [9].

2.3 Previous on Blockchain Adoption in Enterprise Applications

Although much of the existing literature explores blockchain applications in finance, logistics, and cybersecurity, it seldom addresses its broader role in facilitating the transformation of enterprise systems aligned with the Industry 5.0 three pillars.

- Konstantinidis et al. [11] reviewed early blockchain use cases across cryptocurrencies, e-government, and healthcare, focusing on privacy and scalability concerns.
- Song et al. [12] analyzed supply chains and banking, presenting the benefits of blockchain for trust and collaboration, but overlooked ethical decentralization.
- Zrelli and Rejeb [16] reviewed 2,680 logistics papers and emphasized transparency, but overlooked workforce empowerment and democratization.
- Kayan [17] and Shaikh et al. [18] tackled cybersecurity and cryptographic compliance, but overlooked ethical issues.
- Fraga-Lamas et al. [19] addressed sustainability and human-centric goals in sector-agnostic terms and overlooked enterprise-specific contexts, such as regulation and standardization.
- Verma et al. [3] presented blockchain as a security layer in Industry 5.0, but lacked guidance on balancing automation with human agency.
- Hassoun et al. [20] reviewed innovation in the food sector, focusing on technology rather than ethical or resilience concerns.

Previous reviews show a fragmented state of research. Sector-specific studies fail to address the interdependence of sustainability, human-centricity, and resilience. Regulatory proposals are scarce and rarely linked to enterprise applications.

3 Methodology

We conducted a scoping literature review to identify knowledge gaps, examine research trends, and map the potential of blockchain for secure enterprise applications, such as supply chain management. A scoping review is particularly useful in rapidly evolving fields where evidence is still emerging and offers a framework to explore key ideas and synthesize broad insights [21]. This study relies exclusively on peer-reviewed journal publications.

While no universally accepted protocol exists for scoping reviews [21], we adopt the widely cited six-step framework by Arksey and O'Malley [22], further refined by Levac et al. [23], which extends the methodology with practical enhancements to each phase.

3.1 The Six-Step Methodology for Scoping Review

Step 1: Identifying the Research Question. According to Levac et al. [23], this step involves formulating a focused research question based on the core concepts and targeted literature. Our primary research question is as follows:

How is blockchain adoption positioned within enterprise systems in relation to the foundational pillars of Industry 5.0?

This paper explores how blockchain aligns with Industry 5.0 principles, including human-centric, sustainability, and resilience. As Verma et al. [3] note, blockchain serves as a technological enabler of secured and resilient systems within Industry 5.0 ecosystems [3].

Step 2: Identifying Relevant Studies. By applying strict inclusion criteria, we defined our search scope in line with Levac et al.'s [23] guidelines. The review focused on blockchain use in enterprise contexts, guided by Industry 5.0 principles. Only peer-reviewed articles published from 2019 to 2024 were considered. Searches were conducted between August 2024 and December 2024 using Boolean logic Table 1.

Final search string:

```
((Enterprise AND (Application OR Software OR Platform OR
Solution OR System)) OR ((Corporate OR Operational OR
Organisational) AND Software) OR (Business AND (Tools OR
Applications))) AND Blockchain AND (Industry 5.0)
```

The authors are interdisciplinary experts in IoT, digital transformation, and enterprise software systems, making them well-suited to synthesize the literature from these relevant research areas.

Step 3: Study Selection. We employed an iterative selection strategy, guided by the PRISMA framework (Fig. 1), to apply inclusion and exclusion criteria. Studies were retained if they:

- focused on blockchain, enterprise applications, and Industry 5.0;
- were peer-reviewed and published between 2019 and 2024;
- were published in a peer-reviewed academic journal;
- were available in English or had an English summary.

Table 1. List of databases and initial search results

Database	Articles Retrieved
IEEE	22
ACM	24
Web of Science (WoS)	15
Scopus	10
PubMed	8
Total	**79**

We excluded papers focused solely on cryptocurrencies, low-level security algorithms, or general ML methods unrelated to Industry 5.0. Duplicate and non-peer-reviewed entries were removed.

Step 4: Data Charting. A charting form was designed to guide data extraction, based on Levac et al.'s model. Articles were reviewed, and themes were

Table 2. Alignment of Blockchain Technology with the Industry 5.0 Pillars

References (Application Area)	Human-centricity			Resilience			Sustainability		
	RA	WE	GRS	CS	FX	DC	GD	CE	EE
[25] (Healthcare)	I50	**BIO**	I50	**BIO**	I50	**BIO**	I50	I50	**BIO**
[2] (General)		**BIO**	I50	**BIO**	**BIO**	**BIO**	I50	I50	
[26] (Logistics)	I50	I50	I50	I50	I50	I50			
[27] (Agriculture-Food)		*BC*		*BC*	**BIO**	**BIO**			*BC*
[20] (Food Industry)	**BIO**	**BIO**	**BIO**	**BIO**	I50	**BIO**	**BIO**		**BIO**
[28] (Marketing)	**BIO**	**BIO**		**BIO**	**BIO**	**BIO**			**BIO**
[15] (Healthcare)					I50	**BIO**			
[29] (Industrial IoT)	**BIO**	I50		**BIO**	I50	**BIO**	I50	I50	**BIO**
[30] (Future Cognitive Systems)	I50	I50							
[31] (Maritime Logistics)	**BIO**	**BIO**		**BIO**		**BIO**			
[16] (Logistics & Supply Chain)	**BIO**	*BC*		*BC*		*BC*		*BC*	

Legend: RA – Responsible AI, Ethical and Privacy; WE – Worker-centric Ethical and Privacy Issues; GRS – Governance, Regulation and Standards; CS – Cybersecurity; FX – Flexibility; DC – Decentralization; GD – Green Digitalization; CE – Circular Economy; EE – Energy-efficient Technology.

I50 – Industry 5.0 – indicates that the authors discussed aspects of Industry 5.0. where blockchain's capabilities are presented without aligning them with the three pillars.

BC – Blockchain – indicates that blockchain capabilities are discussed without mentioning their alignments with the three pillars of Industry 5.0.

BIO – Blockchain and Industry 5.0 – indicates that the alignment of blockchain and Industry 5.0 is discussed

categorized into the three Industry 5.0 pillars: human-centricity, sustainability, and resilience. Subthemes and identified research gaps were also documented.
Step 5: Collating, Summarizing, and Reporting Results. We applied deductive thematic analysis and grouped the contents of articles under predefined categories, as outlined by Braun and Clarke [24]. The thematic analysis followed the six-step process by Braun and Clarke [24], beginning with familiarization through content review, followed by generating codes based on predefined themes. We identified relevant text for themes, validated themes, and presented the results. Table 2 provides supporting evidence on existing research regarding the alignment of Industry 5.0 with blockchain in enterprise applications. The results of thematic analysis are presented in Sects. 4 (Results), 5 (Discussion), and 6 (Conclusion).
Step 6: Consultation. While Arksey and O'Malley recommend stakeholder consultation [22], this step was omitted due to resource constraints. Future work will include practitioner input for validation.[1]

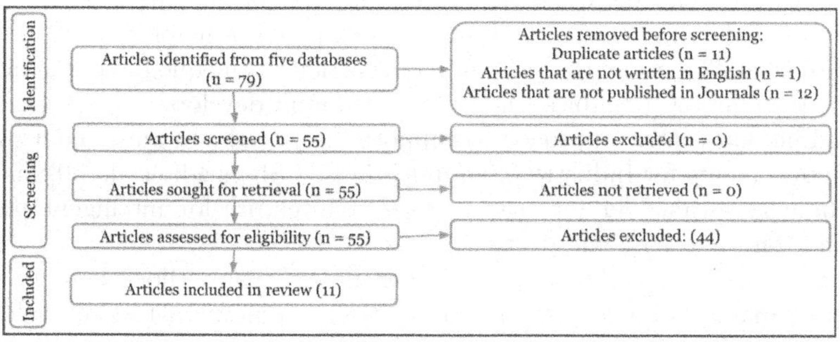

Fig. 1. Literature review process flow diagram based on PRISMA guidelines.[1]

4 Results

This section presents the results of this review. The three pillars, summarized in Sect. 2.2, were used as predefined themes, alongside challenges and research gaps, to outline future research directions. Table 2 unveils gaps in positioning blockchain technology in alignment with the pillars of Industry 5.0.

The adoption of blockchain for enterprise systems to fulfill the three pillars of Industry 5.0 is evident from the results of this study. Two exemplar success stories, one in maritime logistics and one in healthcare, demonstrate blockchain's feasibility, but there are also scalability limitations. For example, according to Zhou et al. [31], maritime logistics systems benefit most by adopting blockchain, enabling them to do risk assessment, supporting them in sustainable maritime

[1] https://www.prisma-statement.org/prisma-2020-flow-diagram.

logistics, and achieving resilience and transparency gains. Also, in healthcare, Abdel-Basset et al. [25] emphasize blockchain's role in ensuring human-centric, resilient, and sustainable design. However, the adoption is constrained by performance and scalability, with Nikseresht et al. [28] arguing that the adoption of blockchain is characterised by scalability and energy consumption issues impacting the climate.

4.1 Blockchain as an Enabler of Human-Centrality in Industry 5.0

The first pillar, human-centricity aspects RA and WE, are relatively well covered. Out of the 11 works, five articles cover each RA and WE, including blockchain and Industry 5.0 discussions. However, Governance, Regulation, and Standards (GRS) appear in only one article in the food industry, revealing a significant research gap.

Adel [2] presents the pillars or principles of Industry 5.0 as: "The fundamental principles of Industry 5.0 are: sustainability, human-centricity, and resilience" In logistics, this means creating solutions that "increase human interaction, enhance SCs'[Supply Chain] resilience and follow sustainable principles" [26]. Similarly, Shahzadi et al. [30] argue that the human-centricity principle in next-generation communications (6G) enables them to "design and develop... applications that relies on human-centric approach to support connected and autonomous intelligent environments for Industry 5.0 applications,". Shahzadi et al. [30] discussed blockchain as an enabler for cross-service architecture for intelligent personal edge and sensor to AI connection.

In marketing, blockchain increases consumer trust. "Blockchain is among the most capable technologies ... providing transparency, trust, decentralization, security, robust data handling, privacy and storage, and many other advantages." [28]. Similarly, in the food sector, the same applies, and Industry 5.0 offers key enablers, namely "transparency and traceability, efficiency and cost reduction, sustainability, consumer engagement, and regulatory compliance" [20]. Human-centricity promotes human social value in a resilient enterprise by creating "a technology-human collaboration environment." [25].

In general, blockchain enables meaningful engagement in value chains and personalization of services by enhancing trust, privacy, engagement, transparency, and agency for individuals and organizations. Hence, blockchain enables human-centricity.

4.2 Blockchain as an Enabler of Resilience in Industry 5.0

The second pillar, resilience, is better covered. For instance, Cybersecurity (CS) is discussed in six of the 11 articles that align blockchain and Industry 5.0, one discusses Industry 5.0 alone, and two discuss blockchain. Decentralization (DC) is extensively addressed in eight applications, while Flexibility (FX) receives less attention.

Resilience is a central pillar in Industry 5.0. Resilience supports Logistics 5.0: According to Andres et al. [26] [Industry 5.0] "I5.0 technologies contributing to the enhanced resilience and sustainability of logistic processes, while also enhancing human decision-making capabilities." [26]. On the other hand, Andres et al. [26] discussed the three pillars of Industry 5.0, they discuss blockchain as an important component for developing a successful blockchain application [26]. In maritime logistics, "Advanced information technologies such as blockchain... are embedded... for risk assessment" supporting sustainable development of the maritime logistics [31]. Transparency and accountability are vital: "Blockchain adoption enhances transparency and security... and facilitates improving the resilience and robustness of supply chains" [31].

Digital twins and IIoT (Industrial IoT) integration facilitate governance from a systems perspective: "A Proof of Authority based blockchain model is suitable... every block can be authorized by Authority Masternodes to enhance the security of the network" [29]. Their evaluation shows: "The proposed PoA-based network reduces end-to-end delay... provides a lesser delay" [29]. Similarly, Cyber Physical Systems (CPS) and Digital Twins (DT) frameworks support resilience through layered data management through the use of blockchain: "blockchain is inherently decentralized, so ther is no need for a central authority making it sutalbe for DT-aided CPS implementations... blockchain also incorporates strong consensus mechanism to validate all data-sharing transaction, ensures data security via encryption, and automates data sharing via smark contracts" [15]. In logistics utilizing IoT, blockchain addresses "security, privacy concerns, trust and acceptance" ensuring traceability and secure sharing of data [16] .

Generally, blockchain contributes to resilience by enabling the development of tamper-proof, transparent, efficient consensus, secure data sharing, and systems governance mechanisms. Also, digital twins combined with IoT reduce vulnerabilities and strengthen organizational robustness.

4.3 Blockchain as an Enabler of Sustainability in Industry 5.0

Sustainability-related topics such as Energy Efficiency (EE), Circular Economy (CE), Green Digitalization (GD), and Decentralization (DC) receive the least attention overall.

Sustainability is formally embedded in Industry 5.0:"Industry 5.0 is promising to use the resources adjusted to the current requirements of the manufacturing industry." [2]. For example, in logistics, Logistics 5.0 principles, which are logistics compliant with Industry 5.0, "contribute to environmental sustainability ... essential for companies to remain competitive and resilient" [26]. Similarly, studies in maritime logistics show a similar focus. This study by Zhou et al. [31] outlines strategies for curbing [CO2] emissions" [31].

Blockchain is cited in food and agriculture contexts for reducing waste:"application of IoT and blockchain in different domains of the agriculture sector, such as food composition, quality, safety monitoring, food supply traceability, and farm and food waste management." [27]. Hassoun et al. [20] reinforce this: "Blockchain provides an immutable ledger... tracing the origin of food products... effectively combats food fraud and mislabeling, thereby building trust among all partners." Blockchain enhances traceability, security, and privacy [16].

Blockchain advances sustainability by enabling provenance tracking, ethical sourcing, and the circular economy, but faces challenges in consensus design. Energy-intensive mechanisms contrast with Industry 5.0's ecological goals, underscoring the need for energy-efficient protocols (Table 3).

4.4 Conceptual Promise of Adopting Blockchain and Industry 5.0 in Enterprise Systems: Requirements

In this section, we list the overarching requirements enterprises should adopt to fulfill the three pillars of Industry 5.0 enabled by blockchain technology. The identified requirements are illustrated in Table 4:

4.5 Identified Research Gap

Blockchain adoption in enterprise systems enables the achievement of most of the requirements of the Industry 5.0 pillars, while facing challenges in aligning. One of the most pressing challenges faced is cross-chain interoperability. The interoperability challenge manifested because of communication vulnerabilities, causing financial losses exceeding $3.2 billion in 2023 alone [4]. The financial loss indicates that blockchain's security guarantees and scalability in enterprise systems are challenging. The adoption of blockchain enables supply chain traceability and healthcare data integrity. Another issue is that blockchain's resource-heavy consensus mechanisms force trade-offs between energy use and its benefits [5,6], conflicting with the sustainability pillar and calling for energy-efficient, lightweight protocols.

Efforts to address blockchain trade-offs (energy consumpiton/performance vs. its other benefits) target wireless optimization, reduced mining energy, and integration with edge computing for IoT (e.g., Proof-of-Work) [7,8]. At the same time, blockchain enhances enterprise security [2,3], in line with compliance regulations and standards, GDPR [9] and ISO 27001 [10]. Besides, Industry 5.0 and regional integrations and standards stresses ethical integration of AI, distributed ledgers, smart contracts, and automation to ensure sustainable growth [9].

This review identifies three critical gaps:

1. **Human-machine governance:** Limited attention is paid to governance, regulations, and ethical frameworks.
2. **Interoperability-resilience nexus:** Cross-chain systems lack standardized protocols for fail-safe operations in dynamic environments.
3. **Energy-latency trade-offs:** Current protocols prioritize security over sustainability, hindering green transitions.

These findings emphasize the need for adaptive consensus mechanisms, human-in-the-loop architectures, and regulatory-compliant AI-blockchain integration to fulfill the potential of blockchain in the Industry 5.0 era.

Table 3. Enterprise systems requirements

System requirements	Supporting evidence	Industry 5.0 pillars
Data Privacy and Security	* Data privacy needs further investigation [28]. * Blockchain can preserve personal data privacy and auditability [25].	Human-Centricity
Transparency and Traceability	* Blockchain provides an immutable ledger, allowing tracing the origin data [20]. * Traceability in IoT applications [27].	Human-Centricity / Sustainability
Governance and Regulatory Compliance	* Governance, Regulation and Standards (GRS) with blockchain and Industry 5.0 [20].	Human-Centricity
Interoperability and Integration	* Blockchain is inherently decentralized and suitable for digital twin-aided cyber physical systems implementations [15]. * Cross-stakeholder systems need integration [31].	Resilience
Consensus Efficiency and Performance	* Algorithms or mechansis reducing end-to-end delay [29]. * Energy-intensive mechanisms are environmentally unfriendly [2] [28].	Resilience / Sustainability
Robustness, security and Risk Management	* Blockchain enhances transparency and security, robustness [31]. * Risk assessment in capabilities [31].	Resilience
Cost Efficiency: less energy consuming design and algorithms and Scalability User acceptance	* Blockchain enables sustainable practices. But, it has higher energy consumpiotn and implementation cost [20]. * Users are hesitant to adopt blockchain [28].	Sustainability
Enabling traceability and Engagement	* Traceability allows make well informed decision [27]. * Consumer engagement Hassoun et al. [20]	Human-Centricity
Standardization	* Abscence of universal digital twins framework [29].	Resilience / Sustainability

5 Discussions and Research Agenda

In this study, we prioritized breadth over depth to provide a comprehensive overview of how blockchain enables the realization of Industry 5.0 pillars rather than offering a detailed system validation and deeper investigation. We identified core research directions that warrant deeper investigation by addressing the guiding research question. The thematic analysis of 11 articles focusing on Industry 5.0 and blockchain highlights key research gaps and challenges. The three pillars of Industry 5.0–**human-centricity**, **resilience**, and **sustainabil-**

ity–are foundational, and blockchain emerges as a key enabler for many of their components.

Industry 5.0 emphasizes **human-centricity** as one of its pillars. Blockchain is adopted in diverse enterprise systems, such as smart manufacturing, logistics, and maritime operations [3,30,31]. Workers of enterprises benefit from adopting blockchain that employs smart contracts by allowing them to focus on value-added tasks and collaboration, as smart contracts automate agreements. In addition, smart contracts enhance trust and transparency [31].

Regarding **resilience**, blockchain ensures secure, real-time data sharing in enterprise domains like logistics, healthcare, and maritime systems. Blockchain maintains data traceability and protects against unauthorized access [3,18]. Moreover, blockchain contributes to decentralization, privacy, and scalability [29].

On the **sustainability** front, blockchain aligns well with Industry 5.0 by improving traceability in green energy and sustainable markets [19]. The 6R framework–Recognize, Reconsider, Realize, Reduce, Reuse, Recycle–supports green manufacturing initiatives [3]. Innovations such as blockchain-based carbon credit systems drive eco-conscious practices (Fraga-Lamas et al., 2024) [19]. However, blockchain's intrinsic energy demands present a paradox, prompting the need for more energy-efficient protocols and architectures.

The reviewed literature shows that blockchain's conceptual promise for Industry 5.0 is beginning to translate into industrial practice, but only in selected domains, such as healthcare, food and agriculture, marketing, IoT, and Maritime logistics. For example, existing research and systems adopting blockchain demonstrate that human-centricity, resilience, and sustainability are addressed in healthcare [25], the food industry [20], marketing [28] [28], and industrial IoT [29]. Besides, the adoption of blockchain enables resilience and human-centricity by providing risk assessment and transparency auditing, demonstrating the practical implementation of the Industry 5.0 traits in maritime logistics [31]. Similarly, Abdel-Basset et al. [25] show that adopting blockchain in healthcare systems enables applications to have privacy-preserving data sharing and human-centered decision support [25]. These successes validate blockchain's role as an enabler of the three Industry 5.0 pillars. Nevertheless, some challenges, such as scalability, energy efficiency, and regulatory standardization, need further research. This results from the gap between experimental implementations and enterprise-wide adoption [28] [20].

There are challenges to adopting blockchain in enterprise systems. One challenge is overcoming resistance to blockchain adoption; many enterprises hesitate to move away from traditional systems, requiring targeted retraining and change management models [3]. Although blockchain enhances transparency, security, and decentralized collaboration, trade-offs persist–especially around scalability and trustless systems [15]. Layer-two technologies may alleviate some burdens, but clear application boundaries in emerging paradigms like Logistics 5.0 remain undefined [26]. For successful enterprise integration, future systems must align with the triad of Industry 5.0 principles while addressing operational and ethical barriers.

Lastly, decentralization bolsters adaptability and interoperability across systems. Smart contracts reinforce secure and authenticated supply chains [3], and blockchain mitigates vulnerabilities in distributed IoT environments [3]. However, integration frameworks, scalability bottlenecks, and regulatory ambiguities still hinder adoption at scale [19]. Continued interdisciplinary research is needed to ensure seamless and compliant blockchain integration into future-ready industrial ecosystems.

6 Conclusions

This paper presented a scoping review of blockchain applications in enterprise systems through the lens of Industry 5.0's three pillars: human-centricity, resilience, and sustainability. The findings show that blockchain is most consistently aligned with resilience, while its contributions to human-centricity are aligned and are emerging, and its sustainability impact remains contested. We argue that to achieve Industry 5.0, system developers and architects should systematically adopt blockchain technologies for developing sustainable, human-centric, and resilient enterprise systems. Doing so requires addressing unresolved challenges of scalability, interoperability, and governance. Ultimately, blockchain offers the potential to transform enterprise requirements into human-centered, resilient, and sustainable practices in Industry 5.0.

Future work must focus on the real-world validation of blockchain in Industry 5.0, particularly to address ongoing issues related to scalability and energy efficiency [18]. Developing standardized blockchain-IoT integration protocols is essential. Likewise, ethical frameworks are needed to ensure fairness, explainability, and transparency in digital industrial ecosystems [29].

Disclosure of Interests. We declare that we do not have any competing interests that could influence the report, particularly the results published in this paper.

References

1. European Commission: Industry 5.0: Towards a sustainable, human-centric and resilient European industry. https://doi.org/10.2777/308407 (2021). publication No. KIBE21005ENN
2. Adel, A.: Future of industry 5.0 in society: human-centric solutions, challenges and prospective research areas. J. Cloud Comput. **11**(1), 40 (2022). https://doi.org/10.1186/s13677-022-00314-5
3. Verma, A., et al.: Blockchain for industry 5.0: vision, opportunities, key enablers, and future directions. IEEE Access **10**, 69160–69199 (2022). https://doi.org/10.1109/ACCESS.2022.3186892
4. Belchior, R., Süßenguth, J., Feng, Q., Hardjono, T., Vasconcelos, A., Correia, M.: A brief history of blockchain interoperability. Commun. ACM **67**(10), 62–69 (2024)

5. Castellon, C., Roy, S., Kreidl, P., Dutta, A., Bölöni, L.: Energy Efficient Merkle Trees for Blockchains, pp. 1093–1099 (2021). https://doi.org/10.1109/TrustCom53373.2021.00148
6. Liu, Y., Su, Z., Wang, Y.: Energy-efficient and physical-layer secure computation offloading in blockchain-empowered internet of things. IEEE Internet Things J. **10**(8), 6598–6610 (2022). https://doi.org/10.1109/JIOT.2022.3181876
7. Chithaluru, P., Al-Turjman, F., Stephan, T., Kumar, M., Mostarda, L.: Energy-efficient blockchain implementation for cognitive wireless communication networks (CWCNs). Energy Rep. **7**, 8277–8286 (2021). https://doi.org/10.1016/j.egyr.2021.10.026
8. Lasla, N., Al-Sahan, L., Abdallah, M., Younis, M.: Green-pow: an energy-efficient blockchain proof-of-work consensus algorithm. Comput. Netw. **214**, 109118 (2022). https://doi.org/10.1016/j.comnet.2022.109118
9. European Commission: Industry 5.0: a transformative vision for Europe. https://ec.europa.eu/info/publications/industry-50-transformative-vision-europe_en (2021), publication No. KIBE21005ENN
10. International Organization for Standardization: ISO/IEC 27001: Information Security Management Systems Requirements. https://www.iso.org (2018). Accessed 07 July 2025
11. Konstantinidis, I., Siaminos, G., Timplalexis, C., Zervas, P., Peristeras, V., Decker, S.: Blockchain for business applications: a systematic literature review, pp. 384–399 (2018). https://doi.org/10.1007/978-3-319-93931-5_28
12. Song, H., Yang, Y., Tao, Z.: Application of blockchain in enterprise financing: literature review and knowledge framework. Nankai Bus. Rev. Int. **14**(3), 373–399 (2023). https://doi.org/10.1108/NBRI-06-2022-0066
13. Grabowska, S., Saniuk, S., Gajdzik, B.: Industry 5.0: improving humanization and sustainability of industry 4.0. Scientometrics **127**(6), 3117–3144 (2022). https://doi.org/10.1007/s11192-022-04360-w
14. United Nations: The sustainable development goals report 2021 (2021). https://unstats.un.org/sdgs/report/2021/The-Sustainable-Development-Goals-Report-2021.pdf. Accessed 07 July 2025
15. Qian, C., Guo, Y., Hussaini, A., Musa, A., Sai, A., Yu, W.: A new layer structure of cyber-physical systems under the era of digital twin. ACM Trans. Internet Technol. (2024). https://doi.org/10.1145/3674974
16. Zrelli, I., Rejeb, A.: A bibliometric analysis of IOT applications in logistics and supply chain management. Heliyon **10**(16), e36578 (2024). https://doi.org/10.1016/j.heliyon.2024.e36578
17. Kayan, H., Nunes, M., Rana, O., Burnap, P., Perera, C.: Cybersecurity of industrial cyber-physical systems: a review. ACM Comput. Surv. **54**(11s), 229–256 (2022). https://doi.org/10.1145/3510410
18. Shaikh, Z.A., et al.: A new trend in cryptographic information security for industry 5.0: a systematic review. IEEE Access **12**, 7156–7169 (2024). https://doi.org/10.1109/ACCESS.2024.3351485
19. Fraga-Lamas, P., Fernandez-Carames, T.M., da Cruz, A.M.R., Lopes, S.I.: An overview of blockchain for industry 5.0: towards human-centric, sustainable and resilient applications. IEEE Access **12**, 116162–116201 (2024). https://doi.org/10.1109/ACCESS.2024.3380249
20. Hassoun, A., et al.: From food industry 4.0 to food industry 5.0: identifying technological enablers and potential future applications in the food sector. Compreh. Rev. Food Sci. Food Safety **23**(6), e370040 (2024). https://doi.org/10.1111/1541-4337.70040

21. Peterson, J., Pearce, P.F., Ferguson, L.A., Langford, C.A.: Understanding scoping reviews: definition, purpose, and process. J. Am. Assoc. Nurse Pract. **29**(1), 12–16 (2017). https://doi.org/10.1002/2327-6924.12380
22. Arksey, H., O'Malley, L.: Scoping studies: towards a methodological framework. Int. J. Soc. Res. Methodol. **8**(1), 19–32 (2005). https://doi.org/10.1080/1364557032000119616
23. Levac, D., Colquhoun, H., O'Brien, K.K.: Scoping studies: advancing the methodology. Implement. Sci. **5**, 1–9 (2010). https://doi.org/10.1186/1748-5908-5-69
24. Braun, V., Clarke, V.: Using thematic analysis in psychology. Qual. Res. Psychol. **3**(2), 77–101 (2006). https://doi.org/10.1191/1478088706qp063oa
25. Abdel-Basset, M., Mohamed, R., Chang, V.: A multi-criteria decision-making framework to evaluate the impact of industry 5.0 technologies: case study, lessons learned, challenges and future directions. Information Systems Frontiers (2024). https://doi.org/10.1007/s10796-024-10472-3
26. Andres, B., Diaz-Madroñero, M., Soares, A.L., Poler, R.: Enabling technologies to support supply chain logistics 5.0. IEEE Access **12**, 43889–43906 (2024). https://doi.org/10.1109/ACCESS.2024.3374194
27. Bhat, S.A., Huang, N.F., Sofi, I.B., Sultan, M.: Agriculture-food supply chain management based on blockchain and IOT: a narrative on enterprise blockchain interoperability. Agriculture **12**(1) (2022), https://doi.org/10.3390/agriculture12010040
28. Nikseresht, A., Shokouhyar, S., Tirkolaee, E.B., Pishva, N.: Applications and emerging trends of blockchain technology in marketing to develop industry 5.0 businesses: a comprehensive survey and network analysis. Int. Things **28**, 101401 (2024). https://doi.org/10.1016/j.iot.2024.101401
29. Sasikumar, A., et al.: Blockchain-based trust mechanism for digital twin empowered industrial internet of things. Futur. Gener. Comput. Syst. **141**, 16–27 (2023). https://doi.org/10.1016/j.future.2022.11.002
30. Shahzadi, S., Iqbal, M., Chaudhry, N.R.: 6G Vision: toward future collaborative cognitive communication (3C) systems. IEEE Commun. Stand. Mag. **5**(2), 60–67 (2021). https://doi.org/10.1109/MCOMSTD.001.2000044
31. Zhou, F., Yu, K., Xie, W., Lyu, J., Zheng, Z., Zhou, S.: Digital twin-enabled smart maritime logistics management in the context of industry 5.0. IEEE Access **12**, 10920–10931 (2024). https://doi.org/10.1109/ACCESS.2024.3354838

Toward Commitment-Driven Enterprise Digital Twins

Lubomír Straka(✉)

Faculty of Information Technology, Czech Technical University in Prague, Prague, Czechia
L.Straka@seznam.cz

Abstract. Enterprises are increasingly challenged to make sense of proliferating digital traces in ways that are semantically coherent, organizationally actionable, and institutionally aligned. This research introduces CoEDiT–a commitment-driven enterprise digital twin–conceived as a reflexive modeling infrastructure that integrates conceptual abstraction, semantic technologies, and empirical data analytics. Grounded in Action Design Research, CoEDiT operationalizes a dialectical loop wherein social commitments serve as ontologically grounded constructs that link strategic intention to operational execution. Applied to air navigation services, the approach demonstrates how latent coordination structures can be surfaced and organizational learning sustained through the semantic reinterpretation of transactional data. Beyond its practical instantiation, CoEDiT contributes to current debates in Information Systems and Business Informatics by proposing a socio-technical modeling grammar that supports institutional sensing, strategic seizing, and organizational transformation. In doing so, it recasts enterprise modeling not as a representational end, but as a dynamic capability for reflexive adaptation in reindustrialized contexts.

Keywords: Reflexive digital twin · Ontology-driven conceptual modeling · Business analytics · Semantic representation · Action design research · Institutional sensemaking

1 Introduction

Conceptual models are increasingly vital in the AI age, especially when treated as dynamic, iterative tools rather than static, one-shot designs [1]. Models now serve not only as design artifacts but as dynamic structures that interpret, contextualize, and validate data-driven outputs. This includes annotating datasets, exposing biases, modeling uncertainty, and supporting the explainability of black-box systems. Conceptual modeling thus reinforces the trustworthiness and relevance of data analytics in complex domains [2]. Concurrently, digitalization is reshaping the architecture of enterprise life. Across industries, data-intensive systems, algorithmic processes, and platform-based infrastructures are transforming how

Published by Springer Nature Switzerland AG 2026
H.-G. Fill et al. (Eds.): PoEM 2025, LNBIP 570, pp. 36–52, 2026.
https://doi.org/10.1007/978-3-032-12063-2_3

enterprises act, decide, and relate [3–5]. Yet, despite this profound shift, many organizations remain unable to fully harness the potential of digitalization [6].

Amid the growing reliance on data-intensive infrastructures, a persistent gap remains: enterprises generate vast streams of digital traces but lack reflexive modeling capacities to convert them into semantically coherent and institutionally meaningful insights. The challenge is addressed here by asking: **How can a dialectical modeling loop of conceptual modeling, data analytics, and reflexive sensemaking reframe routine data artifacts as machine-interpretable commitments, thereby extending enterprise digital twins from process traceability to institutional intelligibility?**

The dialectical modeling loop is conceived as a lean, reflexive infrastructure for organizational learning, where conceptual modeling provides the thesis, data analysis the antithesis, and reflexive sensemaking the synthesis, each cycle generating a refinement that serves as the new thesis for continued inquiry. Anchored in Action Design Research, it is operationalized through the CoEDiT artifact–a commitment-driven enterprise digital twin. Rather than representing enterprise behavior as static processes, CoEDiT models it as networks of evolving social commitments, which are ontologically grounded and semantically rich. These commitments serve as units of analysis that, through data analytics and institutional sensemaking, iteratively align conceptual models with practice, sustaining an ongoing reinterpretation of enterprise essence in dynamic reindustrialized environments.

This research contributes to enterprise modeling literature by introducing a novel commitment-based modeling paradigm that integrates ontological formalism, semantic expressivity, and analytic adaptability within a single learning-oriented infrastructure. It extends the role of enterprise models from design-time artifacts to epistemic scaffolds for situated decision-making and transformation, particularly in sustainability-driven reindustrialization. The paper is structured as follows: Sect. 2 situates the research within related work on conceptual modeling, data analytics, commitment ontologies, and methodological reflexivity. Section 3 outlines the Action Design Research methodology and details the design, enactment, and evaluation of the CoEDiT artifact. Section 4 demonstrates the approach through an interpretive case study in air navigation services. Section 5 reflects on the method's implications, limitations, and avenues for future research. Section 6 concludes by synthesizing the contributions and reaffirming the value of commitment-driven modeling for sustainable enterprise transformation.

2 Background

2.1 Conceptual Modeling and Data Analytics

Conceptual-modeling scholarship increasingly converges with data-analytics research to tame the opacity of data-driven systems and to supply the semantic scaffolding demanded by explainable AI and data governance agendas [2]. Maass & Storey [7] theorize a bidirectional pairing in which conceptual schemas guide machine-learning pipelines while learnt patterns reciprocally refine the schemas, thus linking epistemic transparency with discovery. Schuetz and Schrefl [8] extend this insight across the business-intelligence pipeline, arguing that higher-level models can reduce costly data wrangling and render analytics artefacts intelligible to non-programmers. Together these works recast conceptual models from static blueprints into dynamic mediators that bridge abstraction and implementation in complex, data-intensive contexts.

Design-oriented studies translate this convergence into actionable frameworks. Nalchigar and Yu [9] provide a model-based method for eliciting requirements and structuring analytics architectures; their practitioner evaluation shows improved stakeholder communication and system validation. Park et al. [10] tackle big-data quality by embedding relevance, comprehensiveness, and prioritization criteria into the IRIS conceptual framework, thereby transforming heterogeneous datasets into coherent virtual big-data models. These contributions foreground conceptual modeling as a vehicle for assuring data quality and aligning analytics design with organizational goals.

Collectively, the literature demonstrates that conceptual abstractions enhance explainability, data quality, and stakeholder alignment, yet it treats the organization largely as a static backdrop. The CoEDiT digital-twin framework advances this discourse by modelling enterprises as evolving networks of social commitments expressed in OntoUML and instantiated as RDF knowledge graphs. Its dialectical loop extends prior work from design-time guidance to run-time learning, enabling reindustrializing firms to continuously realign strategic intent, operational data, and sustainability imperatives within a lightweight, reflexive infrastructure.

2.2 Commitment Ontologies, Enterprise Transactions, Methodological Reflexivity

Commitments have long been proposed as the ontological glue that links individual intentions to collective action. Castelfranchi's seminal work [11] reframes organizational coordination as the deliberate management of commitments among autonomous agents, a view operationalized by Telang and Singh [12] through formal criteria for compliance and verification. Enterprise Ontology [13] crystallizes this stance in the DEMO (Design and Engineering Methodology for Organizations) methodology, positing the enterprise as a closed system of actor transactions whose essence is captured by mutually constitutive commitments.

The DEMO Basic Transaction Pattern (BTP) models the minimal structure of a business transaction by through three phases–order, execution, and result–across two domains: coordination (speech-act commitments) and production (material fact creation). It shows how a social commitment unfolds from request (rq), through promise (pm) and declaration of execution (da), to final acceptance (ac). BTP thus provides a semantic backbone for commitment-centered digital twins, rendering the progression of social commitments both observable and ontologically grounded. For extensions beyond this minimal structure, refer to the standard and complete transaction patterns detailed in [13].

Ontological refinements further clarify this pattern. Poletaeva et al. [14] recast the BTP within the Unified Foundational Ontology [15], decoupling structural from behavioral aspects and modelling commitments as OntoUML relators. Service-oriented research has sharpened the commitment lens. Nardi et al.'s [16] UFO-S ontology characterizes a service as the interplay between capability provision and normative engagement: service delivery is possible only because providers and consumers bind themselves through explicit or implicit commitments. Their follow-up analysis of ArchiMate [17] reveals that mainstream architecture languages inadequately capture this duality, prompting a modelling strategy that weaves commitment-based and capability-based views across business, application and technology layers. These results generalize the argument that any multi-layer enterprise representation needs a coherent commitment semantics to remain semantically tractable when moving from strategic intent to operational realization.

Methodological pluralism emerges as a parallel research theme. Kostova et al. [18] critique attempts to reconcile heterogeneous information-system methodologies into a single overarching framework, proposing instead a set of systems-thinking heuristics that promote ongoing, context-sensitive translation among viewpoints. Their interpretivist stance resonates with the phenomenological approach of Jonsson and Enquist [19], who emphasize that conceptual models must reflect the lived, evolving perspectives of enterprise actors rather than abstract, universal structures. Their notion of agreements as socially situated phenomena aligns closely with commitment-based modeling, offering a concise ontological structure that contrasts with the more granular and taxonomically dense models of OntoUML/UFO. Taken together, these interpretive and phenomenological contributions reorient conceptual modeling from a representational exercise toward a reflexive practice–one that privileges lived meaning, shared intentionality, and semantic coherence as foundations for adaptive and accountable information systems.

Across these streams, a consistent narrative unfolds: commitments provide a theoretically robust and empirically actionable unit of analysis that spans micro-level interaction, meso-level service coordination and macro-level organizational design. Building on this foundation, CoEDiT reconceives enterprise digital twins not as static descriptive mirrors, but as epistemic infrastructures, that enable continuous, commitment-centered transformation.

3 Methodology

3.1 Dialectical Action Design Research

The methodological stance adopted in this research is Action Design Research (ADR), underpinned by constructivist epistemology and interpretive paradigm. The designed artifact is a commitment-driven enterprise digital twin (CoEDiT) conceptualized as both a conceptual modeling script and an enterprise knowledge graph. The aim of this section is to outline the four stages of the ADR [20]: (1)

problem formulation, (2) building, intervention, and evaluation, (3) reflection and learning, and (4) formalization of learning.

Problem Formulation. The problem to be addressed is not the scarcity of data or analytical tools [3], but the absence of integrative, reflexive modeling frameworks that can bridge the transactional and trace data and institutional purpose by making explicit the essence of enterprise functioning. Employing Delcambre's reference framework for conceptual modeling [21], we address this challenge by a multi-purpose, multi-language, multi-level conceptual script continuously evolving in response to socio-technical phenomena within enterprise setting.

Building, Intervention, and Evaluation (BIE). The BIE stage unfolds as a dialectical loop in which conceptual modeling establishes the thesis, data analysis provides the antithesis, and reflexive sensemaking mediates as the synthesis, each cycle producing a refined model that serves as the new thesis for continued inquiry. Dialectics here is not vagueness but rigor-in-motion: each thesisantithesissynthesis cycle is disciplined by inference to the best explanation, turning provisional tensions into structured refinements that sustain learning. To unpack the interplay between artifact construction, institutional transformation, and epistemic validation, the following paragraphs detail the methodological foundations underlying CoEDiT's development, enactment, and evaluation.

Building. Unlike conventional static representational models, CoEDiT employs a reflexive method to mediate effectively between formal abstraction and the fluid dynamics of institutional practices. Within the broader taxonomy of digital twins, CoEDiT aligns conceptually with the Digital Twin of an Organization [22] or cognitive digital twins [23]. But it significantly departs from typical applications oriented towards physical systems (cf. [24]) by explicitly targeting social commitments as the foundational ontological elements of enterprise essence [13]. The subsection Way of Modeling articulates CoEDiT's distinctive characteristics as a conceptual script.

Intervention. The purpose of enterprise digital twins is to provide actionable insight into the enterprise essence and its operation; the intervention then means enacting the instantiated twin to reinterpret data, surface commitments, and steer organizational practice–while each enactment simultaneously reshapes the twin itself. Because affordances arise from the interplay of practitioners' capabilities and twin functionalities, the intervention can assume different forms, directing attention to distinct insights and enabling varied paths of organizational adjustment. In the demonstration presented in Sect. 4, the intervention takes shape as the reinterpretation of budgeting data into a network of commitments, with affordances shaped by the authors' dual role as researchers and practitioners. This situated configuration blurs the boundaries between building, intervention, and evaluation, enabling a seamless integration of design and enactment. At the same time, the close coupling of roles constrains the generalizability of the approach, positioning the demonstration as a plausibility proof rather than as an empirically representative case.

EVALUATION. Interpreting and configuring CoEDiT's modeling ensemble involves situated choices guided by reflexive sensemaking, encompassing, among others, formal alignment, contextual framing, ontological anchoring, and semantic articulation of enterprise commitments. These interpretive choices are evaluated through inference to the best explanation (IBE), a method guided by the criteria of unification, explanatory depth, and simplicity [25].

Reflection and Learning. Aligned with the principle of guided emergence, this stage moves beyond solution delivery to critically reassess the problem framing, conceptual assumptions, and representational choices underpinning the ensemble artifact. Rather than seeking a single correct model, the interpretive nature of CoEDiT emphasizes the continuous reconciliation of evolving models [18], with each reconciliation opening the possibility of transcending to a higher level of insight into enterprise essence while retaining and integrating the previous level.

Formalization of Learning. Guided by the principle of generalized outcome, this stage distills situated insights into transferable design knowledge that extends beyond the specific case, articulated in the demonstration's epilogue.

3.2 Way of Modeling

To articulate CoEDiT's distinctive characteristics as a conceptual script, we apply Mayr and Thalheim's [26] schema for eight conceptual model (CM) attributes, adapting attribute names for terminological consistency while retaining the original numbering for reference. The *modeled original* (CM1) is a network of social commitments [11] within an enterprise. As these commitments are not objective features of the world but interpretive constructs, our methodology is firmly rooted in constructivist epistemology and interpretive research tradition. The emergent, situated, and often tacit nature of commitments calls for a careful balance in *model focus* (CM5): formalization ensures ontological clarity, while representational flexibility preserves semiotic fluidity. This methodological tension anchors our approach, requiring reflexivity in how commitments are elicited, represented, and refined.

In its *modeling intention* (CM2), CoEDiT aligns with other conceptual models–facilitating retrospective understanding, perspective communication, and prospective design–yet crucially redefines 'design' as inseparable from use: it entails the dynamic shaping of commitment networks through human-centered interpretation and enactment (UML) and machine-interpretable semantic specification and validation (OWL). This shift naturally leads to the *model affordances* (CM3). Anchored in a machine-interpretable knowledge graph, CoEDiT serves both human and artificial agents–enabling compliance monitoring, semantic querying, constraint validation, and execution of formal specifications. Crucially, its organizational impact hinges on fostering sensemaking: how users perceive, enact, and adapt affordances, shaped by their roles, expertise, and intentionality [27]. Extending this, the *model environment* (CM4) operates in individual and organizational contexts: for practitioners, it demands cross-disciplinary fluency and interpretive engagement; for the enterprise, it bridges formal models with the lived complexity of institutional practice, power dynamics, and normative tensions. In this role, CoEDiT can augment enterprise's management control systems [28] by functioning as both a diagnostic and interactive mechanism for organizational steering [29].

Concerning *model grammar* (CM6), CoEDiT is grounded in a conceptual grammar ensemble, prominently comprising OntoUML (ontology-driven conceptual modeling), RDF (serialization), OWL (inferencing), SHACL (validation), and SPARQL (reasoning and querying). The method involves translating, mapping, and aligning across these diverse modeling grammars. Instead of enforcing strict unification, CoEDiT embraces dialectical synthesis–maintaining diversity while supporting integrated and reflexive modeling across layers and purposes [18]. Within CoEDiT's *concept space* (CM7), social commitments form the core constructs, interpreted variably as definitive [15], sensitizing [30], or ideal-typical [31] constructs depending on contextual needs. Figure 1 illustrates how commitments are framed in a service-oriented architecture using OntoUML grammar. For *concept relationships* (CM8), the primary relational primitives'initiate,' 'access,' and 'wait'give rise to three coordination structures: interaction, interstriction, and interimpediment [13]. The articulation of these relational networks or a holarchy of services constitutes the substance of intervention. Beyond these foundational elements, additional concepts or relationships may be incorporated if they are theoretically grounded or methodologically justified, thereby enriching understanding and analytical depth.

4 Demonstration

4.1 Setting Context

Imagine turning a budgeting spreadsheet into a living map of commitments between organizational units. CoEDiT does exactly that. To illustrate the feasibility and expressiveness of the proposed approach, we conducted an interpretive case study grounded in the domain of air navigation services. The empirical scaffold consists of a constructed dataset inspired by Implementing Regulation 2019/317 [32], which governs cost-efficiency in European air traffic management [33]. The fictionalized data simulates an Air Navigation Service Provider (ANSP) budget over a fiscal year, comprising 125 entries (see a sample in Fig. 2) distributed across organizational units, service categories, and cost types. All underlying research data and modeling artifacts are publicly accessible in accordance with the FAIR principles, curated at https://lustraka.github.io/resources/pechar/, ensuring transparency, reusability, and alignment with open science practices. Although abstracted from real-world entities, the dataset maintains structural fidelity to regulatory logic and operational practice. Its function is not to produce generalizable empirical claims, but to serve as a plausible, bounded arena for modeling intervention. By transforming this compliance-oriented financial data into a semantic network of services, we demonstrate how enterprise digital twins can surface latent coordination structures and render institutional interdependencies intelligible through ontological modeling and semantic reasoning.

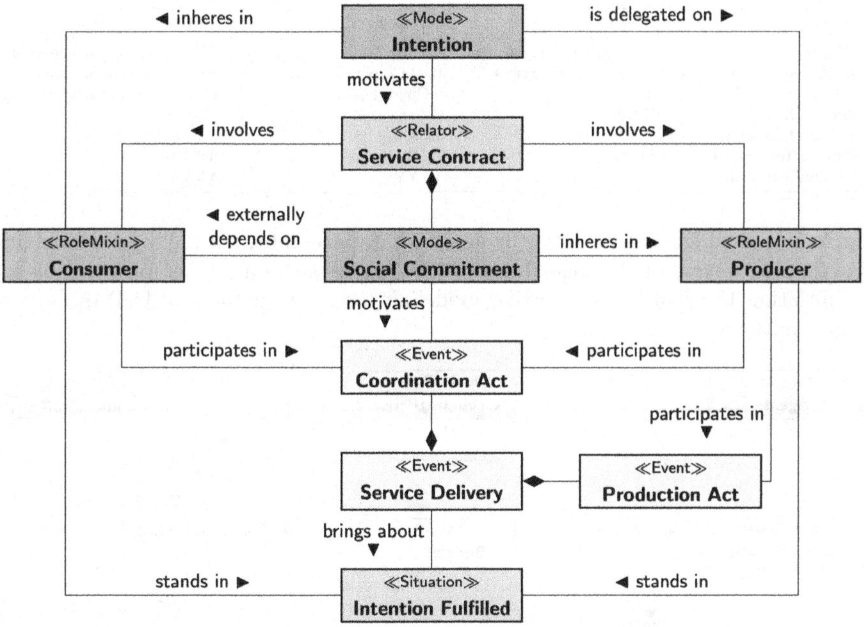

Fig. 1. Simplified OntoUML meta-model depicting a social commitment between a consumer and a producer, capturing both the structural dimension of the service contract and the behavioral dynamics of service delivery–from intention through coordination and production acts to intention fulfillment. Source: authors, based on [14,16].

4.2 Conceptual Modeling

In this stage, flat operational data is reinterpreted as ontologically grounded commitments, transforming descriptive entries into semantically rich constructs. In typical budgeting spreadsheets, cost entries encode the amount, organizational unit, service, and cost type–without exposing their underlying semantics. This flat data structure (Fig. 2) privileges operational expedience but obscures the normative and teleological dimensions of budgeting activity. In contrast, the commitment-oriented model (Fig. 3) reinterprets the budget entries as manifestations of institutionalized commitments. Here, each `BudgetEntry` connects an `OrganizationalUnit` (as agent) to a `Service` (as intentional output), within the context of a given `AccountingPeriod`.

The `Chargeable Service` to `Service` to `CostType` chain of relators (service contacts from Fig. 3) depicts a holarchy of services that structures and embeds commitments between consumers and producers. At the top level, `Chargeable Service` represents the ANSP's commitment to provide air navigation services to flights in a designated airspace. In line with the prohibition of cross-subsidization, these services are strictly separated into En-Route and Terminal categories [33], reflected in the two subkinds of `AmountEUR`. The provision of a `Chargeable Service` requires specific `Service` categories, as defined by [32], whose produc-

Index	bYYe001	bYYe002	bYYe003
Service	201 Air Traffic Management	201 Air Traffic Management	201 Air Traffic Management
OrganizationalUnit	1000 Corporate Services	1000 Corporate Services	1000 Corporate Services
CostType	a Staff Costs	b Operating Costs	c Depreciation Costs
AmountEUR	8752200	624800	18485100
AmountEnRouteEUR	6867900	585300	15084600
AmountTerminalEUR	1884300	39500	3400500
AccountingPeriod	YYYY	YYYY	YYYY

Fig. 2. Initial budget entries from the input dataset exemplify the flat, operational data structure of conventional spreadsheets. These entries serve as the empirical substrate for initiating the dialectical-reflexive modeling loop within the CoEDiT framework. Source: authors.

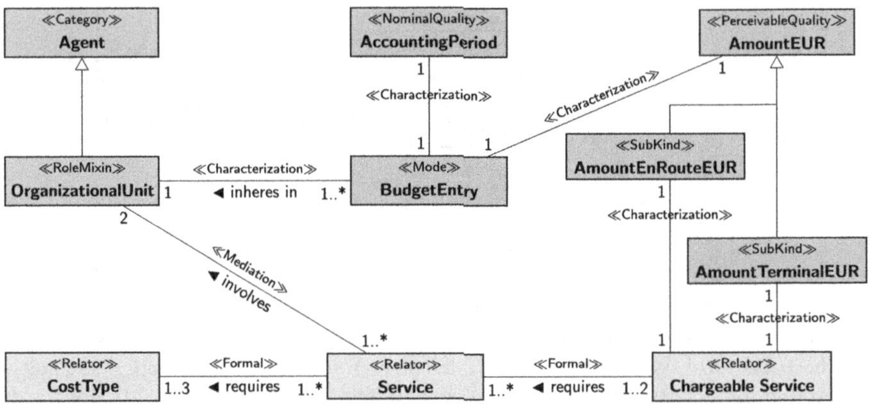

Fig. 3. OntoUML-based conceptual model reinterpreting budget entries as institutionalized commitments linking organizational units, services, and cost types within a specified accounting period. Source: authors.

ers are explicitly modeled as `OrganizationalUnit`. These actors, in turn, act as consumers of underlying sub-services represented by `CostType`, which capture the need for staff, assets and other resources. While not exhaustive, this OntoUML model conveys the essential semantics required to reinterpret otherwise flat budget entries as structured commitments within a service holarchy.

4.3 Data Analytics

In the dialectical movement, data analytics provides the counterpoint to conceptual modeling, confronting abstractions with empirical traces and surfacing patterns that challenge and inform the evolving model. Because the dataset records only amounts without explicit customerproducer links between organizational units, we introduced a pragmatic heuristic: the unit with the highest financial contribution to a service was designated as its proxy agent. This enabled the inference of `deliversTo` relations and the reconstruction of a latent topology of operational interdependence, shown in Fig. 4. In dialectical terms, this analytic move serves as the counterpoint to conceptual modeling: financial traces are mobilized as situated proxies that contest and ground institutional roles, while leaving unresolved the tension between deriving semantics from quantitative dominance or from explicit organizational declarations.

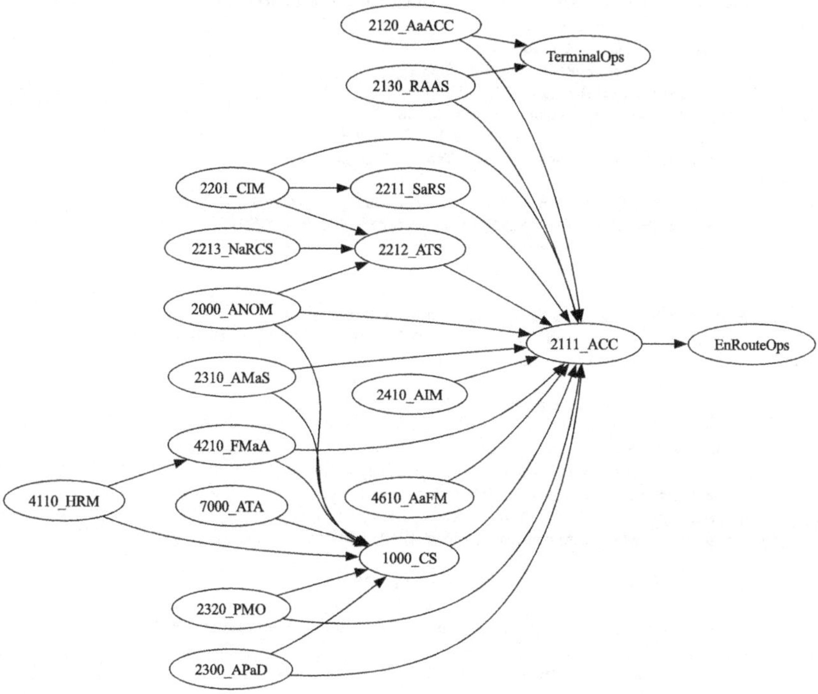

Fig. 4. Inferred coordination network visualizing `deliversTo` relations between organizational units, derived by assigning service ownership to the highest financial contributor per service. This heuristic reconstruction reveals latent patterns of inter-unit operational alignment. Source: authors.

The `deliversTo` relations exemplify the shift along the intensionextension axis: though derived from data, they are reframed as candidate transaction types within the enterprise coordination structure. Interpreted through the lens of the DEMO Basic Transaction Pattern, these relations serve as provisional anchors for analyzing how commitments unfold across order, execution, and result phases. In this way, they consolidate provisional insights into reusable semantic constructs that prepare the ground for the next cycle of the dialectical loop–guiding further data interpretation, model adaptation, and institutional inquiry.

To carry this dialectical tension forward, the inferred coordination patterns are reconstituted within CoEDiT's semantic layer, where the knowledge graph operationalizes them as machine-interpretable relations. In this role, CoEDiT acts both as a conceptual script and as a knowledge graph, instantiated through

```
@prefix gufo: <http://purl.org/nemo/gufo#> .
@prefix pecha: <http://data.europa.eu/eli/reg_impl/2019/317#> .
@prefix pechar: <https://lustraka.github.io/resources/pechar/> .
@prefix schema: <http://schema.org/> .
@prefix ses: <https://eur-lex.europa.eu/eli/reg/2024/2803/oj/> .
@prefix skos: <http://www.w3.org/2004/02/skos/core#> .
@prefix xsd: <http://www.w3.org/2001/XMLSchema#> .

pechar:bYYe001 a gufo:IntrinsicAspect, pechar:BudgetEntry ;
    pechar:AccountingPeriod "YYYY" ;
    pechar:AmountEUR 8752200 ;
    pechar:AmountEnRouteEUR 6867900 ;
    pechar:AmountTerminalEUR 1884300 ;
    pechar:CostType pechar:aStaffCosts ;
    pechar:OrganizationalUnit pechar:1000_CS ;
    pechar:Service pechar:201AirTrafficManagement .

pechar:aStaffCosts a gufo:Relator, schema:DefinedTerm ;
    schema:description "Naklady na zamestnance"@cs ;
    schema:inDefinedTermSet pechar:CostsByNature ;
    schema:name "a Staff Costs" .

pechar:1000_CS a gufo:RoleMixin, schema:DefinedTerm ;
    schema:description "Organizational unit 1000 Corporate Services"@en ;
    schema:inDefinedTermSet pechar:OrgUnits ;
    schema:name "1000 Corporate Services" ;
    pechar:deliversTo pechar:2111_ACC .

pechar:201AirTrafficManagement a gufo:Relator, schema:DefinedTerm ;
    schema:inDefinedTermSet pechar:CostsByService ;
    schema:name "201 Air Traffic Management" ;
    skos:related ses:AirTrafficManagement ;
    pechar:hasTopContributor pechar:2111_ACC .

ses:AirTrafficManagement a schema:DefinedTerm ;
    schema:description "(9) 'air traffic management' or 'ATM' means the
    aggregation of the airborne and ground-based functions and services,
    namely ..." ;
    schema:isPartOf ses:art_2 ;
    schema:name "air traffic management" ;
    schema:termCode "ATM" .
```

Fig. 5. A fragment of RDF serialization of a budget entry modeled as a commitment relator, linking organizational units, services, and cost types. The representation illustrates semantic enrichment through ontological typing (gUFO) and external referencing (e.g., ELI, SKOS), supporting machine-actionable interpretation of budgeting commitments. Source: authors.

RDF. Figure 5 shows how a single budget entry–initially flat and syntactic–can be reframed as a web of typed semantic relations. Leveraging RDF's affordances for integration, interoperability, and reasoning, each element of the entry (organizational unit, service, cost type) is ontologically anchored, interlinked, and externally referenced. This semantic rearticulation stabilizes the provisional insights of data analytics, enabling alignment with domain ontologies and regulatory vocabularies while supporting advanced queries, inference, and cross-context reuse.

4.4 Evaluation

Reflexive sensemaking advances the dialectical loop by treating contradictions as drivers of refinement and organizational learning, while guiding evaluation toward assessing *reflexive sufficiency* across six dimensions. **Accuracy** is demonstrated in the faithful reconstruction of budget entries into ontologically grounded commitments. **Simplicity** emerges in the lightweight heuristics (e.g., financial dominance as proxy ownership) that render the approach usable without heavy data engineering. **Integration** is shown in linking financial traces to institutional commitments, thereby situating operational data within enterprise semantics. **Semantic depth** is achieved by reconstituting flat entries as RDF-encoded commitments that support querying, reasoning, and alignment with external vocabularies. **Reflexivity** lies in surfacing tensions–such as divergences between financial dominance and enacted authority–that drive further model refinement. Finally, **flexibility** is ensured by openly shared artifacts and a modular method ensemble that others can adapt, reuse, and extend. Taken together, these dimensions yield a plausibility proof: CoEDiT is accurate enough to trust, simple enough to use, integrated enough to matter, semantic enough to reason, reflexive enough to learn, and flexible enough to scale. Inference to the best explanation provides the evaluative glue across these six dimensions, ensuring that accuracy, simplicity, integration, semantics, reflexivity, and flexibility are not isolated checkpoints but interdependent virtues weighed together to justify the artifact's plausibility.

4.5 Formalization of Learning

Synthesizing the lessons of CoEDiT enactment, we articulate three design principles for reflexive enterprise digital twins:

Anchor Ontology: Ground modeling in a stable ontological core to safeguard semantic coherence.

This principle emphasizes commitment-based ontology (e.g., DEMO, OntoUML) as the anchor that keeps digital twin enactments intelligible when commitments are re-articulated across enterprise layers and contexts.

Accommodate Reasoning: Support plural reasoning modes to sustain reflexive learning.

The design ensemble must integrate integrity constraints (UML), derivation constraints (OWL), and abductive sensemaking, enabling both human and machine reasoning to coexist and mutually validate.

Assume Formlessness: Treat each instantiation as provisional, enabling adaptive reconfiguration.

A CoEDiT instance is self-exhausting: enactment reshapes the commitments it models. Formalization thus preserves the dialectical loop rather than the artifact itself, ensuring adaptability under evolving institutional realities.

As a final note, this demonstration is offered not as evidence of generalizable findings but as proof of feasibility. Its aim is illustrative: to show how commitment-driven modeling can be applied to real-world inspired artifacts and yield expressive, machine-interpretable representations of institutional structure. The goal is to demonstrate that enterprise digital twins need not be limited to physical or process models–they can represent commitments, obligations, and normative interrelations with ontological rigor. This expands the epistemic reach of digital twins from system traceability to institutional intelligibility, paving the way for reflexive organizational learning in reindustrializing contexts.

5 Discussion and Future Work

The cost budget demonstration crystallizes the dialectical loop by showing how a spreadsheet of budget entries can be re-read as a network of commitments. Translating cost lines into OntoUML relators surfaced latent coordination patterns that fed back into the model, exemplifying the spiral of Conceptual Modelling → Data Analytics → Reflexive Sensemaking → Conceptual Refinement anchoring CoEDiT's stance. The demonstration thus not only illustrates but enacts the reflexivity the loop prescribes.

Revisiting the **research question**–*How can a dialectical modeling loop of conceptual modeling, data analytics, and reflexive sensemaking extend enterprise digital twins from process traceability to institutional intelligibility?*– we argue that the dialectical loop functions as an epistemic infrastructure that integrates abstraction, traceability, and reflexivity. Commitment-driven modeling articulates normative intent, semantic representation ensures logical consistency and interpretability, and data analytics provides empirical grounding. Their interplay fosters a recursive learning process in which institutional commitments are not only documented but critically examined and reconfigured in light of operational realities. This infrastructure supports sustainable reindustrialization by enabling organizations to iteratively align strategic intent, compliance obligations, and resource flows under conditions of volatility.

The study advances three interrelated **theoretical contributions**. First, it reframes enterprise digital twins from descriptive mirrors of reality into epistemic infrastructures centered on social commitments, extending the reach of twins from system traceability to institutional intelligibility. Second, it introduces a method ensemble that dialectically synthesizes integrity-oriented ontology-driven conceptual modeling (UML) with derivation-oriented reasoning (OWL, SPARQL) and data analytics (Python), operationalized through a dialectical Action-Design-Research cycle. Third, it establishes commitment analytics as a distinct unit of analysis that spans micro-level interactions, meso-level coordination, and macro-level organizational design. Underpinning these contributions is a latent but pivotal constructivist-interpretivist stance [18,30,31] that frames models and data not as objective artifacts but as situated mediators of meaning, emphasizing that organizational learning arises through the reflexive negotiation of institutional reality.

Practically, the work offers (i) an actionable script for converting mundane compliance spreadsheets into FAIR knowledge graphs, (ii) lightweight heuristics–such as designating the highest financial contributor as provisional service owner–that expose hidden coordination without heavy data engineering, and (iii) openly shared artefacts (code, dataset, ontology) that lower the barrier for replication and pedagogical uptake. These contributions render commitment-driven modelling accessible to practitioners who face acute sustainability and transparency pressures yet lack extensive semantic-technology expertise.

Several **limitations** delimit the scope of inference. Evidence rests on a single, fictionalized case that functions as a plausibility proof rather than empirical generalization; real-world messiness, power asymmetries, and data incompleteness remain to be confronted. The proxy-ownership heuristic simplifies organizational reality and may misclassify service responsibility where financial dominance diverges from enacted authority. Moreover, bi-directional UML↔OWL transformation and live analytics are only semi-automated, leaving room for human error and interpretive drift. Automated bi-directional transformation between UML and OWL are feasible [34], although not demonstrated in this study.

Future research should therefore extend the CoEDiT framework beyond its demonstrated use in the budgeting context to examine its potential across other organizational domains–such as service delivery, business continuity, and compliance–where latent commitments shape institutional behavior. Applying the framework across diverse enterprises and industries would test its versatility in modeling heterogeneous coordination patterns and institutional logics. Comparative deployments could elucidate how commitment structures differ across organizational cultures and regulatory regimes, offering insight into the portability and limits of commitment-centric modeling. Moreover, the repurposing of operational data for semantic modeling raises important ethical questions around consent, transparency, and representational fairness–particularly when financial traces are interpreted as proxies for institutional intent. Future work should therefore develop normative guidelines for responsible data transformation [3], ensuring that the shift from syntactic to semantic representation remains accountable to affected stakeholders. Finally, incorporating an employee-centric perspective [35,36] would enrich the framework by examining how actors interpret, negotiate, and resist modeled commitments–surfacing the lived experience of enterprise transformation and ensuring that digital twins remain instruments of dialogical engagement, not surveillance.

6 Conclusion

This study advances a commitment-driven approach to enterprise digital twins by embedding conceptual modeling within a dialectical loop of ontological modeling, data analytics, and organizational sensemaking. Through the CoEDiT artifact, commitments are reframed as dynamic, ontologically grounded constructs that anchor reflexive organizational learning in reindustrialized settings. Rather than prescribing static models, CoEDiT supports the continuous rearticulation of enterprise purpose through traceable commitments, fostering sustainable adaptation.

From a broader disciplinary perspective, CoEDiT contributes to ongoing debates about the evolving identity of Information Systems and Business Informatics. As digitalization increasingly permeates organizational life, calls intensify for integrative frameworks that reconcile technical artifacts with institutional dynamics and economic constraints [37]. CoEDiT responds by offering a socio-technical modeling infrastructure that integrates formal abstraction, empirical mining, and reflexive interpretation–recasting enterprise modeling as a dynamic capability for institutional sensing, strategic seizing, and organizational transformation [4,5].

In doing so, CoEDiT demonstrates how operational data can be reframed into commitment-centered structures, illustrating the potential of enterprise digital twins to engage with, rather than merely represent, enterprise transformation.
The authors wish to acknowledge the three anonymous reviewers for their thoughtful remarks, which helped to clarify the ideas and polish their articulation.

References

1. Bork, D., Ali, S.J., Roelens, B.: Conceptual modeling and artificial intelligence: a systematic mapping study (2023)
2. Fill, H.G., Cabot, J., Maass, W., van Sinderen, M.: AI-driven software engineering – the role of conceptual modeling. Enterp. Model. Info. Syst. Archit. **19**, 1–11 (2024)
3. Kitchin, R.: The Data Revolution: A Critical Analysis of Big Data, Open Data and Data Infrastructures. 2nd Edn. SAGE Publications (2021)
4. Vial, G.: Understanding digital transformation: a review and a research agenda. J. Strat. Info. Syst. **28**(2), 118–144 (2019)
5. Kraus, S., Durst, S., Ferreira, J.J., Veiga, P., Kailer, N., Weinmann, A.: Digital transformation in business and management research: an overview of the current status quo. Int. J. Info. Manag.**63**, 102466 (2022)
6. Reddy, R.C., Bhattacharjee, B., Mishra, D., Mandal, A.: A systematic literature review towards a conceptual framework for enablers and barriers of an enterprise data science strategy. Info. Syst. e-Bus. Manag. **20**(1), 223–255 (2022)
7. Maass, W., Storey, V.C.: Pairing conceptual modeling with machine learning. Data Knowl. Eng. **134**, 101909(2021)
8. Schuetz, C.G., Schrefl, M.: Conceptualizing analytics: an overview of business intelligence and analytics from a conceptual-modeling perspective. In: Digital Transformation. Springer Berlin Heidelberg, Berlin, Heidelberg, pp. 311–336 (2023)
9. Nalchigar, S., Yu, E.: Designing business analytics solutions. Bus. Info. Syst. Eng. **62**(1), 61–75 (2020)
10. Park, G., Chung, L., Johng, H., Sugumaran, V., Park, S., Zhao, L., Supakkul, S.: A big data conceptual model to improve quality of business analytics. In: Dalpiaz, F., Zdravkovic, J., Loucopoulos, P. (eds.) RCIS 2020. LNBIP, vol. 385, pp. 20–37. Springer, Cham (2020). https://doi.org/10.1007/978-3-030-50316-1_2

11. Castelfranchi, C.: Commitments : from individual intentions to groups and organizations. In: Proceedings of the First International Conference on Multiagent Systems, pp. 41–48 (1995)
12. Telang, P.R., Singh, M.P.: Business modeling via commitments. In: Kowalczyk, R., Vo, Q.B., Maamar, Z., Huhns, M. (eds.) SOCASE 2009. LNCS, vol. 5907, pp. 111–125. Springer, Heidelberg (2009). https://doi.org/10.1007/978-3-642-10739-9_9
13. Enterprise Ontology. TEES, Springer, Cham (2020). https://doi.org/10.1007/978-3-030-38854-6_20
14. Poletaeva, T., Guizzardi, G., Almeida, J.P.A., Abdulrab, H.: Revisiting the DEMO transaction pattern with the unified foundational ontology (UFO). In: Aveiro, D., Pergl, R., Guizzardi, G., Almeida, J.P., Magalhães, R., Lekkerkerk, H. (eds.) EEWC 2017. LNBIP, vol. 284, pp. 181–195. Springer, Cham (2017). https://doi.org/10.1007/978-3-319-57955-9_14
15. Guizzardi, G., Botti Benevides, A., Fonseca, C.M., Porello, D., Almeida, J.P.A., Prince Sales, T.: UFO: Unified Foundational Ontology. Applied Ontology **17**(1), 167–210 (2022)
16. Nardi, J.C., et al.: A commitment-based reference ontology for services. Info. Syst. **54**, 263–288 (2015)
17. Nardi, J.C., et al.: Service commitments and capabilities across the Archimate architectural layers. In: 2016 IEEE 20th International Enterprise Distributed Object Computing Workshop (EDOCW), IEEE, pp. 1–10 (2016)
18. Kostova, B., Rychkova, I., Naumenko, A., Regev, G., Wegmann, A.: Systems-thinking heuristics for the reconciliation of methodologies for design and analysis for information systems engineering. In: Dalpiaz, F., Zdravkovic, J., Loucopoulos, P. (eds.) RCIS 2020. LNBIP, vol. 385, pp. 112–128. Springer, Cham (2020). https://doi.org/10.1007/978-3-030-50316-1_7
19. Jonsson, T., Enquist, H.: Phenomenological framework for model enabled enterprise information systems. In: Communications in Computer and Information Science, vol. 1064. Springer Verlag, pp. 176–187 (2019)
20. Sein, H.: Purao, Rossi, Lindgren: Action Design Research. MIS Q. **35**(1), 37 (2011)
21. Delcambre, L.M.L., Liddle, S.W., Pastor, O., Storey, V.C.: A reference framework for conceptual modeling. In: Trujillo, J.C., Davis, K.C., Du, X., Li, Z., Ling, T.W., Li, G., Lee, M.L. (eds.) ER 2018. LNCS, vol. 11157, pp. 27–42. Springer, Cham (2018). https://doi.org/10.1007/978-3-030-00847-5_4
22. van der Aalst, W.M.P., Hinz, O., Weinhardt, C.: Resilient digital twins. Bus. Info. Syst. Eng. **63**(6), 615–619 (2021)
23. Zheng, X., Lu, J., Kiritsis, D.: The emergence of cognitive digital twin: vision, challenges and opportunities. Int. J. Prod. Res. **60**(24), 7610–7632 (2022)
24. van der Valk, H., Haße, H., Möller, F., Otto, B.: Archetypes of digital twins. Bus. Info. Syst. Eng. **64**(3), 375–391 (2022)
25. Mackonis, A.: Inference to the best explanation, coherence and other explanatory virtues. Synthese **190**(6), 975–995 (2013)
26. Mayr, H.C., Thalheim, B.: The triptych of conceptual modeling. Softw. Syst. Model. **20**(1), 7–24 (2021)
27. Mesgari, A., Okoli, C., Ortiz de Guinea, A.: Affordance-based information technology sensemaking. Bus. Info. Syst. Eng. (2025)
28. Merchant, K., Van der Stede, W.: Management Control Systems. 5th Edition Edn. Pearson, Harlow (2023)

29. Simons, R.: Levers of Control: How Managers Use Innovative Control Systems to Drive Strategic Renewal. Harvard Business School Press, Boston, Massachusetts (1994)
30. Blumer, H.: What is wrong with social theory? Am. Sociol. Rev. **19**(1), 3 (1954)
31. Sun, Y.: Recontextualizing max weber's ideal type. Innov. Soc. Sciences **2**(2), 194–234 (2024)
32. European Commission: Commission Implementing Regulation (EU) 2019/317 of 11 February 2019 laying down a performance and charging scheme in the single European sky and repealing Implementing Regulations (EU) No 390/2013 and (EU) No 391/2013 (2019)
33. European Commission: Regulation (EU) 2024/2803 of the European Parliament and of the Council of 23 October 2024 on the implementation of the Single European Sky (recast) (2024)
34. Suchanek, M., Pergl, R.: Case-study-based review of approaches for transforming UML class diagrams to OWL and vice versa. In: 2020 IEEE 22nd Conference on Business Informatics (CBI), vol. 1. IEEE, pp. 270–279 (2020)
35. Foundations of Enterprise Governance and Enterprise Engineering. TEES, Springer, Cham (2017). https://doi.org/10.1007/978-3-319-72107-1_4
36. Practicing Enterprise Governance and Enterprise Engineering. TEES, Springer, Cham (2018). https://doi.org/10.1007/978-3-319-73658-7_2
37. Schütte, R., Ahlemann, F., Becker, J., Legner, C., Lehrer, C., Wiesche, M., Richter, G.: Quo Vadis information systems research in times of digitalization? Bus. Info. Syst. Eng. **64**(4), 529–540 (2022)

Towards a Sustainable Modeling Tool for MAL

Thomas Ricardo Pathe and Simon Hacks(✉)

Stockholm University, Stockholm, Sweden
{thomas.pathe,simon.hacks}@dsv.su.se

Abstract. The Meta Attack Language (MAL) provides a framework for creating domain-specific languages tailored to cybersecurity modeling and analysis. However, the discontinuation of graphical editors can disrupt workflows and hinder adoption, necessitating a systematic approach to finding suitable and sustainable replacements. This paper employs Design Science Research to identify, evaluate, and select a suitable graphical modeling tool for the MAL ecosystem. We elicited requirements from five stakeholders familiar with MAL and developed a comprehensive requirements specification artifact. This artifact was then demonstrated by systematically evaluating a set of 26 candidate tools, filtering them based on mandatory criteria. The evaluation led to the identification of ADOxx as the most suitable candidate, balancing MAL's specific meta-modeling needs with crucial sustainable factors.

Keywords: Domain-Specific Language · Meta Attack Language (MAL) · Tool Evaluation · Software Sustainability

1 Introduction

Domain-Specific Languages (DSLs) such as the Meta Attack Language (MAL) provide specialized notations tailored to particular problem domains, facilitating precise communication, formal analysis, and automated processing such as code generation [1–3]. MAL is a framework designed for developing security-focused DSLs, enabling threat modeling and security analysis based on attack graphs derived from system models. Its effectiveness hinges significantly on appropriate tooling that supports both the definition of the language (meta-modeling) and the creation of models (instances) conforming to the language [4]. Graphical user interfaces are crucial for lowering the entry barrier for domain experts lacking extensive technical backgrounds, enabling broader stakeholder participation in modeling activities [5,6].

The development and maintenance of robust tooling for DSLs, especially graphical editors, present considerable challenges [7]. The landscape includes various workbenches and frameworks, often open-source [1]. While beneficial for accessibility and community development, reliance on non-commercial or community-driven tools introduces risks related to long-term support, maintenance, and sustainability. Recently, the primary graphical tool [8] utilized within

H.-G. Fill et al. (Eds.): PoEM 2025, LNBIP 570, pp. 53–61, 2026.
https://doi.org/10.1007/978-3-032-12063-2_4

the MAL framework ceased active development and support, creating a significant gap and necessitating a sustainable replacement.
The objective of this research is to identify, analyze, and evaluate potential graphical modeling tools to address the current limitations within the MAL framework, ultimately proposing a tool that is both functionally suitable and sustainable for supporting MAL-based security analysis and threat modeling processes. This Design Science Research (DSR) study aims to bridge the identified gap by providing a robust and user-friendly interface for MAL's meta-DSL structure.
This objective is guided by the following research objectives (ROs):

- **RO1:** To identify the functional and non-functional requirements for a graphical user interface that supports MAL-based DSLs.
- **RO2:** To define the characteristics of a sustainable tool in the context of MAL.
- **RO3:** To analyze the comparative advantages and disadvantages of existing tools for graphical DSLs and assess their suitability for MAL.
- **RO4:** To identify the most suitable graphical tool for supporting MAL's meta-DSL development and instance modeling based on a comprehensive evaluation.

2 Background and Related Work

2.1 Meta Attack Language

MAL is a framework used to create DSLs for cybersecurity [2]. It functions as a meta-meta modeling approach, allowing security experts to define custom languages for analyzing the security of diverse systems. The core building blocks of any MAL-based DSL are Assets, Attack Steps, Defenses, and Associations. Assets represent system components (e.g., hardware or software), while Attack Steps describe malicious actions that can occur on them. Defenses are countermeasures that can block these steps. The relationships between assets and attack steps are defined by Associations and logical operators, which form potential attack paths. Once a MAL DSL is defined, a specific system's architecture can be represented as an Instance Model using the elements from the DSL. These models can be created either textually or through graphical modeling tools.

2.2 Related Work

Research on DSL tools often maps the landscape of available solutions. Studies have surveyed tools like Xtext, MetaEdit+, Spoofax, and MPS, noting that they differ significantly in their notation (textual, graphical, or projectional) [1,9]. Language Workbenches are comprehensive tools that integrate features for defining language syntax and semantics, but robust meta-modeling support remains a challenge [10,11]. Research into Domain-Specific Visual Language meta-tools, such as Marama, focuses on the visual specification of metamodels and their transformations [12].

The evaluation of modeling tools requires specific frameworks that go beyond general software quality models. Existing approaches focus on usability, expressiveness, performance, and extensibility [6,13,14]. However, for MAL, these evaluation frameworks must be adapted to specifically consider the depth of metamodeling required for language engineering and the long-term sustainability of the tool. The selection of foundational software, like a DSL workbench, is a crucial decision that benefits from a systematic, multi-criteria approach [15,16]. Graphical modeling is widely used in cybersecurity for tasks such as threat analysis. Threat modeling tools like Microsoft TMT[1] and OWASP Threat Dragon[2] often rely on fixed notations and methodologies. Tool sustainability is a critical consideration, particularly for academic and open-source software. It encompasses the long-term viability, usefulness, and accessibility of a tool, beyond its initial functionality [17]. Key factors for sustainability include active maintenance, consistent development, and community support [18]. A lack of sustainability can lead to workflow disruptions, hinder research reproducibility, and introduce security vulnerabilities [19].

3 Methodology

This study adopted a DSR methodology to develop and evaluate a framework for selecting a sustainable graphical modeling tool for MAL. The research process followed five key DSR activities: Explicate Problem, Define Requirements, Design and Develop Artefact, Demonstrate Artefact, and Evaluate Artefact.

The first phase, Explicate Problem, involved a detailed investigation of the practical challenges facing the MAL community. During the Define Requirements phase, a qualitative approach using semi-structured interviews was employed to gather requirements from stakeholders. An interview guide was developed based on established software quality models. Five participants were interviewed, including students at various academic levels (bachelor's, master's, and PhD), a doctoral researcher, and an industry practitioner. Their experience with MAL ranged from novice to several years of expertise. The interviews were transcribed and systematically analyzed to synthesize a set of high-level requirements, which are presented in Sect. 4. The Design and Develop Artefact phase focused on creating the requirements specification and a formal evaluation framework. This involved structuring the synthesized requirements and defining a clear set of assessment criteria to guide the tool selection process.

In the Demonstrate Artefact phase, the developed framework was applied to a set of candidate graphical modeling tools. Each tool was evaluated systematically against the established criteria, with a focus on its ability to represent MAL-specific concepts. The formal evaluation of the integrated tool is planned as a future step and is considered outside the scope of this paper.

[1] https://learn.microsoft.com/en-us/azure/security/develop/threat-modeling-tool.
[2] https://owasp.org/www-project-threat-dragon/.

4 MAL Tool Requirements

The requirements for a suitable MAL graphical modeling tool were systematically derived from stakeholder interviews and guided by the ISO/IEC 25010:2023[3]. These requirements are shown in the following and form the basis for the tool evaluation. They were selected for their relevance to addressing the current gap in the MAL framework and ensuring the long-term viability of a replacement tool. The evaluation criteria used either a binary (0/1) or three-point (0/0.5/1) scale to assess the absence, partial, or full support of a feature.

- **R-1: Functional Suitability - Workflow.** The tool shall cover the whole MAL workflow (language creation, model creation, and simulation possibilities). (0, 0.5, 1)
- **R-2: Functional Suitability - Integration.** The tool shall be able to integrate the MAL framework tools (simulation, compilation, security testing). (0, 0.5, 1)
- **R-3: Functional Suitability - Visualization.** The tool shall provide visualization features (zooming, abstraction, grouping, customizable asset appearance). (0, 0.5, 1)
- **R-4: Functional Suitability - Reuse Motifs.** The tool shall allow definition, identification, and reuse of common graph motifs and attack step structures. (0, 0.5, 1)
- **R-5: Usability - Documentation.** The tool shall provide comprehensive and built-in documentation (guides, tutorials, workflows). (0, 0.5, 1)
- **R-6: Usability - Intuitive GUI.** The tool shall include an intuitive GUI (drag-and-drop, syntax validation, bidirectional switching, interactive tools). (0, 0.5, 1)
- **R-7: Usability - Collaboration.** The tool shall support multi-user collaboration and integration with VCS (e.g., GitHub). (0, 0.5, 1)
- **R-8: Compatibility - Ecosystem.** The tool shall ensure compatibility with MAL compilers, simulators, external cybersecurity databases, and import/export support. (0, 0.5, 1)
- **R-9: Maintainability - Open Source.** The tool shall be open-source to allow community contributions. (0, 1)
- **R-10: Performance - Scalability.** The tool shall efficiently support small and large models. (0, 0.5, 1)
- **R-11: Portability - Platform.** The tool shall be platform-independent. (0, 1)
- **R-12: Security - Data Storage.** The tool shall provide local or on-premise data storage options. (0, 1)

The requirements related to core functionality and usability are critical for enabling the complete MAL workflow. The mandatory criteria for any candidate tool are R-1 (Functional Suitability - Workflow) and R-3 (Functional Suitability - Visualization).

[3] https://www.iso.org/standard/78176.html.

Beyond these mandatory criteria (R-1, R-3), the requirements extend to ensuring modeling efficiency and broad usability. To promote efficient modeling, the tool must support the reuse of common graph motifs (R-4). Usability is further enhanced by requiring an intuitive graphical user interface (R-6) and comprehensive documentation (R-5), catering to both novice and expert users. For collaborative environments, support for multi-user collaboration and integration with version control systems (R-7) is also essential.

A separate set of requirements ensures the tool's compatibility with the broader MAL ecosystem and external systems, alongside its long-term sustainability. The tool must be able to integrate with existing MAL components (R-2), such as compilers and simulators. Furthermore, it should be compatible with the wider cybersecurity ecosystem, including external databases (R-8). For sustainability and practicality, technical requirements were established: the tool must efficiently handle both small and large models without performance degradation (R-10) and be platform-independent (R-11) for broad accessibility. Finally, open-source licensing (R-9) is required to facilitate community contributions, while the option for local or on-premise data storage (R-12) addresses security concerns related to sensitive data.

5 Tool Selection

A systematic search for graphical modeling tools suitable for the MAL ecosystem was conducted through academic literature and web searches. Two tools (AToM3, Kermeta) that were no longer actively maintained were excluded from further consideration. This process identified an initial pool of 26 tools. These candidates were then evaluated against a detailed set of requirements, with a particular focus on the mandatory criteria for functional suitability and visualization. This initial filtering step excluded tools that did not support the core MAL workflow or essential graphical interaction capabilities.

A specific consideration was made for the Eclipse Modeling Framework (EMF) ecosystem. While individual EMF components were assessed, their capabilities were primarily represented through comprehensive platforms such as Sirius and Obeo Designer. These platforms were evaluated as complete toolchains, as they integrate various EMF components to provide a full modeling environment.

The overall evaluation scores, as detailed in Table 1, highlighted several strong candidates. The final ruling focused on the top-scoring tools only, full results can be found here [20].

The final ruling focused on the top two candidates, ADOxx (11.5 points) and JetBrains MPS (11.0 points), after a detailed sustainability analysis. Both are open-source and require custom integration to support the MAL workflow. ADOxx, primarily a graphical modeling environment, scored highest due to its strong native support for graph visualization and web-based accessibility, which aligns closely with the project's main objectives. While JetBrains MPS is a powerful language workbench ideal for deep DSL work, its focus on projectional editing

Table 1. Tool evaluation

	R-1	R-2	R-3	R-4	R-5	R-6	R-7	R-8	R-9	R-10	R-11	R-12	**Overall**
Adoxx[4]	1	1	1	1	1	1	1	0.5	1	1	1	1	11.5
MPS[5]	1	1	1	1	1	1	0.5	0.5	1	1	1	1	11.0
ME+[6]	1	1	1	1	0.5	1	0.5	0.5	0	1	1	1	9.5
Cinco[7]	1	1	1	0.5	1	1	0.5	0.5	1	0.5	0	1	9
ObeoD[8]	0.5	1	1	1	1	1	1	0.5	0	1	0	1	9
Sirius[9]	0.5	1	1	1	1	0.5	0.5	0.5	1	1	0	1	9

[4]https://www.adoxx.org/live/home [5]https://www.jetbrains.com/mps/ [6]http://www.metacase.com/ [7]https://cinco.scce.info/about/ [8]https://www.obeodesigner.com/en/ [9]https://eclipse.dev/sirius/

and steeper learning curve were considered less suitable for the primary goal of creating a user-friendly graphical tool. Therefore, ADOxx was selected as the recommended tool, as it offers a balance of high functional suitability, robust sustainability, and a direct path to integration for the MAL ecosystem's needs.

Obeo Designer and Sirius, both built on EMF, scored 9 points. Their primary limitation is their nature as toolchains rather than single, comprehensive solutions, which introduces complexities and dependencies. MetaEdit+ (9.5 points) and Cinco (9 points) also showed strong capabilities but were ruled out due to their closed-source nature and significant development effort required, respectively, making them less suitable choices given the project constraints and goals.

6 Discussion

The selection of ADOxx as the most suitable tool for the MAL ecosystem, while supported by the evaluation criteria, involves certain considerations. A key challenge is the effort required to integrate ADOxx with the existing MAL toolchain, which includes defining a meta-model, exporting data for compilers, and importing simulation results. This custom development could prolong the deployment timeline. Furthermore, ADOxx's origin in Enterprise Architecture and Business Process Management might necessitate specific adaptations to represent cybersecurity concepts effectively. The tool's sustainability, though considered high due to its open-source nature and the support from the OMILAB Organization, is contingent on the continued commitment of this community.

The research employed a DSR methodology to ensure a systematic and credible tool selection process. Requirements were systematically gathered from stakeholders and used to evaluate 26 candidate tools. However, the study acknowledges certain limitations that could influence the findings. The qualitative assessment of criteria like usability introduces a degree of evaluator subjectivity. Additionally, the lack of explicit weighting for non-mandatory requirements could mean that a different weighting scheme might result in a different final ranking. The requirements were based on input from a limited number of participants, and a larger group might have provided different baseline requirements. The requirements artifact itself represents a snapshot in time and may need to be updated as the MAL community's needs or the tool landscape evolve. Despite these limitations, the methodology is considered reusable for similar tool selection challenges in other domains. The recommendation of ADOxx is specific to the MAL ecosystem and its suitability for other domain-specific languages would depend on their unique requirements.

The research addressed its objectives through a structured process. A comprehensive requirements artifact was developed to address RO1, defining key functional and non-functional requirements. The characteristics of a sustainable tool were defined to address RO2. To fulfill RO3, 26 tools were evaluated against these criteria. Based on this evaluation, RO4 was addressed by recommending ADOxx as the most suitable graphical modeling tool for the MAL ecosystem.

7 Conclusion

This research addressed the need to identify a sustainable replacement for the discontinued graphical modeling tool used by the MAL community. The study utilized a DSR methodology, which involved defining requirements based on stakeholder interviews and established quality models, creating a requirements artifact, and using it to evaluate candidate tools. This systematic approach aimed to find a tool that met both functional and usability needs while also offering long-term sustainability.

The principal finding of this study is the recommendation of ADOxx as the most suitable graphical modeling tool for the MAL ecosystem. This recommendation is based on a comprehensive evaluation against a tailored set of requirements. The research contributes a reusable, context-specific requirements artifact for evaluating graphical modeling tools and provides a practical, evidence-based solution for the MAL community. This study underscores the importance of a systematic, requirements-driven approach for tool selection, particularly when non-functional requirements like sustainability are critical. The adoption of ADOxx has the potential to provide a stable foundation for the future development and application of MAL.

Based on the study's findings and acknowledged limitations, several directions for future work are proposed. The most immediate next step is the technical integration of ADOxx into the MAL toolchain. Subsequent empirical studies with MAL users would be valuable to validate the tool's effectiveness, usability, and impact on the overall workflow.

Acknowledgement. This work has received funding from European Union's HORIZON research and innovation programme under the Grant Agreement no. 101138583.

References

1. Iung, A., et al.: Systematic mapping study on domain-specific language development tools. Empir. Softw. Eng. **25**(5), 4205–4249 (2020). https://doi.org/10.1007/s10664-020-09872-1
2. Wideł, W., et al.: "The meta attack language - a formal description". en. In: Computers & Security, vol. 130, , p. 103284 (2023). issn: 01674048. https://doi.org/10.1016/j.cose.2023.103284. url: https://linkinghub.elsevier.com/retrieve/pii/S0167404823001943 (.Visited 26 Feb 2025)
3. Johnson, P., Lagerström, R., Ekstedt, M.: "A meta language for threat modeling and attack simulations". In: Proceedings of the 13th International Conference on Availability, Reliability and Security (2018). https://doi.org/10.1145/3230833.3232799
4. Grundy, J., et al.: "Generating domain-specific visual language tools from abstract visual specifications". IEEE Trans. Softw. Eng. **39**(4), 487–515 (2013). https://doi.org/10.1109/TSE.2012.33
5. Andrés, F., Lara, J., Guerra, E.: Domain specific languages with graphical and textual views . In:, pp. 82–97 (2008). https://doi.org/10.1007/978-3-540-89020-1_7
6. Dembri,A., Redjimi, M.: Towards a simplified evaluation of graphical DSL workbenches. In: Proceedings of the 2022 5th International Symposium on Informatics and its Applications (ISIA) , pp. 1–6 (2022). https://doi.org/10.1109/ISIA55826.2022.9993580
7. Grundy, J., et al.: Generating domain-specific visual language editors from high-level tool specifications. In: Proceedings of the 21st IEEE/ACM International Conference on Automated Software Engineering (ASE'06), pp. 25–36 (2006). https://doi.org/10.1109/ASE.2006.39
8. Ekstedt, M., et al.: "Securi CAD by Foreseeti: a CAD tool for enterprise cyber security management". In: 2015 IEEE 19th International Enterprise Distributed Object Computing Workshop, pp. 152–155 (2015). https://doi.org/10.1109/EDOCW.2015.40
9. Mernik, M., Heering, J., Sloane, A.M.: Domain-specific languages: a systematic mapping study. Info. Softw. Technol. **51**(4), 766–783 (2009)
10. Erdweg, S., et al.: The state of the art in language workbenches. In: Erwig, M., Paige, R.F., Van Wyk, E. (eds.) SLE 2013. LNCS, vol. 8225, pp. 197–217. Springer, Cham (2013). https://doi.org/10.1007/978-3-319-02654-1_11
11. Rodrigues, I.P., Campos, M.B., Zorzo, A.F.: 'Usability evaluation of domain-specific languages: a systematic literature review. In: Human-Computer Interaction. User Interface Design, Development and Multimodality. Ed. by Masaaki Kurosu. Cham: Springer International Publishing, pp. 522–534 (2017). isbn: 978-3-319-58071-5
12. Liu, N., Hosking, J., Grundy, J.: "MaramaTatau: extending a domain specific visual language meta tool with a declarative constraint mechanism". In: IEEE Symposium on Visual Languages and Human-Centric Computing (VL/HCC 2007), pp. 95–103 (2007). https://doi.org/10.1109/VLHCC.2007.10
13. Alomari, H.W., Vendome, C., Rizkallah, L.: A comprehensive evaluation framework of software visualizations effectiveness. IEEE Trans. Vis. Comput. Graph. **30**(9), 6056–6074 (2024). https://doi.org/10.1109/TVCG.2023.3321211
14. Insfran, E., Pastor, O., Winckler, M.: A usability evaluation framework for software engineering methodologies. In: International Conference on Product Focused Software Process Improvement. Springer, Berlin, Heidelberg (2005)

15. David Estrada-Esponda, R., et al.: Selection of software agile practices using analytic hierarchy process. Heliyon **10**(1), e22948 (2024). issn:2405-8440. https://doi.org/10.1016/j.heliyon.2023.e22948. url: https://www.sciencedirect.com/science/article/pii/S2405844023101563
16. Lucidspark Content Team. Weighted Decision Matrix: How to Use One to Make Better Decisions. Published: Lucidspark Blog. url: https://lucidspark.com/blog/weighted-decision-matrix
17. Costa, J., Meirelles, P., Chavez, C.: On the sustainability of academic software: the case of static analysis tools. In: Proceedings of the XXXII Brazilian Symposium on Software Engineering. SBES '18. event-place: Sao Carlos, Brazil. New York, NY, USA: Association for Computing Machinery, pp. 202–207 (2018). isbn: 978-1-4503-6503-1. https://doi.org/10.1145/3266237.3266243
18. Lasou, P., Neugebauer, T., Carson, P.: "identifying socio-technical risks in open-source software for scholarly communications: tools, metrics, and opportunities for libraries to support sustainable development. EBLIP **20**(1), 20–48 (2025). issn: 1715-720X. https://doi.org/10.18438/eblip30630. url: https://journals.library.ualberta.ca/eblip/index.php/EBLIP/article/view/30630 (visited on 05/07/2025)
19. Boll, A., Vieregg, N., Kehrer, T.: Replicability of experimental tool evaluations in model-based software and systems engineering with MATLAB/Simulink". en. Innov. Syst. Softw. Eng. **20**(3), 209–224 (2024). issn: 1614-5046, 1614-5054. https://doi.org/10.1007/s11334-022-00442-w. url: https://link.springer.com/10.1007/s11334-022-00442-w (visited on 05/07/2025)
20. TP15. TP15/Towards-a-Graphical-Tool-for-MAL: Release 1.0.2. Version v1.0.2. (2025). https://doi.org/10.5281/zenodo.17232507

AI and Model-Driven Approaches for the Next-Generation Enterprise

MODTWIN: A Method for Model-driven Engineering of Digital Twins for SMEs

Benjamin Nast[1(✉)] and Kurt Sandkuhl[1,2]

[1] University of Rostock, 18059 Rostock, Germany
{benjamin.nast,kurt.sandkuhl}@uni-rostock.de
[2] Jönköping University, 55111 Jönköping, Sweden

Abstract. The interest in digital twins (DTs) has recently increased among various industries. Consequently, various methods have been proposed to enhance their development and maintenance. The creation of DTs relies on integrating models and data from a variety of sources, including sensors, Internet of Things (IoT) devices, and other data streams. Model-driven engineering (MDE) is considered an effective approach for developing DTs. Our previous research indicates that current methods focus primarily on the software and systems perspective, often overlooking the importance of organizational integration. Additionally, we identified a growing need for approaches specifically designed to meet the needs of small and medium-sized enterprises (SMEs). In this paper, we introduce a method for MDE of DTs with the corresponding tool support meeting the specific requirements of SMEs. In three case studies from different domains, we demonstrate the applicability and confirm that domain experts are able to develop DTs with domain knowledge using our method.

Keywords: Modeling method · Model-driven engineering · Digital twin · Internet of Things · Domain-specific modeling language · MODTWIN

1 Introduction

In recent years, interest in digital twins (DTs) has increased among various industries [20,39]. The deployment of DTs offers a multitude of advantages, e.g., real-time monitoring, simulating and analyzing data, or remote control [1,20]. The development is contingent upon the integration of models and data derived from disparate sources, including sensors, Internet of Things (IoT) devices, and other data streams. DTs can largely be seen as IoT-intensive systems [35]. Model-driven engineering (MDE) is considered an effective technique for addressing the challenges inherent in the development and management of DTs [4].

Many enterprises face difficulties in extracting business value from technologies such as the IoT or DTs, while others hesitate to invest due to the challenges of organizational integration [36]. We argue that method support for the development of DTs should include organizational aspects to ease the creation of

Published by Springer Nature Switzerland AG 2026
H.-G. Fill et al. (Eds.): PoEM 2025, LNBIP 570, pp. 65–82, 2026.
https://doi.org/10.1007/978-3-032-12063-2_5

business value. However, in previous work [27], we showed through a systematic literature review that MDE approaches for developing IoT applications and DTs tend to focus on technological aspects. This is supported by a study of Fortino et al. [8] investigating IoT development approaches.

Furthermore, development processes in small and medium-sized enterprises (SMEs) differ from those of larger companies. In [27], we derived specifics of SMEs regarding the introduction of new technological innovations (such as DTs) from the perspective of digital innovation readiness. There are notable differences regarding the available resources, IT structure, knowledge, and broader aspects like the strategy or culture of the SME. Currently available model-driven approaches do not specifically consider the special needs of SMEs. A recent literature survey [40] confirms this for adopting DTs in manufacturing. It is concluded that clear guidelines for implementation are lacking and that the staff in those enterprises are often unable to face the resulting challenges.

The aim of our research is to address these problems by proposing a holistic approach for MDE of DTs that is suitable for SMEs and includes organizational aspects. Following the design science research (DSR) paradigm (see Sect. 3), our previous research resulted in a method for MDE of DTs, and a tool support for the heating, ventilation, and air conditioning (HVAC) domain [29]. However, applicability in other domains than HVAC still has to be shown, which requires additional iterations in the DSR design and evaluation cycle. Thus, this paper addresses two more application domains (smart farming and intralogistics), improves the method accordingly, and assesses our artifact for cross-domain applications. The following research questions (RQs) will be addressed:

- RQ1: How to adapt the method for MDE of DTs for cross-domain applications?
- RQ2: What should the technological support look like?
- RQ3: Which organizational aspects need to be considered while and after the development of DTs?

The paper is structured as follows: Sect. 2 provides an overview of MDE of DTs and related work in this field. The methodology applied is described in Sect. 3. Section 4 introduces our method and tool support, and Sect. 5 is concerned with their application and evaluation. We conclude this work in Sect. 6.

2 Background

2.1 Model-Driven Engineering of Digital Twins

DTs can be defined as virtual representations of physical or cyber-physical objects, systems, or processes [14]. A distinguishing feature is the automatic, bidirectional exchange of data between the virtual and physical instances [17]. The fundamental notion is to establish a comprehensible and adaptable virtual (digital) image of a tangible entity in the real world, with the objective of enhancing comprehension, observation, and control of its behavior [30]. They aim to enable the monitoring, understanding, and optimization of the behavior of the physical counterpart [38]. Modifications in the real world are to be automatically transferred to the DT, and vice versa. Consequently, a DT needs to offer both a representation of the physical part and a connection that facilitates communication between the two systems [7].

MDE is an effective technique to tackle the challenges of the development and management of DTs [4]. Automatic code generation resulting from model transformations enhances productivity and ensures consistency [5]. The complexity of development and efficient and (partially) automated implementation can be addressed by metamodels for domain-specific applications. MDE can be enabled by defining a domain-specific modeling language (DSML) to describe system requirements [9]. Model integrity is preserved by a defined syntax or semantics, which also prevents nonsensical models. The clarity and comprehensibility of models can be improved by specific graphical notations.

Current work confirms the growing interest in MDE of DTs (e.g., [19,23]). Tao et al. [39] further highlight the importance of DT modeling but also state that more modeling tools and a unified framework are needed. Lehner et al. [19] state in a systematic mapping study that most MDE approaches for DTs described in current research are still to be evaluated in an industrial context. Another important issue is that the complexity is more challenging for smaller enterprises, and guidelines for implementation are missing [40].

2.2 Related Work: Methods for MDE of Digital Twins

A substantial body of research has already been conducted on MDE of DTs.

In [6], an integrated method for MDE of low-code development platforms for DTs is introduced. It enables domain experts to create and operate customized DTs for cyber-physical systems for a variety of applications using the most appropriate modeling languages. In [3], the authors present a model-driven methodology and reference architecture for the efficient development of DTs for cyber-physical production systems with a specific focus on injection molding processes. It introduces a component and connector architecture using MontiArc (a framework for modeling and simulating software architectures), supplemented by domain-specific languages that enable the specification of event-driven behaviors and the communication interface via Open Platform Communications Unified Architecture (OPC UA), allowing for automation in the design of experiments and process optimizations. Kirchhof et al. [16] suggest a model-driven approach combining MontiArc models and UML/P (a specialized UML language profile) class diagrams to address the need for methods to build DTs of cyber-physical systems. In a practical IoT application, it is shown that this can eliminate repetitive programming activities and promote the systematic engineering of DTs. A model-driven framework to automatically derive specific DT models from existing AutomationML files created during the development of a system is presented by Lehner et al. [18]. In their case study, this reduced the time and effort required by experts to set up the necessary infrastructure by about 50%.

The focus of the aforementioned works is to systematize, simplify, and thus accelerate the development of DTs. A validated method that integrates both technological and organizational aspects throughout all phases of and after the development process, which is tailored for SMEs, has not yet been identified. Another aspect is that the applied standards (e.g., AutomationML) would require additional training for the employees.

3 Research Method

The main objective of this research project is to provide methodical and technological support for SMEs to develop DTs. The overall research strategy follows the ideas and principles of DSR [11]. DSR aims to develop practical solutions by humans that professionals can use in their respective fields [15]. A viable artifact must be produced in the form of a construct, a model, a method, or an instantiation [11,15,22], to fulfill the requirements of DSR. The artifact of the research presented in this work can be regarded as a method [22]. The goal of the method (artifact) development can be described using the *design problem* template proposed by Wieringa [41]:

> ***Improve*** *the development of DTs*
> ***by*** *engineering a method and tool support*
> ***that*** *are applicable by users in SMEs,*
> ***in order to*** *enable development processes, while considering both technological and organizational integration.*

Our development procedure is oriented towards Peffers et al. [34] (see Table 1). We applied a combination of literature study, descriptive case studies, expert interviews, argumentative-deductive, and conceptual-deductive analysis [42] to address our overarching RQs.

As our previous work [25,27] indicated that the specifics of SMEs were not efficiently represented in existing work on MDE of DTs, we decided to perform a qualitative case study to gather information pertinent to the subject area and further address *Problem Identification and Motivation* and *Define Objectives of a Solution*. A qualitative case study is a research approach that facilitates the exploration of a phenomenon within its context using various data sources [2]. This ensures that the subject under consideration is not explored from only one perspective but rather from various perspectives, allowing for multiple facets of the phenomenon to be revealed and understood. Within the case study, we used three different perspectives, which at the same time represent sources of data. We observed the activities during DT development, examined the business model of the case study enterprise, and interviewed people involved in different roles. The case study in which the first versions of our method and tool support were developed [13,24] must be considered descriptive, as it describes the phenomenon of process outsourcing and the real-life context in which it occurs [43].

Concerning *Design and Development* and *Demonstration*, a first version of the method and tool support has been developed and presented in [27]. A central and critical aspect of DSR is *Evaluation* [11,22]. The primary focus is the assessment of outcomes (e.g., artifacts [22]). After a number of iterations of *Evaluation*

Table 1. DSR process applied in this work according to Peffers et al. [34].

Phase	Research Method	Result and Status
Step 1 Problem Identification and Motivation	Systematic Literature Review [27], Case Study and Expert Interviews [25,27]	Defined Problem ✓
Step 2 Define Objectives of a Solution	Expert Interviews [25], Argumentative-deductive Analysis [27]	Requirements ✓
Step 3 Design and Development	Conceptual-deductive Analysis [27,29] and Sect. 4	Method and Tool Support (✓)
Step 4 Demonstration	Case studies [24,27,29] and Sect. 5	Demonstrated Method and Tool Support ✓
Step 5 Evaluation	Case Studies [28] and Sect. 5, Expert Interviews [28], Experiments [26]	Evaluated Method and Tool Support (✓)
Step 6 Communication		Communicated Results in Research and Practice ✓

"✓" = Done, "(✓)" = Mostly done

in the case study in the HVAC domain [13,24], an improved version was presented in [29]. The *Evaluation* of the method and tool support mainly focused on quality, effectiveness, usefulness [26,28], and aspects of digital innovation readiness for SMEs [27], confirming that they are suitable for DT development at least in this domain. It also led to various improvements in the method description and the tool support. The latest version for cross-domain applications is reported in Sect. 4 and evaluated in Sect. 5.

Communication included the publication in academic outlets listed here (e.g., conferences or conference workshops) to report on the tackled problem, the relevance, the applicability, and usefulness of the artifact. In addition, Peffers et al. [34] state that it is also important to share the results with relevant audiences from practice. We consistently involved domain experts from the case study enterprise and partners from a joint research project [13,24] throughout all iteration steps. Since our approach is used in practice in the case study enterprise, the exchange on it led to additional insight that influenced the final design, e.g., with regard to maintenance and evaluation.

The main objective of this work is to present the method and tool support in the iteratively improved version for cross-domain applications. The *demonstration* is broadened by applying the approach in two more domains. This also contributes to preparing the additional *evaluation* episodes with focus on the incorporation of relevant aspects of organizational integration. Further iterations may be necessary if the evaluation and communication in further case studies reveal feedback or areas for improvement, meaning that the design and development must be further advanced.

4 The MODTWIN Method

As outlined in Sect. 3, the objective of the *Modeling Digital Twins (MODTWIN)* method is to facilitate the development of DTs by users in SMEs with no special IT skills. We provide guidelines to support the development and organizational integration. The tool's user-friendly interface enables domain experts to input the domain knowledge (metadata) required for the respective use case and images to create a DSML based on this information. The DSML enables the creation of conceptual models through the utilization of a comprehensible visual notation. The API allows for the automated configuration of the DT based on metadata.

4.1 Approach for Model-Driven Engineering of Digital Twins

Figure 1 presents the approach for MDE of DTs. Our method is structured in accordance with the method conceptualization by Goldkuhl et al. [10]. They define a method as a set of interchangeable and reusable *method components* that address specific subproblems of the overall problem. Additionally, we divided the method into three phases representing different stages of development based on identified related work [12,37] and experiences from our first case study [13, 24]. The upper part of Fig. 1 shows the six method components and a general execution flow. Each phase creates outputs that are utilized in the subsequent phase. The whole method is triggered by identified problems or optimization potential in the physical world and aims to improve it. In addition, the relevant applications and services, as well as the connections to the method and the physical world, can be seen in the middle of the figure.

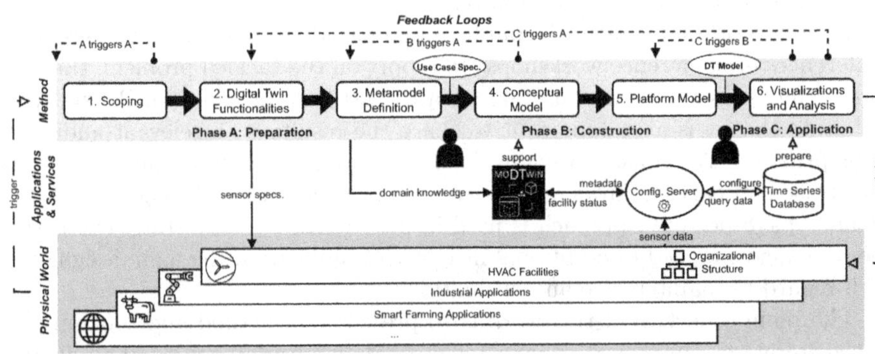

Fig. 1. Approach for model-driven engineering of digital twins.

Phase A: *Preparation* addresses the scope of the specific application, derives requirements, and prepares the tool support. The *Scoping (1)* component is responsible for determining the scope of the application. In order to gain a comprehensive understanding of the problem, a detailed analysis must be conducted. This analysis should identify the causes of the problem and define the problem domain, stakeholders, and individuals responsible for developing the DT. It must be clarified which knowledge and resources are necessary. Once these elements have been established, the overall goals of the application can be defined. The objective of *Digital Twin Functionalities (2)* is to identify the specific functionalities of the DT based on this. It must be clarified what is realistic to be implemented in the given situation, regarding the context and the enterprise. The available and required sensors or further data sources for the application can now be derived. In *Metamodel Definition (3)*, domain experts can create the metamodel with the corresponding DSML and prepare the metadata collection using the *MODTWIN* tool[1], which is based on the ADOxx metamodeling platform [31]. Based on the ADOxx meta-metamodel (*M4*), we defined the *MODTWIN* metamodel (*M3*) for DTs (see Fig. 2, further described in Sect. 5.1). This allows for the simple creation of domain-specific metamodels (*M2*) using domain knowledge, and by adding graphical representations, the DSML can be created to generate conceptual models (*M1*) of the DT instance (*M0*). The output of this phase is the defined *Use Case Specification.*

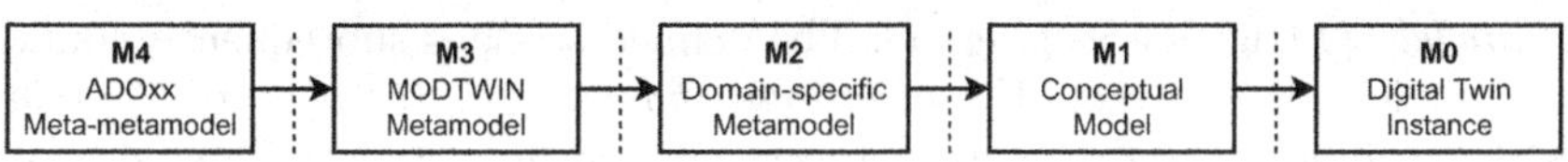

Fig. 2. Five-layer metamodeling architecture based on ADOxx.

Phase B: The objective of *Construction* is to develop the DT. The *MODTWIN* tool used by the domain expert supports both components of this phase. The component *Conceptual Model (4)* aims to create a conceptual model of a facility using the implemented DSML with the domain-specific metamodel. In addition, the data required from the facilities (metadata) was determined in *Phase A* to implement the application. The retrieval of the metadata represents a significant part of the development of the conceptual model of a facility (components and required sensors are created automatically for each type). The model can then be adjusted and converted into the platform model. For this, as well as further data exports, several functionalities are implemented to support the modeling process (e.g., checks for completeness or errors in the data). Component *Platform Model (5)* is responsible for using the entered metadata to convert it into a platform-specific format (*DT Model*), which can then be used to configure the time series database (TSDB), which is required for the last phase of the method.

[1] https://www.omilab.org/activities/projects/details/?id=510.

Phase C: The primary purpose of *Application* is the actual application of the DT. The platform model, which is automatically created with the tool, combines the metadata with the requisite information to configure the TSDB and create visualizations and analyses that are intended to optimize the problems identified in the physical world (component *Visualizations and Analysis (6)*). The metadata is sent to the TSDB (e.g., to InfluxDB as a JSON file). An API token is then automatically created for each customer or enterprise, and the corresponding buckets and dashboards are created based on the metadata. Based on the incoming sensor data, we can define states for sensors and components and visualize them in the conceptual model. In addition, in this phase, it is necessary to assess whether the objectives of the use case are met by the DT, which must be maintained in a current state.

Feedback Loops: The method contains feedback loops that may occur during execution. They are important if the execution of a component generates knowledge that leads to the need to execute a previous component again. These are typical loops we identified while developing this method and applying it in the case studies. They are not intended to prevent users from executing other loops that may occur when the method is executed. Those feedback loops are, for example: *Digital Twin Functionalities (2)* triggers *Scoping (1)*: When it is realized that specific functionalities can not be realized (e.g., sensors can't be utilized or data sources are not available), the scope must be adjusted. *Conceptual Model (4)* triggers *Scoping (1)*: The defined scope is subsequently found to be incomplete or incorrect. *Visualizations and Analysis (6)* triggers *Conceptual Model (4)*: It is realized that the objects created or metadata entered contain errors that need to be adjusted in the conceptual model.

4.2 Organizational Integration

The integration of our method into the organizational context of SME has to be differentiated into at least two aspects: the integration during the phase of MDE of the DT and the preparation of the operation of the DT. For the former, we consider the relevant roles required in the enterprise. For the latter, we investigate what aspects of readiness are relevant and how our method can be prepared for these aspects. The "readiness" of enterprises for innovation aims to identify aspects and factors involved in its introduction. In developing our method, we looked at digital innovation readiness aspects [21] and adapted them to the specific needs of SMEs in prior work [27]:

- **Resource Readiness:** SMEs have less flexibility in allocating resources to technological innovation projects. Consequently, they prioritize projects with clearly defined and stable resource requirements.
  We provide a clear and well-defined method and free-of-charge tool support, contributing to low resource requirements.

- **IT Readiness:** The IT situation in SMEs is strictly determined by organizational needs. IT implementation as such is often equated with innovation or regarded as such.
  IT readiness expectations are reduced to a reasonable level through the use of standard components.
- **Cognitive Readiness:** The focus of SMEs is on the availability of the competencies and knowledge necessary for their core business. Competencies in the areas of innovation are generally available if the subject of innovation is in the core area.
  The DSML and the automatic development of the DT based on the domain knowledge minimize the need for specialized employee training and lower the cognitive readiness threshold.
- **Partnership Readiness:** There is no general pattern, as the partnership readiness highly depends on the domain and business model of the SME.
  In this context, it is unreasonable to expect all partners, suppliers, and customers to provide or receive required information digitally. For example, information about specific components in a facility under consideration. While some customers may be able to provide this information digitally, experience from our case studies shows that most customers either lack access to it or the necessary technical knowledge. Therefore, our method and tool support do not rely on mandatory digital input data from customers or partners. However, the tool allows for the provision of information about a facility from the model and for exporting it.
- **Cultural Readiness:** Cultural readiness for digital innovation refers to the extent to which an organization's values enable innovation. A culture of sharing ideas, decentralized decision-making, or risk-taking is often regarded as an indicator of readiness.
  The method and tool support provided does not serve as a direct means to promote this. However, it is important to note that the materialization of both would not have been possible without the participation of the case study enterprises. Therefore, they can be regarded as indicators of a certain level of readiness.
- **Strategic Readiness:** The capacity of SMEs to engage in new activities is often constrained by the multifaceted responsibilities of their management personnel, which limits the time and resources available for new initiatives.
  As described, our approach offers a range of support for organizational integration (see also the remainder of this section). This reduces the effort required, thereby saving time and resources.

For conducting the method, we identified two superior roles: *Domain Expert* and *System Admin*. Table 2 summarizes the respective tasks in the different method components and results relevant for organizational integration. The *Domain Expert* should have extensive and long-term experience in the domain. This also includes in-depth knowledge of the relevant organizational structures, key business processes, and the IT landscape. The *System Admin* needs to have a good overview of all systems in the organization and their interplay.

The *Domain Expert* has various tasks defined in all method components. In the case studies conducted (see Sect. 5), we have seen that this role can be filled by one person, that the corresponding tasks can be distributed among several people, or that the same tasks can also be performed by several people. In our experience, the role of *System Admin* is often held by one person in SMEs.

In *Scoping (1)*, the resulting elements relevant for integration in multiperspective models (e.g., 4EM) are *Goals*, *Actors*, and *Resources*. It must be examined whether the *Goals* can be meaningfully integrated and to what extent they may influence existing ones. It must also be evaluated which *Actors* are affected by the implementation of the DT and the further usage, what *Resources* are needed for this, and what further effects this has on the organization. After describing *Digital Twin Functionalities (2)*, *Technical Components*, such as sensors and data sources, arise that need to be considered. In *Platform Model (5)*, the *System Admin* first needs to set up the TSDB and create the API token to connect the *MODTWIN* tool. After uploading the data by the *Domain Expert*, the *Technical Component* (TSDB) needs to be integrated. In *Visualization and Analysis (6)*, *Problems* may arise regarding the usage or technical issues that also need to be addressed in the models. Furthermore, novel *Processes* and *Services* are emerging, which necessitate integration into the relevant models.

Table 2. Overview of roles, tasks, and results across MODTWIN method components.

Component	Task	DE	SA	Result
1. Scoping	Problem Analysis, Define Stakeholders (needs) and Responsibilities, Identify Required Knowledge and Resources, Derive Goals	X		Goals, Actors, Resources
2. Digital Twin Functionalities	Derive DT Functionalities, Analyze Required Data Sources	X		Technical Components
3. Metamodel Definition	Supply Domain Knowledge	X		
4. Conceptual Model	Create and Adjust the Conceptual Model	X		
5. Platform Model	DE: Create Platform Model and Upload Data SA: Setup InfluxDB and Configure API	X	X	Technical Components
6. Visualizations and Analysis	DE: Consume and Analyze Data SA: Connect Data Sources to InfluxDB	X	X	Problems, Processes, Services

"DE" = Domain Expert, "SA" = System Admin

5 Method Application and Evaluation

This section presents the application and evaluation of our method and tool support in three real-world case studies. The first case study was conducted in the HVAC domain, in which we evaluated the whole development process and the support for organizational integration. This led to several improvements, and, in the next step, we applied our approach in two further real-world case studies in different domains: smart farming and intralogistics. The focus in the latter two case studies was on the development parts, so the evaluation of the organizational integration parts in these domains remains open for future work.

5.1 Optimizing the Energy Efficiency of HVAC Facilities

The first case study was conducted in collaboration with an SME specializing in the construction, operation, and maintenance of HVAC facilities. These facilities are not mass-produced but individually designed to meet customer-specific requirements. The objective of the DT was to enable energy optimizations with minimal sensor deployment, while also supporting maintenance, error detection, and recognizing operating errors caused by humans. A major challenge in this domain lies in the complexity and quantity of components and sensors. More than 200 attributes with their respective data types, value ranges, and units were considered, covering operator and customer data, component specifications, sensor types, and other metadata critical for contextualizing real-time sensor data. This makes it an excellent case for applying our approach.

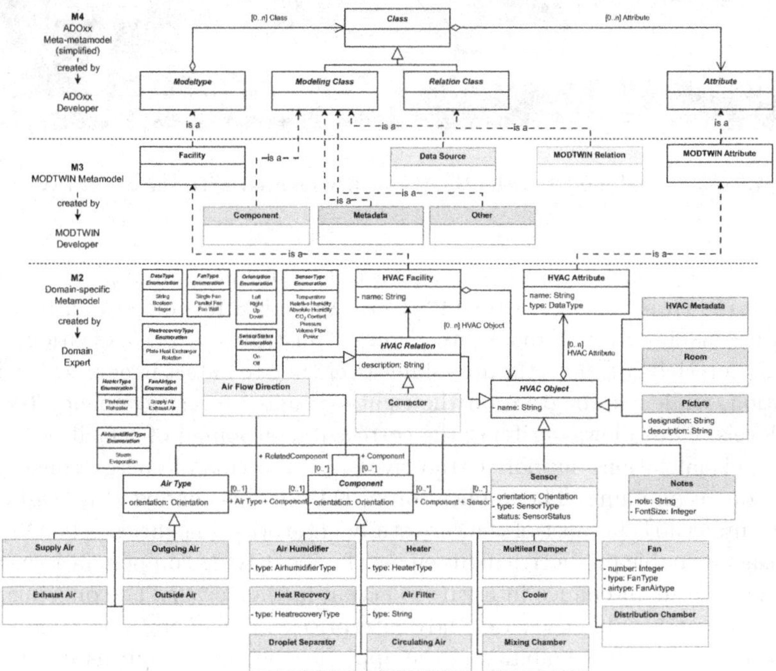

Fig. 3. Instantiation of the HVAC metamodel (from M4 to M2).

Based on the ADOxx meta-metamodel, we developed the *MODTWIN* metamodel to support the creation of a DSML by providing a structure for the relevant elements (see Fig. 3). Some relations (*is-a*) across the metamodel layers *M3* and *M2* are represented visually with colors for improved clarity. All metadata is stored as attributes in the *Metadata* class. The enumeration class attributes are represented on the left side in the *M2* layer. A domain expert provided the necessary domain knowledge (metadata) via the tool. This input automatically generates the domain-specific metamodel, based on the *MODTWIN* metamodel.

The graphical representations of the DSML are also to be uploaded by the domain expert via the tool. The DSML was then used to create a conceptual model of an HVAC facility (see Fig. 4), enriched by a background image of the facility in the tool for greater comprehensibility.

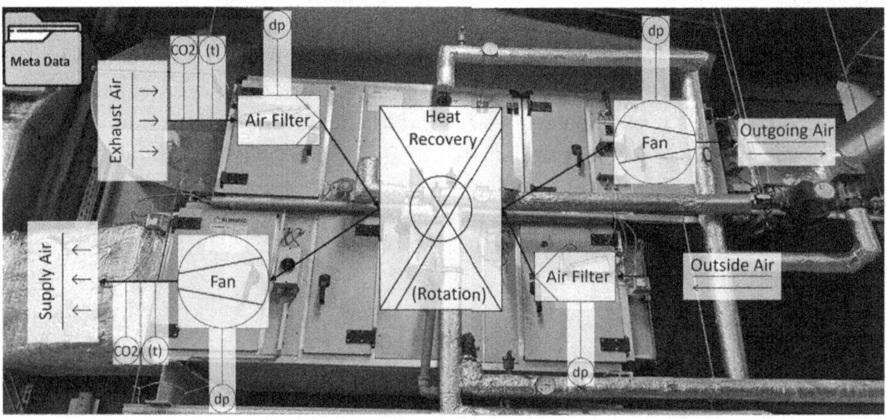

Fig. 4. Conceptual model of the HVAC facility created with the MODTWIN tool.

The conceptual model was subsequently transformed into a platform model. Metadata is transmitted via HTTPS to an InfluxDB instance to automatically configure dashboards and diagrams. Figure 5 illustrates two visualizations: a carpet diagram (left) displays the air volume over time to detect irregularities during operation, while the diagram on the right estimates room occupancy based on CO_2 levels. This allows verifying the correct dimensioning of a facility.

The visualizations support data-driven optimization of energy consumption and resource planning. The application of DTs in this context can yield energy savings up to 30% in most of the case study enterprises' facilities [24]. Moreover, DT insights enable predictive maintenance by identifying component issues early and adapting maintenance intervals to actual facility usage. The ongoing use of our method and tool in the case study enterprises' daily operations demonstrates not only the technical viability of the approach but also confirms its organizational integration support.

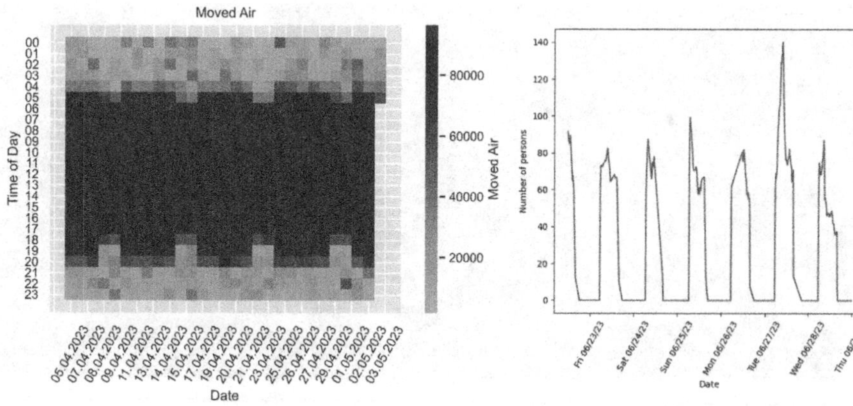

Fig. 5. Diagrams for moved air volume and number of persons present in a room.

5.2 Digital Health Record for Cows

In collaboration with a research institute for farm animals, we have developed two use cases relevant in cowsheds: health monitoring and optimization of milk production. Compared to the other case studies, the metadata required in this context is significantly less complex. Only the *Animal Number*, *Life Mark*, *Name*, *Gender*, *Date of Birth*, and *Breed* are to be collected for each cow. The use cases rely heavily on measured data rather than calculated values, as in the HVAC case study. Each cow is treated as an individual "component", with vital data including *Body Temperature*, *Activity*, *Feed Intake*, and *Milk Yield* continuously collected and analyzed. These values are integrated with treatment records from veterinarians, which include historical diagnoses and interventions.

For the optimization of milk production, additional parameters are monitored, such as milk composition (e.g., *Fat*, *Protein*, or *Lactose*), environmental factors (*Ambient Temperature*), and animal-specific factors (e.g., *Health Status*, or *Feed Quality*). This holistic data integration supports early detection of performance issues and enables targeted interventions to improve both the quality and quantity of milk production. Figure 6 shows an example of an automatically generated dashboard using our tool and visualized in Grafana. The dashboard consolidates sensor data, metadata, and external records to provide real-time insights into herd health and productivity.

These results demonstrate that the *MODTWIN* method effectively supports health monitoring and optimization of milk production in livestock farming by integrating real-time sensor data with structured metadata, laying the groundwork for predictive analysis and simulation, thereby enhancing proactive decision-making in livestock management in future applications.

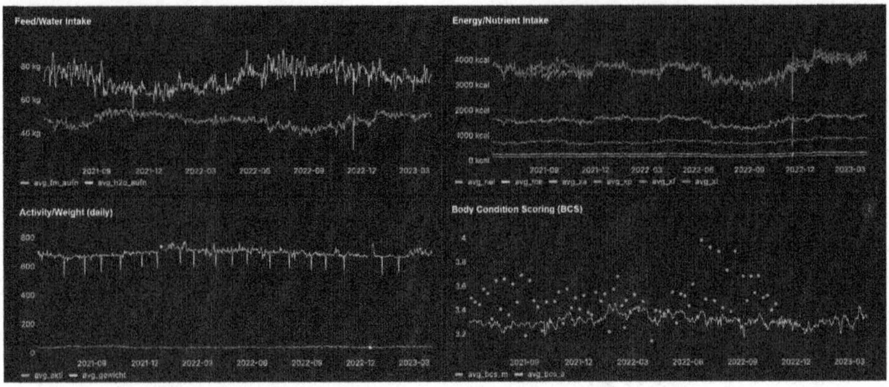

Fig. 6. Automatically generated Grafana dashboard for cowshed digital twin.

5.3 Improving Operational Efficiency in Intralogistics

Intralogistics, encompassing the internal flow of materials within industrial facilities, is a promising domain for the application of MDE of DTs. In collaboration with a practical partner specializing in embedded OPC UA solutions, we explored how MDE can be enhanced by leveraging the inherent knowledge of Industrial IoT communication protocols. This led us to the semantic Industry 4.0 protocol known as OPC UA. Its self-descriptive approach provides context with every piece of information. In combination with standardized domain-specific data models known as Companion Specifications (CSs), e.g., for "Cranes and Hoists" [33] or "Robotics" [32], this protocol can be a valuable data source (metadata) for our approach. OPC UA with the CSs can therefore support DT development in both the design and runtime phases by sending real-time data from the machines. These CSs provide structured information for components like *Brake Type*, *Axis Type*, or *Motion Device Type*, which can be directly used in modeling and configuration.

The case study assumes that (most) of the machines involved have an OPC UA interface with standardized data models, either natively or retrofitted. Intralogistics processes are characterized by their complexity and the need for precise coordination between different systems. The main goal is to improve operational efficiency, predictive maintenance, and real-time monitoring.

We extracted the relevant metadata from the CSs to enable modeling of facilities to allow for supervision, condition monitoring, and asset management. Figure 7 presents a conceptual model that contains four cranes, a robot, and an external system that can request restrictions on the operation of the crane. In this case, it is a body-worn device that can be used to request speed limits for the crane in order to make the working area safer for people and other machines. The relations symbolize the type of communication between the components.

At this stage, we only tested the creation of the conceptual model and the configuration of the TSDB. Analyzing sensor data and organizational integra-

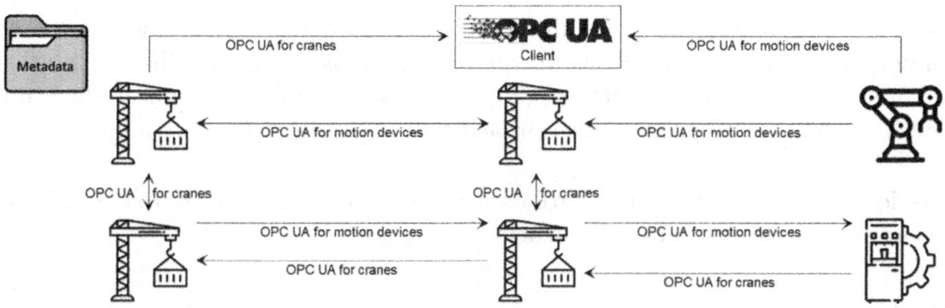

Fig. 7. Conceptual model of a facility for cranes and hoists.

tion has not yet been done. These initial results underscore the feasibility of applying metadata-driven DT modeling in complex industrial domains, laying the groundwork for full integration in future work. The expected improvements here lie in the efficiency and decision-making support. The integration of standardized data models provided by OPC UA CSs will result in a reduction in planning and implementation costs. The ability to visualize and analyze data supports proactive maintenance strategies and enhances the overall agility of intralogistics operations, eventually increasing efficiency.

6 Conclusion

In this paper, we presented *MODTWIN*, a novel method for MDE of DTs for SMEs. The method was demonstrated and evaluated in three case studies in diverse domains: *HVAC*, *Smart Farming*, and *Intralogistics*. This showed that its components effectively support the phases of *Preparation*, *Construction*, and *Application* (RQ1) and the tool enables domain experts to define DSMLs and build conceptual models to configure DTs (RQ2). The support of organizational integration was also confirmed, specifically in the HVAC case study (RQ3).

Overall, *MODTWIN* provides a lightweight, accessible, and structured approach enabling the wider adoption of DT technology in SMEs, bridging a critical gap in current MDE approaches. The findings from the case studies confirm the intuitiveness of use. As the method has been developed in real-world SME settings, it also incorporates considerations for cybersecurity and data protection compliance (e.g., by using HTTPS and token-based API).

Despite these strengths, some limitations should be acknowledged. While the ADOxx platform supports flexible DSML creation, it poses constraints in user interface customization, extensibility, and collaborative modeling. As with many DSR projects, the iterative method development was closely tied to the specific case studies to improve fit and relevance, which may introduce contextual biases and limit generalizability.

For the organizational integration, future work will also have to investigate how to support business model innovation and the required changes in business processes and services. Aspects such as the co-operation forms and parts of the method components (see Goldkuhl et al. [10]) require further specification based on ongoing practical experience. Extending the tools ' compatibility with other TSDBs and visualization platforms, and the creation of more advanced diagrams and dashboards, are promising approaches to expanding the functionality.

Disclosure of Interests. The authors have no competing interests to declare that are relevant to the content of this article.

References

1. Attaran, M., Celik, B.G.: Digital twin: benefits, use cases, challenges, and opportunities. Dec. Anal. J. **6**, 100165 (2023)
2. Baxter, P., Jack, S.: Qualitative case study methodology: study design and implementation for novice researchers. Qualit. Rep. **13**(4), 544–559 (2008)
3. Bibow et al.: Model-driven development of a digital twin for injection molding. In: Advanced Information Systems Engineering, pp. 85–100. Springer, Cham (2020)
4. Bordeleau., et al.: Towards model-driven digital twin engineering: current opportunities and future challenges. In: International Conference on Systems Modelling and Management, pp. 43–54. Springer (2020)
5. Brambilla, M., Cabot, J., Wimmer, M.: Model-driven Software Engineering in Practice. Morgan & Claypool Publishers (2017)
6. Dalibor, et al.: Generating customized low-code development platforms for digital twins. J. Comput. Lang. **70**, 101117 (2022)
7. Eramo, R., Bordeleau, F., Combemale, B., van Den Brand, M., Wimmer, M., Wortmann, A.: Conceptualizing digital twins. IEEE Softw. **39**(2), 39–46 (2021)
8. Fortino, G., Savaglio, C., Spezzano, G., Zhou, M.: Internet of Things as system of systems: a review of methodologies, frameworks, platforms, and tools. IEEE Trans. Syst. Man Cybern. Syst. **51**(1), 223–236 (2020)
9. Frank, U.: Domain-specific modeling languages: requirements analysis and design guidelines, pp. 133–157. Springer Berlin Heidelberg (2013)
10. Goldkuhl, G., Lind, M., Seigerroth, U.: Method integration: the need for a learning perspective. IEE Proc. Softw. **145**(4), 113–118 (1998)
11. Hevner, A.R., March, S.T., Park, J., Ram, S.: Design science in information systems research. MIS Q. **28**(1), 75–105 (2004)
12. Hussein, M., Li, S., Radermacher, A.: Model-driven development of adaptive IoT systems. In: MODELS (Satellite Events), pp. 17–23 (2017)
13. Ivanovic, N., Nast, B., Reiz, A., Sandkuhl, K.: Technologies for a diagnostic technique for HVAC systems using IoT and cloud-based architecture. In: 2023 International Interdisciplinary PhD Workshop (IIPhDW). pp. 1–6 (2023)
14. Javaid, M., Haleem, A., Suman, R.: Digital twin applications toward Industry 4.0: A review. Cogn. Robot. **3**, 71–92 (2023)
15. An Introduction to Design Science. Springer, Cham (2021). https://doi.org/10.1007/978-3-030-78132-3_9
16. Kirchhof., et al.: Model-driven digital twin construction: synthesizing the integration of cyber-physical systems with their information systems. In: International Conference on Model Driven Engineering Languages and Systems, pp. 90–101 (2020)
17. Kritzinger., et al.: Digital twin in manufacturing: a categorical literature review and classification. Ifac-PapersOnline **51**(11), 1016–1022 (2018)

18. Lehner et al.: AML4DT: A model-driven framework for developing and maintaining digital twins with AutomationML. In: International Conference on Emerging Technologies and Factory Automation (ETFA), pp. 1–8 (2021)
19. Lehner., et al.: Model-driven engineering for digital twins: a systematic mapping study. Softw. Syst. Model. **24**(5), 1–39 (2025)
20. Liu, M., Fang, S., Dong, H., Xu, C.: Review of digital twin about concepts, technologies, and industrial applications. J. Manuf. Syst. **58**, 346–361 (2021)
21. Lokuge, S., Sedera, D., Grover, V., Dongming, X.: Organizational readiness for digital innovation: development and empirical calibration of a construct. Info. Manag. **56**(3), 445–461 (2019)
22. March, S.T., Smith, G.F.: Design and natural science research on information technology. Decis. Support Syst. **15**(4), 251–266 (1995)
23. Michael., et al.: Model-driven engineering for digital twins: opportunities and challenges. Syst. Eng. (2025)
24. Nast, B., Reiz, A., Ivanovic, N., Sandkuhl, K.: A modeling approach supporting digital twin engineering: optimizing the energy consumption of air conditioning facilities. In: 2023 ACM/IEEE International Conference on Model Driven Engineering Languages and Systems Companion (MODELS-C), pp. 479–483 (2023)
25. Nast, B., Sandkuhl, K.: Meta-model and tool support for the organizational aspects of Internet-of-Things development methods: organizational aspects of IoT development methods. In: International Conference on Advanced Information Science and System. AISS '21, Association for Computing Machinery, New York, NY, USA (2021)
26. Nast, B., Sandkuhl, K.: Evaluation of the intuitiveness of MIoTA. In: International Conference on Perspectives in Business Informatics Research (BIR 2024). CEUR (2024)
27. Nast, B., Sandkuhl, K.: A method for model-driven IoT application development. In: Evaluation of Novel Approaches to Software Engineering, pp. 141–164. Springer Nature Switzerland, Cham (2024)
28. Nast, B., Sandkuhl, K.: Quality evaluation of a DSML supporting model-driven IoT development for air conditioning facilities. In: Advances in Enterprise Engineering XVII, pp. 52–72. Springer, Cham (2024)
29. Nast, B., Sandkuhl, K., Paulus, S., Schiller, H.: MIoTA: modeling IoT applications for air conditioning facilities with ADOxx. In: Int. Conf. on Perspectives in Business Informatics Research Workshops and Doctoral Consortium, BIR-WS 2023, vol. 3514, pp. 158–168. CEUR (2023)
30. Ogunsakin, R., Mehandjiev, N., Marin, C.A.: Towards adaptive digital twins architecture. Comput. Ind. **149**, 103920 (2023)
31. OMiLAB: The ADOxx Metamodelling Platform. https://www.adoxx.org/live/home (2025). Accessed 1 July 2025
32. OPC Foundation : Robotics. http://opcfoundation.org/UA/Robotics/
33. OPC Foundation: CranesHoists. http://opcfoundation.org/UA/CranesHoists/
34. Peffers, K., Tuunanen, T., Rothenberger, M.A., Chatterjee, S.: A design science research methodology for information systems research. J. Manag. Inf. Syst. **24**(3), 45–77 (2007)
35. Rivera et al.: On the engineering of IoT-intensive digital twin software systems. In: 42nd International Conference on Software Engineering Workshops, pp. 631–638 (2020)
36. Sandkuhl, K., Seigerroth, U.: Digital transformation of enterprises: case studies and transformation paths. In: PACIS, p. 35 (2021)

37. Reyna, S., et al.: Methodology for the model-driven development of service oriented IoT applications. J. Syst. Architect. **90**, 15–22 (2018)
38. Stary, C., Elstermann, M., Fleischmann, A., Schmidt, W.: Behavior-centered digital-twin design for dynamic cyber-physical system development. Complex Syst .Info. Model. Quart. **30**, 31–52 (2022)
39. Tao, F., Zhang, M.: Digital twin shop-floor: a new shop-floor paradigm towards smart manufacturing. IEEE Access **5**, 20418–20427 (2017)
40. Bossuyt, V., et al.: The future of digital twin research and development. J. Comput. Info. Sci. Eng. **25**(8), 080801 (2025)
41. Design Science Methodology for Information Systems and Software Engineering. Springer, Heidelberg (2014). https://doi.org/10.1007/978-3-662-43839-8_20
42. Wilde, T., Hess, T.: Methodenspektrum der wirtschaftsinformatik: Überblick und portfoliobildung. Tech. rep, Arbeitsbericht (2006)
43. Yin, R.K.: Case Study Research: Design and Methods, vol. 5. sage (2009)

Talk to Me! Toward Speech-Based UML Modeling

Simon Schwantler[1], Stefan Klikovits[2], Haydar Metin[3], Philip Langer[3], and Dominik Bork[1(✉)]

[1] Business Informatics Group, TU Wien, Vienna, Austria
simon.schwantler@gmx.at, dominik.bork@tuwien.ac.at
[2] Department of Business Informatics, JKU Linz, Linz, Austria
stefan.klikovits@jku.at
[3] EclipseSource, Vienna, Austria
{hmetin,planger}@eclipsesource.com

Abstract. Modeling is a core task in enterprise systems engineering. The use of graphical modeling editors, however, remains cumbersome in general and poses a significant challenge for users with disabilities. Natural language processing (NLP) and intent recognition are at the forefront of making many technologies more accessible and intuitive by allowing users to engage using natural language. This paper presents a natural language interface (NLI) for speech-based UML model interaction that leverages state-of-the-art NLP technologies to enable speech-based modeling. We provide a workflow for the creation of NLIs for modeling editors, a proof-of-concept integration of this approach into the BIGUML open-source modeling editor, and an empirical evaluation that shows promising results in intent recognition, the effectiveness of model creation, and usability. Thereby, this paper makes significant contributions towards more natural, inclusive, and accessible modeling.

Keywords: Natural language interface · Speech-based interaction · GLSP · Modeling tool · UML · Accessibility

1 Introduction and Background

In the practice of enterprise modeling, the proficient utilization of modeling editors is crucial. The use of graphical modeling editors such as BIGUML [28], Papyrus [24], StarUML[1], or Visual Paradigm[2] is the day-to-day business of software engineers and domain experts in the context of enterprise and software modeling. However, efficient editor-supported modeling typically requires numerous long and complex interaction sequences involving many switches between keyboard and mouse, and the skilled orchestration of both input devices. This form

[1] https://staruml.io/.
[2] https://www.visual-paradigm.com/.

Published by Springer Nature Switzerland AG 2026
H.-G. Fill et al. (Eds.): PoEM 2025, LNBIP 570, pp. 83–101, 2026.
https://doi.org/10.1007/978-3-032-12063-2_6

of interaction, which is common to all current graphical modeling editors, often presents accessibility barriers for users with physical disabilities [36].

While recent years have seen notable efforts to improve accessibility in software engineering and web development[3], the field of conceptual modeling still lags behind [37]. Innovative means of model interaction and improved accessibility in modeling have been largely neglected, making the discipline less inclusive and failing to accommodate all modelers' varied needs and abilities. This oversight not only excludes people with disabilities from participating in conceptual modeling and model-driven engineering, but also neglects the potential benefits that accessible interfaces provide, as seen by the widespread adoption of voice assistants (e.g. Siri, Alexa) in everyday homes. Enhancing accessibility in modeling could thus promote inclusion [8] and enable users of all abilities to engage. It further offers potential for more natural means of editor interaction over traditional mouse and keyboard inputs [26].

Natural language processing (NLP) and intent recognition are at the forefront of making software applications more accessible by allowing users to specify their intent in natural language. Nonetheless, the complexity of human language poses challenges, including e.g., ambiguity, colloquial language (a.k.a. *slang*), regional accents and dialects, and speech impairments. Overcoming these challenges would render conceptual modeling more intuitive, more usable because of an increase in modeling efficiency, and more accessible to users without technical training or users facing some form of disability.

This paper introduces speech-based modeling using a natural language interface (NLI) for BIGUML [29], a web-based, extensible, and open-source UML modeling editor. We chose UML class diagrams as the target language because of the availability of a publicly used modeling editor.

Recently, Large Language Models (LLMs) have been studied for conceptual model creation from natural language descriptions [1,17,18,23,35,39]. These approaches rely on one-shot model generation, with the output in textual format (e.g., PlantUML). This process, however, has three main drawbacks: First, model creation is an iterative process of editing steps (adding, deleting, and refactoring), rather than one-shot generation. Second, LLMs mainly support standard languages such as UML or SysML, with limited support for domain-specific languages (DSLs). Third, for larger models, LLMs frequently hallucinate or diverge from intended meaning (e.g. due to ambiguous input).

Our approach overcomes these drawbacks by relying on purpose-trained BERT models. This renders our approach more generally applicable to other modeling languages. Technically, this research proposes four core contributions:

1. A generic workflow for creating NLIs for modeling editors;
2. a dataset of UML class diagram modeling commands in natural language that can be used as a reference for other NLI models and other modeling languages;
3. a reference NLI implementation in BIGUML that can be adapted for, and integrated into, other languages and tools; and

[3] https://www.w3.org/TR/WCAG21/.

4. an empirical evaluation of our approach.

Our software (incl. installation and usage instructions) is freely available online[4]. Likewise, with this paper, we release the dataset generator we developed to create the NLI training data for natural language modeling commands[5].

In the remainder of this paper, Sect. 2 describes the results of a survey aimed at gathering NL modeling interaction requirements. In Sect. 3 we then discuss the development of a natural language (NL) server for UML modeling. The integration of this server into BIGUML alongside the results of a systematic empirical evaluation is covered in Sect. 4. Section 5 presents a discussion of the key findings, before we conclude this paper with an overview of related works in Sect. 6 and future research directions in Sect. 7.

2 Interaction Requirements Analysis

Figure 1 outlines the process we followed to develop the NLI extension for BIGUML. In particular, we point towards the two user studies (cf. (1) and (6)), which we performed next to the technical development.

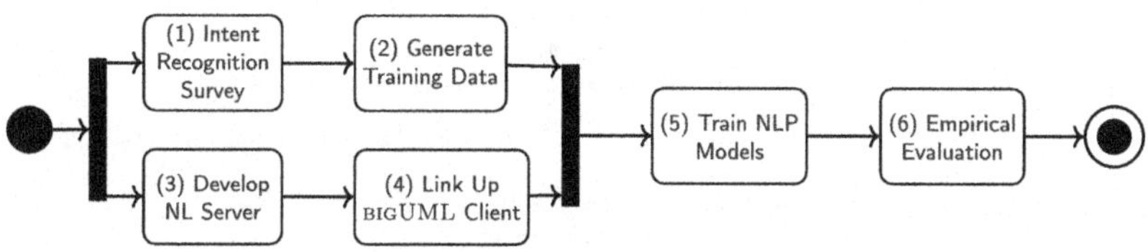

Fig. 1. Research outline

2.1 Intent Recognition Study

The training and the evaluation of the developed NLI are primarily based on a representative dataset of modeling commands and matching *intents* that need to be supported. Thus, we compiled a user survey based on primary UML interaction methods [38], where we asked experienced UML modelers about their choice of voice commands for triggering certain modeling actions on a specific UML model element.

The survey was carried out to learn more about the natural language instructions that modelers intuitively use when engaging with a voice-controlled UML class diagram editor and to identify various ways modelers articulate similar tasks typically performed in UML diagramming tools. The participants were asked to provide full, natural language sentences in response to the modeling scenarios listed in Table 1. We asked the participants to provide as many natural language command examples as they could intuitively think of to steer a modeling tool to execute a certain modeling scenario.

[4] https://github.com/sschwantler/bigUML/blob/main/NLI_README.md.

[5] https://github.com/stklik-org/NLI4UML-DataGenerator.

Table 1. User-provided responses on the survey of natural language commands for UML modeling.

Scenario	# Responses	Sample Responses
Create a Class	29	- *Create a class called car.* - *Insert a class Vehicle into the current diagram.* - *I want to add a new Class to the diagram, where the new class' name is "Car".* - *Generate a class for "train".* - *Declare the class bike.*
Add an Attribute to a Class	25	- *Add an attribute called name of type string to the Employee class.* - *Add the string property name to the class Bike.* - *Attach the attribute motor to the class car.*
Add a Method to a Class	22	- *add a method named CalculateSalary with a return type of decimal to the Employee class* - *Create a new operation for the class Bike, which is named getBikeName. The operation expects two input properties which are both of type string.* - *Define the method accelerate for the class car.*
Rename a Class	23	- *change the class name from Employee to Worker.* - *Set the name of the class Bike to Motorcycle.* - *I want to rename the already existing class "Car" to "Vehicle".* - *The class car should actually be called bike.*
Modify an Attribute Name of a Class	26	- *Rename the property "Color" of the class "Car" to "PrimaryColor".* - *Tyre would be a better name for the car class's wheel attribute* - *Rename the car's doors to door.* - *change the attribute name from name to employeeName in the Worker class.*
Modify an Attribute Visibility of a Class	23	- *make the employeeName attribute in the Worker class public.* - *Change—Update the visibility of the attribute name from the class Bike to public.* - *make the "rail with" visible to everyone* - *Make all attributes of the class car public.*
Modify a Method Name of a Class	23	- *rename the method CalculateSalary to ComputeSalary in the Worker class.* - *Edit the method name of the method getName inside the Bike class to change it to getSerialNr.* - *"go somewhere" should now be called "move tram"*
Modify a Method Visibility of a Class	23	- *set the ComputeSalary method in the Worker class to public.* - *I want to change the accessibility of the method "getPrize" of the class "Car" to "private".* - *Make the car class's start method private.* - *Adjust the visibility of the method 'getSupplierInfo' to public in the 'Supplier' class.*
Modify Method Parameters of a Class	24	- *In the method "DriveVihicle" change the parameter "speed" to "double" "kmh".* - *Add one int to the params of the car class's start method.* - *Update the name of the second parameter of the Bike class' method getWithTwoParams to secondParam.*
Add a Relation	25	- *create an association between the Worker and Manager classes.* - *create a generalization from the base class Person to the subclass Teacher.* - *Let the car inherit from vehicle.* - *Create a new relation between the classes car and driver with the following attributes: 1. The relation is called drives. 2. One driver drives one or more cars. 3. The relation type is dependency. A driver requires a car to drive.* - *Add a one to one association from car to person called drives.*
Modify the Positioning of a Class	32	- *The class "Engine" should be below the class "Car".* - *Put the car class to the top right of the diagram.* - *Position the "Vehicle" class north of "Car" class.*
Other Commands	26	- *Delete/clear entire diagram..* - *Undo the last change.* - *Highlight all classes that are subclasses of the 'Vehicle' class.*

Respondents were encouraged to list alternative phrasings and synonyms to better capture the range of commands. For example, the phrases "Create an attribute *XYZ*" or "add a property *XYZ*" represent the same modeling intent. This is an important piece of information for later steps. To be able to cover a wide range of different wordings and avoid bias in the capability of understanding queries. An open-ended question allowed participants to suggest any other commands they believed would be useful for interacting with a UML editor.

The survey was distributed online between March and April 2024 to academic colleagues and industrial partners, who we could attest had prior experience in UML modeling. We gathered a total of 301 user-defined natural language commands from eleven participants. Table 1 displays an exemplary selection of NL commands for various model interactions, and lists how many synonymous responses we received for each modeling intent.

2.2 Data and Analysis

We reviewed the data to identify common patterns in phrasing and discover how users express modeling commands in natural language. Entries with incomplete or unclear responses were excluded, ensuring that only meaningful data were used in the analysis. Subsequently, different wordings could be derived for each taxonomy entry, which yielded the training data for the NL model.

We then used the Python Natural Language Toolkit (NLTK)[6] scripts to remove stopwords and identify the most frequent terms in all modeling scenarios.

Lessons Learned. Among the survey respondents, we observed a large variety of commands ranging from precise, short instructions to very lengthy commands that are composed of several sub-commands (we discuss the challenge of such composite commands in Sect. 4). In the following, we summarize other findings; the complete generated dataset is available online[7].

Consistency in Basic Commands. Participants showed a clear pattern in command structure across modeling scenarios. Most responses followed a "verb + object" format, e.g. "create class car" or "add an attribute called name".

Use of Synonyms. Participants used diverse synonyms to describe the same intention. For instance, "attribute" was also referred to as "field" or "property", and methods were called "functions".

Modification Complexity and Relationships. Commands related to modifying attributes, methods, or creating relationships are generally more complex. Participants included specific parameters and visibility settings, suggesting the need for the system to accommodate complex instructions and compound commands with clarity and precision.

[6] https://www.nltk.org/.

[7] https://github.com/stklik-org/NLI4UML-DataGenerator/blob/main/intents-to-commands-survey.json.

Positioning and Layout Control. Participants used directional terms such as "below", "next to" or specific coordinates to position elements in the diagram, expecting the ability to adjust layouts relative to other elements.

Focus as a Key Concept. One of the most important survey findings was the need to focus certain diagram elements. As one respondent noted, "being able to set a context for future commands [...] would make using such a system a lot easier." This is particularly relevant in complex diagrams with nested classes, attributes, and methods that would require long prompts that become cumbersome for users to phrase and for the system to understand. Thus, instead of saying "rename the attribute 'weight' in the class Car to 'mass"', the user could say: "focus on attribute weight" followed by "rename to mass".

2.3 Training Data Generation

We use the cleaned survey data for analysis. We developed a training data generator to enable the generation of large randomized data sets based on the data queries. The reasoning behind the randomization is to enforce training generalization and avoid overfitting. Thus, for each individual intent in our survey (Table 1), we created a set of "pattern templates", which we could automatically populate with specific entities (concrete class and attribute names, geometric coordinate positions, etc.). Thus, given that we obtained a set of alternative formulations for each intent, combined with a large number of possible entities in our catalog, it is possible to flexibly re-generate different training data and experiment with the size of the required training data. The employed script for data generation is available in an open source repository (see Footnote 5).

3 NLI Development

Besides gathering training data, we implemented the NLI as a separate component that could be easily integrated into BIGUML. Our goal was to keep the modifications of the existing BIGUML client and Graphical Language Server Platform (GLSP)[8] server to a minimum. Thus, the task was to develop a middleware layer capable of obtaining standardized GLSP commands from natural language inputs, and translating them into actions that BIGUML's current implementation can recognize and execute without altering its core functionality.

Note, however, that even though the remainder of the section focuses on the development of an NLI for UML class diagrams in BIGUML, the developed architecture could easily be reconfigured for other modeling languages and editors, especially but not exclusively those based on GLSP.

3.1 Architecture

Before developing the tool architecture itself, we defined three design constraints for the subsequent implementation:

[8] https://github.com/eclipse-glsp/glsp.

1. Avoiding Feature Interference. Any NL capability must not interfere with existing editor interaction methods. Users should always be able to choose between keyboard & mouse, keyboard shortcuts (cf. [37]), or the new NL interaction.

2. Portability. We envision seamless integration across all tools, editors, and platforms. Thus, the NLI a) exposes its functionality by a *REST API* and b) is *containerized* using Docker[9]. These choices aim to improve portability, testability, and deployment with minimal overhead.

3. Performance. For minimal additional strain on the existing client or connection, all components (e.g. speech-to-text transcription) should be implemented at the NL Server and without online dependencies. Thus, the client's only additional responsibility is to capture the audio input.

The conceptual overall application design is shown in Fig. 2, with components developed in this project highlighted in the darkblue color. From a high-level view, our application consists of three primary components:

- the **NL Server**, which is the core contribution of our technique. It parses user queries to identify modeling intents and extract relevant UML entities. It exposes a REST API for seamless integration with tools such as BIGUML;
- the minimally adapted **bigUML Client**, which enables the speech recording and use of NLI; and
- the **bigUML Server**, which is largely unmodified as the NLI reuses functionality previously developed for modeling use with keyboard and mouse.

3.2 Natural Language Server

Based on the above design decisions, we implemented the NL Server using state-of-the-art NL technologies. Architecturally, the NL Server consists of six components (see Fig. 2), of which the NLP Classifier and the two NL models could be seen as the primary components.

NLP classifier. The NLP classifier interprets a user's transcribed input and maps it to a concrete modeling action. This task is performed using two separate Bidirectional Encoder Representations from Transformers (BERT) [15] models: 1. one BERT model performs intent recognition (IR), i.e. *what* should be done, while 2. another one is tasked with entity extraction (EE), i.e. *which* UML model entity is affected. Both models were trained on the survey response dataset (see Sect. 2.3).

Additionally, the NL Server contains three other components, namely

- the `Speech-to-Text` tool transcribes the user's spoken language into text using OpenAI's Whisper API[10].

[9] https://www.docker.com/.
[10] https://github.com/openai/whisper.

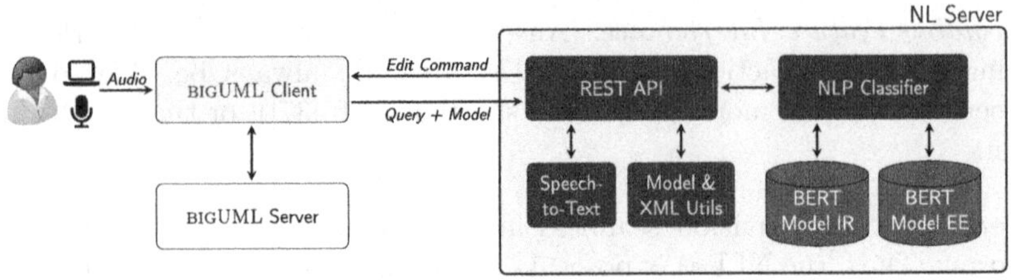

Fig. 2. Application Design and Architecture

- the `Model & XML Utils` component, which parses BIGUML's XML encoding and bridges the NL Server and the model; and
- the FastAPI[11] REST API to communicate with the BIGUML client.

3.3 Frontend Integration in BIGUML

Our prototype requires only minimal changes to the standard BIGUML interface, as seen in (see Fig. 3). Specifically, the new panel contains two buttons to start a voice recording, which is then transcribed and displayed in the `Command` text field. Subsequently, the `Send command` button triggers the command execution. A short screencast showing the tool in action can be seen online[12].

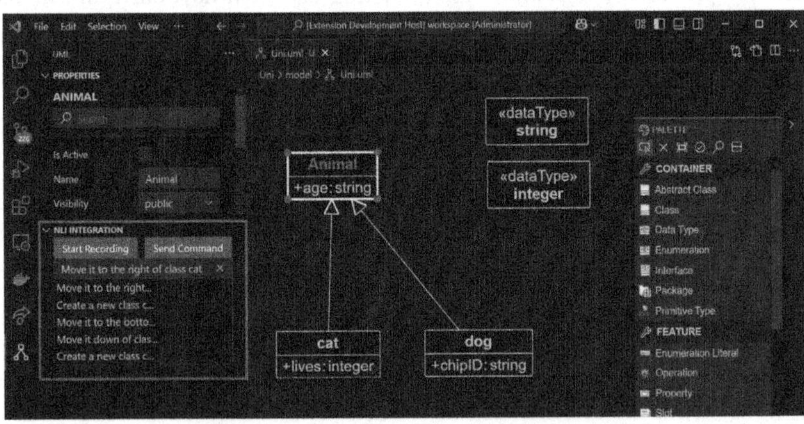

Fig. 3. BIGUML UI Integration of the NL Interface

[11] https://fastapi.tiangolo.com.
[12] https://github.com/sschwantler/bigUML/blob/main/NLI_README.md.

4 NLI Evaluation

To prove the applicability of NLI-based modeling editor interaction and to empirically evaluate our prototype, we conducted experiments with 23 participants from three different institutes (two universities, one industrial partner). Most participants were technically skilled software engineering students, while some participants did not have a technical background. The user study was conducted in March 2025 and consisted of: 1. a *short questionnaire* about the users' experience with speech assistants (e.g., Siri, Alexa), 2. a *modeling task* to test the NLI, and 3. a *system usability scale* (SUS) [9] questionnaire for the prototype. The survey form we used and the entire questionnaire are available online[13].

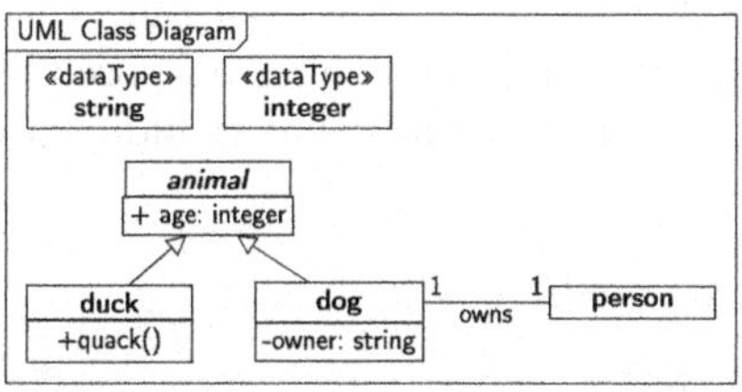

(a) UML diagram in graphical concrete syntax

```
Create a new data type called string.
Create a new data type called integer.
Move it to the right of data type string.
Create a new abstract class called animal.
Move it to the bottom of data type string.
Add a public property called age of type
    integer.
Create a new class called Duck.
Move it to the bottom of class animal.
Add a public method called quack.
Create a new class called dog.
Move it to the right of class duck.
Add a private property called owner of
    type string.
Add a new class person.
Move it to the right of class dog.
Create a generalization from duck to
    animal.
Create a generalization from dog to animal
.
Create an association called Owns from
    person to dog.
```

(b) NL commands necessary for creating the UML diagram

Fig. 4. Solution and NL commands for the example used in the evaluation

4.1 Empirical Evaluation

Our empirical evaluation aims to respond to the following research questions:

RQ1. To what extent are modelers able to create a UML class diagram using NLI?

RQ2. What is the perceived usability of NLI-based UML modeling?

RQ3. How effective is the developed language model in detecting the correct modeling intent expressed in natural language?

We prepared a ready-to-use prototype of BIGUML which includes our NLI extension (the UI extensions and the language model), and also with a *tracking component* that logs all interactions between the modeler and the modeling editor (i.e. timestamped audio clips, derived intents, and the actions performed in

[13] https://forms.gle/oe3BEVss5jid3RoF9.

BIGUML). Using these data, we could systematically evaluate the current prototype and, moreover, learn how humans interact with NLIs. A common modeling use case for all participants ensured comparability amongst the responses. The installation and usage instructions—including a short video that demonstrated how participants could interact with the NLI extension—were distributed as part of the online survey. Furthermore, users were asked to upload the resulting model `.xmi` file, a screenshot of the model, and their usage logs.

Evaluation Use Case. The user study was performed to discover how humans *i*) interact with a UML modeling editor in natural language, and *ii*) perceive this interaction. The former was studied using modeling success rates, while *ii*) used a system usability scale evaluation. Most participants were familiar with UML modeling through university classes or practical use in their job, and many of them were already familiar with the BIGUML modeling editor. Each participant was asked to complete the same example task of creating a UML class diagram (cf. Fig. 4a) using only the NLI ofBIGUML. The example contains a diverse range of UML modeling elements (abstract class, class, generalization, dataType, property, visibility, role, multiplicity), while remaining purposefully compact. Figure 4b shows a minimal set of speech commands that would create this UML class diagram in BIGUML.

4.2 Results

We report on the evaluation results by responding to the three research questions defined at the outset.

RQ1 – Human Modeler Support. The first and primary concern of our evaluation relates to the usage of the NLI. According to the usage data and the screenshots, 13 of 23 participants (57 %) completed the modeling use case by exclusively interacting in natural language. Nonetheless, we observed that several users struggled with the "move" intent, meaning that the model elements were created on top of another. This was also observable by the Move intent's relatively low recognition accuracy of around 46% (cf. Table 3). The 10 users who could not create the model entirely still managed to create partial models, even though some elements (e.g., individual attributes or methods) were missing. As a result, some participants solved the problem by repositioning the elements using the mouse, while others ignored the move command entirely, such that all elements were placed on top of one another.

Overall, we conclude that some users were able to create models using an NLI-only approach. This is a reaffirming result for our prototype. Nonetheless, we noticed that various problems occurred and that the incorrect functionality of one central intent (in our case, 'Move') causes problems.

Answer to RQ1 A majority of our participants succeeded in modeling using the NLI alone, and many of the remaining participants nearly completed the task with the NLI. We conclude that our tool has the potential to serve as an effective alternative input source to the mouse & keyboard of modeling editors. Nonetheless, we remark that there are still more than 40% of users who could not completely solve the task.

RQ2 – Perceived Usability. Despite the early development stage of our prototypical implementation, we applied the System Usability Scale (SUS) [9] to derive an initial usability score, and thus a quantitative measure of the perceived ease of use, for our system. In the following, we briefly summarize the answers to the SUS questions on a five-point Likert scale ranging from *strongly agree* (++), to *agree* (+), to *neither agree nor disagree* (/), to *disagree* (–), to *strongly disagree* (––). Table 2 shows the frequencies of each specific answer. Aggregating these scores by each participant leaves a mean combined SUS of 66.85 with a standard deviation of 16.14 and a median of 70. Minimum and maximum combined SUS are 30 and 87.5, respectively.

We can notice that the tool has potential, given that most users found the system *easy to use*, and that *the various functions were well integrated.* The vast majority of users also think that *most people would learn to use this system very quickly*, and almost 80% of respondents think that they would not *need the support of a technical person to use the system.* It is also promising that a majority of the respondents reject the statement that the NLI was *very cumbersome to use* and that almost half of them *felt very confident using the system.*

The evaluation, however, also confirmed our expectations that, despite the good intent and entity recognition, the tool's usability can be further improved. Table 2 shows the responses to the SUS. Thus, users responded that they would rather not *like to use the system frequently* in its current state and that it is acting *inconsistently.* This critical feedback is unsurprising as usability was not a core focus in this initial work on NLI-based UML modeling. Moreover, the inconsistent behavior seems to correlate with participants being unable to move elements using NL commands.

Answer to RQ2 Given the early stage of development of the BIGUML NLI, it was expected that the usability would point out some limitations. Nonetheless, we do see that users found that the system was easy to use, the functionalities well integrated, and that it would be easy to learn for most people.

RQ3 – Intent Detection. Since every participant provided logging data for their modeling session along with all captured voice recordings, we could analyze them for patterns in natural language understanding performance. The logs are structured with timestamps and contain the transcribed query text as interpreted by our speech recognition system. Each query was processed by the NL server

Table 2. NLI Prototype – System Usability Scale (SUS)

Question	++	+	/	–	– –
I think that I would like to use the system frequently	0	6	4	10	3
I found the system unnecessarily complex	0	1	3	7	12
I thought the system was easy to use	6	9	5	2	1
I think that I would need the support of a technical person to be able to use this system	0	3	2	8	10
I found the various functions in this system were well integrated	2	16	4	1	0
I thought there was too much inconsistency in this system	8	4	4	7	0
I would imagine that most people would learn to use this system very quickly	6	14	1	1	1
I found the system very cumbersome to use	1	4	5	3	10
I felt very confident using the system	1	8	6	6	2
I needed to learn a lot of things before I could get going with this system	0	3	1	14	5

Table 3. Evaluation Modeling Use Case Log Data

Intent	Count of Intent	Avg. Intent Correct	Avg. Entity Correct
AddAttribute	99	78.8%	65.7%
AddMethod	72	55.6%	69.4%
AddRelation	124	95.2%	72.6%
ChangeDatatype	9	22.2%	22.2%
ChangeName	53	100.0%	88.7%
ChangeVisibility	3	100.0%	100.0%
CreateContainer	231	92.2%	85.3%
Delete	53	94.4%	62.3%
Focus	118	85.6%	76.3%
Move	160	100.0%	45.6%
Undo	10	90.0%	90.0%
Total	**932**	**88.7%**	**70.7%**

to extract two core elements: the intended modeling action (*intent*) and the relevant modeling language elements (*entities*).

In total, we obtained 932 intent recordings as shown in Table 3, which we manually matched to the actual user input (speech and transcripts) to the tool-predicted intents and extracted entities, and classified the correct/incor-

Table 4. Examples of Wrong Entity Extraction

Query	Entities
Move animal below data type string	{"element_type": "data type", "element_name": "string"}
Create an owns association between owner and person	{"relation_type ": "owns", "element_name": "association ", "class_name_from": "owner", "class_name_to ": "person"}
Add attribute age integer to animal	{"element_type": "attribute ", "element_name": "age integer "}

rect information by intent. We see that, overall, many of the NL commands operated successfully, such that the intent recognition worked very well (except `ChangeDatatype` and `AddMethod`). Still, we also see that the entity recognition is less capable, leading to an overall decreased accuracy in command interpretation.

Table 4 shows some examples of entities wrongly identified. The first query misses an entity containing the direction to move, the second one extracts the wrong entities (relation type and name are wrong), and the third one displays an incorrect attribute name.

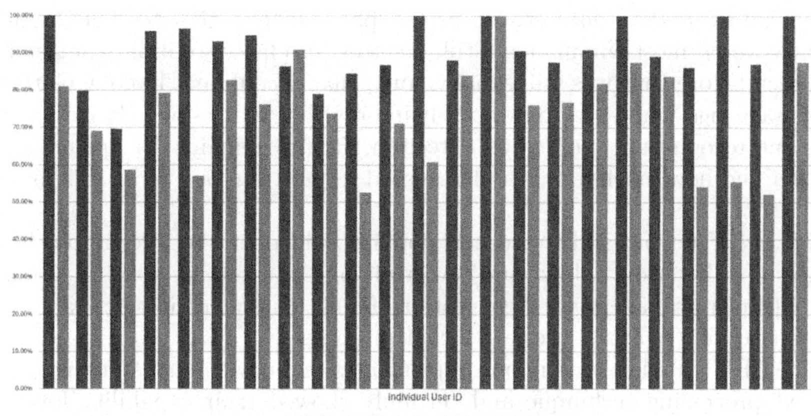

Fig. 5. Average accuracy of intent and entity detection per participant

In a subsequent analysis, we were interested in whether the accuracy changed between different users. As the use of natural language is subjective (dialects, different ways non-native speakers speak English, mumbling, audio quality, etc.), we computed accuracy scores per individual participant. Figure 5 presents the user-specific accuracy metrics for all 23 participants. One can see that the results are quite homogeneous for intent detection, with values ranging from 69.57% to 100.00%. For the entities detection, the values are more diverging with a range from 52.17% to 100.00%.

The heterogeneity of these results made us curious to check the submitted original audio snippets of some participants, especially those for which the accuracy values were low. We present these findings, amongst others, in the subsequent discussion section.

Answer to RQ3 Across all 932 user-defined NL queries, our approach could correctly identify 88.7% of modeling intents and 70.7% of entities. We observe that for specific intents and entities, the recognition requires better training data. We thus conclude that our NL server is capable of handling NL input correctly for many user queries in our evaluation case. We can also state that the accuracy changes between participants.

5 Discussion

The development of the NLI prototype provided insights into how users interact with model editors using speech. Here we discuss some of the lessons learned.

Synonymous Sentences. Primary success factors were the two user surveys (see Sect. 2) through which we discovered a broad set of specific commands that modelers would use to describe a modeling intent. Although we do not claim to have an exhaustive dataset, our prototype evaluation showed that the initial survey covered most commands. Still, our tool also faced an input that had not been seen before (but was still synonymous) that it could not handle. Gathering more usage logs enables us to iteratively improve our tool, especially with respect to intent recognition and entity detection. It also remains an open question whether and how much data should be used to pre-train our two BERT models.

BERT and Model Sizes. The recently popularized Generative Pre-trained Transformers (GPTs) are a robust and powerful competitor technology. In combination with retrieval-augmented generation (RAG), these technologies can also be customized and typically used with chat prompts.

The BERT models used in our implementation build upon a similarly powerful text processing technique and certainly showed their capability for intent recognition and entity extraction. The technology is also customizable and proven capable of specialized tasks such as programming (CodeBERT[14]) or medical domains (e.g. BiomedVLP CXR BERT[15]) recognition.

As we deliberately used small language models that could be deployed directly on the user's computer, an open question is whether larger (pre-trained) models that run on dedicated servers or as SaaS could be capable of comparable or even better results.

[14] https://github.com/microsoft/CodeBERT.

[15] https://huggingface.co/microsoft/BiomedVLP-CXR-BERT-specialized.

Accents and Dialects. Accents and dialects had a strong influence on voice transcription. Table 5 shows example results of wrong transcriptions with their interpretation of what was intended, along with an evaluation comment when listening to the audio recording. Note that every example is from a different participant. Recurring issues were poor pronunciation and poor microphone quality. Moreover, the OpenAI Whisper transcription model did consider that the participants were non-native English speakers, which might explain why these errors were observed across different users.

Table 5. Examples of Wrong Transcriptions

User	Transcript	Interpretation of Intent	Comment
A	Select class stack	Select class duck	Accent
B	Move it to the left of the glass anymore	Move it to the left of class animal	Accent
C	Add a public method for WAC 2	Add a public method called quack to duck	Accent, Quiet and bad Microphone
D	Rename it to any matter	Rename it to animal	Accent, Reverb. and Echo Effects
E	Place it to the left of class torque	Place it to the left of class dog	Accent

5.1 Limitations

While our NLI shows promising results, several limitations remain.

User Selection Bias. Our user surveys relied on personal invitations primarily comprised of academic participants, with some additions from our industry partner. Their feedback might not be fully representative of the general user population.

Exclusion of Accessibility Considerations. Although we aim to increase accessibility, due to our prototype's early development stage, we could not include users with disabilities in our study. We plan to reach out to these users with the upcoming beta version of our software, as their insights are of utmost interest.

Uncontrolled Evaluation Variables. We did not control for factors such as microphone quality or noisy environments, which impact the quality of the recordings, and, subsequently, the intent recognition and entity detection quality.

Evaluation Realism. It remains unclear how well the NLI performs with larger, more complex UML diagrams requiring advanced navigation and layout support, as our current evaluation was based on a compact UML model (cf. Figure 4a).

6 Related Work

Our research towards the integration of a capable NLI for UML editors touches upon several related fields. In this section, we position our contributions relative to the most closely related domains.

Natural Language-Based Modeling. The use of NL input in modeling workflows has been pursued for several decades. Early approaches used a controlled, structured, or restricted natural language to simplify intent processing [2,16,19,40] for requirements, translation to use cases, or data extraction. Previous approaches use NL input for automated derivation of UML diagrams [4,12,13,20,27,30], although these approaches are based on "classical" means of language processing (parse trees, word tagging, phrasal grammars).

Recently, LLMs were shown to be effective for translating natural language into models [10,17], including retrieval-augmented generation (RAG) for domain-specific environments [3]. These approaches, however, lack support for incremental editing and often depend on specific tools. In contrast, our work natively integrates NLI into an existing UML editor. An alternative approach uses chatbots for incremental domain-specific language (DSL) modeling [32,33].

Speech and Voice Input. Speech interfaces for programming have been studied since at least 2006 [14]. Since then, powerful AI and LLM approaches [31] were applied, recently peaking in so-called *vibe coding*[16], whose goal is the exclusive use of LLMs and NL input to complete small-scale programming projects.

Speech-based modeling has also been explored from several directions. [6] integrates voice for Simulink diagram editing, while [21] uses voice to draw on interactive whiteboards, showing user acceptance of voice-enabled software. ModelByVoice [11] combines voice, non-vocal sounds, and gestures for modeling. This project is close to our work, although the tool primarily supports the matching of short voice commands, rather than the use of an NLI with intent recognition.

Accessibility. Other related work [25] explores NLI for accessibility, e.g., developing a model editor for blind people. The TeDUB project [34] spearheaded the accessibility of technical drawings and graphical models, as outlined in [7]. [22] explores blind users' interaction with UML class and state diagrams, while [5] enables their interaction with graph models.

To summarize, we note that existing NL and speech-based modeling approaches often rely on structured inputs, simple commands, or resource-intensive LLMs, which lack incremental editing and offer limited DSL support. Our work instead integrates a lightweight BERT-based NLI into a UML editor, enabling efficient intent recognition and domain-specific adaptability without the computational overhead of LLMs.

[16] https://arstechnica.com/ai/2025/03/is-vibe-coding-with-ai-gnarly-or-reckless-maybe-some-of-both/.

7 Conclusion and Future Work

This paper introduces a natural language interface (NLI) to improve accessibility and usability in enterprise modeling editors. Our approach integrates speech input and state-of-the-art natural language processing (NLP) capabilities into the BIGUML editor, using BERT models for modeling intent recognition and UML entity extraction. The models were trained on a dataset derived from a user survey to capture varied natural language modeling commands. An empirical evaluation with modelers showed that our prototype is capable of fulfilling many modeling tasks, despite the prototype's early-development phase usability problems.

In the future, we will extend our approach using the user feedback to support a more diverse and complex set of modeling actions, including compound multi-intention commands. Finally, we will also reach out to the accessibility community to gain insights and feedback from persons with disabilities.

References

1. Ali, S.J., Reinhartz-Berger, I., Bork, D.: How are LLMs used for conceptual modeling? an exploratory study on interaction behavior and user perception. In: Conceptual Modeling - 43rd International Conference. ER 2024, pp. 257–275 (2024)
2. Ambriola, V., Gervasi, V.: Processing natural language requirements. In: International Conference on Automated Software Engineering, pp. 36–45 (1997)
3. Ardimento, P., Bernardi, M.L., Cimitile, M., Scalera, M.: A rag-based feedback tool to augment UML class diagram learning. In: MODELS Companion (2024)
4. Arora, C., Sabetzadeh, M., Briand, L., Zimmer, F.: Extracting domain models from natural-language requirements: approach and industrial evaluation. In: 19th International Conference on Model Driven Engineering Languages and Systems, pp. 250–260 (2016)
5. Balik, S.P., et al.: Including blind people in computing through access to graphs. In: 16th Int. ACM SIGACCESS Conference on Computers and Accessibility, pp. 91–98 (2014)
6. Black, D., Rapos, E.J., Stephan, M.: Voice-driven modeling: Software modeling using automated speech recognition. In: MODELS Companion, pp. 252–258 (2019)
7. Blenkhorn, P., Evans, D.G.: Using speech and touch to enable blind people to access schematic diagrams. J. Netw. Comput. Appl. **21**(1), 17–29 (1998)
8. Bork, D., Klikovits, S., Michael, J., Netz, L., Rumpe, B.: Inclusive model-driven engineering for accessible software. In: MODELS 2025 NIER (2025)
9. Brooke, J.: SUS-A quick and dirty usability scale. Usabil. Eval. Ind. **189**(194) (1996)
10. Cámara, J., Troya, J., Burgueño, L., Vallecillo, A.: On the assessment of generative AI in modeling tasks: an experience report with ChatGPT and UML. Softw. Syst. Model. **22**(3), 781–793 (2023)
11. de Carvalho, J.F., Amaral, V.: Towards a modelling workbench with flexible interaction models for model editors operating through voice and gestures. In: 45th Annual Computers, Software, and Applications Conference, pp. 1026–1031 (2021)
12. Deeptimahanti, D.K., Babar, M.A.: An automated tool for generating UML models from natural language requirements. In: ASE 2009, pp. 680–682 (2009)

13. Deeptimahanti, D.K., Sanyal, R.: Semi-automatic generation of UML models from natural language requirements. In: India Software Engineering Conference (2011)
14. Désilets, A., Fox, D.C., Norton, S.: Voicecode: an innovative speech interface for programming-by-voice. In: CHI'06 Extended Abstracts, pp. 239–242 (2006)
15. Devlin, J., Chang, M., Lee, K., Toutanova, K.: BERT: pre-training of deep bidirectional transformers for language understanding. In: NAACL-HLT 2019 (2019)
16. Fantechi, A., Gnesi, S., Ristori, G., Carenini, M., Vanocchi, M., Moreschini, P.: Assisting requirement formalization by means of natural language translation. Formal Methods Syst. Des. **4**, 243–263 (1994)
17. Ferrari, A., Abualhaijal, S., Arora, C.: Model generation with LLMs: from requirements to UML sequence diagrams. In: Requirements Engineering Conference Workshops (2024)
18. Fill, H., Fettke, P., Köpke, J.: Conceptual modeling and large language models: impressions from first experiments with ChatGPT. Enterp. Model. Inf. Syst. Archit. Int. J. Concept. Model. **18**, 3 (2023)
19. Giannakopoulou, D., Pressburger, T., Mavridou, A., Schumann, J.: Generation of formal requirements from structured natural language. In: Madhavji, N., Pasquale, L., Ferrari, A., Gnesi, S. (eds.) REFSQ 2020. LNCS, vol. 12045, pp. 19–35. Springer, Cham (2020). https://doi.org/10.1007/978-3-030-44429-7_2
20. Hamza, Z.A., Hammad, M.: Generating UML use case models from software requirements using natural language processing. In: ICMSAO 2019, pp. 1–6 (2019)
21. Jolak, R., Vesin, B., Chaudron, M.R.V.: Using voice commands for UML modelling support on interactive whiteboards: insights and experiences. In: XX IberoAmerican Conference on Software Engineering, pp. 85–98 (2017)
22. King, A., Blenkhorn, P., Crombie, D., Dijkstra, S., Evans, G., Wood, J.: Presenting UML software engineering diagrams to blind people. In: Miesenberger, K., Klaus, J., Zagler, W.L., Burger, D. (eds.) ICCHP 2004. LNCS, vol. 3118, pp. 522–529. Springer, Heidelberg (2004). https://doi.org/10.1007/978-3-540-27817-7_76
23. Kolev, P., Pruss, H.H., Wilken, J.R., Sandkuhl, K.: Grass-root enterprise modelling: how large language models can help. In: PoEM 2024, pp. 123–139 (2024)
24. Lanusse, A., et al.: Papyrus UML: an open source toolset for MDA. In: European Conference on Model-Driven Architecture Foundations and Applications, pp. 1–4 (2009)
25. Lopes, J., Cambeiro, J., Amaral, V.: Modelbyvoice - towards a general purpose model editor for blind people. In: Proceedings of MODELS 2018 Workshops. CEUR Workshop Proceedings, vol. 2245, pp. 762–769 (2018)
26. Lukyanenko, R., Bork, D., Storey, V.C., Parsons, J., Pastor, O.: Inclusive conceptual modeling: diversity, equity, involvement, and belonging in conceptual modeling (short paper). In: ER 2023 Forum. CEUR Workshop Proceedings (2023)
27. Mala, G.A., Uma, G.: Automatic construction of object oriented design models [UML diagrams] from natural language requirements specification. In: 9th Pacific Rim International Conference on Artificial Intelligence, pp. 1155–1159 (2006)
28. Metin, H., Bork, D.: Introducing BIGUML: a flexible open-source GLSP-based web modeling tool for UML. In: MODELS 2023 Companion, pp. 40–44 (2023)
29. Metin, H., Bork, D.: A reference architecture for the development of GLSP-based web modeling tools. Softw. Syst. Model. (2025)
30. More, P., Phalnikar, R.: Generating UML diagrams from natural language specifications. Int. J. Appl. Inf. Syst. **1**(8), 19–23 (2012)
31. Nowogrodzki, A.: Speaking in code: how to program by voice. Nature **559**(7712), 141–143 (2018)

32. Pérez-Soler, S., González-Jiménez, M., Guerra, E., de Lara, J.: Towards conversational syntax for domain-specific languages using chatbots. J. Object Technol. **18**(2), 5:1–5:21 (2019)
33. Pérez-Soler, S., Guerra, E., de Lara, J.: Flexible modelling using conversational agents. In: MODELS Companion 2019, pp. 478–482 (2019)
34. Petrie, H., et al.: TeDUB: a system for presenting and exploring technical drawings for blind people. In: Miesenberger, K., Klaus, J., Zagler, W. (eds.) ICCHP 2002. LNCS, vol. 2398, pp. 537–539. Springer, Heidelberg (2002). https://doi.org/10.1007/3-540-45491-8_102
35. Reinhartz-Berger, I., Ali, S.J., Bork, D.: Leveraging LLMs for domain modeling: the impact of granularity and strategy on quality. In: CAiSE 2025, pp. 3–19 (2025)
36. Sarioglu, A., Metin, H., Bork, D.: Accessibility in conceptual modeling - a systematic literature review, a keyboard-only UML modeling tool, and a research roadmap. Data Knowl. Eng. **158**, 102423 (2025)
37. Sarioğlu, A., Metin, H., Bork, D.: How inclusive is conceptual modeling? A systematic review of literature and tools for disability-aware conceptual modeling. In: Conceptual Modeling: 42nd International Conference. ER 2023, pp. 65–83 (2023)
38. Seidl, M., Scholz, M., Huemer, C., Kappel, G.: UML @ Classroom: An Introduction to Object-Oriented Modeling (2015)
39. Silva, J., Ma, Q., Cabot, J., Kelsen, P., Proper, H.A.: Application of the tree-of-thoughts framework to LLM-enabled domain modeling. In: Conceptual Modeling - 43rd International Conference. ER 2024, pp. 94–111 (2024)
40. Zhang, H., Yue, T., Ali, S., Wu, J., Liu, C.: A restricted natural language based use case modeling methodology for real-time systems. In: 9th International Workshop on Modelling in Software Engineering (MiSE), pp. 5–11 (2017)

The Interim Experiment Report: A Systematic Account of The Experimental Design of Large Language Model-Based Text-to-Model Approaches

Sybren de Kinderen[1(✉)], Qin Ma[2], Jonathan Silva Mercado[2], and Karolin Winter[1]

[1] Department of Industrial Engineering and Innovation Sciences, Eindhoven University of Technology, Eindhoven, The Netherlands
{s.d.kinderen,k.m.winter}@tue.nl

[2] University of Luxembourg, Esch-sur-Alzette, Luxembourg
{qin.ma,jonathan.silva}@uni.lu

Abstract. The increasing advent of approaches that adopt Large Language Models for text-to-model generation is accompanied by a variety of experimental designs for their evaluation. Inspired by "The Prompt Report", which provides a systematic account of prompting techniques for prompt engineering, we present a structured synthesis of experimental designs used to evaluate LLM-based text-to-model approaches.

Through a systematic literature review, we compile a compendium of experimental designs, organized into six tree-structured categories. This compendium integrates both experimental design principles from traditional empirical research and challenges unique to LLM usage. For example, specific to LLMs, we identify studies that conduct an ablation study to isolate the effect of individual prompting techniques, as well as those that address cascading errors introduced by intermediate LLM outputs. The compendium is intended to inform the design of future evaluations in this emerging field, offering researchers structured support and guidance.

Keywords: Experimental design · Text-to-model generation · Large Language Models

1 Introduction

With the increasing use of Large Language Models (LLMs) for conceptual (enterprise) modeling tasks [4,36], we also witness a growing body of approaches using LLMs to support automated translation of texts into a conceptual model. Examples of such LLM-based text-to-model approaches include domain modeling [2,7,12], process modeling [5,27], goal modeling [11] or otherwise.

The increasing advent of LLM-based text-to-model approaches is mirrored by a wide array of experimental designs for their evaluation. On the one hand, this diversity reflects general principles of empirical study design which apply regardless of whether an LLM is used, such as variation in datasets, participant populations, and methodological diversity (e.g., perceived quality assessed

H.-G. Fill et al. (Eds.): PoEM 2025, LNBIP 570, pp. 102–120, 2026.
https://doi.org/10.1007/978-3-032-12063-2_7

through qualitative surveys, as in [13,22,41] vs. ground truth-based quantitative performance metrics, as in [7,12,14,26,27,31]). On the other hand, and more intriguingly, we observe experimental designs specific to the use of LLMs and characteristics thereof. As highlighted by [9], who advocate standardized benchmarks of LLM-based (software) modeling, such considerations include (1) *solution space variability*, acknowledging that modeling tasks often allow for multiple valid solutions; (2) *non-determinism of LLM output*, where identical prompts can yield different results across runs; and (3) *prompting strategy dependency*, recognizing that the variations in prompt formulation, across a spectrum of prompting techniques, can significantly influence the generated LLM output.

Despite the recognition of both general and LLM-specific considerations in the experimental designs of LLM-based text-to-model approaches, a systematic account is still lacking. We argue that a structured synthesis of these experimental design practices, one that integrates both principles from traditional empirical research and challenges unique to LLM usage, holds significant potential. Such an account can serve as a valuable source of inspiration and guidance for experimental design of LLM-based text-to-model approaches, much like "The Prompt Report" [39] has done for prompt engineering. For example, as discussed in Sect. 3.7, [27] exemplifies a good practice by conducting an ablation study to isolate the effects of different prompting techniques on LLM output. Similarly, as discussed in Sect. 3.6 to address the variability of modeling solutions [5] gauges LLM-generated models against a reference model using multiple criteria: strict (exact syntax matching), relaxed (semantic equivalence), and flexible (allowing variation in level of detail). Accordingly, our research question reads *"What are the key considerations in the experimental design of Large Language Model-based text-to-model approaches?"*

To address this gap, we conduct a Systematic Literature Review (SLR) focusing on the experimental designs of studies that (1) employ an LLM, (2) target creating conceptual models from textual descriptions, and (3) provide a dedicated description of their experimental design. We contribute six overarching categories, each comprising of relevant sub-categories. These are:

- **Evaluation Aims**: the goals motivating the evaluation of LLM-based text-to-model based approaches;
- **Evaluation Focus**: what aspect is being evaluated, meaning, either the generated output or the dynamics of the modeling process;
- **Input and Output Dataset**: the nature of the input data and the resulting LLM output;
- **Evaluation Means**: how the approach is evaluated, such as comparison against a reference model or judgment based on specific properties;
- **Scoring Criteria**: the rubric used to grade LLM-generated output;
- **LLM-related Independent Variables**: the LLM specific variables that are systematically varied to assess their impact on LLM performance.

The remainder of this paper is structured as follows. In Sect. 2 we describe our SLR setup. In Sect. 3 we describe the experiment report, as a synthetic effort across the studies found in the SLR. Also we briefly describe the process for

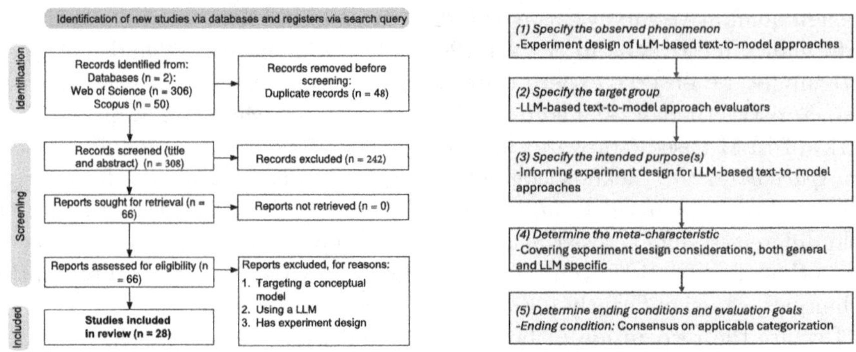

(a) Filtering out the final paper selection according to PRISMA [29]

(b) Creating the categorization, according to [24]

Fig. 1. The SLR: reporting and analysis

deriving the categories. In Sect. 4 we conclude, with a wrap up of key learning, and the most important points going forward.

2 Literature Review Design

In order to provide a systematic account of the experimental design of LLM-based text-to-model approaches, we carry out a systematic literature review. Systematic literature reviews aim at synthesizing and structuring the current state of the art around a given topic, to identify gaps it [19]. For LLMs an example includes "The Prompt Report" [33], which surveys prompt engineering techniques and on which we base the title of this paper.

We report on our review following PRISMA, the Preferred Reporting Items for Systematic reviews and Meta-Analyses [29]. Figure 1a shows our process for arriving at the final paper selection.

Search Query. For our literature review we use the following search query:

("large language model" OR "generative AI") AND ("domain model" OR "conceptual model" OR "business process" OR "goal model" OR "enterprise model" OR "software model")

This keyword selection is primarily driven by our overarching research question (stated in the introduction). We follow our research question in terms of (1) the selection of conceptual enterprise models, of which we include various variants [19], pertaining to enterprise modeling and associated communities, like the business process management community. Also, we include the variants domain model and software model, which are especially prevalent in the Model Driven Engineering community; (2) the focus on LLMs, having generative AI as an associated variant. We have consciously excluded experiment-related keywords. This is because the papers we target are inconsistent in their explicit characterization of the performed experiments in terms of their title, keywords, or abstract. Including experiment-related keywords, therefore, would unnecessarily narrow the selection of query results.

Identification. In the identification step, we queried Scopus and Web of Sciences, being two well established databases for scientific literature. While they exhibit a considerable overlap in terms of the retrieved papers (expressed in the $n = 48$ duplicates), nevertheless both have contributed to unique papers.

Screening. In the screening step, we first reviewed all retrieved unique papers on their relevance in terms of title and abstract. Here we primarily target the use of LLMs, and if the paper seems to address modeling, either directly (by virtue of targeting a modeling technique), or indirectly, by virtue of targeting a broader topic. Regarding the latter, one often mentioned broader topic is business process management, but since modeling is often a part of that, we did not want to exclude it from our initial set. We involved two authors in the screening on abstract and title of each paper, thereby ensuring that paper inclusion is consensus based. We excluded 242 out of 308 papers based on title and abstract, the main reason being that many papers were agreed upon to be thematically out of scope, often targeting a particular non-modeling application of LLMs.

Thereafter, we performed a full text reading of each remaining article. Next to a focus on modeling and LLMs being also important to the full text reading, an important inclusion criterion is the extent to which a paper has a dedicated discussion of its experimental design. We again relied on a consensus between two researchers from the pool of authors of this paper to make a decision.

Final Inclusion. After screening, 28 studies are included in our review.

3 The Interim Experiment Report

3.1 Creating the Categorization

Figure 1b displays an excerpt of the main steps for creating our categorization. Our design process takes cues from [24], though by no means we want to claim an exhaustive implementation of the associated taxonomy design process.

We focus on the experimental design for evaluating LLM-based text-to-model approaches (as a phenomenon, cf. [24]), with the goal of supporting approach evaluators (the target group) and informing their experimental design (the main purpose). To provide a comprehensive guidance, we address general and LLM specific experimental design considerations, and formulate the following meta-characteristic (cf. [24]): Covering both general and LLM specific experimental design considerations for evaluating LLM-based text-to-model approaches.

We define our categories complementarily. Firstly, we follow a conceptual-to-empirical approach, starting from predefined categories driven by (1) existing research like [9] for the category solution space variability, and (2) our research question, like for the category input dataset (as per the input text), output dataset (as per LLM output), evaluation means and scoring criteria (for models, partially as tied to LLMs), and independent variables (which are particular to LLMs). We then adopt an empirical-to-conceptual approach, adding categories as they emerge from the reviewed literature and clustering them accordingly. For example, we added the category cascading error due to an experimental design in a reviewed study [40] that explicitly tackles this issue in a multi-step approach. As an ending condition (see Fig. 1b), we define reaching a consensus on a categorization we deem applicable.

Next, we discuss the resulting six categories.

3.2 Evaluation Aims

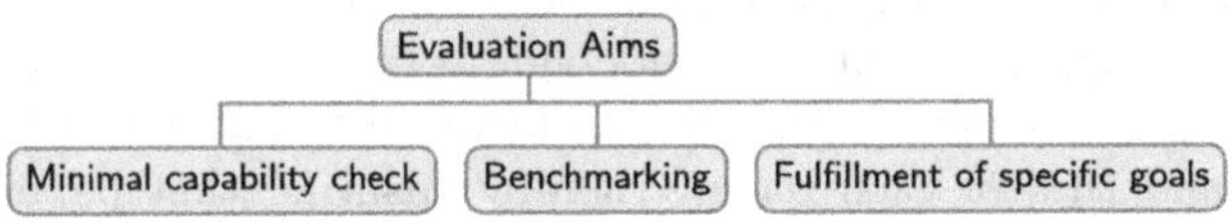

Fig. 2. Evaluation Aims category

The Evaluation Aims category (Fig. 2) captures the goals that motivate the evaluation of the reviewed LLM-based text-to-model approaches.

Minimal Capability Check. This aim investigates whether it is reasonable and practical to employ LLMs for conceptual modeling tasks. A substantial number of studies addressed this aim (e.g., [17,27,34,37]), but have articulated their evaluation goals using a variety of closely related formulations. Some focus on foundational questions, such as "whether it makes sense" to use LLMs for conceptual modeling [21] or to "explore the suitability of LLMs" [15]. Others aim to "check the ability" of LLMs [7] or to "understand the current capabilities of LLMs" in performing modeling tasks [41]. A further group of studies seeks to "assess the effectiveness of LLMs" [30], or to "investigate the extent to which LLMs can" construct accurate conceptual models [11]. Together, these formulations reflect a shared interest in evaluating the potential and readiness of LLMs for supporting conceptual modeling.

Benchmarking. This aim focuses on comparing LLM-based text-to-model approaches with alternative ones, including other LLM-based approaches [13,23], as well as non-LLM approaches such as rules-based systems [7], machine learning-based techniques [7], and human expert level performance [7,20].

Fulfillment of Specific Goals. This subcategory subsumes a diverse range of specific goals pursued in the evaluation of LLM-based text-to-model approaches. For example, in line with the Design Science Research (DSR) paradigm [18,41] takes stakeholder utility, defined as the extent to which stakeholder driven requirements are satisfied, as the primary and concrete evaluation criteria, in their evaluation of a proprietary LLM-based solution for business process modeling within an organization, using its employees as evaluators.

In addition to user-defined requirements, specific purposes are also articulated through research questions or hypotheses. Examples include evaluating multi-perspective modeling and ensuring consistency [21]; evaluating compatibility of generated models with tools that require both XMI and diagrammatic representations [21]; and evaluating prompt effectiveness [5,10,11,25,40]. Other goals involve identifying different types of modeling elements [10,25], generating reusable reference models [30], and producing diverse and scalable synthetic training data [6,14,32]. Further studies examine the ability of LLMs to identify modeling patterns [40], their sensitivity to domains and modeling notations [10,11], the syntactic and semantic quality of generated models [10], the model size limitations [10], and robustness to intermediate result quality [5].

3.3 Evaluation Focus

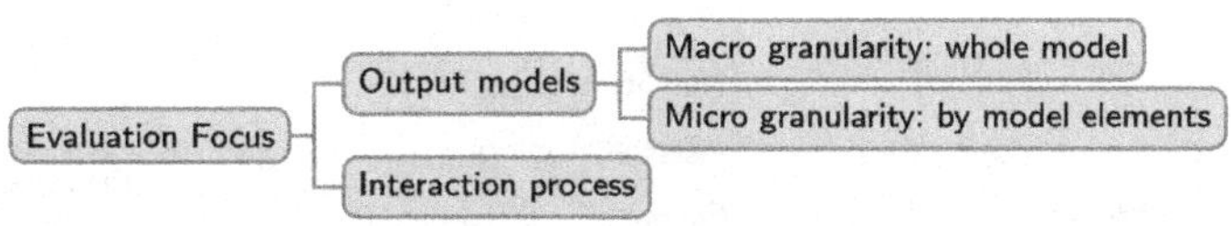

Fig. 3. Evaluation Focus category

The Evaluation Focus category (Fig. 3) classifies the evaluation targets set in experiments on the reviewed LLM-based text-to-model approaches. Specifically, it captures what is being evaluated. We observed a clear distinction between a majority of evaluations (e.g., [1,5,7,11,13,15,20,21,23,25,30,32,40]) focusing on generated output, namely the resulting models, and a relatively smaller number of evaluations (e.g., [10,41]) focusing on the interaction process, e.g., the dynamics of the modeling process itself.

Interaction Process [41] exemplifies an evaluation that puts the interaction, i.e. the modeling process, at the center, assessing user-perceived helpfulness. Another example is [10], which analyzes the complexity of interaction logs and conducts a strength and weakness analysis based on that to identify where LLMs perform well or struggle, and what common mistakes they tend to make.

Output Models. Output-oriented evaluations can be conducted at two levels of granularity: macro and micro. With the macro granularity, the generated models are assessed as a whole. The criteria used are often related to the intrinsic properties of the models, such as syntactic, semantic, or pragmatic validity [30]; understandability, correctness, completeness, relevance, and ease of updating [13]; alignment with the provided textual description [20]; or soundness and executability [23].

With the micro granularity, evaluations focus on individual model elements, often aggregated along the component-relationship dichotomy. For examples in goal modeling [11], components include intentional elements and actors, while relationships include contribution, decomposition, and dependency links. In multi-perspective enterprise modeling [21], components represent entities across different enterprise perspectives such as business, resource and technology, while relationships include both inter- and intra-perspective ones. In business process modeling [1,5,15,32], components include tasks, actors, and gateways, and relationships include flow and actor performer relation. For class diagram modeling [7,25,40], components consist of classes and attributes, while relationships encompass both associations and generalizations.

3.4 Input and Output Dataset

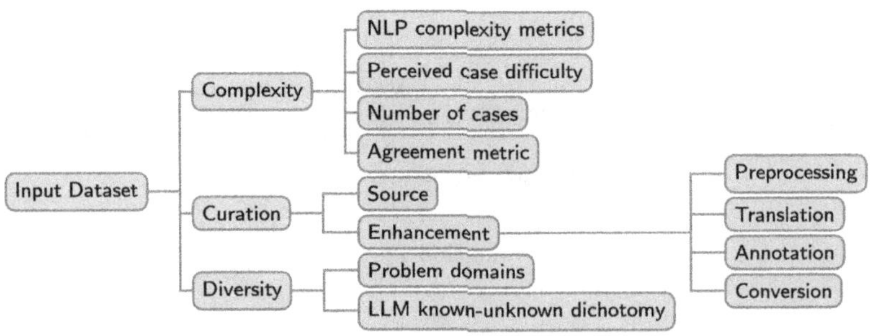

Fig. 4. Input Dataset category

The Input Dataset category (Fig. 4) concerns what LLM-based text-to-model approaches take as input during the experiments, which are mainly textual problem domain descriptions. When preparing input datasets for experiments, we observe efforts along three key subcategories: complexity, curation, and diversity, guided largely by empirical study principles.

Complexity. This subcategory concerns the coverage of different levels of complexity in input datasets. Several studies (e.g., [3,5,6,20,35]) target linguistic complexity using NLP complexity metrics such as the number of sentences, sentence length, number of words, number of unique words, and word length.

Notably, [3] goes beyond linguistic complexity to also consider perceived case difficulty. Specifically, both the readability of a case description measured by the Flesch-Kincaid Ease Score based on the number of sentences and word length and the estimated difficulty of cases as judged by the authors are used as indicators of input data complexity.

Additionally, many studies pay attention to the number of cases [12,13,26, 27,34,40], often of different domains (cf. subcategory diversity below). Of note here is [6] where creating a dataset is part of the paper contribution. They consciously compare their scenarios in terms of number of cases, in addition to ensuring coverage of different domains and levels of NLP complexity.

Finally, [7] uses an agreement metric (Fleiss' Kappa) as a proxy for input data complexity. The authors individually tag elements in an input scenario description to build a gold standard, and the level of agreement among them reflects the complexity of the scenario: the greater the tagging divergence, the higher the complexity.

Curation. This subcategory reflects the efforts made to achieve quality and fit-for-purpose input dataset from various sources. In terms of source, some studies rely on datasets from a curated repository, like the PET dataset for business process modeling [13,22,27], or a use case dataset for goal modeling and use case diagrams [2,7]. Alternative dataset sources include established scenarios from the literature, like in [15,34], from course material [6,7] or textbooks [21], and those created by the authors themselves [31]. Furthermore, [32] relies on LLMs to generate large synthetic datasets (covering 500 random domains).

A few studies [14,21,28,31] source and subsequently curate fit-for-purpose datasets through enhancement. Noteworthy is [14], who enhances a comprehensive Danish healthcare dataset via pre-processing (e.g., to remove duplications), translation (into English), and annotation (to make a PET-like dataset). Of interest, the authors use LLMs to support the annotation process to clarify ambiguities and improve annotating efficiency. When the source dataset lacks sufficient complexity variety (cf. subcategory complexity above), [21] enriches the dataset (which is considered complex) with a conversion of the original one into a simpler counterpart. Additionally, [28] applies three distinct strategies: base, flipped, and random, to convert non-textual source datasets into natural language representations with varying amounts of information incorporated. Finally, [31] converts simple descriptions in three distinct styles: analytical, which is precise and rigorous; eclectic, which is less structured but multi-perspective; and educational, starting with essential concepts only and adding details progressively.

Diversity. This subcategory concerns the range of domains represented in the input datasets. Many studies (e.g., [6,10,22,27,28,34,40]) explicitly report the problem domains covered in their experiments, spanning finance, energy, healthcare, education, transportation, or farming, to name a few. Particularly noteworthy for LLM-based text-to-model approaches, some papers, e.g. [7,10,11,28,37], deliberately accommodate the LLM known-unknown dichotomy in selecting the domains, including both well-represented and underrepresented domains in LLM training data in their input datasets.

In contrast, the Output Dataset category (Fig. 5) focuses on what LLM-based text-to-model approaches produce in the experiments, which of course primarily pertains to conceptual models. However, given the flexibility of LLM-generated text, these models can be represented variously, in terms of covered conceptual scope, used modeling notation, and specific output format.

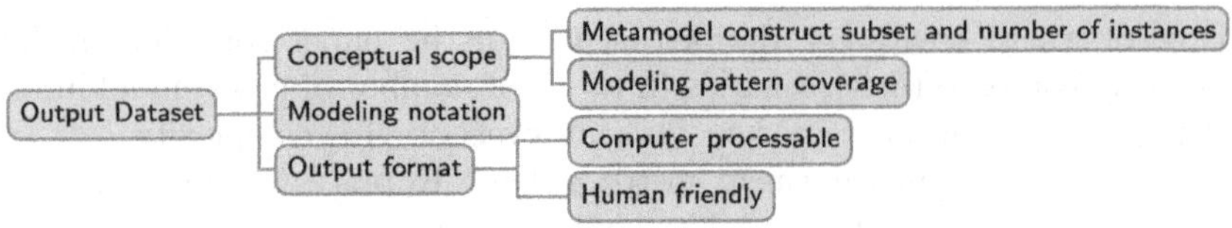

Fig. 5. Output Dataset category

Conceptual Scope. Many studies in their experiments consciously target only a metamodel construct subset, like [7] who, for UML class diagrams, covers only classes and associations, [31] who covers classes, attributes, and associations, whereas for process modeling with BPMN [22,26] cover a subset of process modeling concepts only. There are a few studies that aim at full conceptual coverage, but we find that this tends to be the case for modeling languages of a relatively small scale, like Data Flow Diagrams [17], or goal modeling languages [35].

Interestingly, a few studies explicitly target modeling patterns coverage in the output. Specifically, for UML class diagrams, [12] evaluates the output with respect to player-role and abstraction-occurrence patterns, finding that these patterns are rarely captured by the LLM. [40] follows up with a multi-step iterative automated domain modeling approach using LLMs, which according their evaluation improves the identification of player-role patterns.

Modeling Notation. While the conceptual scope subcategory above addresses variation in the use of the abstract syntax of modeling languages, [10] explores an equally noteworthy dimension in the design of the output dataset in experiments: the choice of modeling notations (i.e., concrete syntax). Specifically, [10] experiments how different UML notations: PlantUML and USE (the UML-based Specification Environment) affect LLM performance, with the finding that ChatGPT tends to make fewer syntactic mistakes when generating models in PlantUML.

Output Format. Experiments also vary in the expected output format. On the one hand, we find computer processable formats. This can be outputs directly importable into a modeling tool such as JUCMNav [34] for goal modeling, or PlantUML [3,31] for domain modeling. Others e.g., [12,22] take an indirect stance by requiring LLMs to generate structured formats, which then can be post-processed into conceptual models.

On the other hand, we observe studies e.g., [7,27] target human friendly formats in their experiments, without the aim of further computer processing. Often the output of these experiments is simply interpreted by the authors to gauge the performance against a reference model (cf. evaluation means, Sect. 3.5).

3.5 Evaluation Means

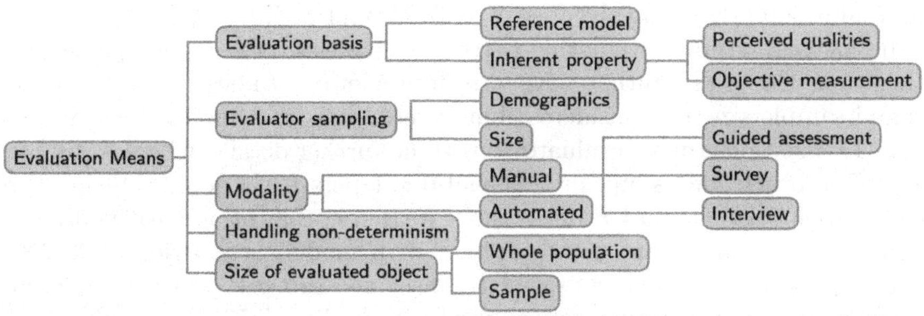

Fig. 6. Evaluation Means category

The Evaluation Means category (Fig. 6) describes how the LLM-based text-to-model approaches are evaluated (whereas the evaluation focus category presented in Sect. 3.3 describes what is being evaluated). We identify five subcategories based on the reviewed studies, detailed in the following.

Evaluation Basis. We observe that a majority of surveyed studies, e.g., [2,5–7,11,12,14,15,21,25–27,31,37,40] compare LLM generated models against a reference model. These studies typically employ information retrieval metrics (such as precision, recall, and F1 score) to gauge the accuracy of generated models, element by element. In addition, model distance metrics quantifying the difference between generated models and reference models to assess models as a whole, are sometimes employed, like in [5,16,26,28,37].

Alternatively, judgments are made based on the inherent properties of what is being evaluated, being either the generated models or the modeling process (cf. Section 3.3). These properties can be assessed subjectively, through perception of human evaluators (e.g., prospective users of the proposed approach [13,22,41] or study authors [3], cf. evaluator sampling subcategory discussed next), or objectively, using objective measurements, elaborated below.

In terms of perceived qualities, for example [13] checks understandability, correctness, completeness, and relevance of the generated business process models, as well as the ease of updating them, a property concerning the modeling process itself. [17] considers perceived completeness and correctness of generated models. And [41] assesses users' perception of the helpfulness, time-saving potential and facilitation of modeling tasks offered by their approach.

In terms of objective measurements, two studies stand out: [10] quantifies interaction complexity by tracking the number of sessions and prompts per session required for successful model generation; [32] measures size, density, separability and variability of generated models to judge how well they fit for constituting diverse and scalable synthetic datasets of declarative process models.

Evaluator Sampling. This subcategory touches on sampling considerations. The studies where LLM output is compared against a reference model often use the study authors as evaluators, who are well versed in the approach being assessed and evaluation criteria involved, such as [7,11,12,14,25,27,40].

In contrast, studies evaluating perceived qualities often recruit participants other than the study authors. Among the reviewed studies, both demographics and sample size are considered, but descriptions of evaluator demographics vary. [17] mentions three "evaluators" with no further details, whereas [13] mention "nine practitioners and professional developers from Bonitasoft and three academics specializing in BPM", without further specification. Others are more explicit in the participant demographics, with modeling experience [20,22] or BPM experience [41] being an explicitly discussed property of the sample. Furthermore, in case a survey focuses on user perceived qualities the population size is often mentioned, but only [22] remark on nòn response.

Modality. When it comes to the mode of evaluation, we find that studies perform their evaluation manually or automatically. Manual evaluation is used by the majority of studies. It is applied both in studies that compare the LLM output to a reference solution and studies in which perceived qualities are in focus (cf. evaluation basis subcategory above). When comparing to a reference model, studies employ guided assessment, following a grading rubric (cf. category scoring criteria discussed in Sect. 3.6 for more details), or established guidelines in the literature. For example, [32] applied two criteria in the Seven Process Model Guidelines (7PMG) to evaluate generated models. Another example is [7], who employ a decision tree for evaluators to qualitatively agree upon the status of a model element. Briefly, the tree evaluates element scope first, if in scope, evaluates redundancy, and if not redundant, considers relevance. When assessing perceived qualities, studies either use a survey as in [13,17,22], or conduct an interview with prospect users such as in [41] to collect feedback.

Only one study [28] conducts an automated evaluation of models (expressed in PDDL, Planning Domain Definition Language, a formal language to represent planning problems). The formal semantics of planning domain models and a heuristic model equivalence metric based on the semantics are essential components that make the evaluation computer amenable. However, as noted by [12], "automated comparison of two domain models is ... non-trivial ..., they either provide an imprecise estimation or work under carefully selected situations."

Handling Non-determinism. This subcategory, being specific to LLMs, considers the extent to which a study explicitly addresses the non-deterministic nature of LLMs, even when all the independent variables are fixed (cf. Section 3.7). Some studies, such as [7,15,23,40] systematically run the experiments multiple times and aggregate the results to account for the non-deterministic nature of LLMs. In contrast, one study [21] in our sample adopts a more pragmatic approach by re-running the experiments until the LLM generates a model importable to the targeted modeling tool, a prerequisite for further evaluation.

Size of Evaluated Object. Evaluation of generated models is often performed on the whole population. For example, studies evaluate all models generated from 7 [20], 15 [1] or 39 examples [5] within the PET dataset. Similarly, evaluations of UML models have covered all 8 [12,40] or 9 [7] exercises derived from university courses. However, when the number of models generated is too extensive to realistically evaluate, only a selected sample is evaluated. For example, in [32], 8 models were sampled for evaluation from a total of 500.

3.6 Scoring Criteria

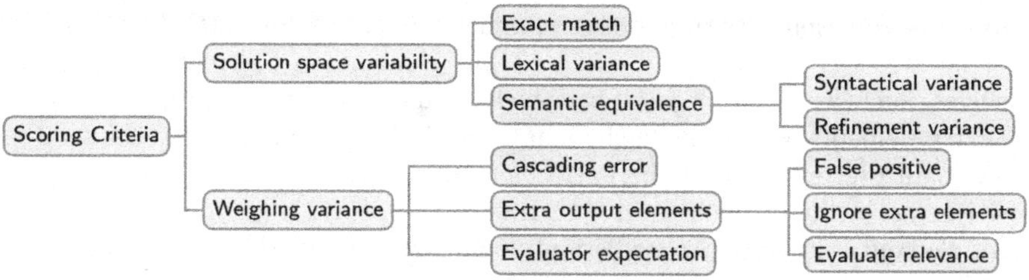

Fig. 7. Scoring Criteria category

The Scoring Criteria category (Fig. 7) encompasses the considerations involved in designing the scoring rubric used to grade LLM generated output.

Solution Space Variability. Conceptual modeling exhibits what [9] terms solution space variability, meaning that for same problem description multiple models can be equally valid. To account for this variability, the reviewed studies adopt a spectrum of scoring strictness levels. These different levels allow for the evaluation of LLM generated models within a broad solution space. As such, this accommodates diverse yet correct models.

Studies e.g., [5,25] use an exact match to check if the output model is identical to the reference. [5] refers to this as a strict comparison, allowing no deviation from the reference solution. [5,11,15,40] goes a step further by permitting lexical variance, namely allowing for synonymous names between the compared model elements. Even more accommodating are studies targeting semantic equivalence instead, realized in two forms. First, syntactical variance allows different model constructs to capture the same meaning [12,40]. For example, the reference model uses a boolean attribute to represent a status, while the LLM solution suggests an enumeration with two literals [12]. Second, refinement variance tolerates model constructs differing in the level of detail but are appropriate in the context. For example, [15] allows combining consecutive activities into a single one, while [5] allows splitting activities containing double action into two.

Weighing Variance. This subcategory addresses various strategies to weigh components (errors in LLM outputs or user perceptions) of evaluation.

When weighing errors, two types of errors are considered: cascading errors and extra output elements. Cascading errors originate from intermediate errors made in early stages of multi-step LLM-based text-to-model workflows. Scoring strategies may either weigh in intermediate errors by accounting for their downstream impact, such as in [40]. Alternatively, some evaluations weigh out intermediate errors by completely ignoring the cascading errors in the final result, as seen in [7]. Interestingly, one study [5] explores both settings: (1) an incremental setup, where early step results are used as input to later ones, allowing cascading errors to occur naturally, and (2) a gold standard setup, where each step is evaluated in isolation using the gold standard as input to prevent cascading errors.

Extra output elements are those generated by the LLM but not present in the reference model, (whereby the subcategory solution space variability discussed above concerns elements that in the reference model but not in the LLM output). A strict strategy for handling extra output elements is to treat them as false positives, such as in [11,40]. Alternatively, a more lenient strategy is to ignore the extra elements in scoring, such as in [7]. In between, there is also the strategy to evaluate the relevance of the extra elements and mark them as true or false positives accordingly, such as in [21]. In addition, [11,21] recommend reporting extra elements explicitly, regardless of how they are scored.

When weighing user perceptions, some studies suggest explicitly considering evaluator expectation and adjusting the weight of their perceptions accordingly. For example, negative opinion from a user with higher expectation should be less weighted than from a user with low expectation [41]. Another factor, highlighted by [20] is the user's awareness of whether a model is created by an LLM or a human, as this awareness can influence their perception and evaluation.

3.7 LLM-Related Independent Variables

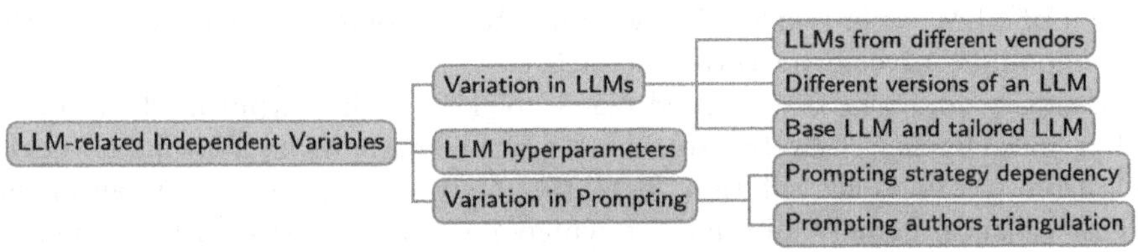

Fig. 8. LLM-related Independent Variables category

The LLM-Related Independent Variables category (Fig. 8) specifies subcategories that are systematically varied in LLM-based text-to-model experiments.

Variations in LLMs. Some studies evaluate the performance of LLMs from different vendors on the same modeling task. Comparisons include open-source models such as Llama and Starcoder [28], closed-source models like GPT and Gemini [23], and comparisons between open- and closed-source models, such as GPT and Mixtral [7], or GPT, Cohere and Llama [34]. Other comparisons involve different versions of an LLM from the same organization. For closed-source, the model name is specified, such as GPT-4 and GPT-3.5-Turbo [16], or GPT-4o and GPT-3.5-0125 [27]. For open-source models, versions are typically categorized by LLM size, such as Llama 7B, 13B and 70B [28]. Finally, variations in LLMs can pertain to the use of both base models and tailored models. These include comparisons between the base model and the fine-tuned model for chat (e.g., Llama vs Llama-chat) [28], models fine-tuned with varying volumes of data [1], and general versus code specific LLMs for SQL generation [37].

LLM Hyperparameters. The behavior and output of LLMs can be configured through hyperparameters such as temperature and top-k. Briefly, the lower the values, the less variety in the generated responses. For example, [5,11,27,32,40] consciously set the temperature close to zero to avoid too variable outputs. [34] evaluates three different settings of temperature, 0.4, 0.6, and 0.8, and reports that the two higher values generated more acceptable goal models. Similarly, [28] adjusts the top-k parameter to manage the diversity of the generated responses.

Variation in Prompting The prompting strategy dependency is emphasized in a recent study [9], which highlights the influence of prompt formulations on the quality of models generated by LLMs. Our observation is that the most common approach is to modify the prompts then assess the impact on the generated models. These techniques include in-context learning approaches such as zero-shot, few-shot [8], and chain-of-thought [38], in which LLMs recognize and execute the task with the context provided in the prompt [8]. We found three studies comparing all three prompting techniques [12,25,27]. Two other studies compare zero-shot and few-shot [5,15]. Others use only one technique, either zero-shot [11,20] or few-shot [16,21,23,28,32,41]. Moreover, when an approach adopts prompting techniques decomposing the modeling task into consecutive steps, comparison with a single-step setting can be observed. For example, [40] divided into four steps, increasing the recall performance. [7] uses a two step decomposition achieving more accurate UML class models. [13] achieves higher accuracy in process models using six steps. Finally, [34] uses eight steps for goal modeling; however, it is not compared with other approaches.

We identified only one study that aimed to isolate the impact of individual prompting techniques through an ablation study. In [27], the authors set the LLM temperature to zero to reduce the model non-determinism so as to establish a baseline for comparison. Then they systematically removed specific prompting techniques from the baseline and reported quantitative results to assess the effect of each change in the prompt. However, other studies with prompt variation resemble an ablation study, even though they do not formally present it as such. These studies follow an approach to modify the prompt and compare the LLM performance. For example, [5,25,28] change the number of examples in few-shot prompting, or [11,20] use different instructions in zero-shot.

Another variation is prompting authors triangulation, where different authors independently create prompts for the same task. This approach evaluates the robustness of LLM outputs in response to variations in prompt formulation [15].

4 Concluding Outlook

In this paper, we used a systemic literature review to provide a synthesis of experimental design considerations of LLM-based text-to-model approaches. We organize our findings along six categories, with subcategories for each. Reflecting upon each category, we find the following observations to be of particular interest.

Evaluation Aims: Align with Research Questions and Stakeholder Needs. When evaluation goes beyond basic reality checks or benchmarking, it is good practice to explicitly articulate the evaluation goals through well-defined research questions and/or hypotheses. Moreover, in stakeholder-oriented context, evaluation should be driven by stakeholder needs, following principles of Design Science Research to ensure relevance and utility.

Evaluation Focus: The Process Can be Just as Important as the Output. Most reviewed studies emphasize evaluating the LLM-generated models, the final tangible artifacts. However, the modeling process itself including user interaction, iteration, and experience, is equally important, as it directly shapes the quality of the output. While the decision to evaluate models or process depends on the specific research focus, we find it valuable to consider both outcome and process when appropriate.

Input and Output Datasets: Address LLM Exposure Alongside Empirical Design Principles. While established empirical study design principles such as ensuring dataset complexity, diversity and quality remain essential, an equally critical factor specific to evaluations of LLM-based approaches is the LLM's prior exposure to the data. Evaluations should intentionally include both "known" and "unknown" datasets to enhance credibility of evaluation results.

Evaluation Means: Mitigate LLM Non-determinism to Support Reproducibility of Experiments. The inherent non-deterministic behavior of LLMs is a challenge for consistent evaluation of the experiments. Some studies address this by running the same experiment multiple times and aggregating the results, while others rely on LLM hyperparameters to reduce its effect to some extent. Clearly specifying the strategy adopted is essential to ensure some degree of reproducibility.

Scoring Criteria: Recognize Valid Solutions Beyond the Reference Models and Make the Criteria Explicit. Evaluating LLM-generated models using a single reference solution is a common practice, which may overlook potential valid alternatives. Moreover, cascading errors, namely errors in later step due to mistakes in early steps may penalize the overall score unfairly. Since there is no standardized scoring rubric, it is essential to clearly define: (1) how alternative correct solutions can be accepted (e.g., through a relaxed grading strategy), (2) how error propagation is handled, and (3) how these choices influence the overall evaluation. Making these assumptions explicit is important for ensuring transparent evaluation.

LLM-Related Independent Variables: Adopt a Formal Ablation Study to Isolate Effects. Multiple studies vary prompts to assess their performance;

however, only one study [27] explicitly presents results as an ablation study. This highlights an opportunity to isolate the impact of individual prompt components, supporting more interpretable and insightful evaluations.

Our goal is to support future evaluation of LLM-based text-to-model approaches by offering a compendium of experimental design considerations, both generally relevant and LLM-specific. In pursuing this goal, this paper has one key limitation: as is inherent to an SLR, our contribution is limited to a synthesis of the reviewed sample. While the sample certainly yields valuable insights into current experimental practice (cf. the summarized observations above), our SLR, at least in the way it was conducted, does not adopt a forward-looking perspective grounded in broader empirical context. For example, we did not incorporate insights from user studies in the empirical software engineering literature. Notably, many of the reviewed studies adopt an "engineering like" stance to evaluation, focusing on benchmarking LLM output on an often predefined dataset, and against predefined qualities. User focused considerations from the broader empirical (software engineering) literature, like an explicit account of user defined requirements, or a focus on user interaction with an LLM, appear underrepresented, at least in our sample.

Future work will aim to develop a final experiment report that includes two additional categories not covered in this paper due to space constraints: "evaluation metrics" and "reproducibility". Furthermore, we plan to integrate general user study guidelines from empirical software engineering to both guide experimental design and provide a forward-looking perspective complementing the findings of this review.

References

1. Apaydin, K., Zisgen, Y.: Local large language models for business process modeling. In: Delgado, A., Slaats, T. (eds.) ICPM 2024. LNBIP, vol. 533, pp. 605–609. Springer, Cham (2024). https://doi.org/10.1007/978-3-031-82225-4_44
2. Arulmohan, S., Meurs, M., Mosser, S.: Extracting domain models from textual requirements in the era of large language models. In: ACM/IEEE International Conference on Model Driven Engineering Languages and Systems. MODELS, pp. 580–587. IEEE (2023)
3. Bari, D.D., Garaccione, G., Coppola, R., Torchiano, M., Ardito, L.: Evaluating large language models in exercises of UML class diagram modeling. In: Proceedings of the 18th ACM/IEEE International Symposium on Empirical Software Engineering and Measurement. ESEM, pp. 393–399. ACM (2024)
4. Barn, B.S., Barat, S., Sandkuhl, K.: Adaptation of enterprise modeling methods for large language models. In: Almeida, J.P.A., Kaczmarek-Heß, M., Koschmider, A., Proper, H.A. (eds.) PoEM 2023. LNBIP, vol. 497, pp. 3–18. Springer, Cham (2023). https://doi.org/10.1007/978-3-031-48583-1_1
5. Bellan, P., Dragoni, M., Ghidini, C.: Process knowledge extraction and knowledge graph construction through prompting: a quantitative analysis. In: Proceedings of the 39th ACM/SIGAPP Symposium on Applied Computing, pp. 1634–1641. ACM (2024)

6. Bozyigit, F., et al.: Generating domain models from natural language text using NLP: a benchmark dataset and experimental comparison of tools. Softw. Syst. Model. **23**, 1493–1511 (2024)
7. Bragilovski, M., Van Can, A.T., Dalpiaz, F., Sturm, A.: Leveraging machines to derive domain models from user stories. In: Requirements Engineering (2025)
8. Brown, T.B., et al.: Language models are few-shot learners. In: NeurIPS (2020)
9. Cámara, J., Burgueño, L., Troya, J.: Towards standarized benchmarks of LLMs in software modeling tasks: a conceptual framework. Softw. Syst. Model. **23**(6), 1309–1318 (2024)
10. Cámara, J., Troya, J., Burgueño, L., Vallecillo, A.: On the assessment of generative AI in modeling tasks: an experience report with ChatGPT and UML. Softw. Syst. Model. **22**(3), 781–793 (2023)
11. Chen, B., et al.: On the use of GPT-4 for creating goal models: an exploratory study. In: 31st IEEE International Requirements Engineering Conference. RE, pp. 262–271. IEEE (2023)
12. Chen, K., Yang, Y., Chen, B., López, J.A.H., Mussbacher, G., Varró, D.: Automated domain modeling with large language models: a comparative study. In: 26th ACM/IEEE International Conference on Model Driven Engineering Languages and Systems. MODELS, pp. 162–172. IEEE (2023)
13. Eldin, A.N., Assy, N., Anesini, O., Dalmas, B., Gaaloul, W.: A decomposed hybrid approach to business process modeling with LLMs. In: Comuzzi, M., Grigori, D., Sellami, M., Zhou, Z. (eds.) CoopIS 2024. LNCS, vol. 15506, pp. 243–260. Springer, Cham (2024). https://doi.org/10.1007/978-3-031-81375-7_14
14. Grathwol, D., van der Aa, H., López, H.A.: Automating pathway extraction from clinical guidelines: a conceptual model, datasets and initial experiments. In: Comuzzi, M., Grigori, D., Sellami, M., Zhou, Z. (eds.) CoopIS 2024. LNCS, vol. 15506, pp. 296–312. Springer, Cham (2024). https://doi.org/10.1007/978-3-031-81375-7_17
15. Grohs, M., Abb, L., Elsayed, N., Rehse, J.: Large language models can accomplish business process management tasks. CoRR (2023)
16. Guan, L., Valmeekam, K., Sreedharan, S., Kambhampati, S.: Leveraging pre-trained large language models to construct and utilize world models for model-based task planning. In: Advances in Neural Information Processing Systems 36: Annual Conference on Neural Information Processing Systems (2023)
17. Herwanto, G.B.: Automating data flow diagram generation from user stories using large language models. In: Joint Proceedings of REFSQ-2024 Workshops, Doctoral Symposium, Posters and Tools Track, and Education and Training Track, vol. 3672 (2024)
18. Hevner, A.R., March, S.T., Park, J., Ram, S.: Design science in information systems research. MIS Q. **28**(1), 75–105 (2004)
19. Kitchenham, B., Budgen, D., Brereton, P.: Guidelines for performing systematic literature reviews in software engineering. Technical report EBSE-2007-01, EBSE Technical report, Keele University and Durham University (2007)
20. Klievtsova, N., Benzin, J., Mangler, J., Kampik, T., Rinderle-Ma, S.: Process modeler vs. chatbot: is generative AI taking over process modeling? In: Delgado, A., Slaats, T. (eds.) ICPM 2024. LNBIP, vol. 533, pp. 637–649. Springer, Cham (2024). https://doi.org/10.1007/978-3-031-82225-4_47
21. Kolev, P., Pruss, H.H., Wilken, J.R., Sandkuhl, K.: Grass-root enterprise modelling: how large language models can help. In: Paja, E., Zdravkovic, J., Kavakli, E., Stirna, J. (eds.) PoEM 2024. LNBIP, vol. 538, pp. 123–139. Springer, Cham (2024). https://doi.org/10.1007/978-3-031-77908-4_8

22. Köpke, J., Safan, A.: Efficient LLM-based conversational process modeling. In: Gdowska, K., Gómez-López, M.T., Rehse, J.R. (eds.) BPM 2024. LNBIP, vol. 534, pp. 259–270. Springer, Cham (2024). https://doi.org/10.1007/978-3-031-78666-2_20
23. Kourani, H., Berti, A., Schuster, D., van der Aalst, W.M.P.: Process modeling with large language models. CoRR (2024)
24. Kundisch, D., et al.: An update for taxonomy designers: methodological guidance from information systems research. Bus. Inf. Syst. Eng. **64**(4), 421–439 (2022)
25. Li, Y., Keung, J., Ma, X., Chong, C.Y., Zhang, J., Liao, Y.: LLM-based class diagram derivation from user stories with chain-of-thought promptings. In: 48th IEEE Annual Computers, Software, and Applications Conference. COMPSAC, pp. 45–50. IEEE (2024)
26. Licardo, J.T., Tankovic, N., Etinger, D.: A method for extracting BPMN models from textual descriptions using natural language processing. In: CENTERIS, vol. 239, pp. 483–490. Elsevier (2023)
27. Neuberger, J., Ackermann, L., van der Aa, H., Jablonski, S.: A universal prompting strategy for extracting process model information from natural language text using large language models. In: Maass, W., Han, H., Yasar, H., Multari, N. (eds.) ER 2024. LNCS, vol. 15238, pp. 38–55. Springer, Cham (2024). https://doi.org/10.1007/978-3-031-75872-0_3
28. Oswald, J.T., Srinivas, K., Kokel, H., Lee, J., Katz, M., Sohrabi, S.: Large language models as planning domain generators. In: Proceedings of the Thirty-Fourth International Conference on Automated Planning and Scheduling. ICAPS, pp. 423–431. AAAI Press (2024)
29. Page, M.J., et al.: The Prisma 2020 statement: an updated guideline for reporting systematic reviews. BMJ (2021)
30. Piller, C.: Meta-prompt engineering in ChatGPT-4 for AI-generated BPM reference models. In: Elstermann, M., Lederer, M. (eds.) S-BPM ONE 2024. CCIS, vol. 2206, pp. 315–331. Springer, Cham (2024). https://doi.org/10.1007/978-3-031-72041-3_22
31. Prokop, D., Stenchlák, S., Skoda, P., Klímek, J., Necaský, M.: Enhancing domain modeling with pre-trained large language models: an automated assistant for domain modelers. In: Maass, W., Han, H., Yasar, H., Multari, N. (eds.) ER 2024. LNCS, vol. 15238, pp. 235–253. Springer, Cham (2024). https://doi.org/10.1007/978-3-031-75872-0_13
32. Santos, W.D.S., Coutinho, J.R., Baião, F., Spyrides, G.M., Lopes, H.C.V.: Terpsichora: a tool to generate synthetic MP-declare process models. In: Delgado, A., Slaats, T. (eds.) ICPM 2024. LNBIP, vol. 533, pp. 624–636. Springer, Cham (2024). https://doi.org/10.1007/978-3-031-82225-4_46
33. Schulhoff, S., eta l.: The prompt report: a systematic survey of prompting techniques. CoRR (2024)
34. Siddeshwar, V., Alwidian, S.A., Makrehchi, M.: A comparative study of large language models for goal model extraction. In: Proceedings of the ACM/IEEE 27th International Conference on Model Driven Engineering Languages and Systems. MODELS, pp. 253–263. ACM (2024)
35. Siddeshwar, V., Alwidian, S.A., Makrehchi, M.: Goal model extraction from user stories using large language models. In: Bertolino, A., Pascoal Faria, J., Lago, P., Semini, L. (eds.) QUATIC 2024. CCIS, vol. 2178, pp. 269–276. Springer, Cham (2024). https://doi.org/10.1007/978-3-031-70245-7_19
36. Snoeck, M., Pastor, O.: Teaching conceptual modelling in the age of LLMs: shifting from model creation to model evaluation skills. Softw. Syst. Model. 1–11 (2025)

37. Song, Y., et al.: Enhancing text-to-SQL translation for financial system design. In: Proceedings of the 46th International Conference on Software Engineering: Software Engineering in Practice. ICSE-SEIP, pp. 252–262. ACM (2024)
38. Wei, J., et al.: Chain-of-thought prompting elicits reasoning in large language models. In: NeurIPS (2022)
39. White, J., et al.: A prompt pattern catalog to enhance prompt engineering with ChatGPT. CoRR (2023)
40. Yang, Y., Chen, B., Chen, K., Mussbacher, G., Varró, D.: Multi-step iterative automated domain modeling with large language models. In: Proceedings of the ACM/IEEE 27th International Conference on Model Driven Engineering Languages and Systems. MODELS, pp. 587–595. ACM (2024)
41. Ziche, C., Apruzzese, G.: LLM4PM: a case study on using large language models for process modeling in enterprise organizations. CoRR (2024)

Automated and LLM-Assisted Conceptual Modeling from Semi-structured Data

Pedro Guimarães[1,2(✉)], António C. Vieira[1,2], Vânia Sousa[1,2], Guilherme Moreira[3], and Maribel Y. Santos[1,2]

[1] ALGORITMI Research Centre, University of Minho, Campus de Azurém, 4800-058 Guimarães, Portugal

[2] CCG/ZGDV Institute, University of Minho, Campus de Azurém, 4800-058 Guimarães, Portugal

pedro.guimaraes@ccg.pt

[3] Bosch Car Multimédia Portugal, S.A. Apartado 2458, 4701-970 Braga, Portugal

Abstract. Conceptual modeling, particularly with Entity-Relationship Diagrams (ERDs), is traditionally a manual and complex task in data engineering. This paper presents a method and tool for automating ERD generation from semi-structured data using Large Language Models (LLMs). The approach follows an iterative cycle, data ingestion, prompt design and execution, and results evaluation, with human-in-the-loop refinement to improve accuracy through expert feedback. Validation was performed on two datasets, assessing model quality via coverage, referential integrity, and Third Normal Form (3NF) compliance. Results showed high scores (0.90 and 0.93), confirming the tool's effectiveness and the need for expert input to resolve complex modeling issues. This work offers an LLM-assisted solution to assist in complex data engineering tasks, while acknowledging the continued importance of expert oversight.

Keywords: Conceptual Modeling · Entity-Relationship Diagrams · Large Language Models · Automated Model Generation · Data Engineering

1 Introduction

Conceptual modeling is central to data engineering and knowledge representation, typically expressed through ERDs or UML diagrams to abstract domain entities and relationships [1,6]. Despite its importance, it remains largely manual, with limited automation efforts [8,12].

The complexity arises from interpreting unprocessed data lacking explicit entity and relationship definitions [3,6]. Challenges include ambiguous naming, incomplete identifiers, and the need for sufficient contextual information, as insufficient context can lead to incorrect mappings, whereas excessive information may compromise performance by overfitting.

Published by Springer Nature Switzerland AG 2026
H.-G. Fill et al. (Eds.): PoEM 2025, LNBIP 570, pp. 121–129, 2026.
https://doi.org/10.1007/978-3-032-12063-2_8

LLMs have recently shown promise in data-centric tasks due to their ability to capture linguistic and semantic patterns [3,5,11]. In conceptual modeling, they can infer structures and generate formal representations like ERDs. However, the automated construction of conceptual models presents unique challenges, as it requires an understanding of domain semantics, the identification of implicit relationships, and the abstraction of relevant entities and attributes from unstructured or semi-structured data.

This paper introduces a method to mitigate these challenges and a supporting LLM-assisted tool for ERD inference. The tool applies the method to two datasets, validating its effectiveness despite variability in LLM outputs.

The paper is organized as follows. Section 2 reviews related work. Section 3 outlines the method. Section 4 defines evaluation metrics. Section 5 describes the tool. Section 6 presents experimental results. Section 7 concludes with findings and future directions.

2 Related Work

This section reviews studies from 2023 to 2025 on LLMs in conceptual modeling, focusing on ERD generation, current capabilities, and open challenges.

[14] evaluated LLMs in tasks like domain modeling and class diagram generation. While LLMs effectively identify entities and attributes, they struggle with complex relationships, consistency, and domain-specific patterns. Outputs often require expert correction and refinement. [7] used ChatGPT to generate ERDs via contextual prompts. Though some results were accurate, modeling expertise was necessary for validation. They concluded LLMs are better suited for draft generation than complete ERDs.

Benchmarking efforts by [4,10,13] show high precision in entity extraction but lower recall for relationships and cardinalities. [10] compared LLM-generated ERDs to reference models, noting frequent errors in implicit relationships and attribute misclassification. Cardinalities were often incorrect or missing due to limited prompt context. [13] benchmarked ChatGPT using Jaccard similarity, finding strong entity recognition but weaker performance on nested or context-dependent relationships. Misclassification of attributes occurred, and prompt tuning had minimal effect. [4] confirmed similar trends.

Only [12] explored file-based inputs, proposing a hybrid tool that combines LLMs with traditional algorithms for schema discovery and constraint detection, reducing manual effort.

Overall, LLMs show strong performance in entity and attribute recognition but face limitations in modeling complex relationships. Their outputs serve best as initial drafts requiring expert refinement. There is limited exploration of leveraging diverse data inputs beyond natural language, such as file datasets, to support the ERD generation.

3 Automated and LLM-Assisted Conceptual Modeling

This section outlines a method for automated ERD generation using an LLM-driven cycle. The approach iteratively refines ERDs based on input data and settings to improve contextual accuracy. As shown in Fig. 1, it involves five steps, incorporating an LLM template and domain expert input. Each step is described in the following subsections.

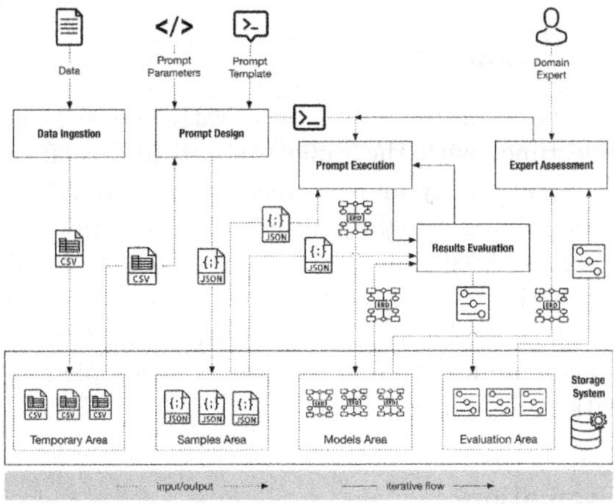

Fig. 1. Proposed Method for Automated and LLM-Assisted Conceptual Modeling.

3.1 Data Ingestion

The ERD generation begins with file ingestion, during which a unique universal identifier (UUID) for tracking is assigned to each file. Submitted files are validated to ensure CSV format and, once confirmed, stored temporarily for use in subsequent steps.

3.2 Prompt Design

A key step involves the extraction of data samples from the data source, adhering to pre-configured parameters used to build the prompt[1]: a float, defaulting to 0.05, representing the fraction of data to sample (`SAMPLE_FRACTION`); an integer, defaulting to 1000, representing the maximum number of sample records to include in the LLM prompt (`SAMPLE_LIMIT`); an integer, defaulting to 3, representing the number of execution runs in the LLM for each dataset (`LLM_RUNS`); a list of float values between 0 and 1 (e.g., `[0.0, 0.35, 0.70]`), representing different temperature settings (`LLM_TEMPERATURES`).

[1] Prompt available at: https://github.com/pedroccg/erdify/prompt.

These samples are stored in the samples area and used in engineering the prompt for the LLM, also considering the dataset name and column structure.

To define the above list of requirements, we ran experiments with LLMs and found that prompting for an ERD in 3NF alone was insufficient. Accurate results required explicit, sometimes redundant instructions. LLMs often missed normalization rules or key entities without detailed guidance, and performed better with iterative reinforcement of concepts like functional dependencies, transitive relationships, and Primary Key (PK) constraints.

3.3 Prompt Execution

To improve ERD generation reliability, an iterative strategy is used: the model is invoked multiple times with the same prompt, and each output is assessed to account for LLM variability and produce diverse candidates. This increases the likelihood of identifying a high-quality ERD. The approach varies the temperature setting across three runs, 0.0, 0.35, and 0.7, to balance deterministic and creative outputs. Lower temperatures yield consistent, focused responses, while higher ones allow exploration of alternative structures. This variation is especially useful when input data is ambiguous or incomplete, helping the model infer implicit entities and relationships.

3.4 Results Evaluation

Each ERD candidate is evaluated using indicators such as Coverage, 3NF Compliance, and Referential Integrity (see Sect. 4). An overall score, based on average F1 scores, is calculated to assess quality. The top-performing ERD is then selected and presented as the final recommendation.

3.5 Expert Assessment

After selecting the top-performing ERD, a domain expert reviews it along with its evaluation report. From there, the expert chooses between two next steps: **Approval,** if the model meets domain requirements, the expert accepts it, concluding the LLM-assisted process; **Refinement,** the expert provides corrections and insights to improve accuracy, which are added to the original prompt, along with dataset details and direct LLM instructions (e.g., "entity X has column Y as its PK"). The approach dynamically updates the original prompt with expert instructions and context. This refined prompt initiates a new generation cycle, combining LLM capabilities with expert insight to iteratively enhance the ERD.

4 Evaluation Indicators

This section outlines the indicators used to evaluate generated ERDs, as detailed in Sect. 3.4. Evaluation focuses on syntactic correctness, while semantic adequacy is assessed by domain experts during iterative refinement.

To assess LLM performance, each indicator is measured using True Positives (TP), False Positives (FP), and False Negatives (FN), from which precision, recall, and F1 scores are calculated. The main indicators are:

1. **FieldCoverage:** Measures how well input dataset columns are represented in the ERD.
   - TP: Columns correctly included.
   - FP: Extra columns not in the dataset.
   - FN: Missing columns from the dataset.
2. **3NFCompliance:** Assesses adherence to the 3NF, a requirement from Sect. 3.2. Evaluation may use LLMs or heuristic methods, with sample data aiding the inference of functional dependencies. Our tool generates synthetic data for this purpose. The synthetic data generator creates records for each ERD entity. PKs are filled with unique values, non-key attributes with random data, and FKs sampled from related PKs. This enables automated 3NF validation, though full implementation is pending.
   - TP: Normalization correctly applied.
   - FP: ERD candidate includes unnecessary 3NF transformations, creating entities misaligned with the input data.
   - FN: ERD candidate omits required 3NF steps, leaving transitive dependencies in entities.
3. **ReferentialIntegrity:** Assesses the ERD's structural soundness by checking PK definitions and FK relationship coherence. It verifies that each entity has a PK and that FKs correctly reference existing entities and valid PKs.
   - TP: PKs are correctly defined, and FKs point to valid entities and PKs.
   - FP: Relationships suggested by the LLM that aren't supported by the input data.
   - FN: Entities missing PKs or lacking expected FK relationships.

After computing each indicator, the Overall Score is derived by averaging their F1 scores, yielding a value between 0 (lowest) and 1 (highest performance).

5 Tool for Automated and LLM-Assisted Modeling

The tool operates as a decoupled, asynchronous service with stateless execution, coordinated via a persistent HDFS backbone. This architecture separates the web interface (Fig. 2), data processing, and LLM interaction.

Web and Application Layer: FastAPI. The main interface is a RESTful API built with FastAPI, supporting async operations and strict validation via Pydantic. An Angular frontend displays the generated ERD (Fig. 3), its score, and evaluation report.

Storage Layer: HDFS. HDFS manages: i) Temporary Storage: CSV uploads stored in request-specific directories; ii) Data Staging: processed subsets saved

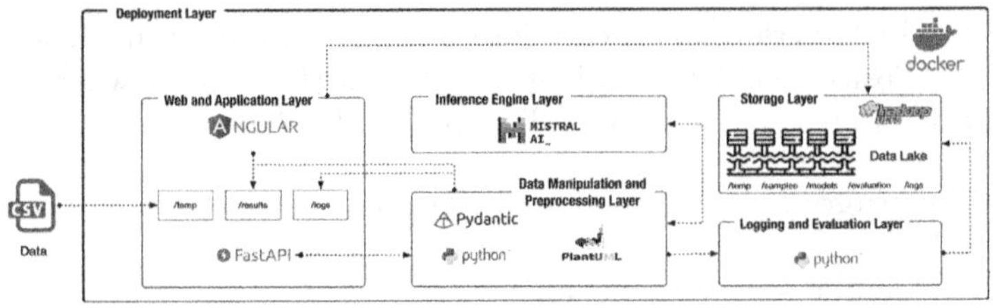

Fig. 2. Technological Architecture of the Supporting Tool.

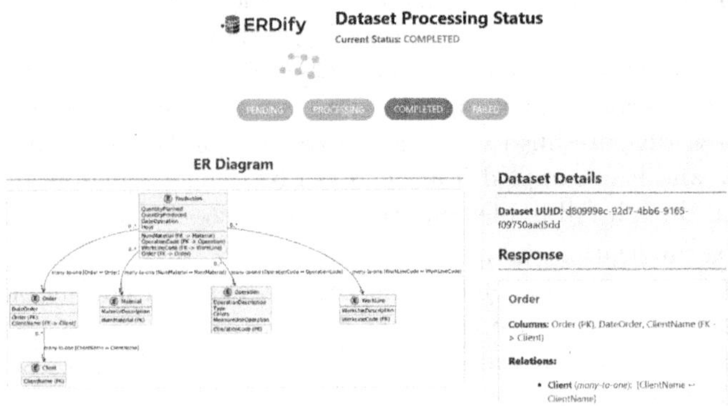

Fig. 3. Screenshot of the proposed tool showcasing a generated ERD.

as JSON samples for LLM input; iii) State Management: job status tracked via JSON files, enabling stateless API scaling; and, iv) Artifact Persistence: final ERDs, evaluation reports, and logs stored for traceability.

Data Manipulation and Preprocessing Layer: Python. Pandas handles in-memory data tasks, including sample generation for prompt enrichment. The ERD is converted to PlantUML and rendered in Angular.

Inference Engine Layer: Mistral AI LLM. ERD generation uses the Mistral AI LLM via its Python client. The tool constructs a context-rich prompt with metadata and staged samples. The LLM's JSON output is passed to the evaluation module.

Logging and Evaluation Layer: Python Logging. Evaluation logs are saved as detailed text files in HDFS.

Deployment Layer: Docker. The entire system runs in a Docker container managed by docker-compose, ensuring portability and reproducibility.

6 Experimental Validation

To evaluate the tool's effectiveness, we ran experiments on two datasets. All resources are available in the GitHub repository[2]. The evaluation took place in a reproducible Docker environment using Python 3.11, along with FastAPI, Pandas, and the Mistralai client to handle inference and evaluation.

Dataset A, Airlines Dataset (synthetic), contains flight, airline, and airplane data, including airport details. It has 18 columns with defined PKs and FKs, requiring multiple normalization steps. Dataset B, Manufactory Dataset (real), sourced from a manufacturing company, includes data on work centers, orders, materials, and production schedules. With 15 columns, it also features clear PKs and FKs and requires normalization. Neither was publicly available to avoid data leakage during LLM evaluation [2,9].

The performance of the method on Datasets A and B is summarized in Table 1. Although the method supports iterative refinement (Sect. 3), only first-iteration results are presented here.

Table 1. Quantitative Evaluation Results at Different Temperatures

Temperature (T)	Indicator	Dataset A						Dataset B					
		TP	FN	FP	Precision	Recall	F1 Score	TP	FN	FP	Precision	Recall	F1 Score
0	FieldCoverage	17	1	0	1.00	0.94	0.97	15	0	0	1.00	1.00	1.00
	3NFCompliance	5	3	0	1.00	0.63	0.77	5	2	0	1.00	0.71	0.83
	ReferentialIntegrity	11	2	0	1.00	0.85	0.92	11	0	1	0.92	1.00	0.96
	OveralScore						**0.89**						**0.93**
0.35	FieldCoverage	18	0	3	0.86	1.00	0.93	15	0	0	1.00	1.00	1.00
	3NFCompliance	5	3	0	1.00	0.63	0.77	5	2	0	1.00	0.71	0.83
	ReferentialIntegrity	10	2	0	1.00	0.83	0.91	10	1	1	0.91	0.91	0.91
	OveralScore						**0.87**						**0.91**
0.70	FieldCoverage	18	0	5	0.78	1.00	0.88	15	0	1	0.94	1.00	0.97
	3NFCompliance	6	2	0	1.00	0.75	0.86	5	2	0	1.00	0.71	0.83
	ReferentialIntegrity	14	1	0	1.00	0.93	0.97	10	1	0	1.00	0.91	0.95
	OveralScore						**0.90**						**0.92**

For Dataset A, the best model scored 0.90 at temperature 0.70. Higher temperatures improved `3NFCompliance` and `ReferentialIntegrity`, while `FieldCoverage` showed a trade-off: precision dropped from 1.00 to 0.78 as recall rose to 1.00. The highest F1 Score for `FieldCoverage` was at $T = 0$ (0.97), but overall performance peaked at $T = 0.70$ due to gains in normalization and relationship accuracy. Compared to the reference model[3], all fields were included, but some were misplaced (e.g., *airplane_model* in Flight). Referential integrity issues included missing associative entities for flight status updates. For 3NF, fields like *city* and *status* were not properly normalized.

[2] https://github.com/pedroccg/erdify/.

[3] https://github.com/pedroccg/erdify/blob/main/results_dataset_a/Comparison_dataset_A.pdf.

Dataset B showed different behavior: best results occurred at T = 0, with performance declining at higher temperatures. Notably, `3NFCompliance` remained constant across all temperatures (Precision: 1.00, Recall: 0.71, F1: 0.83), suggesting temperature had no impact on normalization detection. The reference model[4] revealed a misinferred relationship between *WorkLine* and *Material*, instead of *OrderOperation*. While most normalization was correct, fields like *color* and *type* were not extracted into separate entities.

These findings show temperature affects model quality, but its impact varies by dataset. For complex or denormalized data (like Dataset A), higher temperatures help uncover deeper relationships and normalization opportunities. Each ERD serves as a baseline for expert refinement, enabling iterative improvements.

Some inferred PKs were suboptimal (e.g., categorical fields), which is expected given the denormalized input. However, the creation of new FK columns, even if absent in the original data, is considered a positive sign of intelligent inference. While the models are functionally valid, they do not fully meet 3NF or business rule standards. Simpler datasets tend to yield higher scores, suggesting model complexity influences LLM performance.

7 Conclusion

This paper presented a method and automated tool for generating ERDs from semi-structured data using an LLM. The approach addresses LLM variability through iterative, expert-guided refinement and includes a robust evaluation suite to ensure model quality. Experiments showed the tool can translate semi-structured data into conceptual models, but expert input remains essential for accuracy and domain alignment. Challenges include limited performance in achieving 3NF and capturing business rules.

Results may be affected by factors such as using an open-source LLM, single-iteration evaluation, and prompt design constraints due to token limits. Real-world application may raise concerns around data privacy and sharing, highlighting the need for future work on anonymization strategies.

Acknowledgments. This work has been supported by FCT - *Fundação para a Ciência e Tecnologia* within the R&D Units Project Scope UID/00319/Centro ALGORITMI (ALGORITMI/UM) and national funds through the Operational Competitiveness and Internationalization Programme (COMPETE 2020) [Project no 179826; Funding Reference: SIFN-01-9999-FN-179826]. Generative AI (CoPilot) was used for text summarization. This paper uses icons made available by www.flaticon.com.

Disclosure of Interests. The authors have no competing interests to declare that are relevant to the content of this article.

[4] https://github.com/pedroccg/erdify/blob/main/reference_models/.

References

1. Bernasconi, A., García S., A., Ceri, S., Pastor, O.: PoliViews: a comprehensive and modular approach to the conceptual modeling of genomic data. Data Knowl. Eng. **147** (2025). https://doi.org/10.1016/j.datak.2023.102201
2. Bradbury, J.S., More, R.: Addressing data leakage in humaneval using combinatorial test design. In: 2025 IEEE Conference on Software Testing, Verification and Validation (ICST), pp. 587–591 (2025). https://doi.org/10.1109/ICST62969.2025.10989022
3. Buchmann, R., et al.: Large language models: expectations for semantics-driven systems engineering. Data Knowl. Eng. **152**, 102324 (2024). https://doi.org/10.1016/j.datak.2024.102324
4. Chen, K., Yang, Y., Chen, B., López, J.A.H., Mussbacher, G., Varró, D.: Automated domain modeling with large language models: a comparative study. In: 2023 ACM/IEEE 26th International Conference on Model Driven Engineering Languages and Systems (MODELS), pp. 01–06. IEEE (2023). https://doi.org/10.1109/MODELS58315.2023.00037
5. Fahland, D., Fournier, F., Limonad, L., Skarbovsky, I., Swevels, A.J.E.: How well can a large language model explain business processes as perceived by users? Data Knowl. Eng. **157** (2025). https://doi.org/10.1016/j.datak.2025.102416
6. Guizzardi, G., Fonseca, C.M., Almeida, J.P.A., Sales, T.P., Benevides, A.B., Porello, D.: Types and taxonomic structures in conceptual modeling: a novel ontological theory and engineering support. Data Knowl. Eng. **134** (2025). https://doi.org/10.1016/j.datak.2021.101891
7. Hans-Georg, F., Peter, F., Julius, K.: Conceptual modeling and large language models: impressions from first experiments with ChatGPT. Enterp. Model. Inf. Syst. Archit. **18** (2023). https://doi.org/10.18417/emisa.18.3, cited by: 43
8. Koupil, P., Hricko, S., Holubová, I.: Schema inference for multi-model data (2022). https://doi.org/10.1145/3550355.3552400
9. Li, C., Flanigan, J.: Task contamination: language models may not be few-shot anymore. In: Proceedings of the 38th AAAI Conference on Artificial Intelligence and 36th Conference on Innovative Applications of Artificial Intelligence. AAAI Press (2024). https://doi.org/10.1609/aaai.v38i16.29808
10. Omar, M.A.: Measurement of ChatGPT performance in mapping natural language specification into an entity relationship diagram (2023). https://doi.org/10.1109/ICSC58660.2023.10449869
11. Remadi, A., El Hage, K., Hobeika, Y., Bugiotti, F.: To prompt or not to prompt: navigating the use of Large Language Models for integrating and modeling heterogeneous data. Data Knowl. Eng. **152** (2025). https://doi.org/10.1016/j.datak.2024.102313
12. van Renen, A., Stoian, M., Kipf, A.: Dataloom: simplifying data loading with LLMs (2024). https://doi.org/10.14778/3685800.3685897
13. Stojanović, T., Jovanović, K., Lazarević, S.D.: Evaluation of GPT-generated conceptual models based on verbal descriptions: accuracy and quality analysis (2025). https://doi.org/10.1109/IT64745.2025.10930270
14. Storey, V.C., et al.: Large language models for conceptual modeling: assessment and application potential. Data Knowl. Eng. **160**, 102480 (2025). https://doi.org/10.1016/j.datak.2025.102480

BPMN-Based Business Process Collaboration Modeling Using Large Language Models

Aritha Kumarasinghe(✉) and Marite Kirikova

Institute of Applied Computer Systems, Riga Technical University, 6A Kipsalas Street, Riga 1048, Latvia
{balasuriyage-aritha-dewnith.kumarasinghe, marite.kirikova}@rtu.lv

Abstract. There has been an increasing interest in leveraging the natural language processing capabilities of LLMs within business process modeling tasks. This paper adds to that growing body of knowledge by proposing an LLM-based approach that leverages the role-playing capabilities of LLMs to create data-annotated process collaboration models using the Business Process Model and Notation. The proposed approach consists of decomposing the modeling process into three main steps (process participant extraction, process model element extraction, and collaboration modeling) and results in the definition of Formalized Process Data to represent the process elements. The modeling approach is evaluated on several real-world Standard Operating Procedures to assess its viability in a real-world setting where relatively large documents need to be considered. The result showcases that the proposed approach is capable of creating sufficiently detailed data-annotated collaboration models.

Keywords: Business Process Modeling · BPMN · Large Language Models · LLM-based Modeling

1 Introduction

Business Process Modeling (BPM) seeks to graphically represent the activities, events, control flow logic, and resources that form current or future business processes; it can be considered as one of the prerequisites for business process management initiatives [1]. A key BPM artifact is the process model, which is defined using specific modeling languages or notations such as the Business Process Model and Notation (BPMN). The latest BPMN version v2.0 [2] supports the representation of multiple perspectives, including participant interaction through collaboration models and data flows through data associations. The rich semantic representation capabilities of BPMN made it the modeling notation of choice for this research.

The creation of a process usually requires the extraction of process models from sources such as reports, emails, and ad-hoc documentation, which, when done manually, can be a slow and error-prone process [3]. While there are several approaches that

Published by Springer Nature Switzerland AG 2026
H.-G. Fill et al. (Eds.): PoEM 2025, LNBIP 570, pp. 130–138, 2026.
https://doi.org/10.1007/978-3-032-12063-2_9

are currently used to automate this process (such as rule-based and machine-learning-based methods), in recent years there has been an increased interest in using the Natural Language Processing (NLP) capabilities of Large Language Models (LLMs) [3] for that purpose.

While current research has demonstrated the efficacy of using LLMs for the creation of BPMN models, several gaps remain. Firstly, the current solutions are usually evaluated using relatively short textual descriptions (e.g., PET dataset [4]) rather than longer and more complex real-world documentation such as Standard Operating Procedures (SOPs). Based on this limitation, the first research question is defined: *R1 - Are LLMs able to create process models to represent the processes defined within real-world Standard Operating Procedures?* Secondly, the current works do not explicitly consider the collaboration aspect, which during the modeling process consists of defining multiple pools with each pool representing a single participant within a process (which can be achieved using current solutions) [3] and defining message flows between the process model elements contained within these pools (which has not yet been considered in current research). This gap leads to the second research question: *R2 - Can LLMs be used to generate process collaboration models by defining message flows between process model elements contained in separate BPMN pools?* Finally, the data perspective of business processes has yet to be considered within LLM-based business process modeling and is recognized as a potential direction for future work [5]. While a BPMN diagram without the added data associations represents the order in which activities are completed, it fails to capture the data required to complete them, as well as the data produced by these activities. This data perspective is considered through the third research question: *R3 - Are LLMs able to define the data elements that correspond to task elements defined based on process descriptions?*

The research represented in this paper seeks to address the above-discussed research questions by proposing an approach for generating data-annotated collaboration models from real-world SOPs. This approach consists of participant-based decomposition of activities using role-based LLM prompts to define process elements (including data objects), followed by the definition of message flows between process elements to represent collaboration. The proposed approach is evaluated using several real-world SOPs [6]. The main contributions of this work are as follows:

- Developing a systematic approach that can be used to transform SOPs into BPMN diagrams, using LLM-enabled participant-based decomposition and role-based process modeling.
- Incorporating the data perspective within the proposed approach so that data associations are defined for the extracted business processes using an LLM, enabling the capture of data flows.
- Demonstrating the proposed approach on real-world SOPs made publicly available by the European Food Safety Authority (EFSA) [6].

The remainder of this paper consists of Sect. 2 that presents background knowledge relating to this research; Sect. 3, which introduces the proposed approach for LLM-based collaboration modeling using BPMN; Sect. 4, which demonstrates the validity of the proposed approach by evaluating how well it represents real world SOPs; and Sect. 5 that presents the conclusions drawn from this work and possible future research directions.

2 Background

BPMN allows for the creation of different types of models, including the process collaboration model [7], which links different process models using message flows to represent the interactions (conversations) between participants. These message flows help understand the interactions between different participants [8].

Besides collaboration, the data used when carrying out these processes can be of importance, evidenced by the data association and data object elements being among the 20 most commonly used elements based on an analysis of 38,863 process collaboration models [7].

The approach proposed in this paper seeks to leverage LLMs for the creation of such data-annotated process collaboration models that represent both the interactions between process participants and the data used during these processes.

A literature review conducted on process extraction (which constitutes a large part of the BPM process) automation using NLP [3], presents the 'pre-LLM' era of automated BPM, which relied on rule-based and machine and deep learning methods. An example of rule-based process extraction is the colliery collaboration discovery technique [9], which applied process mining algorithms to create process models based on event logs, with message flows then being defined based on logged exchanges. Instead of using event logs, the proposed approach focuses on the use of more unstructured (free text) data contained as text within SOP documents.

The review [3] also presents the early stages of LLM-based process extraction, where the considered solutions achieved a performance that is comparable or superior to pre-LLM solutions. The review recognizes that previous studies use LLMs to generate process models in concise output formats such as JSON, or Partially Ordered Workflow Language (POWL which are used to define (e.g., through mapping) the final process model/diagram.

Additionally, the review [3] shows the possibility of using LLM-based multi-agent (LLM-MA) systems where specialized LLM agents are used to extract, critique, and integrate process elements. Based on this idea, the approach proposed in this paper seeks to leverage the role-playing capabilities of LLMs [10] to identify participants, generate role-based process models, followed by the definition of interactions using message flows.

Following the above-mentioned systematic review [3], several works have considered LLM-based process modeling. Two of these studies demonstrate the potential for using a tabular intermediary representation of process models. Activity tables (consisting of columns Label, Dependencies, Who, Dependents, Activity, and Condition) are used to represent process elements with conditions shown as if-else elements used in one of them [11]. Formalized Process Data (FPD) is used in another study [12] to represent process elements. A tabular format will be applied as an intermediary representation of process model elements in the approach proposed in this paper as well, with this representation also being used to transfer process data between LLM agents.

While previous studies [3, 11, 12] showcase that LLMs are capable of creating process models, they mainly focus on single-pool process models and not collaboration models that include message flows between participants. With regards to the data perspective, although not explicitly explored, the authors of [13] demonstrated that LLM can be used to define process information that would allow a heuristic algorithm to create process models that include data associations. However, this work has the limitation of using datasets for evaluating the proposed prompt template (which will be discussed in more detail in the next paragraph). Additionally, [13] does not consider the use of decomposed prompt which can result in better performance [14] and is implemented in the proposed approach through the use of multiple instances of an LLMs with three different prompts.

Another aspect of automated business process modeling is the evaluation of the solutions. The PET dataset [4] was proposed as a benchmarking dataset for evaluating business process extraction from text and has been used in several studies, such as [13]. It consists of 45 process descriptions that have been annotated to specify segments of the text that represent various process elements. A major drawback of the PET dataset is the relatively short textual descriptions when compared to real-world SOPs. This is demonstrated in Table 1, which compares the PET dataset (adopted from [4]) and 5 SOPs made publicly available by EFSA [6] and used to evaluate the approach proposed in this paper. The EFSA was selected due to its publicly available repository, currently consisting of 42 SOPs, allowing for future research to carry out further evaluation.

Table 1. Statistics of the documents used to evaluate automated process modeling.

Statistic	Value	
	PET Dataset	EFSA SOPs
Total Documents	45	5
Total Sentences	417	392
Average sentences per document	9.27	78.40
Average words per document	168.20	2299.40
Average words per sentence	18.15	29.33

3 BPMN-Based Data Annotated Collaboration Modeling Using LLMs

This section describes the process of how LLMs are used to generate BPMN-based data-annotated collaboration models. The process consists of three main steps that are initiated by the user inputting an SOP document.

Step 1: Process Participant Extraction. In this step, an LLM is prompted to play the role of process modeling expert and is tasked with identifying the main participants mentioned in the process documents (e.g., SOPs), the entire text of which is included in the prompt. These participants correspond to the pools that are included in the process model, while the lanes which are 'used to organize and categorize activities within a pool' [2] being considered out of the scope of this research, since the main focus is identification of only essential collaboration participants while disregarding 'noise' that can be in form of general collective statements (e.g., 'all relevant participants') or those mentioned in relation to the maintenance of process documentation itself. This step produces a list of participants that is used in the next step of the modeling process, which consists of sequential role-based prompting.

Step 2: Process Entity Extraction. For each of the participants identified a new instance of the LLMs is prompted using a prompt template (see Fig. 1), which assigns the role of process modeling expert and one of the participants (persona), and also outlines format in which the output must be given (formalized output format) based on all the text contained in the process documentation (context management), which, in this case, is a FPD table consisting of columns (that specify the meta language to be used) labeled Object Type, Object Name, Predecessor, Successor, Input Data, Output Data, and Additional Information. The specification of the output format also contains format examples of how each BPMN model element must be represented, which, in the context of this research, include Start Event, Task, Send Task, Receive Task, Gateway (Parallel), Gateway (Exclusive), Intermediate Event, and End Event. This step produces a markdown table of BPMN elements that represents the processes carried out by a single participant.

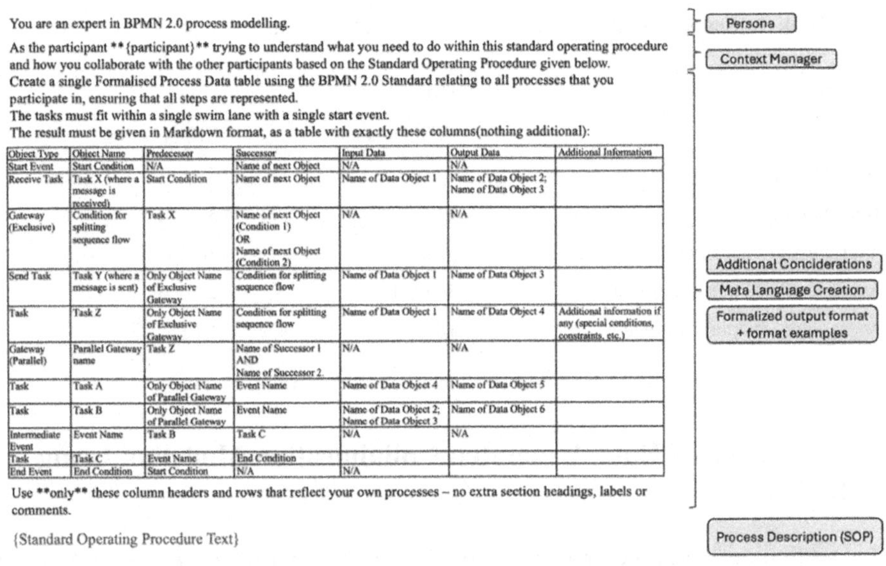

You are an expert in BPMN 2.0 process modelling.

As the participant **{participant}** trying to understand what you need to do within this standard operating procedure and how you collaborate with the other participants based on the Standard Operating Procedure given below.
Create a single Formalised Process Data table using the BPMN 2.0 Standard relating to all processes that you participate in, ensuring that all steps are represented.
The tasks must fit within a single swim lane with a single start event.
The result must be given in Markdown format, as a table with exactly these columns(nothing additional):

Object Type	Object Name	Predecessor	Successor	Input Data	Output Data	Additional Information
Start Event	Start Condition	N/A	Name of next Object	N/A	N/A	
Receive Task	Task X (where a message is received)	Start Condition	Name of next Object	Name of Data Object 1	Name of Data Object 2; Name of Data Object 3	
Gateway (Exclusive)	Condition for splitting sequence flow	Task X	Name of next Object (Condition 1) OR Name of next Object (Condition 2)	N/A	N/A	
Send Task	Task Y (where a message is sent)	Only Object Name of Exclusive Gateway	Condition for splitting sequence flow	Name of Data Object 1	Name of Data Object 3	
Task	Task Z	Only Object Name of Exclusive Gateway	Condition for splitting sequence flow	Name of Data Object 1	Name of Data Object 4	Additional information if any (special conditions, constraints, etc.)
Gateway (Parallel)	Parallel Gateway name	Task Z	Name of Successor 1 AND Name of Successor 2.	N/A	N/A	
Task	Task A	Only Object Name of Parallel Gateway	Event Name	Name of Data Object 4	Name of Data Object 5	
Task	Task B	Only Object Name of Parallel Gateway	Event Name	Name of Data Object 2; Name of Data Object 3	Name of Data Object 6	
Intermediate Event	Event Name	Task B	Task C	N/A	N/A	
Task	Task C	Event Name	End Condition			
End Event	End Condition	Start Condition	N/A	N/A		

Use **only** these column headers and rows that reflect your own processes – no extra section headings, labels or comments.

{Standard Operating Procedure Text}

Fig. 1. Prompt template for defining process elements.

Step 3: Collaboration Modeling. A new instance of the LLM is prompted (template is shown in Fig. 2) to play the role of a process modeling expert and to define message flows between the send and receive tasks that were defined in Step 2, which should be outputted as a formalized process data table.

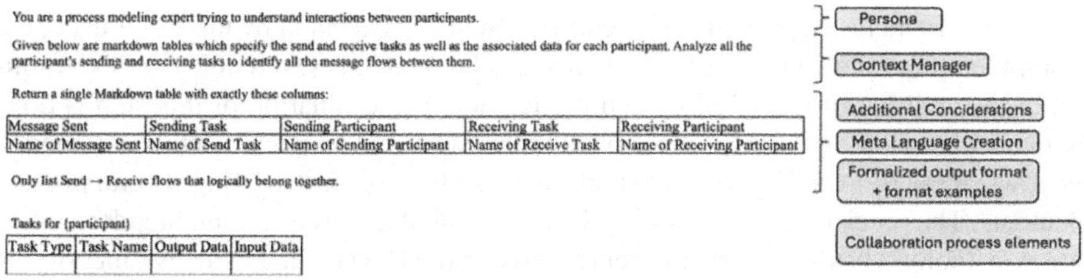

Fig. 2. Prompt template for defining message flows between process elements.

By the end of Step 3, the proposed solution will create an FPD table for each of the participants recognized in Step 1 and a single FPD table defining message flows between participants. Using the cells of the FPD tables, a diagrammatic representation of the BPMN model can be created by mapping FPD to diagram elements [11].

4 Evaluation of the LLM-Based Data-Annotated Collaboration Modeling Approach

The evaluation of the proposed approach is done using a Python script that implements the proposed solution (available on GitHub [15]) with the pdfplumber library being used to extract text from SOPs [11] and the openai library being used to invoke the GPT-4o model selected as the LLM for this evaluation due to its high input context window of 200000 tokens and relativity low cost. The user should manually specify the path to one of the SOPs issued by the European Food Safety Authority [6], which are saved as PDF files.

The script initiates the modeling process by prompting the LLM to list the main participants involved in the processes mentioned in the SOP. The evaluation of this step is done manually by comparing the LLM-identified participants with those mentioned in the SOP. Precision, recall, and F1-Score are then calculated (see the Participant Recognition column of Table 2) based on the participant correctly identified as executing processes (True Positives), incorrectly identified as executing processes (False Positives), and omitted despite executing processes (False Negatives).

Table 2. Statistics of the documents used to evaluate automated process modeling.

SOP	Participant Recognition			Step Representation			Collaboration Perspective			Data Perspective		
	Pre	Rec	F1	Pre	Rec	F1	Pre	Rec	F1	Pre	Rec	F1
SOP-001	1.00	1.00	1.00	0.94	0.94	0.94	0.75	0.94	0.83	0.98	0.97	0.97
SOP-002	1.00	1.00	1.00	0.99	1.00	1.00	0.78	0.48	0.59	0.94	0.94	0.98
SOP-003	0.92	1.00	0.96	0.99	0.99	0.99	0.92	0.38	0.54	0.96	0.95	0.96
SOP-004	0.86	1.00	0.92	0.99	0.99	0.99	1.00	0.44	0.61	0.96	0.95	0.96
SOP-005	0.86	1.00	0.92	0.80	1.00	0.85	1.00	0.33	0.50	1.00	0.98	0.98

Based on the list of participants identified, Step 2 is executed by the script using the prompt template shown in Fig. 1. The generated FPD table is saved in CSV files, resulting in the creation of one file for each participant. The evaluation of this step is done by manually mapping the steps mentioned in the SOP to process elements mentioned in the rows of the FPD tables, where a single step can be represented using several process elements. The precision, recall, and F1-Score are calculated (see column Step Representation in Table 2) based on the steps represented in the FPD (True Positives), incorrectly identified in the FPD (False Positives), and omitted in the FPD (False Negatives).

The results of these two steps provide insight into R1, which relates to the capacity of LLMs in representing the processes described in the larger contexts contained in SOPs. The results indicate that none of the metrics fall below 0.80, demonstrating that most participants were identified, and most steps described in the SOPs were represented. This result indicates that the proposed approach is capable of creating nearly complete and correct data annotated process collaboration models, but the modeling process must still have a human in the loop.

Focusing specifically on the collaboration modeling capabilities of LLMs, the message flows defined between the send and receive tasks identified in Step 2 must be evaluated. These message flows are defined by the script prompting a new instance of the LLM using a prompt created based on the prompt template shown in Fig. 2, with the prompt including FPD table rows that have an object type 'send task' or 'receive task' filtered by the script using string comparison. To evaluate the results, precision, recall, and F1-score were calculated based on whether a pair of send and receive tasks created by the defined message flow made logical sense together (True Positives), did not make logical sense together (False Positives), or pairs of send and receive tasks were not combined by message flows (False Negatives). The result of this evaluation is presented in column Collaboration Perspective in Table 2, with the results being varied across the five SOPs. The precision in all five of the SOPs is higher than 0.75, meaning that most of the message flows that were defined were identified correctly. The LLM seems to struggle with missing message flows caused by the definition of send tasks without a receive task that logically belong together, or vice versa. For instance, in the FPD representing SOP-001, a send event labelled 'Receive Public Consultation Closure' is defined for the participant 'Potential Applicant' and there is no corresponding send task (e.g., 'Send Public Consultation Closure') defined for any of the other participants. With regards to R2, the evaluation results indicate that defining the send and receive tasks for each participant in isolation and then defining message flows between can produce unsatisfactory results.

The final research question (R3) considers the data perspective representing capabilities of LLMs. To answer this question, each of the data objects defined for the task elements was evaluated manually based on the coherence between the label of the data object and the label of the task. The metrics used are precision, recall, and F1-score, calculated based on the data object input and output associations defined correctly (True Positives), defined incorrectly (False Positives), and missing associations (False Negatives). The results of this evaluation are presented in the column Collaboration Perspective in Table 2. With all the F1-Scores being above 0.95, meaning that an LLM has defined a complete representation of the data perspective of business processes.

These results also present the first steps to address the potential data leakage associated with using standard evaluation datasets that can potentially be used in training foundational models [16], by using SOPs that have not yet been previously used for the evaluation of process modelling tasks.

The formalized process data, as well as the evaluation of this data, is made available on GitHub [15].

5 Conclusions and Future Works

This research proposes an approach for generating BPMN-based data-annotated collaboration models using LLM instances, consisting of three main steps. In the first step, an LLM is used to extract a list of process participants. In the next step, each participant is assigned to a new LLM instance, which defines BPMN model elements representing participants' activities and the data created by or used during the activity as Formalized Process Data (FPD). In the final step, another LLM instance defines message flows between the previously identified send and receive tasks. Executing this approach results in the creation of an FPD table for each participant and an FDP table representing message flows. The approach was evaluated on five SOPs published by the European Food Safety Authority, through manual review of the LLM-defined elements. Findings indicate that while the approach captures the broader process and data perspectives of SOPs, it still yields inconsistent message flows, often due to defining send tasks without corresponding receive tasks and vice versa. This problem occurs because the send and receive tasks are defined for each participant in isolation, which can potentially be addressed by having another step within the modeling process that updates the FPD to ensure that every send task has a receive task and vice versa.

While this work demonstrates the viability of the proposed approach to defining the BPMN process model using an LLM-based decomposed modeling approach, more testing is required to fully assess its capabilities.

Disclosure of Interests. The authors have no competing interests to declare that are relevant to the content of this article.

References

1. Indulska, M., Recker, J., Rosemann, M., Green, P.: Business process modeling: current issues and future challenges. In: van Eck, P., Gordijn, J., Wieringa, R. (eds.) Advanced Information Systems Engineering. CAiSE 2009. Lecture Notes in Computer Science, vol. 5565, pp. 501–514. Springer, Berlin, Heidelberg (2009). https://doi.org/10.1007/978-3-642-02144-2_39
2. Object Management Group: Business process model and notation specification version 2.0.2. https://www.omg.org/spec/BPMN
3. Van Woensel, W., Motie, S.: NLP4PBM: a systematic review on process extraction using natural language processing with rule-based, machine and deep learning methods. Enterp. Inf. Syst. **18**(11), 2417404 (2024)

4. Bellan, P., Dragoni, M., Ghidini, C., Ponzetto, S., van der Aa, H.: Process extraction from natural language text: the PET dataset and annotation guidelines. In: NL4AI 2022: Sixth Workshop on Natural Language for Artificial Intelligence. CEUR, vol. 3287, pp. 177–191 (2022)
5. Kourani, H., Berti, A., Schuster, D., van der Aalst, W.M.P.: Process modeling with large language Models. In: van der Aa, H., Bork, D., Schmidt, R., Sturm, A. (eds.) Enterprise, Business-Process and Information Systems Modeling. BPMDS EMMSAD 2024 2024. Lecture Notes in Business Information Processing, vol. 511, pp. 229–244 (2024). Springer, Cham. https://doi.org/10.1007/978-3-031-61007-3_18
6. European Food Safety Authority Standard Operating Procedures. https://www.efsa.europa.eu/en/corporate/pub/sops. Accessed 10 May 2025
7. Compagnucci, I., Corradini, F., Fornari, F., Re, B.: A study on the usage of the BPMN notation for designing process collaboration, choreography, and conversation models. Bus. Inf. Syst. Eng. **66**(1), 43–66 (2024). https://doi.org/10.1007/s12599-023-00818-7
8. Khmelyarchuk, M., Zhukovska, S., Weigang, G., Myronchuk, K.: BPMN diagrams as an essential tool for enhancing business process management and team collaboration. Eur. Res. Stud. J. **27**(Special A), 652–682 (2024)
9. Corradini, F., Pettinari, S., Re, B., Rossi, L., Tiezzi, F.: A technique for discovering BPMN collaboration diagrams. Softw. Syst. Model. **23**(6), 1323–1343 (2024). https://doi.org/10.1007/s10270-024-01153-5
10. Tseng, Y.M., et al.: Two tales of persona in LLMs: a survey of role-playing and personalization. arXiv preprint arXiv:2406.01171 (2024)
11. Ajmal, F., Wijekoon, P., Dhanamina, H., Ravishan, Y., Nawinna, D., Attanayaka, B.: Automated BPMN diagram generation. In: 2024 6th International Conference on Advancements in Computing (ICAC), pp. 7–12. IEEE (2024)
12. Daclin, N., Mallek-Daclin, S., Zacharewicz, G.: Generative AI for business model generation (GAI4BM): from textual description to business process model. In: Proceedings of the 10th International Food & Operations Simulation Workshop (FOODOPS 2024), p. 013 (2024). https://doi.org/10.46354/i3m.2024.foodops.013
13. Neuberger, J., Ackermann, L., van der Aa, H., Jablonski, S.: A universal prompting strategy for extracting process model information from natural language text using large language models. In: International Conference on Conceptual Modeling, pp. 38–55. Springer Nature Switzerland, Cham (2024). https://doi.org/10.1007/978-3-031-75872-0_3
14. Khot, T., et al.: Decomposed prompting: a modular approach for solving complex tasks. arXiv preprint arXiv:2210.02406 (2022)
15. Kumarasinghe, A.: GitHub repository: LLM based Collaboration Modeling. https://github.com/ArithaRTU/LLM-based-Collaboration-Modeling.git
16. Fettke, P., Houy, C.: Evaluating the process modeling abilities of large language models--Preliminary foundations and results. arXiv preprint arXiv:2503.13520 (2025)

Human and Cognitive Dimensions of Enterprise Modeling

Exploring Practitioner's Perception of Conceptual Modelling in Agile Software Development

Yaimara Granados Hondares[1,2](✉), Monique Snoeck[2], Gheisa Ferreira Lorenzo[1], and Jenny Ruiz de la Peña[3]

[1] Central University of Las Villa, Villa Clara, Santa Clara, Cuba
ygranados@uclv.edu.cu
[2] KU Leuven, Leuven, Belgium
[3] University of Holguin, Holguin, Cuba

Abstract. Agile Software Development (ASD) has become the dominant approach for delivering value in iterative cycles, managing changing requirements, and coordinating distributed teams. Nevertheless, requirements management and technical debt persist as challenges. Conceptual models (CM) have been proposed as a means to address these issues; however, there is a paucity of empirical evidence regarding their systematic use and effectiveness in agile contexts. The present study investigates the perceptions of software practitioners regarding the use of CM in ASD. A total of 88 professionals actively working in software development, including project managers, analysts, developers and architects, participated in the study. Descriptive statistics were used to explore general trends, and Partial Least Squares Structural Equation Modeling was employed to examine relationships between constructs and to identify key predictors of intention to use conceptual models. The findings reveal a consistent and positive perception of CM among practitioners, with the highest ratings related to their usefulness for software requirements and system design. However, perceptions regarding their contribution to agile-specific tasks were less favorable. The findings of the present study underscore the notion that perceived usefulness and habit are the strongest predictors of intention to use CM. Furthermore, cultural factors appear to influence these perceptions. A comparison between Cuban and non-Cuban participants reveals significant disparities, particularly with regard to their propensity to adhere to organizational expectations. This study provides empirical insights into the role of CM in ASD and establishes a foundation for future work aimed at supporting their adoption and addressing cultural variations in perception.

Keywords: Agile Software Development · Conceptual Models · Survey

1 Introduction

The software development industry has moved towards agile approaches that have proven effective in delivering value to stakeholders in short cycles, managing constantly changing requirements, and coordinating distributed teams [1]. Among the most prominent

Published by Springer Nature Switzerland AG 2026
H.-G. Fill et al. (Eds.): PoEM 2025, LNBIP 570, pp. 141–158, 2026.
https://doi.org/10.1007/978-3-032-12063-2_10

agile methodologies are XP and Scrum, often used in combination and with additional tools such as Kanban [2]. The agile manifesto [3], or agile software development methods in general, do not prescribe to use conceptual models, but their utility has been highlighted as a way to gain a better and more comprehensive understanding of user stories, improved system design and enhanced software architecture [4]. Also, Agile Modelling [5] promotes simple, just-in-time models to support communication and quick decision-making in agile development, demonstrating the relevance of including models in Agile Software Development (ASD).

Despite the known advantages of conceptual modelling, their use as part of ASD is not commonplace. In itself, this is not a problem, but ASD is confronted with a number of challenges for which conceptual modelling could possibly offer a solution [6]. In particular, 'requirements management' and 'technical debt' are two well-known challenges that could (at least partially) be addressed through conceptual modelling [6]. Furthermore, within and enterprise context, such models can serve as a vital bridge, ensuring that agile projects remain aligned with overarching business goals and processes. Given that conceptual models are not natively incorporated in the ASD workflow, and that their use or creation could address certain ASD challenges at both technical and requirements level, it's important to explore practitioners' perceptions of conceptual modelling, especially within agile software development, before further exploring introducing conceptual models in the ASD workflow. The key questions to be answered in this paper are:

RQ1: What are software practitioners' current perceptions regarding the use of conceptual models in ASD?

RQ2: What factors influence the adoption of conceptual modeling in ASD?

RQ3: How do cultural factors influence the perception of and willingness to use conceptual models in the context of ASD?

To this end, a survey was designed based on the Technology Acceptance Model (TAM) [7] and distributed among active developers in the software industry. The survey was extended to professionals in general, but users of agile approaches constituted the large majority of the respondents, allowing us to analyze the perception of agile practitioners. The paper is structured as follows: Sect. 2 reviews related work on software industry practitioners' current perceptions of the use of conceptual models in software development. Section 3 describes the design of the questionnaire and the selection of constructs. Section 4 presents the results of the survey. Section 5 discusses how the results relate to the identified ASD challenges and discusses threats to validity. Section 6 concludes the paper and provides an outlook to further research.

2 Related Work

This section provides an overview of the existing research on modelling practices in software development, paying particular attention to agile contexts. The review distinguishes between studies that examine modelling in agile development more broadly, and those that focus specifically on conceptual modelling. Particular attention is given to studies that capture the perspectives of practitioners through surveys.

A meta-analysis of 26 previous studies on agile methodologies explored the use of modeling in agile contexts [8]. This synthesis indicated that, while agile methodologies often oppose documentation, visual and modelling tools continue to play a significant role in practices such as requirements engineering and hybrid development approaches. The utilization of visual aids, incorporating diagrams, was regarded as a strategy to enhance team communication and align development initiatives. While modelling is not universally adopted, it remains relevant in real-world software development, especially when supported by tools that reduce the cost of model creation and maintenance. This study provides a comprehensive overview of modelling in agile settings, however without addressing the practitioner's perspective. Furthermore, it does not consider the contextual influences that shape modelling practices in agile environments.

A number of survey-based studies have been conducted to assess software engineers' perceptions and practices regarding modelling in real-world development contexts. While none of these surveys focused specifically on ASD, the results provide preliminary insights that might be relevant for the ASD context as well. A large-scale survey across 27 countries [9] found that 68% of embedded systems developers reported using models at least occasionally, mainly for communication purposes; however, manual modeling was often viewed as laborious and not cost-effective. A study focused on 151 Italian developers [10] revealed that larger companies tend to adopt modelling more frequently, whereas smaller organizations often lack the necessary skills or perceive a low return on investment. A survey of 222 Brazilian professionals from 140 IT companies [11] showed that only 28.2% of respondents used UML regularly, despite more than half of respondents agreeing that UML acts as the "lingua franca" of software modelling. This study highlighted the limited adoption of UML in practice and suggested that automatic diagram generation could enhance its usage. Furthermore, a survey of 113 software practitioners [12] investigated the circumstances, motivations and methods by which developers utilize or refrain from utilizing software modelling. The results indicated that UML remains the dominant notation, but is primarily used informally for documentation and upfront design rather than full code generation. The key barriers identified included tool limitations, the suboptimal quality of generated code, and developer preferences for code-centric workflows. The study concluded that enhanced tool support and textual modelling options that are aligned with developer habits could foster wider adoption.

In a similar vein, an online survey of 96 practitioners around the world [13] examined the use of conceptual modelling languages such as UML and BPMN, confirming UML as the dominant language. The study revealed that models were employed extensively by a wide range of stakeholders, particularly software architects. The study identified three distinct modelling usage modes: informal (most frequent), semi-formal, and formal (least common). A more specialized survey of 109 practitioners [14] analyzed UML usage for modelling software architectures across six viewpoints: functional, information, concurrency, development, deployment, and operational. Popular UML diagrams varied by viewpoint, including class diagrams for data and concurrency structures, sequence diagrams for data lifecycle, deployment diagrams for physical structure, and activity diagrams for data flow.

While [12–14] share major contact points with the present study through their exploration of practitioners' perceptions, [13] is the most closely aligned, as it investigates practitioners' perceptions of conceptual modelling (CM) in real-world settings and the use of modelling in software development. Nevertheless, the subject under discussion does not pertain to agile contexts. The existing body of research does therefore not provide an answer to the question of how conceptual modelling is perceived specifically by ASD practitioners, which factors might influence the broader acceptance and integration of conceptual modelling practices, and to what extent cultural factors could have an impact. The present study contributes to the existing body of knowledge by examining CM perceptions within agile environments, identifying predictors of adoption, and incorporating cultural comparisons.

3 Methodology

To investigate ASD practitioners' perceptions and willingness to use conceptual modelling, a survey was conducted to enable a larger sample size. This section outlines the survey's constructs, design, distribution strategy, and data analysis methods.

3.1 Survey Constructs

To identify the different aspects of perception related to using Conceptual Models (CM), including the factors that may influence the willingness to use CM, we adopted an extended model based on the original TAM [7]. As illustrated in Fig. 1, the model includes the three main TAM constructs: Perceived Ease of Use (PEoU), Perceived Usefulness (PU), and Intention to Use (IU), and includes constructs from TAM2 [15] and TAM3 [16]. Specifically, it includes Subjective Norms (SN) and Motivation to Comply (MC) from TAM2 [15] and TAM3 [16], and Enjoyment from TAM 3. This selective inclusion aimed to maintain model parsimony by simplifying the model and avoiding redundancy, while focusing on constructs with the highest theoretical and contextual relevance to the research setting. Additionally, we included the Habit (Hab) construct, understood as the tendency to perform behaviors automatically based on prior learning and repeated experience [17]. Rather than conceptualizing Habit as part of UTAUT2 [18], it is introduced here as an independent predictor of both PEoU and PU, based on the assumption that repeated use of conceptual modeling practices may increase perceived fluency and perceived benefits of such tools. Similar extensions have been made in previous research [19, 20], which found that Habit can play a significant role in shaping user perceptions.

The integration of these components fosters a understanding of the framework employed to analyze the acceptance of conceptual models. Below we motivate the different constructs.

PEoU: This construct assesses practitioners' perceptions regarding the ease or difficulty of using or creating conceptual models, alongside their perceived proficiency in doing so based on their modelling skills. The latter aspect is associated with self-efficacy theory [21], which emphasizes perceived personal competence and outcome expectations and can influence individual behavior. In this study, we chose to integrate self-efficacy theory with the concept of perceived ease of use, given the strong interrelation between the two. When practitioners feel competent in using or creating conceptual models, they are more likely to perceive these models as easier to use. This combined approach offers a more comprehensive understanding of practitioners' interactions with conceptual models. The construct was measured using three questions (PEoU1, PEoU2, PEoU3) presented in Table 1. The last item is directly adapted from TAM [7], while the first two draw on concepts from self-efficacy theory [21], and have been aligned to the modeling context of this study.

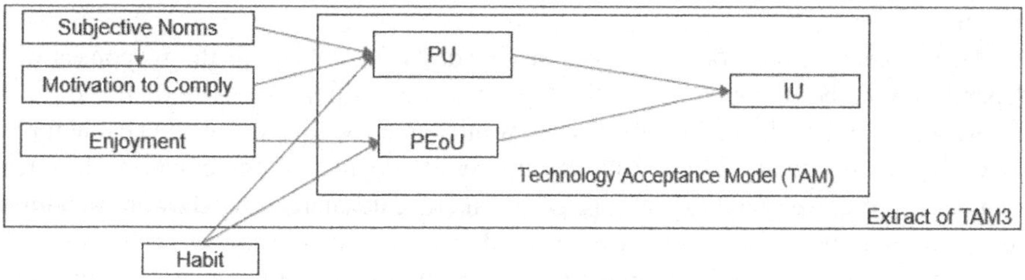

Fig. 1. Extended model from TAM

PU: This concept refers to the perceived usefulness of using or creating conceptual models in software development. In addition to the original TAM question (PU1), the construct was further refined by addressing three key perspectives on the impact of **software requirements** (PU2, PU3, PU4): ambiguity, completeness, and agreement. These aspects align with the three core dimensions of requirements engineering [22], adapted to the context of conceptual model usage. Additional dimensions of perceived usefulness include the impact on **software quality** (PU5, PU6) and the **influence on agile processes** (PU7, PU8, PU9). The **agile process dimension** covers practitioners' perceptions of how conceptual models support handling continuous changes in requirements, delivering increments within short timeframes, and prioritizing requirements to ensure the value of the delivered product.

Intention to Use (IU): This concept was included to assess the intention to use conceptual models in software development.

Habit (Hab): This construct refers to the use or creation of conceptual models as part of daily activities. The habit of repeatedly using or creating models can influence practitioners' perceptions of modeling in software development. The two questions (Hab1, Hab2) were adapted from [18].

Enjoyment (E): Enjoyment or intrinsic motivation drives effort and enhances results. It can be viewed as an alternative to utility, capturing how enjoyable it is to use or create conceptual models and the level of satisfaction derived from doing so. Two questions (E1, E2) were adapted from [15].

Social Influence: Includes questions related to subjective norms (SN1, SN2, SN3) and motivation to comply the norms (MC1, MC2, MC3) adapted from [15, 23]. This construct is used to assess the extent to which social elements (e.g., peers, project managers vision, or corporate policies) can influence to use or create conceptual models.

3.2 Survey Design

The initial section of the survey collects information on demographic aspects, company characteristics, and the distribution of the development team. The second section, presented in Table 1, includes questions related to the use of conceptual models in software development, designed to measure the defined constructs. We decided to use close questions in order to be more efficient while processing the survey and reducing respondent burden.

The choice between odd and even scale points for collecting the responses may depend on whether the goal is to allow for a neutral midpoint or to guide respondents toward a particular side. In this research we wanted to provide a design choice that forces a non-neutral stance and effectively captures subtle degrees of agreement or disagreement. Therefore, we opted to use a six-point Likert scale characterized by an even number, to measure attitudes,. This format is methodologically advantageous for our study as it mitigates central tendency bias [24–27]. From a behavioral standpoint, this compels respondents to engage more deeply with the content, reducing non-discriminating answers. Statistically, this design enhances data variability and differentiating power. Thus, it provides more nuanced and discriminative data on participant perceptions.

In order to validate the questionnaire, it was subjected to evaluation by five IT and survey experts in order to ensure both clarity and comprehensibility. The experts, from Cuba and Belgium, included academics, practitioners, and researchers and their feedback allowed improving the formulation of the questions.

3.3 Survey Distribution

The survey was distributed via a Google Form starting on April 4, 2024, with data collection continuing until July of the same year, spanning approximately four months. A range of methods was employed to distribute the questionnaire, including outreach to software industry professionals at academic events in Cuba: the survey was first applied in a scrum master training at the University of Computer Sciences (UCI), then in a workshop with developers at the UCI, and later in events at the Central University of Las Villas as well as in a workshop of the Union of Computer Scientists of Cuba (UIC). We also made an open call through the LinkedIn platform, and direct contact with specific individuals whose perspectives were considered particularly valuable.

3.4 Data Analysis

Prior to statistical analysis, the dataset was cleaned to identify participants who may have provided uniform responses across all items without proper attention. The frequency distribution of each item was also reviewed to ensure the absence of data entry errors. Conservative winsorization was applied to mitigate the influence of outliers by replacing extreme values with those at specific percentiles, thereby reducing variance without altering the sample size. This strategy was considered appropriate due to the small sample size and the sensitivity of PLS-SEM to such deviations.

As a preliminary step, descriptive statistics were examined using Python to understand the distribution and overall trends in the data. This facilitated the identification of general patterns, potential biases, and anomalies prior to conducting more advanced analyses. Partial Least Squares Structural Equation Modeling (PLS-SEM) was then used to estimate the model, offering increased reliability with small sample sizes [28].

Table 1. Survey Items Used to measure each construct

Concept	ID	Measurement Question	Area in SD
Perceived Usefulness (PU)	PU1	In general, conceptual models are useful for software development	
	PU2	Using conceptual models helps to resolve ambiguities in requirements	Software requirements
	PU3	Using conceptual models helps to achieve more complete requirements	
	PU4	Using conceptual models helps to achieve an agreed-upon understanding of requirements	
	PU5	Using conceptual models improves software design	Software quality
	PU6	Using conceptual models helps to achieve better software quality	
	PU7	Using conceptual models helps to set priorities during sprint planning	Agile-SD
	PU8	Using conceptual models speeds up delivery time	
	PU9	Using conceptual models reduces continuous changes in requirements	
Perceived Ease of Use (EoU)	PEoU1	I'm feeling proficient in conceptual modeling	
	PEoU2	I can understand, build, and maintain conceptual models	
	PEoU3	It's easy for me to work with conceptual models	
Habit	Hab1	The use of conceptual models is a common practice for me	
	Hab2	I always use conceptual models when developing software	
Enjoyment	E1	I don't like to use conceptual models, I prefer to go straight to coding	

(*continued*)

Table 1. (*continued*)

Concept	ID	Measurement Question	Area in SD
	E2	I don't like modelling at all	
Subjective Norms	SN1	My co-workers think conceptual modelling is important	
	SN2	The use of conceptual models is a corporate policy	
	SN3	The project managers do not require the use of conceptual model	
Motivation to Comply	MC1	The opinions of my co-workers and direct colleagues are important to me	
	MC2	I feel it's important to comply to corporate policy	
	MC3	Usually, I have my own opinion on what are best practices, and don't care about the guidelines of project managers	
Intention to Use	IU	I would use conceptual models when developing software	

4 Results

4.1 Participants

After data cleaning, we had a total of 88 valid responses from participants from different regions of the world. Of these, 57.3% (n = 50) were from Cuba, 14.6% (n = 13) from the United States, 13.5% (n = 12) from Belgium, and smaller contributions came from countries such as Canada, Mexico, Uruguay, Ecuador, Iran, Germany, and Chile. The majority of participants were between the ages of 30 and 65 (68.5%, n = 60), with the remaining 31.5% (n = 28) between the ages of 18 and 30.

The profile of the respondents solidly aligns with the agile focus of this study. First, an overwhelming majority of participants (95%, n = 82) reported actively employing agile methodologies in their work (AUP, XP, Scrum). This high prevalence of agile practitioners ensures that the collected data accurately reflects perceptions from within the target domain of ASD. While Scrum was confirmed as the dominant framework (69%, n = 61), consistent with its widespread industry adoption [29], the sample also included users of other methodologies. This variation, inherent to the broad umbrella term 'Agile', acknowledges the spectrum of practices in the field.

Furthermore, the participants are highly experienced software professionals. 98% (n = 86) hold direct software development roles. Their experience in software development is diverse, 31% (n = 27) have less than 5 years of experience in software development, 17% (n = 15) between 5 and 10 years, 42% (n = 36) between 10 and 20 years, 7% (n = 6) between 20 and 30 years, and two participants (2%) have extensive experience in SD (more than 30 years). This blend of roles and experience provides a foundation for assessing the practical utility of conceptual modeling in ASD. For answering the RQs, only the answers of the 82 ASD practitioners were considered.

4.2 Perception of Using Conceptual Models in ASD (RQ1)

To answer RQ1, we consider the answers to the different questions of the survey.

Usefulness. It is widely acknowledged among practitioners that conceptual models play a significant role in software development. According to the results of the study, 77% of the participants (n = 63) (strongly) agreed with usefulness in general (**PU1**), and even 97% of the participants (n = 80) if we include those who "Mostly Agree". The mean of approximately 5.0 indicates a high level of perceived usefulness. According to the three dimensions of usefulness delineated in Table 1, addressing the dimensions of requirements engineering evidences analogous results to **PU1**. Specifically, 97% (n = 80) of practitioners deem the utilization of conceptual models indispensable for comprehending requirements (**PU2**), ensuring their completeness (**PU3**, 93%, n = 76)), and attaining consensus on them (**PU4**, 98%, n = 81). This tendency to agreement is noteworthy. The survey results indicate that a significant majority of the participants hold a favorable opinion regarding the role of conceptual models in software design (**PU5**, 93%, n = 76) and software quality (**PU6**, 90%, n = 74). With regard to the items concerning agile practices, such as prioritizing (**PU7**), rapid delivery (**PU8**), and managing requirements changes (**PU9**), practitioners have expressed a greater degree of skepticism. While a substantial majority of practitioners, ranging from 68% to 78%, concur (mostly agree to strongly agree) that agile practices exert a favorable influence, the results suggest a highest level of strong agreement (58%, n = 48) relates to their role in setting priorities during sprint planning. However, this perception appears to decrease slightly when considering other aspects: less than half of respondents (47%, n = 39) strongly agreed that conceptual models contribute to faster delivery and reducing continuous changes in requirements.

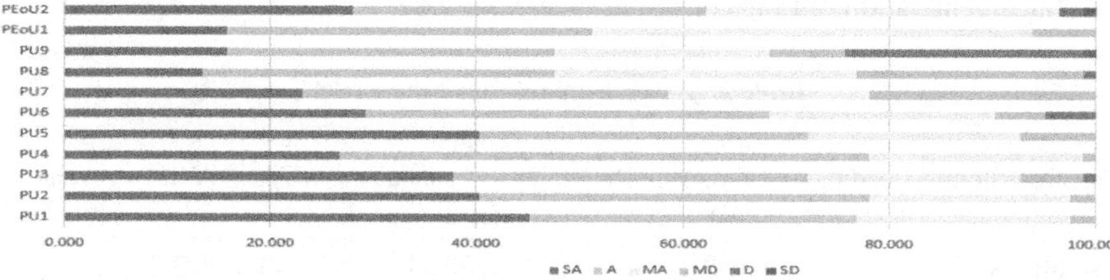

Fig. 2. General perception about the items

Ease of Use. A large majority of around 94% expressed proficiency in using, understanding, building, and maintaining conceptual models (**PEoU1,** n = 77, **PEoU2,** n = 79), and 91% of the respondents (n = 75) reported that they find it easy to work with conceptual models (**PEoU3**).

Habit. Around 70% of practitioner express that using conceptual models is a common practice for them and to always use it when developing software (**Hab1,** n = 59, **Hab2,** n = 58).

Enjoyment. Both enjoyment questions were negatively formulated. Fig. 2 shows the reverse-coded results: 79% (n = 65) of the respondents disagreed to disliking modelling (**E2**), and 90% (n = 74) disagreed with going straight to coding (**E1**).

Social Influence. A significant proportion of respondents (84%, n = 69) expressed concurrence with the notion that their colleagues place significant value on conceptual modelling (**SN1**), with a majority of 93% (n = 77) acknowledging the importance of their colleagues' perspectives (**MC1**). Half of the subjects recognize the existence of a corporate modelling policy (**SN2**), while 78% (n = 64) of them expressed a preference for compliance with such policies (**MC2**). Despite the fact that 57% (n = 47) of respondents stated that project managers do not require model use (**SN3**), 76% (n = 63) reported caring about their guidelines (**MC3**).

Intention to Use. In terms of intention to use (IU), although 73% of respondents (n = 60) express a generally positive intention to use CM in software development, only 43% (n = 35) report having a strong intention to do so. Regarding the types of models used by agile practitioners, entity-relationship models were reported as the most commonly used, followed by UML class diagrams. These two diagram types are consistent with the findings reported in [13, 14].

While practitioners generally perceive CM as useful, easy to use, and even enjoyable, the lower percentages in strong intention to use in an agile contexts, suggest a significant intention-behavior gap.

4.3 Intention to Adopt CM in Agile Software Development (RQ2)

Given that 95% of the valid sample (n = 82 out of 88) consists of agile practitioners, this subset will be used to address RQ2. PLS-SEM was applied to identify the latent constructs that most strongly influence the adoption of conceptual modeling practices in agile software development. The evaluation includes an assessment of the reliability and convergent validity of the constructs (see Table 2).

Table 2. Assessment results of the model

Construct/Item	Loadings	Composite Reliability (CR)	Cronbach's α (CA)	AVE	p-value
Usefulness		**0.909**	**0.903**	**0.567**	
PU1	0.752				< 0.001
PU2	0.786				< 0.001
PU3	0.816				< 0.001
PU4	0.734				< 0.001

(continued)

Table 2. (*continued*)

Construct/Item	Loadings	Composite Reliability (CR)	Cronbach's α (CA)	AVE	p-value
PU5	0.796				< 0.001
PU6	0.832				< 0.001
PU7	0.727				< 0.001
PU8	0.644				< 0.001
PU9	0.666				< 0.001
EaseOfUse		**0.705**	**0.747**	**0.62**	
PEoU1	0.771				< 0.001
PEoU2	0.751				< 0.001
PEoU3	0.838				< 0.001
Habit		**0.752**	**0.816**	**0.797**	
Hab1	0.853				< 0.001
Hab2	0.93				< 0.001
Enjoyment		**1.042**	**0.775**	**0.802**	
E1	0.959				< 0.005
E2	0.827				< 0.005

The evaluation of the measurement model demonstrates satisfactory psychometric properties across all latent constructs. The outer loadings of the indicators were statistically significant ($p < 0.001$ or $p < 0.005$) and exceeded the recommended threshold of 0.70 in most cases, indicating that each question reflects its construct well. Two items (PU8 = 0.644, PU9 = 0.666) exhibited loading thresholds that are proximate to, or marginally below, the commonly accepted benchmark. Both items were retained despite their lower loading, on the basis of their theoretical relevance to the construct of usefulness in agile practices. The internal consistency of the scale was confirmed, with composite reliability (CR) values ranging from 0.705 to 0.909, confirming that the sets of items consistently measured their intended constructs. In the case of the construct Enjoyment, the CR is 1.042, which exceeds the commonly recommended upper threshold of 0.95. This result should be interpreted with caution [30], particularly given that the construct is measured using only two items, which exhibit a moderate inter-item correlation ($r = 0.633$). The Cronbach's alpha (CA) values were between 0.733 and 0.902, both exceeding the commonly accepted cutoff of 0.70. All constructs demonstrated levels of Average Variance Extracted (AVE) that met or exceeded the established standard threshold (AVE = 0.50), with values ranging from 0.567 (Usefulness) to 0.802 (Enjoyment), meaning that a large proportion of variance in the indicators are explained by their construct. This finding provides substantial support for the notion of convergent validity.

Table 3 shows the path coefficients of the different relationships in the model. The findings indicate that Perceived Ease of Use (PEoU) exerts a positive influence on both

Intention to Use (IU) and Perceived Usefulness (PU), exhibiting statistically significant relationships. In contrast, the variable of Enjoyment does not have a significant effect on these variables. Habit emerges as a significant predictor, demonstrating considerable positive effects on PEoU, IU, and PU. This finding suggests that repetitive behavior has a profound impact on perception and system usage. It is important to note that, although Motivation to Comply and Subjective Norms are not directly related to IU or PU, Subjective Norms exerts a strong and significant effect on Motivation to Comply. This suggests that perceived social pressure is mediated by the individual's willingness to meet external expectations.

Table 3. Total and Indirect Effects in the Model

	Total effect	p-value	Result
PEoU ~ IU	**0.307**	**< 0.05***	**Supported**
PEoU ~ PU	**0.253**	**< 0.05***	**Supported**
Enjoyment ~ PEoU	-0.152	0.284	Unsupported
Enjoyment ~ IU	-0.047	0.599	Unsupported
Enjoyment ~ PU	-0.038	0.621	Unsupported
Habit ~ PEoU	**0.385**	**< 0.05***	**Supported**
Habit ~ IU	**0.246**	**< 0.05***	**Supported**
Habit ~ PU	**0.350**	**< 0.05***	**Supported**
Motivation to Comply ~ IU	0.057	0.302	Unsupported
Motivation to Comply ~ PU	0.112	0.293	Unsupported
Subjective Norms ~ IU	0.095	0.134	Unsupported
Subjective Norms ~ Motivation to Comply	**0.448**	**< 0.001****	**Supported**
Subjective Norms ~ Usefulness	0.187	0.097	Unsupported
PU ~ IU	**0.505**	**< 0.001****	**Supported**

4.4 Influence of Cultural Factors on Perceptions Toward Conceptual Models in ASD (RQ3)

In order to explore potential cultural or regional influences on the perception and use of conceptual models in ASD, we performed a comparative analysis of the mean responses of Cuban and non-Cuban participants across the items (see Fig. 3). It was reported by respondents from both the Cuban and non-Cuban groups that the usefulness of conceptual modelling was perceived to be high in general. While responses across items measuring usefulness (**PU1** to **PU9**) were consistent between groups, some variation was observed, suggesting slightly different emphasis on specific perceived benefits depending on regional context. The responses to ease of use items (**PEoU1 to PEoU3**) indicate that non-Cuban participants perceived conceptual models as easier to use. With regard to the utilization of conceptual models (**Hab1**, **Hab2**), non-Cuban participants exhibited a more pronounced propensity for habitual use.

The enjoyment of using/developing conceptual models (**E1**, **E2**) was moderately high in both groups, with non-Cuban participants reporting marginally more positive experiences. Significant variations were observed in items pertaining to subjective norms (**SN1** to **SN3**), whereas motivation to comply (**MC1** to **MC3**) appears the same.

Despite the observed differences across other constructs, responses to intention to use (**IU1**) were almost identical between Cuban and non-Cuban respondents. This finding suggests a shared willingness to adopt conceptual modelling in ASD.

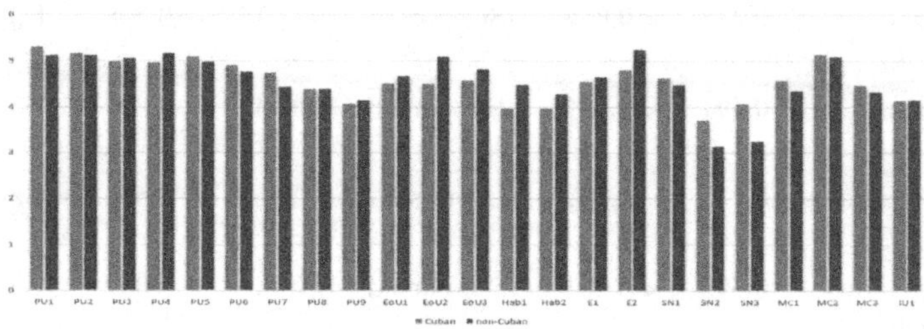

Fig. 3. Responses by Region: Cuba vs. Non-Cuba

In the Cuban sample statistically significant relationships were identified between perceived ease of use (**PEoU**) and intention to use (**IU**) ($\beta = 0.354$, $p < 0.05$), **Habit** and **IU** ($\beta = 0.234$, $p < 0$). The results of the study demonstrated a statistically significant relationship between **Habit** and **PEoU** ($\beta = 0.44$, $p < 0.05$), as well as between **Motivation to Comply** and **IU** ($\beta = 0.217$, $p < 0.05$) and **Motivation to Comply** and **PU** ($\beta = 0.491$, $p < 0.05$) (see Table 4). A significant effect was also identified between **Subjective Norms** and **Motivation to Comply** ($\beta = 0.596$, $p < 0.001$), and between **Subjective Norms** and **PU** ($\beta = 0.298$, $p < 0.05$). In contrast, within the non-Cuban sample, significant relationships were observed only between **PU, IU** ($\beta = 0.597$, $p < 0.001$) and **Habit** and **IU** ($\beta = 0.333$, $p < 0.05$) and Habit and PU ($\beta = 0.552$, $p < 0.05$). The remaining relationships in both samples were not statistically significant ($p > 0.05$).

Table 4. Cultural effects in adoption of CM in ASD

	Cuban sample			Non-Cuban sample		
	Total effect	p-value	Result	Total effect	p-value	Result
PEoU ~ IU	**0.354**	**< 0.05***	**Supported**	0.221	0.309	Unsupported
PEoU ~ PU	0.027	0.848	Unsupported	0.333	0.096	Unsupported
Enjoyment ~ PEoU	0.089	0.676	Unsupported	-0.234	0.324	Unsupported
Enjoyment ~ IU	0.032	0.69	Unsupported	-0.049	0.531	Unsupported

(*continued*)

Table 4. (*continued*)

	Cuban sample			Non-Cuban sample		
	Total effect	p-value	Result	Total effect	p-value	Result
Enjoyment ~ PU	0.002	0.937	Unsupported	-0.078	0.385	Unsupported
Habit ~ PEoU	**0.44**	**< 0.05***	**Supported**	0.288	0.154	Unsupported
Habit ~ IU	**0.234**	**< 0.05***	**Supported**	**0.333**	**< 0.05***	**Supported**
Habit ~ PU	0.189	0.209	Unsupported	**0.552**	**< 0.05***	**Supported**
Motivation to Comply ~ IU	**0.217**	**< 0.05***	**Supported**	-0.026	0.798	Unsupported
Motivation to Comply ~ PU	**0.491**	**< 0.05***	**Supported**	-0.043	0.801	Unsupported
Subjective Norms ~ IU	0.131	0.139	Unsupported	0.066	0.552	Unsupported
Subjective Norms ~ Motivation to Comply	**0.596**	**< 0.001****	**Supported**	0.34	0.097	Unsupported
Subjective Norms ~ Usefulness	**0.298**	**< 0.05***	**Supported**	0.11	0.581	Unsupported
PU ~ IU	**0.442**	**< 0.001****	**Supported**	**0.597**	**< 0.001****	**Supported**

5 Discussion

5.1 General Perception

The findings of this study indicate that software practitioners generally hold a favorable perception of conceptual modelling, perceiving it as useful, accessible, and enjoyable. It is evident that the majority of respondents recognize the value of modelling for key software development tasks, including requirements comprehension, ensuring completeness, building consensus, and improving architectural quality. These results corroborate earlier research [8, 11] indicating the importance of conceptual models in enhancing the communication processes in software projects in general [6] or as a way to address requirements engineering challenges experienced in ASD [31, 32]. However, a more nuanced picture emerges when considering the intention to use CM, particularly in agile environments. Despite the high perceived usefulness of CM in ASD processes, only 43% of practitioners report a strong intention to use it. This intention discrepancy highlights a salient tension: practitioners recognize the advantages of modelling, yet are reluctant to fully incorporate it into fast-paced, iterative workflows. This hesitation is especially evident in activities associated with core agile principles such as rapid delivery, continuous change, and lightweight documentation.

5.2 Factors that Influence in the Adoption of CM in ASD

The discrepancy between PU and IU calls for a deeper understanding of factors influencing the adoption of CM. A structural model was developed to analyze the factors influencing the intention to use conceptual modelling in ASD. Among the latent constructs, perceived usefulness emerged as the strongest direct predictor of intention to use, irrespective of culture. This finding lends further support to the notion that practitioners are more inclined to adopt conceptual models if they perceive a practical, beneficial outcome in their work. The ease of use of a system has been demonstrated to exert a significant positive effect on perceived usefulness. This finding suggests that the facilitation of the modelling process, through the provision of enhanced tools, guidelines, or simplification of the models, may indirectly promote a greater propensity to adopt modelling practices.

Furthermore, the study revealed that habit, understood as the periodic utilization of CM, exerted a substantial influence on intention to use. This finding indicates that familiarity and repeated exposure to modelling practices can reinforce positive attitudes. In contrast, the study established that enjoyment did not demonstrate a statistically significant influence on ease of use. This suggests that intrinsic motivation alone is not sufficient to drive adoption, and that usability and utility must also be considered.

5.3 Cultural Factors

A comparative analysis of Cuban and non-Cuban participants reveals that both groups generally perceive CM as useful in ASD. Nonetheless, it is evident that cultural divergences exert an influence on particular attitudes and factors associated with adoption. Cuban practitioners demonstrated stronger effects of perceived ease of use, habit, motivation to comply, and subjective norms on their intention to use CMs. This observation underscores the significance of social and organizational influences within this group. In contrast, non-Cuban participants exhibited a significant relationship between perceived usefulness, habit, and intention to use, suggesting a more task-focused adoption driven by the pragmatic advantages of CMs.

These findings imply that cultural context exerts an influence on the manner in which practitioners engage with CM in ASD. For Cuban teams, external pressures and social expectations have been identified as key drivers. It is therefore vital that successful implementation strategies consider organizational culture and social dynamics. However, in non-Cuban settings, it may be more effective to enhance perceived usefulness and habitual use. It is imperative to comprehend these variations in order to customize interventions and frameworks to optimize the adoption of CM and, consequently, enhance agile practices across a range of cultural contexts.

5.4 Threats to Validity

Conclusion Validity: A possible limitation of this study is the relatively modest sample size. However, under the assumption of a medium effect size ($f2 = 0.15$), the model attains an acceptable statistical power of 82.9%, a value that is sufficient for detecting medium effects in the most complex structural path. While satisfactory, these results could be enhanced through complementary qualitative methods, such as interviews or focus groups, to enable deeper insights and triangulation.

Internal Validity: The six-point Likert scale employed may have introduced response bias from participants selecting options without strong opinions, potentially affecting accuracy.

Construct Validity: Some constructs were operationalized using only two items. Whilst this approach may be considered pragmatic in terms of reducing survey length and participant fatigue, it does have the potential to compromise the robustness of the constructs. Another potential threat is concerns the respondents' understanding of the term "conceptual modeling" as opposed to the broader notion of "modeling". Nevertheless, the consistent use of the term "conceptual modeling" in the questionnaire context provides a clear basis for interpretation.

External Validity: The participant sample is skewed towards Cuban practitioners, introduces a potential cultural bias and limits the generalizability of the findings to broader international contexts. Nevertheless, this imbalance enabled a comparative analysis between Cuban and non-Cuban respondents, offering valuable insights into how cultural context influences perceptions of CM in Agile environments.

6 Conclusion and Future Work

This study addressed three research questions. The first (**RQ1**) established a clear intention-behavior gap, revealing that while practitioners perceive conceptual models as useful, ease of use, and enjoyable, particularly in requirements engineering and design, this positive attitude does not translate into a strong intention for their adoption within agile methodologies, where their value is viewed more skeptically. The second research question (**RQ2**) directly builds upon this finding by identifying the pivotal factors that mediate this gap, demonstrating that habit, ease of use, and perceived usefulness are key drivers of adoption intention. Furthermore, the third question (**RQ3**) contextualizes these factors by identifying multifaceted barriers; it concludes that practitioners' intentions are significantly shaped by and often hindered by a complex interplay of socio-cultural influences, organizational policies, and cognitive barriers, despite the widely recognized benefits of conceptual modelling. Addressing this gap will require targeted action, including the promotion of lightweight modelling practices, integration into agile toolchains, and educational efforts that clearly demonstrate practical benefits. Organizational support through clearly defined policies aligned with agile principles may also foster sustainable and balanced modelling use. It is recommended that future research focuses on refining the survey instrument to mitigate response bias and improve construct validity, particularly by increasing the number of items per construct. Moreover, expanding the sample size and ensuring greater participant diversity would enhance the external validity of the results and minimize potential cultural or contextual bias. Further research into the interplay between conceptual modelling and agile methodologies is essential to understand how modelling can be effectively adapted across different agile settings, organizational structures, and cultural environments.

References

1. Islam, M.A., Hasan, R., Eisty, N.U.: Documentation Practices in Agile Software Development: A Systematic Literature Review. In: Proceedings - 2023 Ieee/Acis 21st International Conference On Software Engineering Research, Management And Applications, SERA 2023, Institute of Electrical and Electronics Engineers Inc., 2023, pp. 266–273 (2023). https://doi.org/10.1109/SERA57763.2023.10197828
2. Al-Saqqa, S., Sawalha, S., Abdelnabi, H.: Agile software development: methodologies and trends. Int. J. Interact. Mobile Technol. **14**(11), 246–270 (2020). https://doi.org/10.3991/ijim.v14i11.13269
3. Beck, K.: "Manifesto for Agile Software Development," (2001) Accessed Dec 17 2024. [Online]. Available: https://agilemanifesto.org/
4. Mornie, M.N., Jali, N., Junaini, S.N., Mit, E., Shiang, C.W., Saee, S.: Visualisation of User Stories in UML Models: A Systematic Literature Review (2023) Prague University of Economics and Business. https://doi.org/10.18267/j.aip.212
5. Ambler, S.: Agile modeling: effective practices for extreme programming and the unified process. John Wiley & Sons (2002)
6. Gupta, A., Poels, G., Bera, P.: Using conceptual models in agile software development: a possible solution to requirements engineering challenges in agile projects. IEEE Access **10**, 119745–119766 (2022). https://doi.org/10.1109/ACCESS.2022.3221428
7. Davis, F.D.: Perceived Usefulness, Perceived Ease of Use, and User Acceptance of Information (1989)
8. Al-Zewairi, M., Biltawi, M., Etaiwi, W., Shaout, A.: Agile software development methodologies: survey of surveys. J. Comput. Commun. **05**(05), 74–97 (2017). https://doi.org/10.4236/jcc.2017.55007
9. Akdur, D., Garousi, V., Demirörs, O.: A survey on modeling and model-driven engineering practices in the embedded software industry. J. Syst. Architect. **91**, 62–82 (2018). https://doi.org/10.1016/j.sysarc.2018.09.007
10. Delishi, A., Lila, R., Ciccozzi, F., Cicchetti, A.: An Empirical Study on Software Modeling Curricula (2022)
11. Farias, K., Gonçales, L., Bischoff, V., Da Silval, B., Guimarães, E., Nogle, J.: "On the UML use in the brazilian industry: A state of the practice survey." In: Proceedings of the International Conference on Software Engineering and Knowledge Engineering, SEKE, Knowledge Systems Institute Graduate School, 2018, pp. 372–375 (2018). https://doi.org/10.18293/SEKE2018-183
12. Forward, A., Badreddin, O., Lethbridge, T.C.: Perceptions of software modeling: a survey of software practitioners. In: 5th workshop from code centric to model centric: evaluating the effectiveness of MDD (C2M: EEMDD), 2010
13. Störrle, H.: "How are conceptual models used in industrial software development? A descriptive survey," In: ACM International Conference Proceeding Series, Association for Computing Machinery, pp. 160–169 (Jun 2017). https://doi.org/10.1145/3084226.3084256
14. Ozkaya, M., Erata, F.: A survey on the practical use of UML for different software architecture viewpoints," Inf Softw Technol, vol. 121 (May 2020). https://doi.org/10.1016/j.infsof.2020.106275
15. Venkatesh, V., Davis, F.D.: A theoretical extension of the technology acceptance model: four longitudinal field studies. Manage. Sci. **46**(2), 186–204 (2000)
16. Venkatesh, V., Bala, H.: Technology acceptance model 3 and a research agenda on interventions. Decis. Sci. **39**(2), 273–315 (2008). https://doi.org/10.1111/j.1540-5915.2008.00192.x

17. Limayem, M., Hirt, S.G., Cheung, C.M.K.: How habit limits the predictive power of intention: the case of information systems continuance. MIS Q. **31**(4), 705–737 (2007). https://doi.org/10.2307/25148817
18. Venkatesh, V., Thong, J.Y.L., Xu, X.: Consumer acceptance and use of information technology: extending the unified theory of acceptance and use of technology. MIS Q. **36**(1), 157–178 (2012). https://doi.org/10.2307/41410412
19. Kim, B.: An empirical investigation of mobile data service continuance: incorporating the theory of planned behavior into the expectation-confirmation model. Expert Syst. Appl. **39**(18), 12333–12339 (2012). https://doi.org/10.1016/j.eswa.2012.04.031
20. Liao, C., Chen, J.-L., Yen, D.C.: Theory of planning behavior (tpb) and customer satisfaction in the continued use of e-service: an integrated model. Comput Human Behav **23**(6), 2804–2822 (2007). https://doi.org/10.1016/j.chb.2006.05.006
21. Bandura, A., Adams, N.E.: Analysis of self-efficacy theory of behavioral change. Cognit Ther Res **1**(4), 287–310 (1977)
22. Pohl, K.: The three dimensions of requirements engineering: a framework and its applications. Inf. Syst. **19**(3), 243–258 (1994). https://doi.org/10.1016/0306-4379(94)90044-2
23. Sukackė, V.: "Towards extending the original technology acceptance model (tam) for a better understanding of educational technology adoption," *society. In:* Integration. Education. Proceedings of the International Scientific Conference, vol. 5, p. 525, May (2019). https://doi.org/10.17770/sie2019vol5.3798
24. Garland, R.: The mid-point on a rating scale: Is it desirable? Mark. Bull. **2**(1), 66–70 (1991)
25. Weijters, B., Cabooter, E., Schillewaert, N.: The effect of rating scale format on response styles: the number of response categories and response style in Likert-type scales. Int. J. Res. Mark. **27**(3), 236–247 (2010). https://doi.org/10.1016/j.ijresmar.2010.02.004
26. Johns, R.: One size doesn't fit all: selecting response scales for attitude items. J Elect Public Opin Parties **15**(2), 237–264 (2005)
27. Kulas, J.T., Stachowski, A.A.: Middle category endorsement in odd-numbered Likert response scales: associated item characteristics, cognitive demands, and preferred meanings. J. Res. Pers. **43**(3), 489–493 (2009)
28. Cepeda, G., Roldán, J.L., Sabol, M., Hair, J., Chong, A.Y.L.: "Emerging opportunities for information systems researchers to expand their PLS-SEM analytical toolbox," (Jun 18 2024), Emerald Publishing. https://doi.org/10.1108/IMDS-08-2023-0580
29. Habib, B., Romli, R., Zulkifli, M.: Identifying components existing in Agile software development for achieving 'light but sufficient' documentation. J. Eng. Appl. Sci. **70**(1)(Dec 2023). https://doi.org/10.1186/s44147-023-00245-1
30. Hair, J.F., Hult, G.T.M., Ringle, C., Sarstedt, M.: A Primer on Partial Least Squares Structural Equation Modeling (PLS-SEM). SAGE Publications, 2016. [Online]. Available: https://books.google.be/books?id=JDWmCwAAQBAJ
31. PS, G., Cholli, N.G.: "Streamlining Agile Development: The Role of Conceptual Models in Requirements Management," *Available at SSRN 4945245* (2024)_
32. Kasauli, R., Knauss, E., Horkoff, J., Liebel, G.,de Oliveira Neto, F.G.: Requirements engineering challenges and practices in large-scale agile system development. J. Syst. Softw. **172** (Feb 2021). https://doi.org/10.1016/j.jss.2020.110851

Using Biometric Data to Investigate the Cognitive, Behavioural and Emotional Effects of Ambiguities in Business Process Models

Jesper Barfod, John Krogstie(✉), and Kshitij Sharma

Norwegian University of Science and Technology (NTNU), Trondheim, Norway
{John.Krogstie,Kshitij.Sharma}@ntnu.no

Abstract. Much research has been done on the comprehension and development of enterprise process models. In this paper, we follow up on work done previously by others on the effect of ambiguities on model comprehension. Ambiguities might lead to multiple alternative process interpretations by the readers of process models.

In this paper, we will present research on techniques for collecting biometric data to investigate how we work with visual process models, some of which include lexical or visual ambiguities. We report an experiment with data from 26 persons as they interpret both unambiguous and ambiguous process models. The approach, which is based on techniques used in multi-modal learning analytics (MMLA), investigates how the type of ambiguity is correlated with data collected in parallel from EEG, eye-tracking and cameras (tracking facial landmarks).

When working with ambiguous models, we generally find significantly higher memory load, cognitive load, convergent thinking, attention, information processing index, stress and confusion. Visual ambiguous models provide significantly higher numbers on these measures than lexically ambiguous models. In contrast, we find no difference in other cognitive, behavioural, and affective measures such as frustration and boredom.

This work reports early investigations on the impact of ambiguity in process model comprehension. A deeper understanding of how individuals process ambiguous models can inform the design of more precise and effective visual representations, improving the usability of modelling and reducing misinterpretation.

Keywords: Business Process Modelling · BPMN · Multi-modal biometric data · Ambiguity · Neuro-conceptualisation

1 Introduction

Descriptions of enterprise processes are found at various levels in all organisations. They are often represented as visual models using modelling languages such as BPMN and Archimate, combined with textual process descriptions. Comprehension of visual models

Published by Springer Nature Switzerland AG 2026
H.-G. Fill et al. (Eds.): PoEM 2025, LNBIP 570, pp. 159–174, 2026.
https://doi.org/10.1007/978-3-032-12063-2_11

such as process models are also central in many enterprise IT-solutions, as exemplified in [19] where company procedures are structured in more than 2000 process models, being the centre of the company quality system. Since people change jobs internally quite often, it is important that they can quickly familiarize themselves with the new work processes to ensure safe, compliant operations, and thus can understand the new work process correctly with limited effort. Providing a clear visual representation of processes, business process modelling languages allow us to understand the flow of activities, identify redundancies, and spot bottlenecks more easily [25].

Modeling involves the construction of abstract visual representation that capture the structure, behaviour, and relationships of real-world entities or phenomena, and the two-dimensional layout allows to play with both the primary and secondary notation [26] to externalize, create and communicate knowledge. On the other hand, there is an increasing awareness of that business process models may be susceptible to ambiguity [6, 7, 24]. Ambiguity is a characteristics of any knowledge representation that can lead to multiple possible interpretations. Recently, a comprehensive study of ambiguity in business process models highlighted possible sources of ambiguity [9], and in [8] it is documented how cognitive load increases due to different types of ambiguities. Our paper follows up [8], investigating both cognitive, behavioural and affective effects of ambiguity in process models, comparing ambiguities found in the labels of the models (lexical ambiguity) and the visual layout. Whereas [8] studied the phenomena using eye-tracking to capture cognitive load, we have used a broader set of biometric sensors, utilizing multi-modal learning analytics (MMLA).

We present in this paper an experiment using biometric techniques that can be used in a close to normal usage situation to provide better understanding of the effect of different types of ambiguities on comprehension of process models. The experiment is based on the work reported in [8]. That study proposed a categorization of BPMN ambiguities into four types: syntactic, semantic, lexical, and pragmatic (referred to here as empirical) ambiguities. This paper focuses specifically on lexical and empirical (visual) ambiguities and addresses the following research questions:

- RQ1: How do lexical and visual ambiguities affect model readers' comprehension?
- RQ2: Do lexical or visual ambiguities affect model comprehension the most?

In the next section, we will provide background on ambiguities in process models, multi-modal learning analytics and how biometric data has been used for understanding the modelling process in previous research. In Sect. 3 we describe the experiment and in Sect. 4 we highlight the results on how data from the different sensors can improve our understanding of the effect om ambiguities on model comprehension. In Sect. 5 we discuss the results, whereas Sect. 6 provides a conclusion and points out future work.

2 Background and Related Work

An *ambiguity* is the situation with something being perceived to have more than one possible meaning and therefore possibly causing confusion. A related term is *vagueness*. In an ambiguity, specific and distinct interpretations are permitted (although some may not be immediately obvious), whereas with vague information it is difficult to form any interpretation at the desired level of specificity.

Franceschetti et al. [8] differentiate 4 types of ambiguities:

1. Pragmatic ambiguity (Adapted from [2, 13]) is a phenomenon that occurs at the layout level allowing for multiple interpretations without affecting the behaviour of the process model. This we call empirical ambiguity based on the use of these terms in SEQUAL [17]. An example of a layout-issue that can result in ambiguity is if lines depicting flows cross each other.
2. Semantic ambiguity (Adapted from [7, 13, 17]) where a process model lacks validity or completeness, allowing for multiple interpretations.
3. Syntactic ambiguity (Adapted from [2]) occurs when a process model written in a modelling language L can be parsed using more than one grammatical structure of L, allowing for multiple possible interpretations.
4. Lexical ambiguity (Adapted from [24]) is related to that a textual label in a process model can be interpreted in multiple ways.

Although partly basing our experiment on some of the same models as in [8], we differentiate in our work between lexical and visual (empirical) ambiguities. Lexical ambiguities are as above rooted in an issue because of the textual labels. The issue can result in either empirical, syntactic and semantic quality concerns. The visual ambiguities relate to issues connected to the visual layout of the model, which in most cases are dealt with as part of empirical quality. In this paper the visual ambiguities were connected to issues connected to the empirical quality of the model, thus we use these terms interchangeably below.

To investigate the effect of ambiguities we collect multi-modal biometric data (MMD) while interpreting ambiguous models. According to [20], MMD have been used to capture, analyse, and predict learners' behaviour, task-performance and learning gains. Most of the research carried out for instance to provide feedback to learners is based on measurements rooted in unimodal data streams such as, emotions, content (log data), and attention (gaze data).

MMLA combines several data streams and theoretical frameworks [10]. Two of the main ones are Cognitive Load Theory (CLT) [15] and the Affective Learning Framework (ALF) [5]. MMLA looks at these in concert with traditional methods to, in our case, understand the effect of ambiguities of process models [8, 9]. CLT considers the cognitive processes of learning to explain the learner's behaviour. The working principle of CLT is that humans have a limited information processing capacity when they engage with a task. To represent the modeler's behaviour using the principles of CLT, one can use EEG and eye-tracking (ET) data streams. EEG and ET are two main data sources that reveal mental processes involved in the comprehension, construction, and organization of schemas including models.

The second theoretical framework supporting our work is the Affective Learning Framework (ALF). ALF is mostly concerned with how modelers feel while they are processing the information presented. ALF is also concerned with how learning experiences are internalized.

To incorporate ALF in the methodology, we use facial data. Using so-called facial landmarks, one can capture several sets of emotions. The two widely used sets are 1) based on the Control Value theory (anger, happiness, sadness, surprise, fear, disgust) and 2) based on the educational expressions (confusion, boredom, frustration, delight, engagement).

A recent structured mapping study on use of MMLA-techniques in connection to (conceptual) modelling identified 43 papers in the period 2014–2024 that reported empirical work [18]. 42 of the 43 investigations used eye-tracking. Early use of eye-tracking for researching model comprehension is found in [23, 30], but these works focus on capturing area of interest (AOI) (i.e. what the modeler is looking at). Later, eye-tracking is also used for capturing other characteristics such as cognitive load in process model comprehension. The sensor-toolset has lately been extended to include wristbands for capturing for instance electro-dermal activity (EDA) and heart-rate variability (HRV). Some use of EEG is also reported. In some experiments, ET is combined with (retrospective) think-aloud. [27] used facial cameras. In [20] an example of the combined use of all four modalities in MMLA (EEG, ET, facial and physiological data) is reported in connection to process model comprehension. The findings from the experiment reported in [20, 21] demonstrate that particular cognitive-affective states detected from using all the four different sensors in combination is relevant and influential to understand both the cognitive and affective process of model comprehension and the performance of model interpreters.

The majority of studies (40) included model comprehension tasks, in some cases combined with model validation and model creation. Those not including model comprehension explicitly looked at model creation. Independent variables have been.

- aspects of the model (e.g. ambiguities in models, model complexity, model layout, model modularization and usage of colour in the model or modelling language notation).
- modelling language (comparing performance using different modelling languages).
- modelling method.
- characteristics of the modeler (including gender and expertise).

Most experiments are done in a lab with individual students. One study describes an experiment using ET with health practitioners but also conducted in a lab environment. An example of following pairs of modellers with ET is found to investigate joint visual attention.

Whereas the BPMN models in [20] are reported to be made in Signavio and those in [8] in Camunda, few papers on model comprehension report the original tool. Typically, the models are made in a standard tool and exported using a standard format and then imported to a special environment for doing the experiment such as the EyeMind tools used in [8] and which we are also using in the experiment reported in this paper. The tools used in the reported modelling tasks are custom made tools for easier integration with the experimental environment.

Other works include the use of other ways of collecting data, including video and sound of the modeler doing think-aloud, combined with tracking the activities done on screen and retrospectives of activities done. Subjective measures of cognitive load (e.g. NASA TLX [28]) is found in some work [20].

3 Method

We have collected data from an experiment investigating the comprehension of visual business process models, some including visual or lexical ambiguities.

Our study partly replicates and extend the work of Franceschetti et al. [8], who examined how ambiguous BPMN models affect user comprehension using eye-tracking data. We adopted a similar within-subject experimental design in a laboratory setting but expanded the sensor setup to include electroencephalography (EEG), and facial expression analysis, integrating the facial data with the ET-handling of EyeMind [1, 8].

The added modalities enable intuitive analysis of ambiguity within a multimodal learning analytics (MMLA) framework: EEG and eye-tracking are used to investigate processes related to Cognitive Load Theory (CLT), while facial expression analysis serve to operationalize elements of the Affective Learning Framework (ALF).

In addition to replicating the original study with new sensor modalities, we also aimed to enable statistical comparisons between the effect of different types of ambiguity. As we saw above, Franceschetti et al. [8] categorized ambiguities into four types: However, they analysed each category in isolation: their comparisons focused on contrasting each ambiguity type with a control condition (i.e., no ambiguity), rather than statistically comparing the ambiguities themselves. To allow for such comparisons within our study, we narrowed the focus to two ambiguity types (lexical and visual as described above).

3.1 Sensor Modalities

EEG Data. The EEG signals were recorded using a 20-channel Enobio EEG cap following the international 10–20 system [14]. The raw EEG data were recorded at 500 Hz and subsequently divided into the following frequency band powers: delta (δ, below 4 Hz), theta (θ, 4–7 Hz), alpha (α, 8–12 Hz), and beta (β, 18–30 Hz). The built-in Fz electrode served as the signal reference. Additionally, two channels were used for electrooculogram (EOG) correction, and one channel for electric ground reference. The device also incorporated a 3-axis accelerometer with a sampling rate of 100 Hz.

Eye-Tracking. To record gaze, we used a Tobii X3–120 eye-tracking device operating at a 120 Hz sampling rate. Prior to data collection, a 5-point calibration procedure was performed through Tobii's Eye Tracking Manager software. The device was mounted at the bottom of a Dell G2410t 24-inch monitor (1920 x 1080 resolution). Participants were seated approximately 50–70 cm away from the screen.

Facial Video Data. Facial expressions were recorded using a simple WideCam F100 webcam, which was mounted above the monitor, facing directly toward the participants' faces. The camera recorded at 30 frames per second (FPS), with a resolution of 640 x 480. Participants were instructed to exhibit minimal movement during the tasks to ensure high-quality facial expression data.

3.2 Data Preprocessing

EEG Data. An independent component analysis (ICA) was used to remove noise caused by jaw movements. ICA separates the EEG signal into independent components, allowing us to identify and remove those associated with jaw muscle activity, thereby reducing noise. Additionally, an EOG filter built-in the Enobio software was used to remove the noise from eye blinks and eyebrow movements. A separate filter was also added to reduce noise generated by tongue movements. Finally, a 60 Hz line filter was used to remove any noise coming from the interference within the EEG wires.

Eye-tracking Data. The raw eye-tracking data were processed using the EyeMind's default fixation filter, which applies the Velocity-Threshold Identification (I-VT) algorithm [1]. This rule-based algorithm classifies gaze points based on movement speed: slower eye movements below a predefined velocity threshold are labelled as fixations, indicating focused visual attention on a specific area. Faster movements exceeding the threshold are classified as saccades, representing rapid shifts in gaze from one location to another.

Facial Video Data Facial expression data were extracted using OpenFace [3], which processes the video frame-by-frame to detect facial landmarks and Action Units (AUs), based on the Facial Action Coding System (FACS) [3]. To do this, OpenFace uses the Conditional Local Neural Fields (CLNF) algorithm for landmark detection, in addition to trained regression and classification models to detect the presence and intensity of AUs.

3.3 Dependent Variables

The dependent variables in this study were derived from multiple sensor modalities. This section details each measurement, which are further described in [20], including the sources of the argumentation. For measurements computed using time windows – such as average attention – each window was set to 10 s.

Backtracks (ET). Are saccades in which the gaze returns to a previously visited area of the screen, opposite to the typical forward reading direction. In this study, the number of backtracks were used as a scan-path variable to indicate rereading behaviour during BPMN model interpretation. Backtracks indicate that the participant did not fully understand the stimuli and needs to reprocess it. A high frequency of backtracks may suggest that the material is ambiguous, complex, or poorly structured.

Information Processing Index (ET). Visual information processing during task engagement can be characterized by two distinct strategies: Global Information Processing and Local Information Processing. Global Information Processing (GIP) is defined as a pattern of short fixations combined with long saccades. This behaviour is typically observed when users initially encounter a model and reflects a rapid initial visual sweep to grasp the overall layout and get a "gist" of the material. GIP thus reflects broad attentional guidance, indicating which features attract attention at a broader level. Conversely, Local Information Processing (LIP) involves long fixations and short saccades, indicating sustained attention and an in-depth examination of specific regions or items.

This behaviour provides insight into how participants engage with details, including how long they focus on particular elements and the depth of cognitive processing involved in interpreting them. The Information Processing Index (IPI) is then calculated as the ratio of global to local visual processing within a given time window (IPI = GIP/LIP). A higher IPI value indicates broader visual scanning and more extensive screen exploration per unit time, suggesting a greater amount of information processed or received by the observer.

Average Attention (ET). Is the average fixation duration of a participant in each time window, indicating the average attention exerted by them on the task. Longer fixations usually suggest deeper cognitive processing or interest, while short fixations with frequent saccades may indicate confusion or scanning behaviour.

Saccadic Velocity (ET). Refers to the speed at which the eyes move during saccades. It serves as an indicator of perceived task difficulty, the intuitiveness of a visual stimulus, and mental effort. Generally, higher saccadic velocity reflects lower cognitive load and easier task processing. Conversely, slower saccadic velocity signals increased mental effort, confusion, or fatigue, indicating a more challenging or less intuitive visual processing experience.

Cognitive Load (ET). We use eye-tracking data to compute cognitive load based on pupillary activity. Pupil dilation is a well-established physiological marker of mental effort during tasks such as problem-solving. Increases in pupil size have been linked with heightened attention, arousal, and cognitive workload. Because pupillary responses are largely involuntary and occur below conscious awareness, they offer a more objective measure of mental effort than self-reports. As such, the measure is also less susceptible to intentional or unintentional manipulation.

Stress (ET). Is the most common manifestation of increased arousal with negative valence, and it typically emerges during high- demand situations, correlating with high cognitive load and shifts in attentional strategies. Stress was measured based on eye-tracking data. The measure was computed by aggregating our stress-related eye-tracking metrics; (1) High pupil dilation, (2) Blink rate, (3) Short fixations, and (4) Short saccades. Higher values of this composite value would indicate elevated stress levels.

Frustration, Boredom, Confusion (Face). These emotional expressions were derived from facial action units (AUs) extracted from the recorded facial videos using OpenFace. Specific combinations of action units correspond to distinct emotional expressions – for example, boredom is associated with AU4, AU7, and AU12. For this study, emotion intensity was quantified by averaging the intensities of the relevant AUs. The emotions chosen for this study – frustration (AU12 + 43), confusion (AU1 + AU4 + AU7 + AU12), and boredom (AU4 + AU7 + AU12) – are grounded in the Cognitive Disequilibrium Theory (CDT), which links emotional states to cognitive challenges. The theory states that learning is driven by transitions between equilibrium and disequilibrium. In a state of equilibrium, comprehension proceeds smoothly.

Delight (Face). While Cognitive Disequilibrium Theory (CDT) emphasizes negative emotions arising from disequilibrium, a complete understanding of participants' affective and cognitive states also requires accounting for positive emotions. For this reason, we also measured delight which is theorized to occur when equilibrium is restored, signalling the successful outcome of productive struggle – when challenges are overcome and insights are gained.

Engagement (Face). The broader concept of engagement was also computed using facial action units. Engagement is distinct from specific emotions, representing the overall quality and intensity of interaction with the task. Engagement provides a broader measure of sustained investment and attention, including during challenging phases, extending beyond discrete emotional peaks like delight.

Convergent Thinking (EEG). Refers to a problem-solving process focused on narrowing down possibilities to identify a single correct solution. To measure convergent thinking from EEG signals, we followed a standard signal-processing approach: a) a discrete Fourier transform (DFT) was applied to the raw EEG signals; b) two band pass filters were applied to isolate the different frequencies (δ: 1- 3 Hz, θ: 3 – 7 Hz, α: 8–13 Hz, β: 13 –30 Hz); c) inverse DFT was applied to the output signals from the filters. Then two distinct metrics was calculated for the beta activity: d) power, calculated as the root mean square (RMS) of the signal, and e) the mean of all positive slopes of the beta waves, indicating rising activity.

Beta activity is characterized by irregular patterns that emerge during periods of active thinking and focused attention. It has been linked to decision-making, problem solving, and information processing, and is known to increase during states of concentration and intense mental effort.

Memory Load (EEG). To compute memory load from EEG signals, we followed the same four initial signal-processing steps (a–d) as in the convergent thinking analysis but focused on the theta frequency band (θ: 4–7 Hz). The mean theta band power was used as an indicator of working memory load, as previous studies have identified it as a reliable marker.

Drowsiness (EEG). To compute drowsiness from EEG signals, we followed the same four initial signal processing steps (a–d) as in the convergent thinking analysis but focused on the delta frequency band (δ: below 4 Hz). The mean delta band power serves as a reliable indicator of drowsiness and decreased alertness, as identified by previous studies.

Mental Effort and Comprehension Efficiency (Behavioural / ET). In the study by Franceschetti et al. [8], two dependent variables were used to assess cognitive load and one to assess comprehension. Cognitive load was measured using (1) self-reported perceived difficulty and (2) the mean number of fixations lasting 250 ms or longer. Although these metrics are regarded as less robust than alternatives such as pupil dilation that we used, they were included in our study to allow direct comparison with the original findings. Comprehension was also assessed by measuring task completion time, replicating their approach.

3.4 Experiment Material

In our experiment, which focused on empirical and lexical ambiguities, we aimed to use a consistent format for all tasks to allow for comparisons between ambiguity types.

We therefore standardized all tasks as valid trace tasks, which required modifying the original lexical ambiguity models.

A total of 11 process models were created for our experiment: three models for each ambiguity type, three unambiguous control models, and two models used during the training phases to help participants familiarize themselves with the task setup, structure, and software.

The models followed the structure used in Franceschetti et al.'s study [8]. All models represent simplified manufacturing processes. Activity labels were randomly generated using a verb-object format to reduce reliance on domain knowledge. Each label consisted of a randomly selected manufacturing-related verb followed by a generic "piece" name; a string of three random uppercase letters (e.g., Forge piece LDF).

All models were built using Camunda Modeler and featured a standardized number of gateways, activities, and intermediate events, similar with the original study [8]. This standardization aimed to ensure comparable model complexity, reducing the risk of confounding effects where observed differences could be attributed to model complexity rather than the ambiguity type itself.

Before launching the main experiment, three full-scale in-lab pilot trials were conducted to uncover potential weaknesses in the study design. These sessions were held in conditions closely resembling those of the final study, albeit in a more relaxed setting, and resulted in updates of some of the models used.

3.5 Experiment Procedure

Each experiment was designed to last approximately 45 min and was divided into several distinct phases, as illustrated below. The structure was refined based on insights gained during pilot testing. A substantial portion of the session was devoted to familiarizing participants with the setup and calibrating the biometric sensors. In total, the main experiment accounted for only about 20 min of the session. Figure 1 illustrate the process for each experiment which will be further described below.

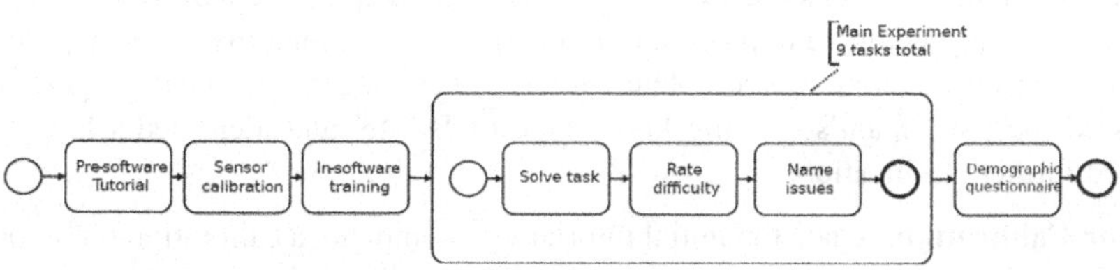

Fig. 1. Process model of individual experiment

Figure 2 illustrates the in-laboratory experiment setup. The participant (A) and experimenter (B) are positioned opposite each other at the main table. Supplementary experiment materials, such as the introductory paper task (C) are arranged on a side table. There are also two plastic flasks (D) on the side table containing anti-bacterial solution (for hygiene) and saline solution (to ensure optimal EEG conductance). The experimental software is operated by the experimenter from a laptop (G). All peripheral devices, specifically the computer mouse (E), the monitor with its mounted Tobii X3–120 eye-tracking device and WideCam F100 webcam (F), and the Neuroelectrics Enobio 20 EEG cap worn by participant (A), are connected to the laptop via a USB hub (H).

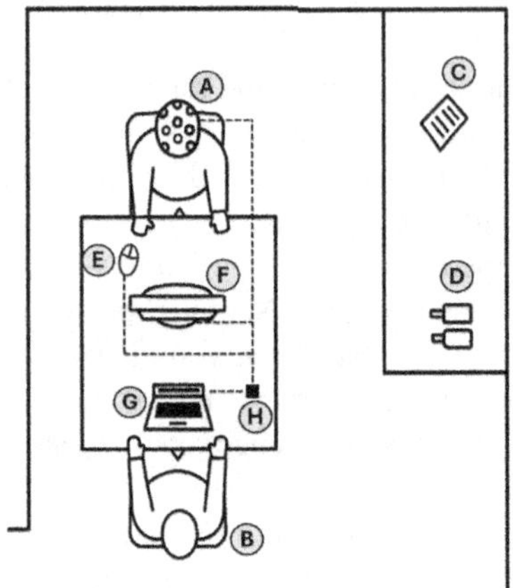

Fig. 2. Experiment setup

Prior to the Experiment. Before attending the experiment, participants were asked to complete a few preparatory steps, including watching a 5-min video tutorial introducing the parts of BPMN being used, wash their hair and wear contact lenses instead of glasses, if possible, as thick glasses could interfere with the eye-tracking system.

Pre-software Tutorial. Upon arrival at the laboratory, participants were given a brief introduction outlining the procedures involved in the experimental session, as well as the overall purpose of the study. Informed consent was obtained through a signed consent form. Participants were told that the research focused on BPMN comprehension using multimodal biometric sensors. However, the specific emphasis on BPMN ambiguities was intentionally withheld to prevent bias and preserve the integrity of the experiment.

Once the introduction was complete, a tutorial phase began in which the experimenter assessed the participant's existing knowledge of BPMN and identified which topics needed further clarification.

Sensor Calibration. Once the initial tutorial was complete, a calibration phase began, during which the three sensors were introduced and calibrated.

In-software Training. Before the experimental tasks began, participants completed a final tutorial task using the integrated computer application while wearing all three sensors.

Main Experiment. Once the in-software training task was completed, participants were given a final opportunity to ask questions, as the experimenter would not provide assistance during the main experiment.

The main experiment consisted of nine tasks. Similarly to the in-software training, each task was followed by three accompanying questions: (1) identify a valid trace through the model, (2) rate the task's difficulty (on a 1–10 scale), and (3) report any issues encountered.

Once all tasks were completed, the biometric sensors were disconnected, and the participants completed a short questionnaire regarding participant demographics (e.g., gender, age, prior experience with modelling, etc.).

Before the study, we received ethical approval based on an assessment by NSD (Norwegian Centre for Research Data), confirming compliance with data protection regulations.

In the end, we ended up with data from 26 participants that carried through the full experiment, with data we could use.

4 Results

To analyse the relationship between ambiguity type and multimodal measurements, we conducted one-way ANOVAs with ambiguity type as the independent variable and each multimodal measurement as the dependent variable. We also used post hoc ANOVAs for pairwise comparisons.

To analyse the relationship between performance levels (High / Low), those who failed to identify ambiguity in one or more cases were classified as having low performance), separately for overall, lexical, and empirical tasks, we used independent-samples t-tests with performance as the independent variable and multimodal measurements as the dependent variables.

Prior to running the ANOVAs and t-tests, we assessed the normality of the data using the Shapiro-Wilk test. We also tested for homoscedasticity (equal variances): Levene's test was used for comparisons between ambiguity groups, and the Breusch–Pagan test was used for comparisons between performance groups.

To examine whether background variables influenced performance, a series of chi-square tests were conducted. First, the association between BPMN familiarity and performance was tested, revealing no significant relationship ($\chi 2(3) = 3.50$, $p = .31$; A second test assessed the relationship between gender and performance, with results indicating no evidence of gender bias ($\chi 2(1) = 0$, $p = 1.00$; Finally, we tested whether having completed a formal BPMN course affected performance; this analysis also showed no significant association ($\chi 2(1) = 0.74$, $p = .38$).

As mentioned, we first conducted an ANOVA using the ambiguity types (lexical / visual) as the independent variable and the multimodal measurements as dependent variables. The analysis revealed significant differences across ambiguity levels for the following variables: time on task, memory load, convergent thinking, attention, cognitive load, information processing index, stress, and confusion. Similar to [8], fixation-based mental effort turned out to be significant, although with a much higher p-value than our own measure for cognitive load. On the other hand, the following variables showed no significant differences: drowsiness, saccadic velocity, backtracks, engagement, boredom, and delight. Subsequent post hoc pairwise ANOVAs (Table 1) revealed that, in all cases except time usage, visual tasks elicited the highest values, and control tasks the lowest. The difference was significant for the differences between visual and lexical ambiguities (except for time usage). We found no significant differences between the fixation-based mental effort on visual vs lexical ambiguities.

Lastly, a manipulation check was performed to examine whether the three independent variables were perceived differently by the participants or not in regard to difficulty. A pairwise t-test between the control, lexical and visual (empirical) ambiguity cases show the following:

- the self-reported difficulty for control condition is significantly lower than that for lexical ambiguity ($t(44.87) = -6.58$, $p = 0.00001$).
- the self-reported difficulty for control condition is significantly lower than that for visual ambiguity ($t(49.54) = -7.46$, $p = 0.00001$).
- there is no significant difference in the self-reported difficulties for the lexical and visual ambiguity ($t(54.47) = -0.02$, $p = 0.98$).

Table 1. Results from post hoc pairwise ANOVA using multimodal measurements as dependent variable and ambiguity type as an independent variable. NA = not applicable because there was no significant main effect.

Measurements	Empirical vs Lexical		Control vs Empirical		Lexical vs Control	
	F[1,24]	P	F[1,24]	P	F[1,24]	P
Backtracks	NA	NA	NA	NA	NA	NA
Information processing index	522.6	< .00001	883.7	< .00001	60.64	< .00001
Attention	628.6	< .00001	1115.6	< .00001	85.96	< .00001
Saccade Speed	NA	NA	NA	NA	NA	NA
Cognitive load	239.93	< .00001	964.8	< .00001	73.93	< .00001
Stress	95.59	< .00001	371.36	< .00001	98.84	< .00001
Frustration	NA	NA	NA	NA	NA	NA
Boredom	NA	NA	NA	NA	NA	NA
Confusion	305.17	< .00001	568.5	< .00001	58.21	< .00001
Delight	NA	NA	NA	NA	NA	NA
Engagement	NA	NA	NA	NA	NA	NA
Convergent Thinking	79.75	< .00001	135.95	< .00001	13.133	< .00001
Working Memory load	78.09	< .00001	362.84	< .00001	120.8	< .00001
Drowsiness	NA	NA	NA	NA	NA	NA
Self-reported mental effort	< 0.01	0.97	74.24	< .00001	51.41	< .00001
Fixation-based mental effort	0.63	0.43	10.09	.002	6.48	.01
Comprehension efficiency	1.75	0.19	23.74	< .00001	18.71	< .00001

5 Discussion

Also, in [8] the cognitive load was higher on models with ambiguities then those without (for all sorts of ambiguities), thus we are with our result replicating their results on this account. We also see how the visual ambiguities (pragmatic ambiguity in [8]) provide significantly higher cognitive load than lexical ambiguities. Of other cognitive measure it is not surprising that ambiguous models have significantly higher information processing index, memory load, convergent thinking and average attention, and again for these, that the visual ambiguities give the highest level. Of behavioural measures, we notice that there are no changes in backtracks and saccadic velocity, thus the models are approached in a similar way, even when they had ambiguities. This can be related to the similar overall layout of all models.

Two affective measures, stress and confusion, were significantly higher for ambiguous models, and significantly higher for visual ambiguities than lexical ambiguities. On the other hand, we found no difference regarding boredom, delight, engagement, frustration, and drowsiness. Thus, confusion was temporary as ambiguities was reasonably quickly dealt with (although the processing time was longer) and not leading into frustration. The lacking influence of drowsiness can be interpreted with that drowsiness did not influence the handling of ambiguities more than models without ambiguities. That engagement, delight and boredom were not influenced by ambiguities strikes us as that we have avoided potential unwanted effects of having too long sessions. Looking at [20], we see that performance in model comprehension can be influence negatively by frustration, boredom, backtracks and drowsiness, thus this not being a factor here is an interesting result in itself. In general, the models worked with in our experiments was simpler than those in [20].

We have above illustrated the potential of using MMLA to capture the complexities of cognitive engagement (compared to the long-standing self-report measures [12], as we saw the self-reported measures only partly showed the same results), utilizing process-related data generated with sensors from the moment-to-moment facial expressions, gaze, and EEG activity. We note that all sensors provide additional information on aspects being influenced by ambiguous models. None of measurements used for analysis can be tracked back to the individual, even if e.g. the facial camera feed needs to have a video of the person before extracting the facial landmarks that are used in the analysis. The actual video is not stored, only the extracted facial landmarks.

Considering the effects on the affective, cognitive, and behavioural dimension of model comprehension of ambiguous models, our method has implications for those communicating knowledge through model representations, indicating the negative effect on e.g. cognitive load and workload with ambiguous models, which will leave less cognitive capacity for other tasks. In addition, ambiguities can easily be interpreted differently by different persons, resulting in possibly undetected disagreement. Tool support to identify ambiguities of models should be improved, since as we see it has significant impact on the processing and understanding of models.

The experiment had some limitations. The testers were all students. On the other hand, a focus was on model comprehension, and as the case in [19] illustrated, all types of workers can be expected to be able to interpret process models. The prior knowledge of BPMN was low among many of the participants, but we did not find any effect of this, given the preparation done to educate all participants of the parts of BPMN used in the models in the experiment.

A challenge when collecting and analysing biometric data is that noise can make the data unusable. In Sect. 3.3 we provided an overview of the data preprocessing done, illustrating how we have tried to avoid this. In this process we also had to remove five sessions due to noisy data, which is to be expected in these kinds of experiments. Thus, we had more subjects than we needed to do the statistical analysis taking this into account, although even more participants would have been an additional strength.

Our method provides researchers and practitioners with a set of multimodal data measures which have been extracted from related works and allows them to consider the model interpreters cognitive, affective, and behavioural processes. The list of dependent variables is not exhaustive but provides a set of measures that are widely accepted in the learning technology literature.

6 Conclusion and Further Work

We have in this paper investigated the effect of lexical and visual ambiguities on affective, behavioural, and cognitive aspect of model comprehension. The broad set of features have been investigated by the use of biometric techniques found in Multi-modal learning analytics (MMLA). Revisiting our research questions we have:

- **RQ1: How do lexical and visual ambiguities affect model readers' comprehension?** Both lexical and visual ambiguities resulted in higher time on task, memory load, convergent thinking, attention, cognitive load, information processing index, stress, and confusion. The following variables showed no significant differences: drowsiness, saccadic velocity, backtracks, engagement, boredom, and delight. Both for lexical and visual ambiguities, we find a significantly higher self-reported difficulty.
- **RQ2: Do lexical or visual ambiguities affect model comprehension the most?** For all areas with a significant difference, the difference was largest on the visual ambiguities. There was no significant difference on self-reported difficulties for interpreting models with lexical and visual ambiguities though.

In previous investigations we have also included wristbands to capture stress and engagement. In this study we deduced these from the ET and facial camera but think more accurate results might be found if we also could look at this using wristbands investigating HRV and EDA.

We have also only touched upon the issue of ambiguities and how they affect the use of models. Other studies could look on the differences between syntactic and semantic ambiguities. From a socio-technical point of view, how to deal with ambiguities in a modelling situation e.g. to find and agree upon how to deal with ambiguities can form another strand of research not focusing on the collection of biometric data but rather study the negotiation processes involved in disambiguation.

References

1. Abbad-Andaloussi, A., Daniel, L., Barbara, W.: "Conducting eye-tracking studies on large process models using EyeMind." In: SoftwareX 101564 (2023). https://github.com/ElsevierSoftwareX/SOFTX-D-23-00482
2. Amna, A.R., Poels, G.: Ambiguity in user stories: a systematic literature review. Inf. Softw. Technol. **145**, 106824 (2022)
3. Baltrusaitis, T., Zadeh, A., Lim, Y.C., Morency, L-P.: Openface 2.0: Facial behavior analysis toolkit. In: 2018 IEEE International Conference on Automatic Face and Gesture Recognition (FG2018), pp. 59–66. IEEE (2018)
4. Clore, G.L., Huntsinger, J.R.: "How emotions inform judgment and regulate thought." In: Trends in Cognitive Sciences 11.9 (Sept. 2007), pp. 393–399. https://doi.org/10.1016/j.tics.2007.08.005

5. D'Mello, S., Graesser, A.: Dynamics of affective states during complex learning. Learn. Instr. **22**, 145–157 (2012)
6. Dijkman, R.M., Dumas, M., Ouyang, C.: Semantics and analysis of business process models in bpmn. Inf. Softw. Technol. **50**(12), 1281–1294 (2008)
7. Fan, S., Hua, Z., Storey, V.C., Zhao, J.L.: A process ontology-based approach to easing semantic ambiguity in business process modeling. Data Knowl. Eng. **102**, 57–77 (2016)
8. Franceschetti, M., Abbad-Andaloussi, A., Schreiber, C., Lopez, H.A., Weber, B.: Exploring the Cognitive Effects of Ambiguity in Process Models Proceedings BPM 2024, Krakow (2024)
9. Franceschetti, M., Seiger, R., Lopez, H.A., Burattin, A., Garcıa-Banuelos, L., Weber, B.: A characterisation of ambiguity in bpm. In: International Conference on Conceptual Modeling. pp. 277-295. Springer (2023)
10. Giannakos, M., Cukurova, M.: The Role of Learning Theory in Multimodal Learning Analytics. British J. Educ. Technol. (2023)
11. Giannakos, M.N., Sharma, K., Papavlasopoulou, S., Pappas, I.O., Kostakos, V.: Fitbit for learning: towards capturing the learning experience using wearable sensing. Int. J. Hum. Comput. Stud. **136**, 102384 (2020)
12. Greene, B.A.: Measuring cognitive engagement with self-report scales: reflections from over 20 years of research. Educ. Psychol. **50**(1), 14–30 (2015)
13. Haisjackl, C., Pinggera, J., Soffer, P., Zugal, S., Lim, S.Y., Weber, B.: Identifying quality issues in bpmn models: an exploratory study. In: International Workshop on Business Process Modelling, Development and Support. pp. 217–230. Springer (2015)
14. Jasper, H.H.: The ten-twenty electrode system of the international federation. Electroencephalogr. Clin. Neurophysiol. **10**, 371–375 (1958)
15. Jermann, P., Nüssli, M. =A.: Effects of sharing text selections on gaze cross-recurrence and interaction quality in a pair programming task. In: Proceedings of the ACM 2012 conference on Computer Supported Cooperative Work, (pp. 1125–1134) (2012)
16. Keenan, T., Evans, S., Crowley, K.: An Introduction to Child Development. 3rd. London: SAGE Publications (2016)
17. Krogstie, J.: Quality in Business Process Modeling, Springer (2016)
18. Krogstie, J.: Using Techniques from Neuroscience in Information Systems Modelling Research: A Systematic Mapping Study. Proceeding NOKOBIT 2024, November (2024)
19. Krogstie, J., Heggset, M., Wesenberg, H.: Business Process Modeling of a Quality System in a Petroleum Industry Company Business Process Management Cases Springer (2017)
20. Krogstie, J., Sharma, K. Using Biometric Data to Improve our Understanding and Support of Business Process Model Comprehension Accepted in SoSym (2025)
21. Krogstie, J., Sharma, K.: Enhancing our understanding of business process model comprehension using biometric data. In: NeuroIS Retreat 2024, Springer, Cham (2024)
22. Malinova, M., Mendling, J.: Cognitive diagram understanding and task performance in system analysis and design. Manage. Inform. Syst. Quart. **46** (2022)
23. Nordbotten, J.C., Crosby, M.E.: The effect of graphic style on data model interpretation. Inf. Syst. J. **9**, 139–155 (1999)
24. Pittke, F., Leopold, H., Mendling, J.: Automatic detection and resolution of lexical ambiguity in process models. IEEE Trans. Softw. Eng. **41**(6), 526–544 (2015)
25. Reijers, H.A., Mansar, S.: L: Best practices in business process redesign: an overview and qualitative evaluation of successful redesign heuristics. Omega **33**(4), 283–306 (2005)
26. Schrepfer, M., Wolf, J., Mendling, J., Reijers, H.A.: The impact of secondary notation on process model understanding. In: Persson, A., Stirna, J. (eds) The Practice of Enterprise Modeling. PoEM 2009. Lecture Notes in Business Information Processing, vol 39. Springer, Berlin, Heidelberg (2009)

27. Shalev, L. et al. (2025). Using facial expressions to predict process mining task performance. In: Delgado, A., Slaats, T. (eds) Process Mining Workshops. ICPM 2024. Lecture Notes in Business Information Processing, vol 533. Springer, Cham. https://doi.org/10.1007/978-3-031-82225-4_41
28. TLX - https://humansystems.arc.nasa.gov/groups/TLX/. Accessed 16 Mar 2023
29. Van Lehn, K., et al.: "Why do only some events cause learning during human tutoring?" In: Cognition and Instruction 21.3 (2003), pp. 209–249. http://www.jstor.org/stable/3233810
30. Weber, B., et al.: Fixation patterns during process model creation: initial steps toward neuro-adaptive process modeling environments. In: 49th Hawaii International Conference on System Sciences (HICSS), Koloa, HI, USA (2016)

On the Influence of Collaboration and Visualization on the Outcome of Goal and Problem Modeling

Anne Gutschmidt[1](✉), Charlotte Verbruggen[2], and Monique Snoeck[3]

[1] University of Rostock, Albert-Einstein-Str. 22, 18059 Rostock, Germany
anne.gutschmidt@uni-rostock.de

[2] TU Wien, Erzherzog-Johann-Platz 1, 1040 Vienna, Austria
charlotte.verbruggen@tuwien.ac.at

[3] KU Leuven, Naamsestraat 69, 3000 Leuven, Belgium
monique.snoeck@kuleuven.be

Abstract. Participatory modeling is considered more effective for creating higher-quality enterprise models with broader stakeholder acceptance compared to traditional approaches. However, involving stakeholders directly requires more time and effort. To elaborate on the benefits, we conducted an experiment to compare the outcome of participatory enterprise modeling and traditional modeling, e.g., by interviewing stakeholders separately. We let groups of participants work in three different settings, varying the possibility of collaborating and working on a preliminary model. Considering the different conditions, we addressed the following research questions: 1) Do the models differ in size? 2) How well-elaborated are the models in terms of connections made between the elements? 3) Are the contributions of the various participants linked differently across the conditions? We found that collaboration slows down the process, which results in smaller models. Collaboration, however, leads to models that are better integrated. We found no evidence that visualization significantly supports the modeling.

Keywords: Participatory Enterprise Modeling · Collaboration · Model Visualization · Experiment · Conceptual Modeling

1 Introduction

One of the goals of enterprise modeling is to create a joint vision of the enterprise among all the stakeholders. To express this vision, enterprise modelers are tasked with creating different kinds of models to describe the various aspects of the enterprise. The information needed to create the models can be sourced from artifacts such as documentation and enterprise policy documents. But very likely these documents do not contain all the information, and therefore additional information needs to be collected from various domain experts using requirements elicitation techniques such as interviews or requirements workshops

Published by Springer Nature Switzerland AG 2026
H.-G. Fill et al. (Eds.): PoEM 2025, LNBIP 570, pp. 175–191, 2026.
https://doi.org/10.1007/978-3-032-12063-2_12

[29]. This raises the question of how to organize the interaction with the domain experts: should the information gathering be based on one-to-one interaction, or should this be better done in a participatory setting? Should the domain experts have the opportunity to work on a model visualization instead of being merely interviewed? In previous research, we investigated the impact of different working methods for modeling (ranging from individual to fully participatory settings) on the sense of ownership towards the models [6]. Besides understanding the sense of ownership, it is also important to investigate to what extent different forms of collaborative modeling support the creation of a "joint" vision on the enterprise. On the one side of the spectrum, one-to-one interactions between modelers and individual domain experts could lead to large models that capture the specific view of each individual domain expert, but simply superpose these views and fail to integrate these individual views into a joint understanding. On the other end of the spectrum, a fully collaborative modeling workshop could lead to a more simple model that pretends to provide a unified view, but is in fact the view of the participants who dominated the conversation during the workshop. The impact of the different settings on the level to which the resulting artifacts are actually constituted of "shared" elements as opposed to being an additive superposition of "individual" elements was left for future research. This paper addresses this gap by re-analysing the data collected during the former experiment set-up. The settings we study differ in two essential characteristics, i.e., the opportunity to collaborate with other stakeholders and the opportunity to work on a model visualization. In particular, we investigate to what extent these characteristics lead to different model properties as stated in the following research questions:

1. Do the models differ with regard to their size?
2. How well-elaborated are the models in terms of connections made between the elements?
3. Are the contributions of the various participants linked differently?

In the next section, we will present some background about participatory enterprise modeling (PEM), including the related topics of collaboration, model visualization, and the role of the method consultant. Section 2 concludes with our detailed hypotheses. In Sect. 3, we describe our research method, followed by our results in Sect. 4 that we finally discuss in Sect. 5.

2 Background

2.1 Participatory Enterprise Modeling

In Participatory Enterprise Modeling (PEM), not only stakeholders' active involvement in creating enterprise models, but also the collaboration among them represents the essential core. In workshops, the stakeholders, in their role as domain experts, exchange knowledge and ideas, negotiate conflicts that might arise, and find a joint agreement manifested in the resulting models [21,24]. Because of this process, PEM is said to lead to a greater acceptance and better quality of the models [24,25]. PEM can be considered as a special form of collaborative modeling, also because the domain experts do not work on their own, but are supported by method consultants [22]. Usually, PEM workshops are joined by a facilitator who leads the discussion and masters the modeling method. Furthermore, another method consultant may support the group in handling the modeling tool. That way, the stakeholders can concentrate on the content [24].

PEM is suitable when a common agreement is to be reached, but the organizational culture has to allow for such practice [22,24]. Moreover, PEM is very consuming in terms of time and labor. During the workshops, the domain experts dedicate their resources solely to this task instead of their usual work. Furthermore, the organization of the workshops represents a considerable effort for the method consultants.

As an alternative, the method consultants can interview the domain experts separately and, in an iterative manner, create the enterprise models, without collaboration among the domain experts. Luebbe and Weske suggested using models during the individual interviews, i.e., they already visualize the content. That way, the domain experts would get more involved in the model creation process. In fact, this approach made the domain experts suggest more corrections to the model [12]. Nevertheless, with this approach, the method consultants will still have to negotiate the different views of several stakeholders, which may also represent a complex and time-consuming task.

This has led us to compare different settings for knowledge elicitation for enterprise modeling. First, in a **consultative setting**, the domain experts are interviewed separately, and the method consultants have to merge the different contributions into one model. Second, in a similar setting that we refer to as **individual/participatory setting**, a method consultant also conducts individual interviews, but lets the respective domain expert participate in creating a visualization in the form of a preliminary model. Third, in a **collaborative/participatory** setting, the domain experts collaboratively create a joint model, supported by method consultants, as suggested in the PEM approach. In a former paper, we already compared the stakeholders' perception of the modeling process and outcome [6]. Although we did not find significant differences in the perception of ownership feeling towards the models, we found that the participants in the consultative interview setting felt a lower possibility to participate in the model creation, and they perceived the value of the model as lower, and the method consultant's contribution as higher. In this paper, we will present an analysis of the outcome of the different settings, in particular, the size of the models and special characteristics that reflect how well-connected the contributions of the different domain experts are.

As the main differences between the settings lie in the possibility to collaborate and to share a visual representation during knowledge elicitation, we will elaborate on these aspects in the next subsections. Moreover, we consider the role of the method consultant as very important, which is why we have added a corresponding section.

2.2 The Role of Collaboration

PEM is a form of group work, although with a special distribution of roles. PEM involves several tasks that the participants have to work on, often depending on the goal of the modeling project, starting from documenting an as-is state, to generating ideas, or discussing goals, future changes, and measures. McGrath developed a typology of tasks performed in a group, defining four quadrants: Generate, Choose, Negotiate, and Execute, which are again subdivided into more specific task types [13]. **Generate** tasks include *planning tasks*, e.g., creating a to-be process, and *creativity tasks*, e.g., brainstorming for tasks in a process model or for goals in a goal model. **Choose** tasks comprise *intellective tasks*, such as finding the right sequence of actions for a process model, and *decision-making tasks*, such as choosing one out of a pool of alternatives for process improvements. **Negotiate** tasks comprise *cognitive conflict tasks* and *mixed motive tasks.* In enterprise modeling, an example of the first could be to decide how an issue is to be modeled when different participants have different, maybe contradicting knowledge or experience about an issue. The latter refers to resolving conflicts of interest, i.e., when the participants have different interests that influence the content of the model to go in one direction or the other. McGrath's **Execute** quadrant is not really applicable to the enterprise modeling context as these task types refer to physical actions, whereas enterprise modeling involves mainly cognitive actions. Yet, our examples for McGrath's task types show how suitable it may be to work collaboratively in enterprise modeling instead of separately, e.g., when having to negotiate different views or look for an optimal solution. Ideation in a group can also bring more diversity to the pool of ideas, e.g., Nijstad and Stroebe found that group members could inspire each other [15].

Nevertheless, collaboration, i.e., PEM, might not only have benefits but also hurdles that are difficult to overcome. Steiner tried to explain why, in some cases, a group performed worse than individuals in non-group settings. He distinguishes between coordination losses and motivation losses [23]. Motivation losses comprise phenomena like free-riding or social loafing, where individuals working in a group show a lower performance compared to a non-collective, so-called co-active setting [17]. This happens especially in unitary, non-divisible tasks where individual contributions are no longer distinguishable. Group members may get the impression that their contribution does not make a difference. That is why an effective measure against social loafing is to make individual contributions identifiable [11,17]. Social loafing can also be reduced when group members notice that their contribution is essential for the whole outcome [7,11], and in some cases, when they can compare their performance to that of others [11].

Consequently, in PEM, the procedure has to be designed in such a way that everyone can voice their ideas and that individual contributions are recognizable. Stirna and Persson suggested phases of card writing, where the participants can work individually, alternating with phases of group discussion [24]. Such an approach might also mitigate the negative effects of so-called social facilitation, an effect on individual performance caused by the presence of others. Social facilitation is connected with a better performance for simple tasks, whereas in more complex tasks, individuals show a lower performance in groups than if they worked separately [2,28]. So, for more difficult tasks, there should be room for the participants to work without feeling observed. This, however, speaks in favor of the two co-active settings we want to compare the PEM setting to. What speaks against these co-active settings is that the participants would not be able to compare their performance with that of others and see their contribution in the whole context.

A well-known negative effect related to coordination that might decrease performance in a PEM setting is called production blocking. Researchers found that the performance of individuals suffers if they cannot express their ideas straight away, but have to wait for their turn [16]. Again, the card-writing approach mentioned above is supposed to mitigate this effect, but working completely separately might be even more effective.

Nevertheless, Reagans et al. [20] stated that if experts in a team, with different specialized knowledge, are not able to communicate effectively, the expert knowledge cannot lead to high team performance. The expert knowledge might even undermine team performance, i.e., teams with low expert knowledge and low coordination even performed better in their study. Reagans et al. suspect that experts with high and diverse knowledge create a more complex solution space, and they may not be able to join their efforts. Thus, it might take them longer to produce an outcome, or the outcome may not be of good quality.

In our context, this could influence the individual settings, where there is no communication between the domain experts. The complex task of coordinating the individual contributions and merging them is up to the method consultants. This can be seen as a major drawback of the two individual settings we suggest.

To sum up, there are effects in group work that speak in favor, but also against a collaborative/ participatory setting. The individual (co-active) settings also have both advantages and disadvantages, which is why it is important to empirically examine the effects of collaboration on the resulting model.

2.3 The Role of Visualization

As mentioned previously, PEM involves several different tasks, such as problem-solving, ideation, and decision-making. Previous research has examined how visualizations can have a supportive but also hindering role in such tasks.

The human mind processes pictorial information differently from verbal information [1]. The main advantage of pictorial information over verbal information is that pictorial information is processed in two steps: perceptual processing, which occurs automatically and very quickly, and cognitive processing, which takes more effort [14]. Via computational offloading, some of the processing effort is executed by the perceptual system, easing the effort for the cognitive system [9].

In modeling, and PEM in particular, ideation corresponds to coming up with new model elements. Decision making plays a role in all three settings we want to study, for example, when deciding whether to include a proposed element and how model elements are best linked, but especially in collaborative settings where different views of different stakeholders need to be consolidated. In such cases, both the domain experts and the modelers can benefit from visualizations to make quicker and/or more effective decisions (see also the "Choose" and "Negotiate" tasks in Sect. 2.2).

Padilla et al. [18] present a cognitive framework for decision making with visualizations. They argue that using visualizations reduces the load on the working memory and creates more capacity for complex decision making. Nevertheless, Padilla et al. [18] report several limitations of decision making with visualizations. The first consideration is that visualizations guide the viewer's bottom-up attention. As a consequence, information that is visualized more prominently will guide the viewer's attention and can therefore introduce bias in their decision-making. Moreover, when there is a low cognitive fit between the visualization and the concept/problem at hand, this can even require additional working memory, leading to slower decision-making and a higher chance of errors.

Vasconcelos et al. [26] investigated the effect of visualization on ideation. In two of three studies, they found that participants who were given example visualizations came up with more elaborate ideas that included drawings, but participants who were not given these visualizations came up with more ideas that were mostly expressed in written text. Välk et al. [27] found that providing a visualization of discussed topics in interdisciplinary idea generation sessions helps participants identify gaps in their ideas and cover more diverse domains.

Furthermore, Crapo et al. [4] underline visualization as a means of communication, an important element when comparing individual and collaborative settings. Modeling requires the collaboration of at least two people: the domain expert and the method consultant; in the collaborative setting, it also requires collaboration between the domain experts. As each individual comes with their own mental model, modeling requires the method consultants and domain experts to arrive at a joint understanding. The idea is that with a joint visualization, a common understanding is more easily reached.

Besides the advantages of graphical visualization, the act of modeling also contributes to different dimensions of requirements engineering [19]: models provide a more formal representation of requirements compared to natural language, which in itself contributes to the accuracy of the requirements. Because of this need for formality and higher accuracy, the act of modeling raises additional questions, thus contributing to a higher engagement of the stakeholders and more complete capture of the requirements.

All in all, we expect visualizations to have a positive effect on the outcome of the modeling process. Nevertheless, research has shown that visualizations may also have a limiting effect.

2.4 The Role of the Method Consultant

Like requirements engineers, method consultants in PEM take on different roles [29]: they act as *facilitators* by guiding and assisting the participants in addressing the relevant issues in order to obtain correct and complete requirements. In a participatory setting, they may act as *mediators* in case of conflicts between requirements and/or stakeholders, and search for a suitable resolution through negotiation and compromise. Finally, they are *responsible for documenting* the requirements either in textual or graphical form [19]. This documentation represents the actual product resulting from the requirements elicitation phase and, depending on the context, may even form a contractual basis. Depending on the setting, the three roles might change in relative importance. In a fully individual setting, during the requirements elicitation activities, the role of facilitator will prevail, as well as the role of responsible for documenting (in either natural language or model format). The role of mediator comes into play only when the views of different stakeholders have to be merged, insofar the method consultant will attempt to resolve conflicts rather than simply document them. In a collaborative setting, besides the roles of facilitator and documenter, the role of mediator may become important, depending on the level of alignment (or conflict) between the different participants to a collaborative modeling workshop. The use of visual notation will impact the role of the method consultant as responsible for documenting requirements. The use of natural language comes with the advantage of simplicity, but the danger of inherent ambiguity. Ensuring a perfect mutual understanding using natural language only is hard, if not impossible. The use of a visual notation will help to avoid misunderstandings and foster a joint understanding of the requirements, provided the notation is sufficiently simple and/or mastered well by all stakeholders.

2.5 Hypotheses

We want to compare three settings that differ with regard to the opportunity to work on a model, i.e., a visualization, and the opportunity to collaborate: 1) the consultative setting (no collaboration, no visualization), 2) the individual/participatory setting (no collaboration, with visualization), and 3) the collaborative/participatory setting (with collaboration, with visualization). We are interested in the differences in the resulting models that are caused by these settings. We will present our hypotheses according to our basic research questions.

Do the Models Differ with Regard to Their Size? We hypothesize that the different settings will lead to a different number of model elements and relations. For ideation tasks like coming up with elements for the model and relations between these, collaboration may be beneficial because participants may be inspired by others' ideas. Nevertheless, in the collaborative setting, the groups have to take on additional group-related tasks such as negotiating, e.g., when they have different perspectives on a subject, and choosing, e.g., when they have come up with a similar goal and need to decide whose wording is most fitting. This takes additional time compared to the other settings, where the participants have to deal with just their own worldview. Thus, we expect these groups to generate fewer elements and relations compared to the other settings.

Visualization may help in the collaborative setting for communicating the ideas and discovering connections between ideas, but we do not expect this to counterbalance the increased time expense due to the additional group-related tasks mentioned above. The visualization of the model may, however, play a role when comparing the individual/participatory setting and the consultative setting. We hypothesize that seeing the model will relieve working memory, such that participants in the individual/participatory setting will be able to generate more elements and more relations. To sum up, we state the following:

H1: The number of elements contained in a model is different depending on the work setting consultative versus individual/participatory versus collaborative/participatory.

H1a: Models generated in a collaborative/participatory setting contain fewer elements compared to the other settings.

H1b: Models generated in an individual/participatory setting contain more elements compared to the other settings.

H2: The number of relations between the elements of a model is different depending on the work setting consultative versus individual/participatory versus collaborative/participatory.

H2a: Models generated in a collaborative/participatory setting contain fewer relations compared to the other settings.

H2b: Models generated in an individual/participatory setting contain more relations compared to the other settings.

This leaves the consultative setting in a middle position for H1 and H2.

How Well-Elaborated are the Models in Terms of Connections Made Between the Elements? We hypothesize that both collaboration and visualization help generate relations in the model. This is not necessarily reflected in the overall number of relations, but in the number of relations in proportion to the number of elements. This should be an indicator of how well the participants have identified logical connections between the elements in general, also excluding the effect of model size. Our reasoning is again that seeing the model relieves the working memory, thus connections can be identified more easily compared to maintaining a view in mind all the time. In collaborative settings, relations can be generated not only for one's own elements but also for the elements of the other participants. To sum up, we state the following:

H3: The number of relations in proportion to the number of elements contained in a model is different depending on the work setting consultative versus individual/participatory versus collaborative/participatory.

H3a: Models generated in a collaborative/participatory setting show a greater number of relations in proportion to the number of elements compared to the other settings.

H3b: Models generated in a consultative setting show a smaller number of relations in proportion to the number of elements compared to the other settings.

This leaves the individual/participatory setting in a middle position for H3.

Are the Contributions of the Various Participants Linked Differently? All models consist of the contributions of several participants, but how well-connected are these contributions in terms of summarized elements expressing the same idea and relations linking elements from different authors? In the collaborative setting, participants may generate similar elements during the individual work phases, e.g., goals or problems describing the same issue. During discussions, the group, with the assistance of the facilitator, should discover content-related overlaps. They must decide whether corresponding elements must be merged and choose the final wording for the description of the final element. In the other settings, the method consultants have to take on this task based on single interviews or isolated individual models, respectively. This task requires the correct interpretation of the participants' contributions. Moreover, the method consultants should be neutral and not interfere with regard to the content. Consequently, we hypothesize that in the collaborative setting, the merging of elements will be done more frequently. The visualization of the model will most likely support this because seeing the element, including the exact wording, with the option to re-read it, facilitates understanding and interpretation. Thus, visualization might lead to a greater number of merged elements in the individual/participatory setting compared to the consultative setting, facilitating the task of understanding and interpretation of an element for the method consultant.

Similarly, we hypothesize about the number of relations between elements from different contributors. While method consultants may be more reluctant or not able to identify such connections, a group working collaboratively may do so more easily. Visualization is an additional supportive factor, such that we may expect more relations between elements from different participants in the individual/participatory setting than in the consultative setting.

As we expect collaboration to influence model size, we need to exclude the effect of model size. Thus, we consider the number of merged elements in proportion to the overall number of elements and the number of relations between elements from different authors in proportion to the overall number of relations. To sum up, we state the following:

H4: The proportion of merged elements contained in a model is different depending on the work setting consultative versus individual/participatory versus collaborative/participatory.

H4a: Models generated in a collaborative/participatory setting contain a greater proportion of merged elements compared to the other settings.

H4b: Models generated in a consultative setting contain a lower proportion merged elements compared to the other settings.

H5: The proportion of relations connecting elements of different participants is different depending on the work setting consultative versus indi vi dual/participatory versus collaborative/participatory.

H5a: Models generated in a collaborative/participatory setting contain a greater proportion of relations connecting elements of different participants compared to the other settings.

H5b: Models generated in a consultative setting contain a lower proportion of relations connecting elements of different participants compared to the other settings.

The individual/participatory setting is in a middle position for H4 and H5.

3 Method

3.1 Experimental Setting

In this study, we examine the effect of the opportunity to collaborate with other stakeholders and of the opportunity to work with a model visualization on selected properties of the resulting models. We designed an experimental setup where the independent variable is represented by the work setting, combining these two factors.

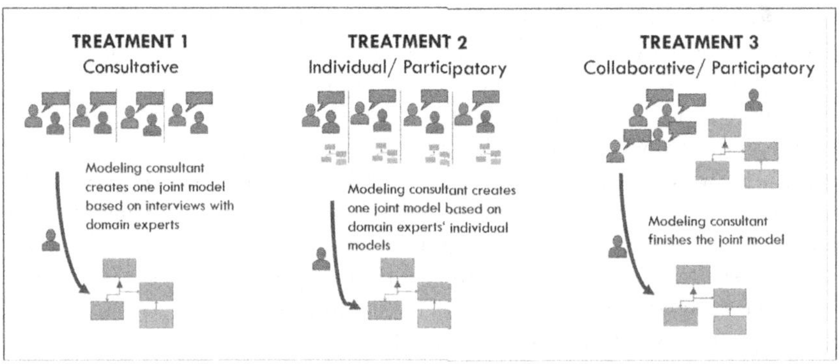

Fig. 1. Experimental design of the study.

In Fig. 1, we depict the design comprising three treatments. For all treatments, we determined groups of four people who should contribute to creating a joint goal model. A goal model fits well with PEM as it requires the participants of the modeling session to discuss and negotiate agreements [21].

In the first treatment, we used a consultative setting where a method consultant interviewed all members of the group individually. The participants would not see any visual representation during the interview. The method consultant summarized the interview material in one joint model. The second treatment, the individual/participatory setting, was similar to the consultative setting in that the method consultant would elicit the knowledge from each group member individually. The participants could, however, see and work on their individual model together with the method consultant. The latter would eventually merge all individual models to one joint model. In the third treatment, the collaborative/participatory setting, all members of a group met with two method consultants having the roles of facilitator and tool operator. We structured the modeling session similar to the procedure suggested by [24]. Phases of individual card writing, e.g., where the participants would write down possible goals or problems, would alternate with phases of presenting and discussing the cards/ideas and arranging them in the model. If the participants found that one idea, e.g., a goal, would be identical to another, they would merge these elements.

The goal models had to be created following the 4EM notation [21]. The task was to explore how learning and teaching at the university could be improved through the use of technology, drawing from the experience gained during the pandemic. Each group consisted of students and at least one university teacher. The intention was to set a task that was of relevance to the participants to raise sufficient interest and motivation. We set different time limits for the three treatments, taking into consideration that modeling and discussing would take additional time. In the consultative setting, the interviews took 20 min, the individual/participatory setting took 30 min, and the collaborative/participatory setting took 45 min.

At the time of the experiment, contact restrictions due to the Covid 19 pandemic were still in place. So, we conducted the study online and met the participants via video conference. For treatment 2 and 3, we used Miro as a modeling tool, which allows for the collaborative modeling we needed for treatment 3. To enable the participants to write down their ideas in private during the card writing phases, we set up private workspaces separate from a joint workspace.

In order to trace individual contributions, each element was marked with a colored frame where each color corresponded to a specific author. Elements to which several participants had contributed had multiple colors. In two models that were created in a collaborative manner, the method consultants had marked "joint" elements with a black frame or no frame, respectively. In these cases we considered the elements as created by all group members.

The method consultants were mostly master's students trained in conceptual modeling. They took the role of facilitator. In the settings involving model visualizations, they additionally acted as tool operators, sharing the role of documenter with the workshop participants. We prepared the method consultants in pre-tests and provided them with a script describing the procedure and rules of behavior for all treatments. For the collaborative sessions, it was important that the method consultants knew how to lead the participants through the process, determining when they should work alone or in plenum. It was their task to ensure speaking times for each individual participant and to allow working out agreements in the group when needed. One collaborative session and two individual meetings were facilitated by one of the authors. Further details about the experimental design can be found in [6].

3.2 Dependent Variables and Methods of Data Analysis

For each model, we could identify all elements, i.e., goals, problems etc., and all relations. With the exception of one model in the consultative setting, the elements had color codes indicating authorship. Thus, we could determine all the elements created by a specific person, all the elements that originated from several participants' contributions, and the relations connecting elements from

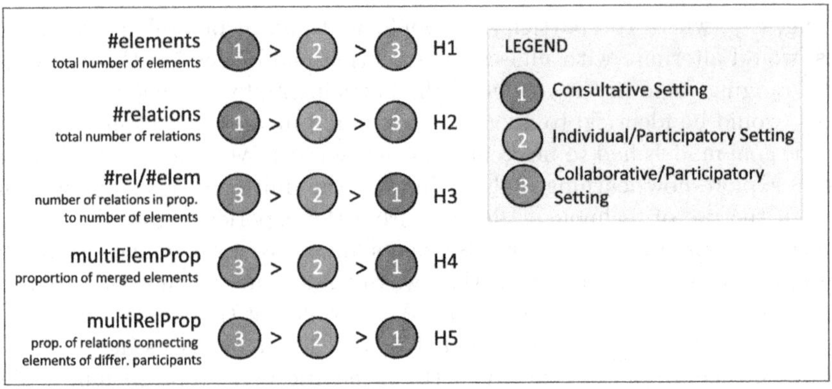

Fig. 2. Overview of the variables and corresponding hypotheses.

different authors.[1] To exploit the whole data set, we calculated the variables that were not related to authorship with all models, including the model mentioned above. For variables that were related to authorship, we excluded this model in our calculations and analyses. Figure 2 gives an overview of all the variables and the hypotheses they correspond to. Due to a small sample size, we cannot expect a normal distribution in our data. That is why we used the non-parametric Kruskal-Wallis test to test for a general difference between the three treatments. In case a general difference was found, we used the Mann-Whitney-U test for pairwise comparisons, including Bonferroni correction [5].

3.3 Sample

Fourteen groups took part in the study, five in the consultative setting, four in the individual/participatory setting, and five in the collaborative/participatory setting. Each group consisted of four people: at least one university teacher and the other members being students. For one collaborative group, one student did not show up for the trial, resulting in a group of two students and one teacher. The participants had different backgrounds, e.g., computer science, business information systems, medicine, educational science, biological sciences, economics etc. According to the questionnaire distributed to the participants, their average enterprise modeling expertise was 2.35 ($\sigma = 1.5$), on a scale from 1 (novice) to 5 (expert). In the collaborative setting, we also assessed whether the participants had met before. In two groups, some of the participants had met before; in one group, the participants did not know each other, and in two groups, all participants knew each other before. In total, 55 people took part in the study (25 female, 29 male, 1 diverse). The participants' average age was 26.8 ($\sigma = 6.4$).

[1] Example models can be found here: https://doi.org/10.5281/zenodo.13772912.

4 Results

Table 1 shows the descriptive statistics for all variables, separated by treatment. It also contains the p-values of the Kruskal-Wallis test and, depending on the latter, the p-values of the pairwise comparisons with the Mann-Whitney-U test. A star indicates statistical significance. Colored rows indicate variables where a reduced data set was used due to missing authorship markings in one model in the consultative setting.

Table 1. Descriptive statistics and Kuskal-Wallis and Mann-Whitney-U test.

	1:Consult.		2:Individ.		3:Collab.		Kruskal-Wallis	Mann-Whitney-U		
	μ	σ	μ	σ	μ	σ		1–2	1 – 3	2–3
✓ H1: #elements	57.4	13.6	57.8	10.4	28.8	6.3	0.011 *	1.000	0.027 *	0.033 *
✓ H2: #relations	71.0	16.6	72.5	9.9	39.2	10.7	0.011 *	1.000	0.034 *	0.026 *
✗ H3: #rel/#elem	1.2	0.1	1.3	0.1	1.4	0.3	0.793			
✗ H4: multiElemProp	0.06	0.06	0.05	0.08	0.22	0.22	0.243			
✓ H5: multiRelProp	0.03	0.04	0.02	0.04	0.40	0.19	0.010 *	1.000	0.054	0.018 *

5 Discussion

5.1 Summary and Interpretation

We will structure our findings according to our three research questions.

Do the Models Differ with Regard to Their Size? In our study, those groups that worked in a collaborative manner created models that were significantly smaller than those created in the consultative and the individual/participatory settings, with regard to the number of both elements and relations drawn. Thus, Hypotheses 1 and 2 were supported, but only in part. We did not find a difference between the consultative and individual/participatory settings. We assume that collaboration slows down the modeling process, e.g., the participants have to present and discuss their ideas, identify and merge similar suggestions, and find connections between their own and others' contributions. This is also mirrored in the great proportions of merged elements and relations between elements from different authors. Participants who worked on their own did not have to consider the views of others and negotiate these with their own. Whether the participants inspired each other, as was found in [15], we cannot say. For this, we will have to conduct further content-related analyses, e.g., whether a participant suggested a problem element as a reaction to a goal suggested by another participant.

Visualization did not seem to have a significant supportive function in the individual/participatory setting, thus, we could not observe any effects of relieving the working memory. We, however, presume that the method consultants have played a special role in our experiment. We cannot rule out that the method consultants did not feel confident enough to merge redundant elements. For this, we also need a further content-related analysis of the models.

How Well-Elaborated are the Models in Terms of Connections Made Between the Elements? To analyze how well-elaborated a model was, we considered the number of relations in proportion to the number of elements. This should indicate how intensely the participants thought about logical connections between their elements. We did not find any differences between the settings with regard to this model attribute; thus, we reject Hypothesis 3. In the collaborative/participatory setting, the participants might not have had enough time to discover all possible connections due to collaboration-related tasks. Another reason could lie in phenomena like social facilitation [28]. Discovering relations may be complex, such that the presence of the other participants might have impaired the process. This underlines the importance of providing a private space and time for complex tasks that could, however, also be integrated into a collaborative session.

Visualization did not seem to support the participants significantly in coming up with relations either. In the study, we, however, used simple goal models. The benefits of a visualization might have shown more clearly if we had used, for example, a process model, with the difficulty of determining sequences of action, alternatives of control flow, or different roles. Consequently, we assume that with growing complexity, the need for relieving the working memory and, thus, the value of a visualization will increase [18].

Are the Contributions of the Various Participants Linked Differently? Hypothesis 4 has to be rejected. Although the collaborative/participatory setting showed a higher average proportion of elements authored by several authors, the variance between the groups in this treatment does not allow a clear distinction. Our results support Hypothesis 5 insofar as the collaborative/participatory can be distinguished from the other settings, but we did not find any difference between the consultative and the individual/participatory setting. Models in the collaborative/participatory setting may be smaller, but the contributions of different participants are better connected in terms of relations connecting elements from different participants. This indicates that collaboration helps create a joint model. Visualization did not seem to significantly support the method consultants in the individual/participatory setting to connect the contributions of the different participants. But this may also be caused by a lack of confidence and experience of the method consultants.

All in all, our study has shown that collaboration may have a slowing effect, but the contributions are better connected. Visualization did not have a significant supportive function in our study, yet this may be due to the low complexity of the models. We still believe that visualizations in the form of models not only facilitate the communication between domain experts but also help the method consultants in case they have to work with the stakeholders separately and consolidate their views, especially when they have different and high expertise [20].

5.2 Limitations

Given the students' relative inexperience as method consultants, one might question the extent to which this negatively impacted the knowledge elicitation process. However, research on trust in requirements engineering shows that, overall, stakeholders do not expect high levels of expertise from requirements engineers during the elicitation of requirements [3]. We therefore expect that the stakeholders' articulation of ideas was not overly influenced by the relatively junior age of the method consultants. Conversely, in consultative and individual/participatory settings, the method consultants are responsible for transferring interviews into a model or merging individual models into a joint model. This requires interpretation work, so the method consultant needs to feel confident about their interpretation of the interview notes or individual models. Due to their inexperience, the method consultants may have been more hesitant, refraining from merging elements that more confident and experienced method consultants would have combined. Their level of experience will likely have affected the outcome, resulting in fewer elements being merged than would have been possible. Conversely, a method consultant who was overly confident might have been inclined to merge requirements too quickly, resulting in a bias in the opposite direction. On the whole, these conditions applied to all settings alike, so this cannot explain the noticed differences between settings.

5.3 Conclusions and Implications

In this paper, we have studied the impact of collaboration and visualization, manifested in different work settings, on the outcome of an enterprise modeling task. While in previous work [6], we had focused on the effect on the participants' perception of the process and outcome, we now examined objective properties of the models. Collaboration in enterprise modeling has many advantages, e.g., we showed that the different views of the participants are better connected in the resulting models. This does not necessarily equate to consensus among the participants, but it reflects a better integration of their ideas. This should have a positive impact on the semantic model quality in terms of completeness and (less) redundancy [8,10]. Collaboration can, however, also have negative effects. Some of these are already being addressed with best practices in PEM, like using a card writing method instead of free brainstorming [24]. Generally, for some stages in the process of participatory modeling, phases of individual work should be considered, e.g., as a countermeasure against the negative effects of social facilitation. Above all, our study has shown that collaboration takes time, which has to be taken into account when planning participatory enterprise modeling projects. Nevertheless, relying on a non-collaborative setting will be significantly more time- and labor-consuming for the method consultants. Moreover, the task of consolidating the different views of the stakeholders is very complex. Future method consultants need to be prepared for this. Although our study does not give evidence of the value of visualizations, we still believe that with growing complexity, the value of a model will increase for generating a shared understanding between method consultants and domain experts. So far, we have only examined quantitative properties of the models. Our next step will be a qualitative analysis of the material to deepen our understanding of the effects of the different work settings, e.g., how model elements addressing the same or similar topics were merged.

References

1. Bertin, J.: Semiology of Graphics. University of Wisconsin Press (1983)
2. Bond, C.F., Titus, L.J.: Social facilitation: a meta-analysis of 241 studies. Psychol. Bull. **94**(2), 265–292 (1983). https://doi.org/10.1037/0033-2909.94.2.265
3. Burnay, C., Snoeck, M.: Trust in requirements elicitation: how does it build, and why does it matter to requirements engineers? In: Proceedings of the Symposium on Applied Computing. SAC '17, pp. 1094–1100. Association for Computing Machinery, New York, NY, USA (2017). https://doi.org/10.1145/3019612.3019750,
4. Crapo, A.W., Waisel, L.B., Wallace, W.A., Willemain, T.R.: Visualization and the process of modeling. In: Ramakrishnan, R., Stolfo, S. (eds.) KDD-2000, pp. 218–226. Association for Computing Machinery, New York NY USA (2000). https://doi.org/10.1145/347090.347129
5. Field, A.: Discovering statistics using IBM SPSS statistics, vol. 6. Sage Publishing, Thousand Oaks (2024)
6. Gutschmidt, A., Verbruggen, C., Snoeck, M.: A study on the impact of the level of participation in enterprise modeling. Softw. Syst. Model. (2025). https://doi.org/10.1007/s10270-025-01275-4
7. Hüffmeier, J., Wessolowski, K., van Randenborgh, A., Bothin, J., Schmid-Loertzer, N., Hertel, G.: Social support from fellow group members triggers additional effort in groups. Eur. J. Soc. Psychol. **44**(4), 287–296 (2014). https://doi.org/10.1002/ejsp.2021
8. Krogstie, J.: Model-Based Development and Evolution of Information Systems: A Quality Approach. Springer, New York (2012). https://doi.org/10.1007/978-1-4471-2936-3
9. Larkin, J.H., Simon, H.A.: Why a diagram is (sometimes) worth ten thousand words. Cogn. Sci. **11**(1), 65–100 (1987). https://doi.org/10.1016/S0364-0213(87)80026-5. https://www.sciencedirect.com/science/article/pii/S0364021387800265
10. Lindland, O., Sindre, G., Solvberg, A.: Understanding quality in conceptual modeling. IEEE Softw. **11**(2), 42–49 (1994). https://doi.org/10.1109/52.268955
11. Lount, R.B., Wilk, S.L.: Working harder or hardly working? Posting performance eliminates social loafing and promotes social laboring in workgroups. Manag. Sci. **60**(5), 1098–1106 (2014). https://doi.org/10.1287/mnsc.2013.1820
12. Luebbe, A., Weske, M.: Determining the effect of tangible business process modeling. In: Leifer, L.J., Plattner, H., Meinel, C. (eds.) Design thinking research, pp. 241–257. Understanding innovation, Springer, Heidelberg (2012). https://doi.org/10.1007/978-3-642-21643-5_14
13. McGrath, J.E.: Groups: Interaction and performance. Prentice-Hall, Englewood Cliffs, NJ (1984)
14. Moody, D.: The "physics" of notations: toward a scientific basis for constructing visual notations in software engineering. IEEE Trans. Softw. Eng. **35**(6), 756–779 (2009). https://doi.org/10.1109/TSE.2009.67

15. Nijstad, B.A., Stroebe, W.: How the group affects the mind: a cognitive model of idea generation in groups. Person. Soc. Psychol. Rev. Off. J. Soc. Personality and Social Psychology, Inc **10**(3), 186–213 (2006). https://doi.org/10.1207/s15327957pspr1003_1
16. Nijstad, B.A., Stroebe, W., Lodewijkx, H.F.: Production blocking and idea generation: does blocking interfere with cognitive processes? J. Exp. Soc. Psychol. **39**(6), 531–548 (2003). https://doi.org/10.1016/S0022-1031(03)00040-4
17. Ohlert, J., Zepp, C., Eys, M.: Group performance. In: Schüler, J., Wegner, M., Plessner, H., Eklund, R.C. (eds.) Sport and Exercise Psychology, pp. 397–424. Springer, Cham (2023). https://doi.org/10.1007/978-3-031-03921-8_16
18. Padilla, L.M., Creem-Regehr, S.H., Hegarty, M., Stefanucci, J.K.: Decision making with visualizations: a cognitive framework across disciplines. Cogn. Res. Principles Implicat. **3**, 1–25 (2018)
19. Pohl, K.: Requirements Engineering. Springer, Berlin (2010)
20. Reagans, R., Miron-Spektor, E., Argote, L.: Knowledge utilization, coordination, and team performance. Organ. Sci. **27**(5), 1108–1124 (2016). https://doi.org/10.1287/orsc.2016.1078
21. Sandkuhl, K., Persson, A., Stirna, J., Wissotzki, M.: Enterprise modeling: tackling business challenges with the 4EM method. In: The Enterprise Engineering Series, 1st edn. Springer, Heidelberg (2014)
22. Sandkuhl, K., Seigerroth, U.: Participative or conventional enterprise modelling? Multiple-case analysis on decision criteria. In: 28th European Conference on Information Systems - Liberty, Equality, and Fraternity in a Digitizing World. ECIS 2020 (2020)
23. Steiner, I.D.: Group Process and Productivity. Social Psychology. Academic Press, New York (1972)
24. Stirna, J., Persson, A.: Enterprise Modeling: Facilitating the Process and the People, 1st edn, 2018 edn. Springer, Cham (2018). https://ebookcentral.proquest.com/lib/kxp/detail.action?docID=5528930
25. Stirna, J., Persson, A., Sandkuhl, K.: Participative enterprise modeling: experiences and recommendations. In: Krogstie, J., Opdahl, A., Sindre, G. (eds.) Advanced Information Systems Engineering, pp. 546–560. Springer, Heidelberg (2007)
26. Vasconcelos, L.A., Neroni, M.A., Cardoso, C., Crilly, N.: Idea representation and elaboration in design inspiration and fixation experiments. Int. J. Des. Creat. Innov. **6**(1–2), 93–113 (2018). https://doi.org/10.1080/21650349.2017.1362360
27. Välk, S., Thabsuwan, C., Mougenot, C.: The ideation compass: supporting interdisciplinary creative dialogues with real time visualization. Int. J. Des. Creat. Innov. **11**(2), 99–116 (2023). https://doi.org/10.1080/21650349.2022.2142674
28. Zajonc, R.B.: Social facilitation. Science (New York, N.Y.) **149**(3681), 269–274 (1965). https://doi.org/10.1126/science.149.3681.269
29. Zowghi, D., Coulin, C.: Requirements elicitation: a survey of techniques, approaches, and tools. In: Aurum, A., Wohlin, C. (eds.) Engineering and Managing Software Requirements, pp. 19–46. Springer, Berlin (2005). https://doi.org/10.1007/3-540-28244-0_2

Mind the Gaps: Which EA Modeling Notations Does Industry Actually Use? A Quantitative Investigation

Alice Forsberg, Gabriella Larsson, and Simon Hacks(✉)

Stockholm University, Stockholm, Sweden
simon.hacks@dsv.su.se

Abstract. Technology is rapidly evolving in modern society. A key solution for organizations to keep up with the development of technology and retain market share is to implement EA. Organizations use Enterprise Architecture (EA) to stay competitive by aligning IT with business goals. This study aimed to identify which EA-modeling notations are used in practice, focusing on how choices relate to industry, implementation year, and organizational size. A global survey with 40 EA professionals was conducted using a quantitative approach.

The most commonly used modeling notations were Archimate, Business Process Modeling Notation (BPMN), and Unified Modeling Language (UML). Statistical analysis through Pearson's Correlation test showed no significant correlation between modeling notation and industry, EA implementation year, or organizational size. However, it was noticeable that people within the public sector often used BPMN and Business Model Canvas (BMC). Furthermore, all organizations surveyed had implemented EA after 2000, and most were large companies with over 250 employees.

Keywords: Enterprise Architecture · Modelling Notations · Empirical Survey · Adoption Factors

1 Introduction

The ongoing technological development affects companies of various structures worldwide. Companies constantly improve and develop their technical capacity, leading to high competition and rapid changes in the market [4]. Businesses that are not quick to adapt to this development risk being outcompleted. Therefore, companies must optimize and streamline their resources and processes. Integration of information systems is essential for maintaining competitiveness in the market, which is where Enterprise Architecture (EA) becomes relevant. EA functions as a tool to integrate IT with business strategies and processes within an organization [20]. Organizations use EA to gain a better understanding of their operations and to create value for their customers [23]. EA tools help optimize and streamline an organization's ability to achieve its business goals. According to ISO/IEC/IEEE 42010:2022, EA is defined as:

Published by Springer Nature Switzerland AG 2026
H.-G. Fill et al. (Eds.): PoEM 2025, LNBIP 570, pp. 192–206, 2026.
https://doi.org/10.1007/978-3-032-12063-2_13

"Enterprise Architecture is a discipline that manages the fundamental organization of an enterprise, which is embodied in its components, their relationships to one another and the environment, and the principles that govern its design and evolution."

The foundations of modern EA were established already in the 1960s [3], but it wasn't until the 1980s when computers became more common in workplaces that EA developed into its own practice. The launch of EA as a concept came in 1987 when John Zachman published an article about architectural frameworks in information systems [29], establishing EA as a recognized term and practical approach.

EA can be structured through Enterprise Architecture Frameworks (EAF), which have been developed by two main groups [19]. The first group is Enterprise Integration (EI), focusing on production and logistics to ensure productive and efficient processes within organizations. The second group is Information Systems (IS), which works with various methods for developing software systems as part of the architecture. EI originally developed the first version of EA, initially covering only production and production control in the early 1960s, and documented it manually. Later, the EA perspective expanded to cover the entire organization, including governance structures and the people working within it.

In a modern context, a modeling notation refers to the visualization of processes through diagrams and represents functions in a business process. Modeling languages represent the rules and structure that determine how the visual notation is constructed [22]. There are several modeling notations used to visualize and document EA [5]. One prominent notation is ArchiMate [16], an independent EA modeling notation standard with open-source support, aiming to assist in the analysis and visualization of enterprise architecture.

It is important to understand that organizations have varying demands and needs. Different structures and processes require different types of solutions, making it essential to be informed about the organization's internal processes and structure. ArchiMate is used to connect areas of expertise across multiple domains, such as business and IT. Other modeling notations, like BPMN and UML, are more domain-specific, where BPMN is more business-oriented [2] and UML is more IT-oriented [6].

EA practice has evolved significantly since the 1980s [14] when it primarily consisted of static models, graphs, and diagrams. Today's organizations are increasingly dependent on digital technology, which means they must adapt to the fast-paced development of technology. Adapting to constantly changing technologies and customer needs contributes to the creation of more complex business structures. As a result, EA has had to evolve to fit this dynamic environment. Modern EA focuses on delivering tailored decision input for all situations, in real time, to facilitate decision-making in complex business issues. This increases operational efficiency.

Usually, studies focus on notations used in scientific articles [5,10]. Therefore, researchers do not know what is used in practice, making it a challenge to conduct research that is relevant to practice. Therefore, we want to close this research gap by exploring which EA modeling notations are applied by organizations.

Moreover, there is limited knowledge about which modeling notations are used across different industries. Additionally, it is interesting to understand when an organization implemented EA to understand if there is a correlation between the adoption of EA and the modeling method used.

This study aims to explore which modeling notations are actually used in practice. Furthermore, the study will examine the reasons behind choosing a specific modeling notation in relation to industry, organizational size, and the year EA was implemented. The results will help researchers conduct research based on real needs and provide organizations with better tools to manage their architecture effectively. Accordingly, we formulate our research question: ***RQ:*** *What EA modeling notations do organizations use in practice?*

To make the research question better explorable, we define the following sub-questions and related hypotheses:

1 Is there a correlation between the selected modeling notation and specific industries?
  - H0 There is no correlation between the selected modeling notation and specific industries.
  - H1 There is a correlation between the selected modeling notation and specific industries.

2 Is there a correlation between the selected modeling notation and the year the organization implemented EA?
  - H0 There is no correlation between the selected modeling notation and the year the organization implemented EA.
  - H1 There is a correlation between the selected modeling notation and the year the organization implemented EA.

3 Is there a correlation between the selected modeling notation and the size of the organization?
  - H0 There is no correlation between the selected modeling notation and the size of the organization.
  - H1 There is a correlation between the selected modeling notation and the size of the organization.

The remainder of this paper is organized as follows. Section 2 surveys prior studies on enterprise-architecture modelling and positions our work in that debate. Section 3 describes the quantitative research method, including the survey design, sampling strategy, and statistical tests. Section 4 presents the empirical findings, starting with descriptive statistics and then reporting the correlation analyses. Section 5 discusses these results in light of earlier work and outlines practical implications. Finally, Sect. 6 summarizes the main contributions, notes limitations, and proposes avenues for future research.

2 Related Work

Garroz Novoa [11] conducted a case study on decision-making processes regarding modeling language choices in Swedish organizations. The study identified a wide variety of standards as a source of reduced understanding, which creates uncertainty when selecting a language. The findings show that such decisions are not always rationally grounded but often influenced by prior experience or entrenched practices that may not align with the current organization's needs.

Undén and Lyckestjärn [26] investigated the use of Enterprise Architecture in Swedish organizations through qualitative interviews. Their results highlight that organizations adopt different frameworks and approaches tailored to their needs, while also pointing to fragmentation in the use of modeling notations.

Barbosa et al. [5] reviewed 120 academic papers on enterprise-architecture (EA) analysis, built a four-dimensional taxonomy (architecture layer, analysis focus, analysis technique, modeling language), and validated it on an additional 46 papers.

Gampfer et al. [10] analyzed roughly 4,000 EA publications since the late 1980s using text mining and classification. They traced the evolution of EA research from descriptive to management-focused studies and forecasted emerging topics such as cloud computing, IoT, agile EA, and big data, while identifying a misalignment between academic focus and industry practice.

Bruls et al. [8] critiqued existing research streams on Business–IT alignment, pointing out the limitations of both high-level "fit" studies and detail-heavy enterprise engineering approaches. They proposed a middle-ground framework for practitioners, developed through design science, that includes domain models, alignment artifacts, and layered knowledge structures.

Zhou et al. [30] systematically reviewed 112 studies on EA visualization, classifying them by purpose, technique, and evaluation, and proposed a generic visualization method to address identified research gaps.

Petersen et al. [18] examined four years of master-level assignments to derive criteria for choosing between 4EM and ArchiMate modeling methods, producing a checklist designed to support teaching and novice use.

Taken together, these studies reveal several important gaps. Prior research has largely examined decision-making in specific contexts, mapped research taxonomies, or proposed conceptual frameworks and methods. While valuable, these contributions either focus on theoretical constructs, literature aggregation, or student-level education rather than empirical insights into actual professional practice. What remains underexplored is how practicing enterprise architects in organizations choose and use modeling notations, and whether these choices relate to contextual factors such as industry sector, the maturity of EA practice, or organizational size. Our study addresses this gap by surveying 40 EA professionals and statistically analyzing their notation choices, thereby offering an empirically grounded view of modeling practice in the field.

3 Research Method

This study explores the practical use of EA modeling notations in different organizations. Because the focus is not on individual attitudes or experiences, a quantitative approach was chosen. To collect data efficiently during the limited research period (four weeks in March/April 2025), a web-based survey was used. This allowed for the broad distribution and collection of structured data in a time-effective way.

The survey included 10 questions[1], with both single- and multiple-choice formats. It began with questions to identify respondents and ensure they came from different organizations. It then covered sector, revenue, organization size, country, notations used, reasons for choosing them, and perceived EA maturity. Respondents rated their EA maturity on a scale from *Explorer* to *Legend* [17], based on how established EA practices and tools were within the organization. There was also an optional open-ended comment field to gather further feedback.

A pilot test of the survey was conducted with seven university students, all studying Marketing Communication and IT.

The study used purposive sampling, targeting professionals with knowledge and experience in EA. The aim was to get responses from various industries and organization sizes globally, to improve generalizability and relevance. To find suitable candidates for our survey, we reached out to our network, e.g., by reaching out to enterprise architects directly and sharing the survey with professional networks specialized in direct exchange between enterprise architects.

For analysis, Pearson's correlation test was used to assess relationships between the chosen notation and three variables: industry, year of EA implementation, and organizational size. Although some data were categorical (nominal or ordinal), it was numerically encoded to allow correlation testing.

4 Results

4.1 Descriptive Results

A total of 40 respondents participated in the survey, each representing one unique organization. All were professionals actively working with EA in various organizations around the world (cf. Fig. 1). The survey had no geographical limitation, and responses were collected globally. Most respondents were employed in large organizations (over 250 employees) (cf. Table 3), and a majority reported that their organizations had an annual turnover exceeding 90 million (cf. Fig. 2).

In terms of EA maturity, most respondents placed their organization at the "Rising Star" level on the EA maturity scale. This means that EA tools are implemented and explored, and that EA is increasingly gaining attention from stakeholders. The second most common level was "Explorer", which represents early-stage exploration of EA with limited implementation.

The organizations represented a broad range of industries, including public sector, IT, finance, energy, education, manufacturing, telecommunications, and more (cf. Table 1).

[1] See Appendix.

4.2 EA Modeling Notations in Industry

The main objective of the study was to identify which EA modeling notations are most commonly used in practice. The results showed that the most frequently used notations among the respondents were (cf. Table 1):

- **Archimate**
- **Business Process Modeling Notation (BPMN)**
- **Unified Modeling Language (UML)**

Many respondents indicated that they use a combination of notations rather than relying on a single one.

The most common reasons for choosing a specific modeling notation were:

- Access to tools and software that support the notation
- The notation is considered "best practice"
- The notation can be adjusted to fit the organization's specific needs
- It is commonly used in the respondent's industry

Free-text responses added further context, such as using the native language of business stakeholders or choosing notations for educational or research purposes.

To test whether the choice of modeling notation was related to industry, year of EA implementation, or organization size, Pearson's correlation test was used.

No statistically significant correlation was found between modeling notation and industry. However, notations such as BPMN and BMC appeared more frequently among respondents from the public sector, although the results were not statistically significant.

All organizations had implemented EA between 2000 and 2025 (cf. Table 2). The test showed no significant correlation between the year of implementation and the choice of modeling notation.

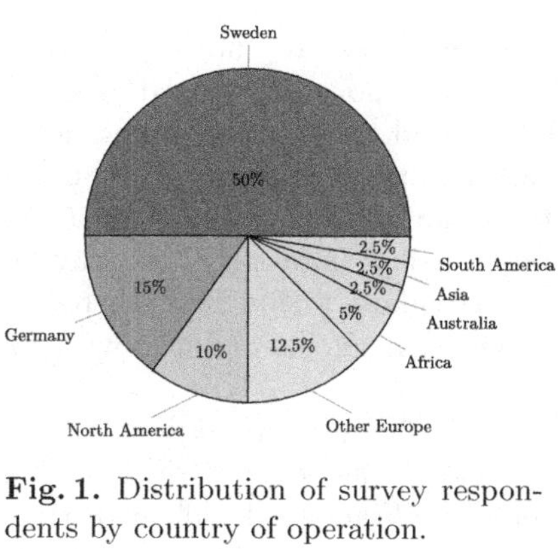

Fig. 1. Distribution of survey respondents by country of operation.

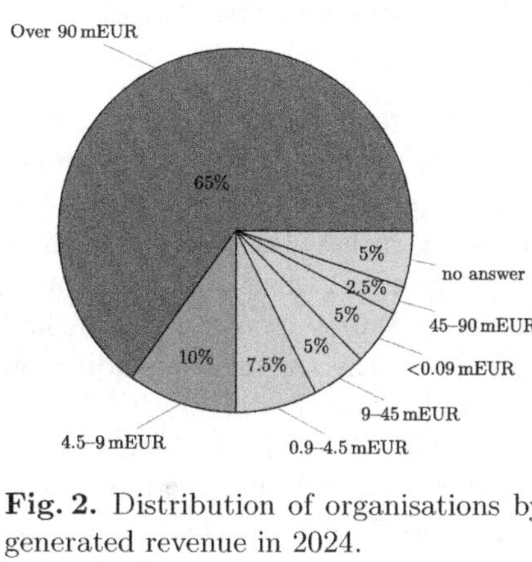

Fig. 2. Distribution of organisations by generated revenue in 2024.

Table 1. Use of modelling notations by industry

Industry	Archimate	UML	BPMN	ERD	BCM	BMC	IDEF	SysML
Construction and Real Estate	0	0	0	0	0	0	0	0
Consulting Services	2	2	3	2	1	0	0	0
Education and Research	1	2	2	2	1	1	1	0
Energy and Environment	2	0	0	0	0	0	0	0
Finance and Banking	2	1	1	1	0	0	0	0
Healthcare and Medical Services	2	2	2	0	0	0	0	1
Insurance	1	0	0	0	0	0	0	0
IT and Software Development	0	1	2	2	2	0	0	0
Manufacturing and Industry	2	2	3	1	1	1	0	0
Media and Entertainment	1	1	0	0	1	1	0	0
Public Sector	5	7	5	4	3	5	2	1
Public Transport	1	1	0	0	0	0	0	0
Retail and E-commerce	2	2	1	0	1	1	0	0
Telecommunications	2	2	2	1	0	0	0	0
Total	23	23	21	13	11	9	3	2

Regarding organization size, most respondents worked in large enterprises (cf. Table 3). Pearson's test showed negative correlations, suggesting that larger organizations tend to use certain notations more often. The strongest trend was found for IDEF, but the p-value was slightly above the threshold for statistical significance ($p > 0.05$).

5 Discussion

5.1 Analysis of the Findings

The modeling notations most commonly used according to the respondents' answers are Archimate (23 responses), UML (23 responses), and BPMN (21 responses). This aligns with previous research [5] and the three modeling notations highlighted in the literature review as some of the leading modeling notations within EA. Based on the collected data, it can also be concluded that the majority of organizations use more than one modeling notation. This may be due to the absence of an established industry standard within EA—there are different paths to take depending on an organization's goals or focus with its EA implementation [24].

Despite the lack of a common industry standard, there are various frameworks within EA. For example, Archimate is closely associated with the EA framework TOGAF (The Open Group Architecture Framework) [9]. A distinctive feature of TOGAF is that it provides tools for developing different types of IT architectures [25]. Archimate is a modeling notation that bridges domains and provides a unified representation of several different modeling notations [28]. Unlike Archimate, UML and BPMN are tailored for specific domains; BPMN is designed for business processes, while UML is used to concretize software [15]. Therefore, it can be assumed that Archimate is one of the most widely used modeling notations in practice due to its non-domain-specific nature, making it more flexible.

Table 2. Modelling notations by EA implementation period

Implementation period	Archimate	UML	BPMN	ERD	BCM	BMC	IDEF	SysML
2000–2009	3	4	3	3	2	1	1	0
2010–2019	9	9	9	4	4	3	1	1
2020–2025	11	10	8	5	5	5	1	1
Unknown	0	0	1	1	0	0	0	0
Total	23	23	21	13	11	9	3	2

Table 3. Modelling notations by organisation size

Organisation size	Archimate	UML	BPMN	ERD	BCM	BMC	IDEF	SysML
Large enterprise (250+ employees)	21	20	18	10	9	9	2	2
Mediumsized (50–249 employees)	0	1	1	1	1	0	0	0
Micro enterprise (0–9 employees)	1	2	1	1	0	0	1	0
Small enterprise (10–49 employees)	1	0	1	1	1	0	0	0
Total	23	23	21	13	11	9	3	2

Due to the fact that only 40 respondents participated in the survey, the dataset was not large enough for the statistical tests to yield high significance. Therefore, it cannot be confirmed that Archimate is actually the most widely used modeling notation in practice alongside UML. However, if one considers only the collected data, the answer to the research question is: Archimate and UML are the modeling notations most commonly used in practice.

5.2 Correlation Between Chosen Modeling Notation and Industry Sector

The sub-question regarding which industry the organizations operated in yielded highly varied responses. However, the majority indicated that they operated within the public sector. Within this sector, the most commonly used modeling notations were UML (7 responses), followed by ArchiMate, BPMN, and BMC, each with 5 responses.

It was noteworthy that most respondents worked in the public sector, considering that previous research has highlighted significant challenges for public organizations in implementing and maintaining EA [13]. Such challenges include difficulties in obtaining management support due to limited resources and concerns that digitalization may pose risks to personal data. Research also suggests that there are numerous opportunities for the public sector if awareness of the value of digitalization increases, along with recognition of the disadvantages of falling behind in digital development [13].

From this, it can be concluded that more public organizations have enhanced their understanding of both EA and its value. Finally, the survey results showed that organizations from several different industries are using EA. However, no significant correlation was found between the variables "chosen modeling notation" and "industry sector." The collected responses, in this case as well, can only be classified as random. **Accordingly, the hypothesis that the choice of modeling notation depends on the industry sector must be rejected.**

5.3 Correlation Between Chosen Modeling Notation and the Year of EA Implementation

EA has its origins as far back as the 1960s and became an established practice in the 1980s due to the increasing digitalization of workplaces [3]. With this context in mind, it is notable that the results showed that none of the respondents had implemented EA prior to the year 2000. The respondents were asked to indicate the year in which EA was implemented in their organization, and the majority of the 40 participants stated that implementation took place after 2010. This supports the conclusion that EA is becoming increasingly necessary as technology continues to evolve [3].

In today's society, it is essential for organizations to implement EA in a timely manner in order to maintain competitiveness on the market [20]. Modern EA is adapted to today's ever-changing needs, in contrast to earlier times when EA consisted solely of static models, graphs, and diagrams [3]. Today, EA contributes to reducing the risk of issues such as non-operational solutions and high maintenance costs. It also facilitates better integration between business processes and IT structures [7]. The significant development of both EA and technology since the 1980s can be assumed to influence why more organizations today are choosing to invest in EA.

The statistical test revealed no significant correlation between the variables "year of EA implementation" and "chosen modeling notation," suggesting that the responses may be considered random. Additionally, the collected data did not indicate any observable pattern between these two variables. What stands out, however, is that ArchiMate, UML, and BPMN are the most commonly used notations, regardless of the year in which EA was implemented. **Consequently, the hypothesis that the choice of modeling notation depends on the year EA was introduced must be rejected.**

5.4 Correlation Between Chosen Modeling Notation and Organizational Size

Regarding the sub-question about the size of the respondents' organizations, 35 out of 40 respondents indicated that they were part of a large organization with 250 or more employees. This aligns with previous research, which shows that larger organizations are more likely to invest in EA [1]. Two respondents reported being part of a small organization with 10–49 employees, two respondents belonged to a micro organization with 0–9 employees, and one respondent indicated a medium-sized company with 50–249 employees.

EA projects require significant resources and high expertise, which most smaller organizations lack. Smaller organizations tend not to prioritize EA, as they often focus on short-term goals, whereas EA aims to create a functioning and integrated enterprise in the long term. The challenge today is that EA is less accessible for smaller organizations due to a lack of knowledge about EA and the value it can provide [1].

When the variable "organization size" was tested against the variable "chosen modeling notation," it was observed that ArchiMate, UML, and BPMN are most commonly used by large organizations. It is important to highlight that the distribution of organization sizes in this study is uneven. Therefore, it is not possible to establish a correlation between organization size and chosen modeling notation. **Accordingly, the hypothesis that the choice of modeling notation depends on organization size must be rejected.**

5.5 Insights from Respondents on the Current EA Practice

The study's survey consisted of multiple-choice questions where respondents were also given the option to provide their own answers. The final section of the survey invited respondents to share their personal thoughts and opinions. The initial analysis draws on a respondent working professionally in a large organization within retail and e-commerce in the USA. The following statement was made:

"Tooling is moving towards collaborative modeling based on virtual whiteboards like Miro or Lucidchart. EA modeling frameworks like Archimate are underrepresented. I would say very few companies can use these frameworks effectively to get data out of them; it's more about productivity and collaborative design."

This respondent highlights a challenge where larger frameworks like Archimate miss an important aspect of modeling, as users feel that not all functionalities are available. However, the respondent seems to blend here the notion of modeling notation and the tool that provides the capabilities to perform the modeling. His answer indicates that established, more formalized notations such as Archimate are usually used with tools that are not perceived as the state of the art anymore.

The conclusion drawn from this is that while major modeling notations such as Archimate and UML are in use, issues regarding the lack of vital functions and efficiency result in related modeling tools not always being the first choice for all EA practitioners. Even though the financial capability to use more resource-intensive modeling tools exists, simpler modeling tools appear more attractive in this case.

Furthermore, another respondent expressed similar views regarding not wanting to be constrained by the language limitations and functions of notations during modeling. This respondent works professionally within EA in the healthcare sector in Sweden:

"Our strategy has been to implement a standard, open, free, and feature-rich notation. We don't want to be hindered by the language to express fidelity in our models."

Organizations choose EA frameworks that best fit their requirements and needs, which serve as templates to help organizations understand these [27]. This case clearly illustrates that there is no consistent industry standard since different frameworks are being used within the EA field, as previously discussed [21]. Despite the respondent's organization having selected the Unified Architecture

Framework, there are still obvious shortcomings and limitations that affect EA practitioners in their work.

The survey also included an EA maturity scale used to assess where organizations stand within EA. A respondent from Sweden, working in the public sector, described the scale as not fixed but rather fluid. This means that reaching higher maturity levels such as *legend* or *leader* does not preclude falling back to lower levels like *explorer*. The respondent described it as follows:

"It's always fluid, one year we can be a leader, the other an explorer of kind."

Another respondent working in the Swedish healthcare sector indicated that their organization was at the *rising star* level, the second-lowest maturity level:

"We implemented organization, processes and governance before we selected and implemented tools. We are the least mature in how the architecture tool is integrated in our way of work."

This highlights how organizations do not always use EA from the start to create and optimize internal business processes and corporate governance. Previous literature has described EA as providing a holistic overview of all parts of an organization [12]. Moreover, EA has been described as vital since information systems are no longer merely supportive functions but central to an organization [7]. This respondent's answer illustrates how a late EA implementation can contribute to a lower maturity level. It suggests that modeling notations have been explored and relevant data identified, emphasizing the challenge of how to use EA effectively. The results indicate that organizations need to implement business processes and increase general EA usage to reach higher maturity levels.

6 Conclusions

This study aimed to investigate which modeling notations are used in practice. Furthermore, the study's sub-questions examined whether the variable "chosen modeling notation" is associated with the variables "industry sector," "year of EA implementation," and "organizational size."

The results showed that Archimate and UML are the most commonly used modeling notations in practice. It also became evident that EA professionals tend to use a combination of notations rather than relying on a single one. The sub-question exploring the potential correlation between modeling notation and industry sector led to the rejection of the alternative hypothesis, indicating no significant relationship between these variables. However, based on the collected data, it became apparent that professionals in the public sector predominantly use BPMN and BMC. This suggests that EA usage within the public sector constitutes a substantial part of this study's sample.

The second sub-question examined the relationship between modeling notation and the year EA was implemented. Here, the alternative hypothesis is rejected, meaning no statistically significant correlation was found. However, the results showed that all respondents implemented EA after the year 2000.

Lastly, the third sub-question addressed whether there is a correlation between modeling notation and organizational size. Once again, the alternative hypothesis was rejected. No significant relationship between the variables was identified. Nevertheless, it is important to highlight that the majority of respondents were employed in large organizations. This could be attributed to their greater access to resources, which likely contributed to the higher volume of data gathered from large organizations in this study.

This study was subject to several limitations. Pearson's correlation test is most effective when applied to large datasets. Therefore, had the dataset been more extensive, the statistical tests might have yielded more conclusive results and potentially identified significant relationships between the variables. This limitation can largely be attributed to the restricted time frame of the study.

The time constraint also had implications for the selection and number of respondents who participated in the study. Ideally, a greater number of professionals working within the EA field globally would have participated in the survey, thereby contributing to more generalizable results. Unfortunately, due to the authors' network, most of the participants were from Europe, with a focus on Sweden, making it difficult to fully achieve the study's external validity.

The results of the study showed that EA professionals tend to use a combination of modeling notations. However, the findings could not be confirmed as statistically significant, which leaves room for future research. Upcoming studies could benefit from adopting a qualitative approach, focusing on in-depth interviews. These interviews could be designed based on this study's survey, while also allowing for more detailed discussions about the rationale behind choosing specific modeling notations. Such an approach would contribute to a deeper understanding of the choices highlighted in this research.

Alternatively, a quantitative study could be conducted with access to a larger portion of the target population. Future research might also focus more specifically on the use of modeling notations within individual industries. One suggestion would be for future researchers to investigate a particular industry sector, rather than examining all sectors within a single study. This would provide a more nuanced perspective on the reasoning behind modeling notation choices in relation to specific professional contexts.

Finally, this study has offered an international perspective on how EA is practiced. Gaining insight into the global application of EA serves as a valuable analytical starting point. A more extensive study, with access to relevant respondents and conducted over a longer period, would yield richer data. A larger dataset would likely produce clearer and more significant results, beneficial not only for EA practitioners but also for researchers and entrepreneurs interested in advancing the field. Such a study could foster greater interest in developing a shared and unified standard for EA in future organizations.

Acknowledgments. The authors have no competing interests to declare that are relevant to the content of this article.

Appendix - Questionnaire

Introductory note to respondents: This survey explores the practical use of enterprise-architecture (EA) modelling notations. All responses are anonymous and will be used solely for research purposes.

#	Item (as shown to respondents)	Response format / options
1	*Please enter the first 2 digits of your organisation-number + the first 2 letters of your company name + the year the company was founded* (e.g. "56HE2000").	Open text
2	*In which industry is your company established?*	Single choice: IT & Software/Finance & Banking/Insurance/Manufacturing & Industry/Energy & Environment/Healthcare & Medical Services/Public Sector/Telecommunications/Retail & E-commerce/Transportation & Logistics/Construction & Real Estate/Consulting Services/Media & Entertainment/Education & Research/Other
3	*Where on this scale does your organisation fit?*	Single choice: Micro (0–9 employees)/Small (10–49)/Medium (50–249)/Large (250+)
4	*What was your organisation's generated revenue for 2024?*	Single choice: < 0.09 m/0.09–0.9 m/0.9–4.5 m/4.5–9 m/9–45 m/45–90 m/> 90 m
5	*Where is your company established?*	Multiple choice (continents): Scandinavia/Europe/Asia/South America/North America/Australia/Africa
6	*Specify the country where you are professionally active, within the chosen continent(s).*	Open text
7	*Which EA modelling notation(s) does your company use?*	Multiple choice: ArchiMate/BPMN/UML/SysML/DMN/IDEF/BCM/BMC/ERD/Other
8	*What is/are the reason(s) your company chose these notation(s)?*	Multiple choice: Best practice/Tool availability/Fits organisation size/Adaptable to needs/Cost-effective/Prior expertise/Facilitates communication/Recommended by advisors/Common in industry/Limited choice at EA introduction/Other
9	*What year did your company implement EA?*	Single choice: 1960–69/1970–79/1980–89/1990–99/2000–09/2010–19/2020–25
10	*Where do you assess your company to be on the EA maturity levels?*	Single choice with descriptors: **Explorer** (isolated data, no EA tool) / **Rising Star** (EA tool in place, growing stakeholder attention) / **Pro** (organised data, EA supports operations) / **Leader** (data-driven decisions, fully integrated EA tool) / **Legend** (EA is central to real-time strategy execution)
11	*Is there anything you would like to add?*	Open text

References

1. Abarca, L., Killander, E., Rollén, C.: Enterprise architecture i små och medelstora företag (2022)
2. Allweyer, T.: BPMN 2.0: introduction to the standard for business process modeling. BoD–Books on Demand (2016)
3. Ardoq: The evolution of enterprise architecture. Ardoq Blog (2022). https://www.ardoq.com/blog/evolution-of-enterprise-architecture
4. Azevedo, C.L., Iacob, M.E., Almeida, J.P.A., van Sinderen, M., Pires, L.F., Guizzardi, G.: Modeling resources and capabilities in enterprise architecture: a well-founded ontology-based proposal for archimate. Inf. Syst. **54**, 235–262 (2015)
5. Barbosa, A., Santana, A., Hacks, S., Stein, N.V.: A taxonomy for enterprise architecture analysis research. In: 21st International Conference on Enterprise Information Systems, vol. 2, pp. 493–504. SciTePress (2019)
6. Booch, G., Jacobson, I., Rumbaugh, J., et al.: The unified modeling language. Unix Rev. **14**(13), 5 (1996)
7. Brown, A.: The value of enterprise architecture (2004). https://cioindex.com/wp-content/uploads/nm/articlefiles/61096-value_of_ea.pdf. Accessed 20 Feb 2025
8. Bruls, W., et al.: Business it alignment—where should we go: a view from practice. Enterp. Model. Inf. Syst. Archit. (EMISAJ) **20** (2025)
9. Franke, U., et al.: EAF2-a framework for categorizing enterprise architecture frameworks. In: 2009 10th ACIS International Conference on Software Engineering, Artificial Intelligences, Networking and Parallel/Distributed Computing, pp. 327–332. IEEE (2009)
10. Gampfer, F., Jürgens, A., Müller, M., Buchkremer, R.: Past, current and future trends in enterprise architecture—a view beyond the horizon. Comput. Ind. **100**, 70–84 (2018)
11. Garroz Novoa, M.: Påverkande faktorer vid valet av modelleringsspråk (2022). https://www.diva-portal.org/smash/get/diva2:1676451/FULLTEXT01.pdf
12. Hacks, S., Brosius, M., Aier, S.: A case study of stakeholder concerns on EAM. In: 2017 IEEE 21st International Enterprise Distributed Object Computing Workshop (EDOCW), pp. 50–56. IEEE (2017)
13. Hedlund, L., Nilsson, A.: Utmaningar och möjligheter med enterprise architecture: inom offentliga verksamheter (2024)
14. Kotusev, S.: The history of enterprise architecture: an evidence-based review. J. Enterp. Archit. **12**(1), 29 (2016)
15. Lankhorst, M., et al.: Enterprise Architecture at Work, vol. 352. Springer, Cham (2009)
16. Lankhorst, M.M., Proper, H.A., Jonkers, H.: The anatomy of the archimate language. Int. J. Inf. Syst. Model. Des. (IJISMD) **1**(1), 1–32 (2010)
17. LeanIX: Enterprise architecture maturity stages and assessment (2025). https://www.leanix.net/en/wiki/ea/enterprise-architecture-maturity-stages-and-assessment. Accessed 28 Apr 2025
18. Petersen, S.A., Quayyum, F., Krogstie, J.: Criteria for selecting an enterprise modelling method-students' perspectives on archimate and 4em. Enterprise Modelling and Information Systems Architectures (EMISAJ) **18**, 5–1 (2023)
19. Romero, D., Vernadat, F.: Enterprise information systems state of the art: past, present and future trends. Comput. Ind. **79**, 3–13 (2016). https://doi.org/10.1016/j.compind.2016.03.001, https://www.sciencedirect.com/science/article/pii/S0166361516300483, special Issue on Future Perspectives on Next Generation Enterprise Information Systems

20. Rouhani, B.D., Mahrin, M.N., Nikpay, F., Nikfard, P.: A comparison enterprise architecture implementation methodologies. In: 2013 International Conference on Informatics and Creative Multimedia, pp. 1–6 (2013). https://doi.org/10.1109/ICICM.2013.9
21. Saint-Louis, P., Lapalme, J.: An exploration of the many ways to approach the discipline of enterprise architecture. Int. J. Eng. Busi. Manag. **10**, 1847979018807383 (2018)
22. Sandkuhl, K., Stirna, J., Persson, A., Wißotzki, M.: Enterprise Modeling. Springer, Cham (2014)
23. Tamm, T., Seddon, P.B., Shanks, G.: How enterprise architecture leads to organisational benefits. Int. J. Inf. Manag. **67**, 102554 (2022)
24. The Open Group: Introduction to the TOGAF Architecture Development Method (2002). https://pubs.opengroup.org/architecture/togaf8-doc/arch/chap01.html. ASccessed 17 Feb 2025
25. The Open Group: Overview of TOGAF (2002). https://pubs.opengroup.org/architecture/togaf8-doc/arch/chap02.html. Accessed 17 Feb 2025
26. Undén, M., Lyckestjarn, M.: Användningen av enterprise architecture på tre svenska storföretag: Ea, teoretisk utopi eller konkretiserad verklighet (2015). https://lup.lub.lu.se/luur/download?func=downloadFile&recordOId=8146485&fileOId=8146486
27. Urbaczewski, L., Mrdalj, S.: A comparison of enterprise architecture frameworks. Issues Inf. Syst. **7**(2), 18–23 (2006)
28. Vicente, M., Gama, N., da Silva, M.M.: Using archimate and TOGAF to understand the enterprise architecture and ITIL relationship. In: Franch, X., Soffer, P. (eds.) CAiSE 2013. LNBIP, vol. 148, pp. 134–145. Springer, Heidelberg (2013). https://doi.org/10.1007/978-3-642-38490-5_11
29. Zachman, J.A.: A historical look at enterprise architecture with John Zachman. Bus. Rules J. **16**(9) (2015). https://www.brcommunity.com/articles.php?id=b828
30. Zhou, Z., Zhi, Q., Morisaki, S., Yamamoto, S.: A systematic literature review on enterprise architecture visualization methodologies. IEEE Access **8**, 96404–96427 (2020)

Contextual and Process-Oriented Modeling

Context-Enriched Process Discovery from IoT Data Sources for Human Behavioral Monitoring

Zahra Ahmadi[1(✉)], Mohsen Shirali[2], Jochen De Weerdt[1], and Estefanía Serral[1]

[1] Research Centre for Information Systems Engineering (LIRIS), KU Leuven, Warmoesberg 26, 1000 Brussels, Belgium
{zahra.ahmadi,jochen.deweerdt,estefania.serralasensio}@kuleuven.be
[2] ICTeam, UCLouvain, Louvain-la-Neuve, Belgium
mohsen.shirali@uclouvain.be

Abstract. The increasing availability of data from diverse sources presents new opportunities for inclusive and data-driven modeling, particularly in the area of human behavior analysis. Process discovery, as a data-driven technique of Process Mining (PM), can be used to extract behavioral and workflow models from event logs. However, this technique requires well-structured event logs that accurately reflect actual processes. In many cases, discovery approaches rely on single-source datasets and rarely integrate heterogeneous data and contextual information. This lack of integration limits the ability to extract deeper insights into human behavior and hinders comprehensive and interpretable modeling. To address this, we propose a methodological approach called **H**uman **B**ehavior Monitoring with **Uni**fied Log and **Contex**tualized Process Discovery (HB-UniContex). HB-UniContex consolidates data from multiple sources, including smart sensing systems, multimedia data streams and human-generated data sources, into a unified event log that supports context-aware process discovery and detailed visualization. HB-UniContex enables a clear extraction and interpretation of human behavior in relation to contextual information. We demonstrate the applicability of this method through a case study in an Ambient Assisted Living (AAL) setting, analyzing human behavior models and examining the relationship between mood states and daily activities. Our findings reveal specific behavior patterns associated with different mood states, providing precise insights into how an individual's daily mood correlates with certain daily activities.

Keywords: Data Integration · Contextualization · Process Mining · Mood Analysis · Internet of Things · Human Behavior

1 Introduction

The analysis and deeper understanding of human behavior has become one of the most significant research areas in recent years and plays a key role in improving

Published by Springer Nature Switzerland AG 2026
H.-G. Fill et al. (Eds.): PoEM 2025, LNBIP 570, pp. 209–226, 2026.
https://doi.org/10.1007/978-3-032-12063-2_14

health-related systems. Behavior analysis can help individuals identify habits that may increase the risk of diseases and this insight enables preventive actions that can slow the decline in functional health [2,3]. An effective approach to analyzing and gaining insights into human behavior is Process Mining (PM), which utilizes event logs to discover, monitor and improve processes. Event logs capture the execution of process activities and may also contain contextual variables, the situational characteristics that affect how a process operates [23]. In PM, contextualization incorporates these variables to enhance the interpretability of process models.

However, event logs often lack contextual and multi-modal information, making it challenging to understand processes, particularly in complex human behavioral systems [14]. Due to the complexity and variability of human behavior, the relationships between human factors and other process elements, such as shifts in mood, cultural events, and environmental changes, often remain hidden or ambiguous. Therefore, simply combining data to create a comprehensive view is insufficient; it is equally crucial to understand the context in which the data was generated. Without effective strategies for data integration and contextualization, generating deep insights and identifying deviations or trends remains a significant challenge [21].

By integrating diverse data streams, we can construct a unified, human-centric and contextualized representation that captures deeper insight into process activities and interactions. Despite advancements, the integration of IoT data and human-generated inputs, along with effective contextualization, remains limited in current PM approaches. This gap leads to challenges in developing comprehensive process models that accurately reflect real-world scenarios. There is a need for a comprehensive and innovative method that combines different data sources and incorporates contextual information into process models, enabling enhanced process analysis. However, the applicability of these contextualized process models to analyze human behavior, which represents insights from different sensor modalities, has not yet been thoroughly investigated, and this paper contributes to this issue.

To address this challenge, we propose **H**uman **B**ehavior Monitoring with **Uni**fied Log and **Contex**tualized Process Discovery (HB-UniContex), a methodological approach that integrates multiple data sources and applies a contextualization method to discover detailed process models and analyze them to uncover human behavior. The HB-UniContex approach consists of four key steps: (1) **Data collection** from multi-modal sources such as IoT systems, system logs, and human self-reports; (2) **Preprocessing and transformation** into a unified event log; (3) **Contextualized process discovery** using domain knowledge and contextual variables inspired from a method presented in [1]; and (4) **Analysis and visualization** to reveal interpretable relationships between human behavior and other process elements. We demonstrate HB-UniContex using a real-world case study in an Ambient-Assisted Living (AAL) setting. We provide a more detailed analysis of specialized activities by integrating contextual information into behavioral process models, derived from smart sensors, a wearable device, a smartphone, and psychological self-reports. The resulting models offer valuable insights into the relationship between mood patterns and an individual's daily activities, showing the practical applicability of our method in real-world scenarios and processes.

The remainder of this paper is structured as follows: Sect. 2 reviews related work, and Sect. 3 details the proposed method. The case study, along with its evaluation and results, is presented in Sect. 4. Key discussion points are explored in Sect. 5, and conclusions are drawn in Sect. 6.

2 Related Work

To support our goal of analyzing human behavior, this section reviews prior research in three domains: IoT systems that utilize multi-source data, process analytics of human behavior in PM and contextualization in PM.

Multi-modal IoT Data Integration: Integration of heterogeneous data sources in IoT is a research area where various methods and their applications in different domains have been widely investigated. Some studies focused on the advantages of merging multiple data sources. For instance, Stikic *et al.* used a combination of RFID devices for tagging key objects and a single accelerometer on the dominant wrist for accurate activity recognition [28]. He *et al.* [17] developed a care system by using video processing technology as the core, combined with sound, infrared, and pulse detections. In other work, Ullah *et al.* in [29] discuss various data fusion approaches in IoT environments, highlighting methods of aggregating data to enhance decision-making processes. In addition, Gavric *et al.* in [14] introduced a method and tool for transforming raw, unstructured data from modalities like video, audio, and sensor data into a structured and unified event log, while maintaining human-in-the-loop. These studies highlight the significance and potential of multi-modal data fusion in IoT systems, enabling the development of more accurate and adaptive applications.

Process Analytics of Human Behavior in PM: PM is employed in a wide range of studies, such as in [12,13,15,19,20], to recognize and analyze individual daily behaviors. Behavioral data collected by wearable devices and AALs are being investigated in several research projects in PM as a way to monitor the health of older adults and track the progression of certain diseases. For instance, researchers assess the relationship between daily activity routines and achieving sufficient levels of physical activity in [25]. In another work [27], mobility patterns are used as indicators of physical health and the ability to live independently in elderly care. Fernandez *et al.* [11] further analyzed the behavioral data to evaluate the impact that PM can have on personalized healthcare and understanding human behavior. Furthermore, health-related process models can aid in selecting appropriate treatments based on patient characteristics. They also have the potential to detect illnesses in their early stages, where behavioral changes may serve as early symptoms of disease onset, such as erratic movements in dementia and adherence to treatment protocols [7,8].

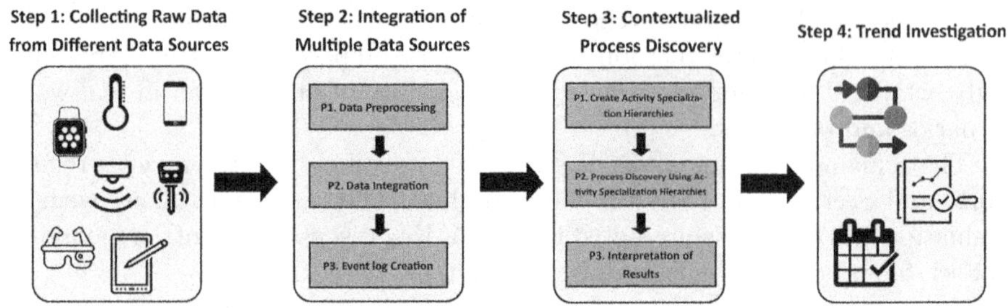

Fig. 1. HB-UniContext methodological approach.

Contextualization in PM: Contextualization methods involve integrating information about the environment in which processes occur, allowing us to obtain better insights from the discovered process models. Several studies have explored the use of context in PM. Van der Aalst *et al.* [30] emphasize the importance of considering the context in which events occur, arguing that contextual information is essential for accurate process analysis. Further, Koschmider *et al.* [18] highlight the significance of understanding event-activity mappings to improve the quality of PM outcomes, and they propose methods to incorporate contextual information effectively. Elali *et al.* [9] demonstrate a practical application of contextualization in PM by using sensor data to create contextual process models in smart home environments. Lately, in our work [1], we introduced a method for extracting contextualized process models by embedding contextual information into process activities and using different levels of contextual detail.

These scholarly contributions highlight that integrating different data sources and using context variables into process models not only enhances their accuracy but also aligns them more closely with real-world scenarios. They highlight that a better representation of real-world context is crucial for advancing the effectiveness of PM in analyzing human behavior. None of the three areas (multi-modal IoT data integration, process analytics of human behavior, and contextualization in process modeling) directly addresses the gap of collecting data from multiple heterogeneous sources to contextualize process models and use this information to identify tendencies and patterns in human behavior.

3 Human Behavior Monitoring with Unified Log and Contextualized Process Discovery (HB-UniContex)

This section presents our four-step methodological approach: (1) Data collection, (2) Preprocessing and transformation, (3) Contextualized process discovery, and (4) Analysis and visualization. Figure 1 shows the steps and their components. Details for each step are provided below.

Step 1: Data Collection. The objective of the first step involves collecting behavior-related raw data from a diverse set of sources as inputs, which include:

- **Smart sensing systems:** These systems are equipped with environmental sensors (which measure temperature, humidity, light levels, etc.), wearable devices (that track metrics like heart rate, skin temperature, sleep patterns) and smart home systems (featuring door sensors, room presence sensors, low-level activity detectors, etc.). Together, these systems generate continuous data that capture environmental conditions, physiological signals, movement patterns and labels for low-level activity.
- **Multimedia data streams**: Richer data can be extracted from sources such as video (used for detecting posture, gestures, facial expressions, etc.) and audio recordings (analyzing speech patterns, tone, etc.) to provide deeper insights into behavior.
- **Human-generated data sources**: This includes structured questionnaires or self-reports that capture subjective experiences such as mood, preferences, stress levels and so on. Additionally, digital diaries or logs offer temporal context and explanations for behaviors not captured by sensors, providing qualitative insights into internal experiences, intentions and preferences.

At this stage, the output is either unstructured or semi-structured and comes in various formats.

Step 2: Preprocessing and Transformation. To address the demand for an event log before process discovery, it is essential to integrate diverse data from various sources into a single, unified event log. The objective of this step is to preprocess and transform the input multi-modal data into an event-centric format suitable for process discovery. Our methodological approach for this integration is divided into three phases:

Phase 1. Data preprocessing: The preprocessing phase ensures that all datasets are consistent and ready for integration. Raw data from IoT devices, multimedia data streams and human-generated data sources is transformed into a high-level and unique format using custom-designed methods to ensure consistency, accuracy and quality. First, to normalize data formats, different data structures (e.g., JSON, XML and CSV) are converted into a unified schema. Next, raw data fields are parsed to extract numerical or categorical values for various parameters, such as time values or sensor measurements. Data cleaning is then performed by addressing errors, duplicates, and missing values through filtering and imputation techniques. In addition, to support process-centric analysis, case identifiers must be determined to differentiate between separate instances of process execution. Finally, specific event abstractions tailored to individual IoT devices are applied to convert raw data into high-level representations.

Phase 2. Data Integration: In this phase, the preprocessed data is combined into a coherent format that aligns heterogeneous sources both temporally and semantically. Temporal alignment ensures that data streams are synchronized along a common time axis, making it easier to correlate events meaningfully.

Semantic alignment is carried out to match equivalent events across diverse sources using mapping strategies, such as ontology-based alignment or schema matching. These strategies help bridge the semantic gap between heterogeneous modalities. For instance, physical activity logs can be mapped to self-reported states like "energetic" or "fatigued". Heart Rate Variability (HRV) or stressful moments recorded by a smartwatch can be synchronized and cross-checked with facial expression data from video to analyze emotional reactions during specific activities.

Phase 3. Event Log Creation: This phase focuses on converting the integrated data into an event log suitable for PM. This log typically includes a sequence of events, each containing a case identifier, activity, and timestamps, potentially enriched with additional relevant contextual layers such as temporal, spatial, physiological, and environmental information captured from diverse data modalities. These contextual elements are added as variables, including device source, location, emotional state, activity type, and quality of activity completion. The resulting log provides a comprehensive view of what occurred and under what conditions, supporting advanced process discovery, behavioral pattern recognition, and in-depth analysis of human behavior in dynamic environments.

Step 3: Contextualized Process Discovery. The objective of this step is to allow the discovery of context-aware process models at varying levels of abstraction, ranging from general overviews to detailed behavioral representations. The input of this step is the event log, and the output is a set of context-aware process models. This step utilizes a previously developed contextualization method [1] to enhance the interpretability of process models. The method employs activity specialization hierarchies to refine activity labels using relevant contextual variables. This step is organized into three phases:

Phase 1. Create activity specialization hierarchy: This phase constructs a hierarchical structure for specialized activities by utilizing contextual details in five sub-tasks: (1) selecting activities to be specialized based on their relevance to the analysis objectives, (2) determining context variables associated with each specialized activity, (3) prioritize context variables by assigning an order of importance to them, which will determine the structure of the specialization hierarchy, (4) categorize context variable values by grouping possible values of each context variable into meaningful categories, and (5) generate the specialization hierarchy by combining the selected activities with the ordered context values to form a tree structure, where each node represent a more context-specific version of the parent activity.

Phase 2. Process discovery using hierarchy structure: In this phase, the hierarchy tree is used for process discovery through: (1) level selection: analysts choose a level of granularity based on the analysis objectives, and (2) model generation: where discovery techniques are applied to the event log using activity labels at the selected level.

Additionally, this paper contributes to our previous contextualization method by introducing an extension that incorporates custom Key Performance Indicators (KPIs) defined by domain experts to enhance the clarity of discovered process models in visualizations. These expert-driven and custom KPIs improve the interpretability of process models by emphasizing the behavioral or contextual dimensions most relevant to the problem domain and analysis objectives. KPIs should be defined based on the attributes or features that experts aim to understand better. For example, to investigate stressful situations in work environments, experts might define KPIs related to the frequency of tasks per day and the transitions between them, as indicators for comparing the pressure on different roles within a company. These KPIs will then be calculated and illustrated in the process models discovered from logs, enabling further analysis.

Phase 3. Interpretation of Results: The final phase focuses on interpreting the contextualized process models discovered in the previous phase. The models are evaluated to identify consistent patterns across similar contexts, variations in process paths influenced by execution with different context variables, and any anomalies or deviations that occur under specific conditions. These insights can uncover previously hidden correlations between different contexts and process behaviors.

Step 4: Analysis and Visualization. The objective of the last step involves visualizing and understanding the result of contextualized process models over time. This step takes contextualized process models as inputs and generates output in the form of visualizations that help identify key trends, patterns, and relationships within the data. There are different visualization techniques, such as those presented in [16,31], which can be used to support multi-level analysis. Alternatively, domain-specific or customized visualizations can be developed to highlight key dimensions relevant to the use case. In this paper, we use a calendar view to provide a temporal visualization perspective that supports intuitive exploration of human behavior over time. It enables the identification of trends in specialized activities by highlighting patterns linked to specific contextual values in the dataset.

4 Case Study Evaluation

To evaluate our proposed method, we present a case study from an IoT application in AAL and evaluate it in this section.

4.1 AAL Case Study

We applied the HB-UniContex method to the problem of analyzing the relationship between daily behavior and mood states in an AAL domain. The goal is to enrich behavioral process models with context-specific information, including mood indicators, to enhance the interpretability of behavior changes over time. Utilizing HB-UniContex in this case study enables a more detailed examination of whether the observed behavioral patterns reflect normal variations, contextual influences or concerning deviations from typical behavior that require thorough inspection by health experts. This case study leverages a real-world dataset capturing the daily behavior of a 60-year-old subject living alone over a period of 146 d [24][1]. We utilized two data sources: a smart sensing system and human-generated inputs, to capture various dimensions of the individual's behavior, environment and internal state. The dataset contains behavioral patterns alongside key contextual events, including the COVID-19 lockdown on day 44, the Nowruz celebration beginning on day 72, and Ramadan occurring from days 109 to 137. The details of this case study are presented in the following section.

4.2 Evaluation

This section provides a detailed, step-by-step explanation of how the method is applied in the described AAL case study.

Step 1: Data Collection Data sources in the dataset are ambient sensors, a wearable wristband, a smartphone, and daily psychological questionnaires. The ambient sensors comprised 15 binary devices installed on furniture, appliances, and doors. These included Passive Infra-Red (PIR) sensors for detecting motion and presence in rooms such as the bedroom, kitchen, and living room. In addition, there were contact sensors that monitor the opening and closing of doors, a power sensor for detecting TV usage, and a gas sensor for identifying cooking activities. The wristband, a Xiaomi Mi Band-3, provided insights into sleep patterns, recording sleep duration and overall quality. The smartphone recorded application usage, including the names of applications, and their respective start and end times. The daily psychological reports were derived from a questionnaire that was designed by incorporating three well-known psychological questionnaires: the General Health Questionnaire (GHQ-28), Beck Depression Inventory, and the Pittsburgh Sleep Quality Index (PSQI). Each day, this questionnaire was filled based on the subject's responses to questions regarding their social activities, food intake, sleep, relaxation, praying, physical condition, and emotional well-being [10].

Step 2: Preprocessing and Transformation Phase 1. Data Preprocessing: Initially, time synchronization, data format normalization, and data cleaning methods are applied to all datasets. Next, high-level activity events are extracted from ambient sensors using the rule-based abstraction technique outlined in [26]. The preprocessed dataset captured high-level activity labels, such as "Sleeping", "Eating", "Watching TV", "Hygiening", "Cooking", "Sitting" and "Praying", along with their corresponding location contexts. We then process the smartphone log to extract key information, including the application name, and start and end times for each application's usage. For the wristband data, sleep events are monitored to determine the start and end times of sleep, including any interruptions. Additionally, to explore the relationship between behavior and individual mood, we consider happiness as a fundamental aspect of mental health. It is

[1] The dataset is not publicly available but can be requested for research purposes.

influenced by daily activities and reflects subjective well-being, which makes it an ideal context variable for our AAL case study. As a result, happiness-related responses provided by the subject in the daily questionnaires are preprocessed to extract mood contexts. The questionnaire of our dataset assessed happiness in six dimensions: "Not feeling sad", "Being happy", "Enjoying normal daily activities", "Not feeling angry", "Not feeling bored", and "Feeling hopeful about the future".

Phase 2. Data Integration: To create a unified dataset, preprocessed events from each data source were combined based on temporal alignment. Two integration techniques were applied: *vertical concatenation* and *horizontal merging*. First, vertical concatenation is applied to temporally combine events that are semantically unrelated, such as sensor logs and smartphone usage. Second, horizontal merging is used to combine semantically related data, such as sleep quality from the wristband, with sleep activity detected by ambient sensors. For example, sleep events from ambient sensors and the wristband were cross-validated against smartphone usage to subtract awake times caused by interruptions, thereby enhancing accuracy.

Phase 3. Event Log Creation: To facilitate daily behavior analysis, each day was modeled as a separate case in the event log, using the date value as a case identifier. High-level activities, along with their start and end times and contextual data from other sources for each day, were linked together. For instance, smartphone application types were associated with the activities conducted that day, and daily step counts and sleep quality were added as contextual information to the cases. This process resulted in an enriched event log with contextual variables, including activity details and mood data, ready for contextualized process discovery.

Step 3: Contextualized Process Discovery Phase 1. Create activity specialization hierarchy: Based on expert recommendations and prior research [6,22], we identified three key daily activities with behavioral and psychological significance: "Eating", "Sleeping", and "Using Phone". These activities are selected for specialization due to their relevance to daily routines, psychological state and digital behaviors. For each selected activity, we identified relevant contextual variables that support multi-level abstraction within the hierarchy. The chosen variables and their priorities for each activity are as follows: for "Eating", *Meal type* and *Mealtime duration* (based on [22]); for "Sleeping", *Sleep time* and *Sleep quality*; and for "Using Phone",*Type of application*. These contextual variables have the following possible values: *Meal Type*,"Breakfast", "Lunch", or "Dinner"; *Meal Duration*, "Short" (<15 min) or "Normal" (>15 min); *Sleep Time*, "Day" Sleep or "Night" Sleep; *Sleep Quality*, "Good" or "Poor"; *Type of Application*, "Call & Msg", "Entertainment", or "Others". The hierarchical tree that incorporates these specialized activities and their relevant contextual variables is illustrated in Fig. 2.

In parallel, we categorized daily happiness levels by assigning a happiness label to each day based on the subject's responses to happiness-related items in daily questionnaire reports. We defined the following categories: "Sad", indicating lower happiness (68 d in total over the whole period of 146 d in our dataset); "Neutral", indicating a moderate emotional state (68 d in total); and "Happy", representing higher happiness (10 d in total). An example of the final event log for this study is provided in Fig. 3.

Phase 2. Process discovery using hierarchy structure: Using the hierarchy tree, we conducted process discovery with both unspecialized and specialized activities, along with their corresponding contextual attributes and hierarchical levels. The PM4Py[2] library, a powerful tool for discovering process models, was utilized to generate process models in the format of Directly Follows Graphs (DFGs). To visualize the custom-designed DFGs proposed in HB-UniContex, we used Gephi[3], a visualization software that allows us to transform the extracted graphs into visually comprehensible models. In the discovered models, activities are represented as nodes (circles) in the graph, and transitions between activities are visualized as directed edges (arrows). Nodes of specialized activities that share the same context variable are drawn in the same colors to indicate contextual grouping. Additionally, Gephi enables us to enhance the visualization of graphs based on two distinct expert-defined KPIs.

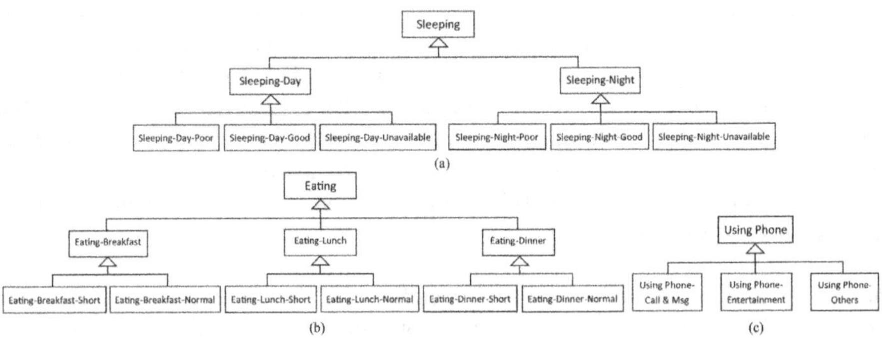

Fig. 2. Hierarchy trees for specialized (a) Sleeping, (b) Eating and (c) Using Phone.

Day	Source	Location/Events	StartTime	EndTime	Duration	Activity	EatingType	Mealtime Duration	PhoneAppType	SleepQuality	SleepType	Happiness
09/01/2020	RawSensorData	BR-Sleeping	2020-01-09 01:37:04	2020-01-09 04:27:05	02:50:01	Sleeping				Poor	Night Sleep	Neutral
09/01/2020	Mobile	Tools	2020-01-09 04:27:05	2020-01-09 04:27:28	00:00:23	Using Phone			Others			Neutral
09/01/2020	Location	Bathroom	2020-01-09 04:45:02	2020-01-09 04:48:59	00:03:57	Hygiening						Neutral
09/01/2020	RawSensorData	BR-Praying	2020-01-09 04:54:03	2020-01-09 06:05:21	01:11:18	Praying						Neutral
09/01/2020	Mobile	Religious	2020-01-09 05:53:04	2020-01-09 05:53:26	00:00:22	Using Phone			Others			Neutral
09/01/2020	RawSensorData	BR-Sleeping	2020-01-09 06:05:21	2020-01-09 08:25:59	02:20:38	Sleeping				Poor	Night Sleep	Neutral
09/01/2020	Location	Bathroom	2020-01-09 08:26:02	2020-01-09 08:27:59	00:01:57	Hygiening						Neutral
09/01/2020	RawSensorData	Cooking	2020-01-09 08:33:04	2020-01-09 09:12:13	00:39:09	Cooking						Neutral
09/01/2020	Mobile	Social Media	2020-01-09 08:49:12	2020-01-09 08:51:17	00:02:05	Using Phone			Entertainment			Neutral
09/01/2020	RawSensorData	K-Eating and Watc	2020-01-09 08:57:52	2020-01-09 09:05:02	00:07:10	Eating	Breakfast	Short				Neutral

Fig. 3. Snapshot of the preprocessed event log with activity and mood contexts.

[2] PM4Py is a Python library for process mining [5].

[3] Gephi is an open source software for graph and network analysis (https://gephi.org/) [4].

The KPIs we considered for visualizing our custom-designed graphs are:

- ***Arrow Thickness:*** The thickness of each arrow shows the frequency of transitions between activities. Thicker arrows represent more frequent transitions, highlighting important and common behavior patterns and routines.
- ***Circle Size:*** The size of each circle corresponds to the average time spent on that activity per day. Larger circles indicate activities that the subject spent more time on doing them, offering a clear view of how the individual's daily time is distributed across different behaviors.

Phase 3. Interpretation of Results: Fig. 4 presents the discovered contextualized process model derived from the unified event log. Blue circles represent the unspecialized activities, while red circles show contextualized variants of "Sleeping", differentiated by sleep duration and quality factors. Yellow circles depict contextualized "Eating" refined by meal type and duration, and green circles represent "Using Phone" categorized by the type of application used.

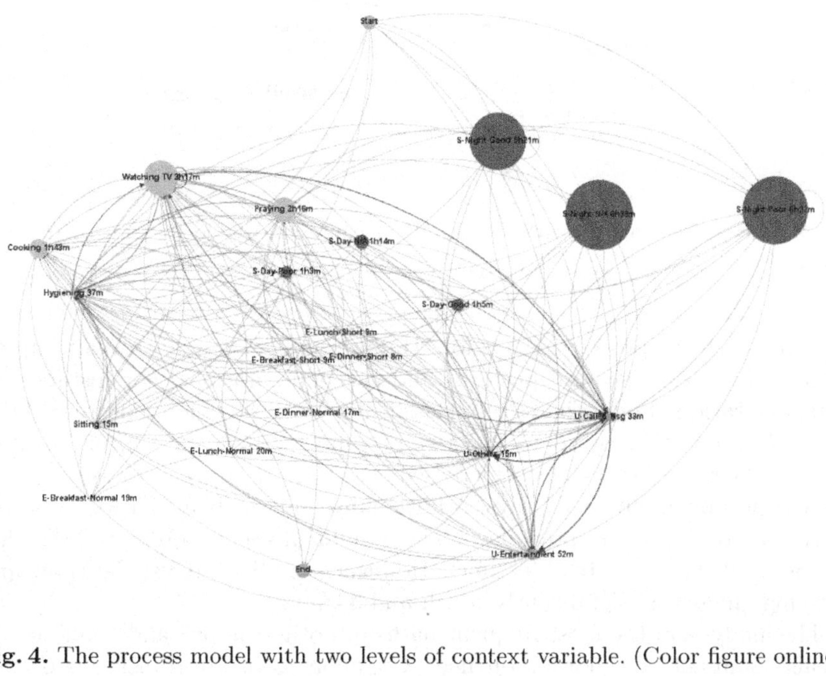

Fig. 4. The process model with two levels of context variable. (Color figure online)

Furthermore, to explore the relationship between daily mood and the daily specialized activities, which is the central focus of this case study, we generated separate process maps for different mood categories. For this analysis, we filtered the log according to mood categories. "Happy" (Fig. 5) and "Sad" (Fig. 6) mood states were selected here as examples. These two emotional extremes provide a clearer understanding of how mood relates to specialized activities. To enhance clarity and emphasize important behavioral patterns, we applied a frequency threshold, displaying only the two most frequent arrows for each activity. This filtering highlights the most common behavioral sequences for each emotional context, reducing visual complexity while highlighting significant differences in the process model.

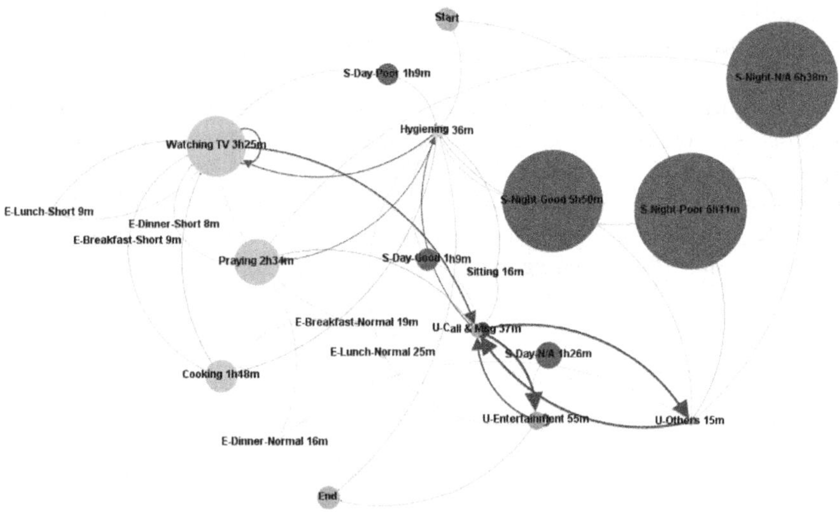

Fig. 5. The process model with two levels of context variable for days with "Sad" mood.

Comparing the process models for "Happy" and "Sad" days reveals interesting insights into behavioral patterns and activity durations. For instance, the average duration of nighttime sleep, classified as "Good" quality, decreased from 6 h and 6 min on "Happy" days to 5 h and 50 min on "Sad" days, while the duration of "Poor" nighttime sleep increased. Daytime sleep, regardless of quality, was also prominent on "Sad" days. Additionally, shifts in behavior were observed in other activities on "Happy" days. The individual spent more time "Watching TV" and allocated 1 h to "Praying". However, on "Sad" days, the time spent "Praying" increased significantly to 2 h and 34 min.

The analysis of the most frequent paths in both "Happy" and "Sad" models reveals dominant behavioral sequences. Common paths are transitions between "Call & Msg" and "Entertainment", as well as "Call & Msg" and "Others" within "Using Phone". Other notable paths are "Hygiening" to "Watching TV" and "Watching TV" to "Call & Msg". These patterns suggest that the individual frequently engaged with her phone while "Watching TV", rather than before or after sleep (those arrows are filtered out due to their low frequency of occurrence). This behavior aligns with medical recommendations aimed at minimizing sleep interruptions and preventing insomnia, highlighting the impor-

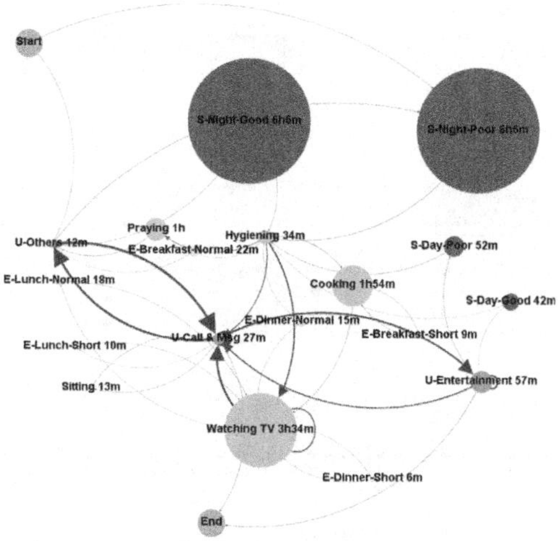

Fig. 6. The process model with two levels of context variable for "Happy" days.

tance of understanding such transitions and individuals' interactions with smart devices.

Step 4: Analysis and visualization: To investigate potential trends in the case study, nighttime sleep was selected as an example. This choice is motivated by our findings from the previous analysis, which highlighted noticeable differences between "Happy" and "Sad" days. For this purpose, we have selected a customized visualization as a calendar view to graphically represent the value of nighttime sleeping in terms of *Sleep quality* to illustrate the variations and patterns of this context.

The calendar view in Fig. 7 focuses on daily duration and quality to identify the overview of the sleeping pattern. To further distinguish between sleep quality, each cell is coded by "Good" (G) and "Poor" (P) through color coding based on total sleep duration, where yellow represents durations of less than 3 h, orange indicates sleep between 3 and 6 h, and red signifies more than 6 h of sleep. The calendar also integrates mood states, providing a view of the factors that may influence sleep patterns and moods. Mood states in the calendar are represented by three types: happy, neutral and sad emoji icons. In addition, certain days are marked with icons representing specific events: the mask icon for days affected by the COVID-19 lockdown, the flower icon for the Nowruz holiday, and a mosque icon for Ramadan-related days. Days with missing sleep data are left unannotated, indicating the absence of available sleep quality information for those days.

This calendar view illustrates that days with "Good" and "Poor" sleep quality are distributed throughout the data collection period and do not completely belong to a specific interval. However, days with better sleep quality are notably more frequent during Nowruz at the end of March and Ramadan in April. These

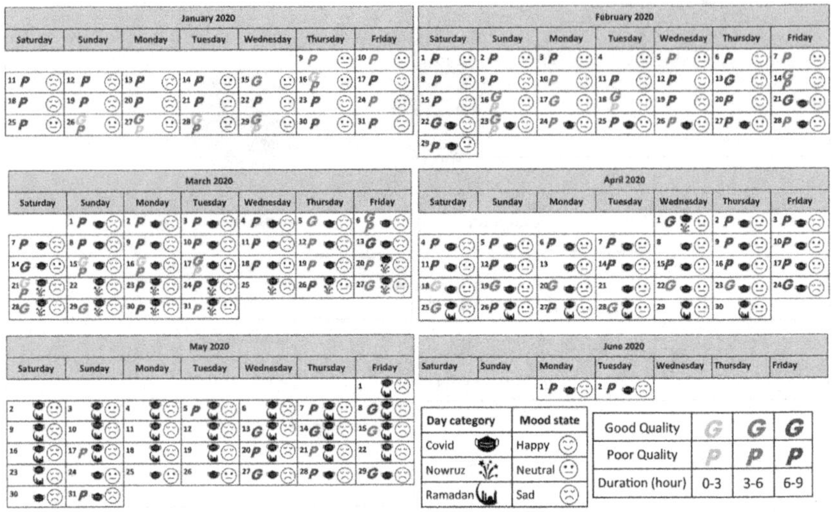

Fig. 7. Calendar view based on mood state and category of day.

trends suggest that cultural and religious events may temporarily influence sleep quality, likely due to changes in daily routines or increased emotional engagement during these times. Interestingly, Fridays (considered weekends in the region from which the data was collected) often correspond to "Happy" moods, showing a possible end-of-week positive trend, regardless of other occasions. However, these improvements in sleep quality tend to be short-lived, as instances of "Poor" sleep continue in the subsequent days. Moreover, the impact of the COVID-19 lockdown is particularly evident from March onward, with days that are consistently associated with "Poor" quality sleep and either "Neutral" or "Sad" moods. This suggests that pandemic-related restrictions likely disrupted regular sleep patterns and adversely affected emotional well-being. Additionally, the increased frequency of "Sad" moods during Ramadan likely reflects emotional or cultural challenges linked to fasting and altered sleep-awake cycles.

5 Discussion

One of the main strengths of HB-UniContex is the ability to integrate heterogeneous data from various sources, enabling a multidimensional perspective on human behavior. This perspective is particularly valuable in domains such as healthcare and behavioral monitoring, where understanding the relationships between multiple factors influencing is crucial to interpret complex processes. Mood analysis, as a perfect example of such a complex process is used in our case study, as it is influenced not only by external factors but also by psychological attributes, including personality traits and cognitive tendencies. Variables such as engagement in physical activities, participation in social interactions, physical health, workload and stress, though not accounted for in this case study, are also significant in impacting mood and are intended for consideration in future research. In addition, the proposed method incorporates contextual information and generates context-rich process models to offer deeper insights into behavior patterns. Furthermore, the study demonstrated the value of custom visualizations in enhancing model interpretability, particularly in the representation of process models based on expert-defined KPIs to show influential factors and calendar views for a detailed investigation of trends over time. Investigating behaviors or activities in relation to various occasions or external events can contribute to a better understanding of how cultural, religious, and global events affect mood states and daily activities. This perspective is valuable in AAL environments, where personalized support systems can be designed to consider the influence of social, temporal, and environmental contexts on individual behavior.

Despite its advantages, the method has several limitations. First, the dependency on IoT and human-generated data introduces challenges related to data quality and completeness. IoT devices may experience technical issues, such as data loss or sensor failures (like the unavailability of sleeping quality for some days). Similarly, human-generated data can be subjective or inconsistent, particularly in self-reported inputs like questionnaires. Individuals may be hesitant to disclose their true feelings to protect their privacy or avoid embarrassment. While the integration of multiple data sources in our case study showed an improvement in overall data reliability and contextual richness, it also introduced technical complexity. The integration phase requires effort to standardize, align, and synchronize heterogeneous data, which needs domain knowledge, careful preprocessing, and often manual intervention. Another challenging aspect involves the method chosen for visualizing contextualized process models and the tools provided for interpretation and further investigation. For instance, illustrating transitions in a process model requires a trade-off: filtering infrequent transitions may create a simplified model that ignores important information, while displaying all transitions may result in a complex and difficult-to-interpret spaghetti-like process model. In our implemented visualization, we aimed to show all activities with the most frequent transitions between them.

While this work considers two types of IoT data and human-generated data, future extensions are needed to support a broader range of data types. To extend the applicability and robustness of the approach, future research should focus on handling various modalities such as continuous numerical data, categorical attributes, video, and image data. In addition, developing a dynamic tool that allows experts to toggle between simplified abstract views and detailed comprehensive models is a potential solution. Such a tool would enable even non-expert users to interactively adjust the level of contextualization according to their specific analytical needs and preferences. Furthermore, the presented method has been validated in a single case study due to the limited availability of public multi-modal datasets to analyze human behavior. We plan to apply this approach to a variety of case studies in different domains and environments to further assess the generalizability of the proposed method.

6 Conclusion

We proposed HB-UniContex that combines diverse datasets from smart sensing systems, multimedia data streams and human-generated data sources, using a contextualization process discovery method to extract contextually enriched, interpretable behavioral models. Using activity specialization hierarchies, we showed how contextual information such as mood states, sleep quality, and activity types can be effectively incorporated into process models to support multi-level behavioral analysis. The method was validated through an in-home monitoring case study, showing its effectiveness in uncovering meaningful relationships between daily activities and emotional states in a smart environment. This research highlights the potential of integrating diverse data modalities, context-aware modeling techniques and interactive visualizations, such as calendar view, to improve process analytics in real-world AAL scenarios.

Acknowledgments. This research was supported by the Flemish fund for scientific research (FWO) with grant number G0B6922N.

References

1. Ahmadi, Z., De Weerdt, J., Serral Asensio, E.: A novel contextualization method for process discovery using activity specialization hierarchies. In: International Conference on Business Process Modeling, Development and Support. pp. 143–155. Springer (2024)
2. Alberdi, A., et al.: Smart home-based prediction of multidomain symptoms related to Alzheimer's disease. IEEE J. Biomed. Health Inform. **22**(6), 1720–1731 (2018)
3. Aramendi, A.A., Weakley, A., Goenaga, A.A., Schmitter-Edgecombe, M., Cook, D.: Automatic assessment of functional health decline in older adults based on smart home data. J. Biomed. Inform. **81**, 119–130 (2018)
4. Bastian, M., Heymann, S., Jacomy, M.: Gephi: an open source software for exploring and manipulating networks. In: Proceedings of the International AAAI Conference on Web and Social Media, vol. 3, pp. 361–362 (2009)
5. Berti, A., van Zelst, S., Schuster, D.: Pm4py: a process mining library for python. Softw. Impacts **17**, 100556 (2023)
6. Chen, Y., Nilforooshan, R., Barnaghi, P.: Predicting poor sleep in people living with dementia: An analysis of in-home activities and physiology measurements during the daytime. Alzheimer's & Dementia **19**(S19) (2023)
7. Di Federico, G., Fernández-Llatas, C., Ahmadi, Z., Shirali, M., Burattin, A.: Identifying variation in personal daily routine through process mining: A case study. In: International Conference on Process Mining, pp. 223–234. Springer (2023)
8. Dogan, O., et al.: Individual behavior modeling with sensors using process mining. Electronics **8**(7), 766 (2019)
9. Elali, R., Kornyshova, E., Deneckère, R., Salinesi, C.: Mining contextual process models using sensors data: a case of daily activities in smart home. In: European, Mediterranean, and Middle Eastern conference on information systems, pp. 409–425. Springer (2022)

10. Falah Rad, M., Shakeri, M., Khoshhal Roudposhti, K., Shakerinia, I.: Probabilistic elderly person's mood analysis based on its activities of daily living using smart facilities. Patt. Anal. Appl. 1–14 (2022)
11. Fernandez-Llatas, C.: Interactive process mining in healthcare. Springer (2021)
12. Fernández-Llatas, C., Benedi, J.M., García-Gómez, J.M., Traver, V.: Process mining for individualized behavior modeling using wireless tracking in nursing homes. Sensors **13**(11), 15434–15451 (2013)
13. Fernandez-Llatas, C., Valdivieso, B., Traver, V., Benedi, J.M.: Using process mining for automatic support of clinical pathways design. Data mining in clinical medicine, pp. 79–88 (2015)
14. Gavric, A., Bork, D., Proper, H.A.: Enriching business process event logs with multimodal evidence. In: Paja, E., Zdravkovic, J., Kavakli, E., Stirna, J. (eds.) The Practice of Enterprise Modeling, pp. 175–191. Springer Nature Switzerland, Cham (2025)
15. Günther, C.W., Van Der Aalst, W.M.: Fuzzy mining–adaptive process simplification based on multi-perspective metrics. In: International Conference on Business Process Management, pp. 328–343. Springer (2007)
16. Guo, Y., Guo, S., Jin, Z., Kaul, S., Gotz, D., Cao, N.: Survey on visual analysis of event sequence data. IEEE Trans. Visual Comput. Graphics **28**(12), 5091–5112 (2022). https://doi.org/10.1109/tvcg.2021.3100413
17. He, Z., Lu, D., Yang, Y., Gao, M., et al.: An elderly care system based on multiple information fusion. J. Healthcare Eng. **2018** (2018)
18. Koschmider, A., Mannhardt, F., Heuser, T.: On the contextualization of event-activity mappings. In: Business Process Management Workshops: BPM 2018 International Workshops, Sydney, NSW, Australia, September 9-14, 2018, pp. 445–457. Springer (2019)
19. Lull, J.J., Bayo, J.L., Shirali, M., Ghassemian, M., Fernandez-Llatas, C.: Interactive process mining in IoT and human behaviour modelling. Interactive process mining in healthcare, pp. 217–231 (2021)
20. Ma'arif, M.R.: Revealing daily human activity pattern using process mining approach. In: 4th International Conference on Electrical Engineering, Computer Science and Informatics (EECSI), pp. 1–5. IEEE (2017)
21. Minor, B., Greeley, C., Holder, R., Thomas, B., Holder, L.B., Cook, D.J.: A feature-augmented transformer model to recognize functional activities from in-the-wild smartwatch data. IEEE J. Biomed. Health Inform. 1–10 (2025). https://doi.org/10.1109/JBHI.2025.3586074
22. Morshed, M., et al.: Food, mood, context: Examining college students' eating context and mental well-being. ACM Trans. Comput. Healthcare **3**(4) (2022)
23. Mounira, Z., Mahmoud, B.: Context-aware process mining framework for business process flexibility. In: Proceedings of the 12th International Conference on Information Integration and Web-based Applications & Services, pp. 421–426 (2010)
24. Rad, M.F., Roudposhti, K.K., Khoobkar, M.H., Shirali, M., Ahmadi, Z., Fernandez-Llatas, C.: Dammi:daily activities in a psychologically annotated multimodal Iot dataset (2024). https://arxiv.org/abs/2410.04152
25. Shirali, M., Ahmadi, Z., Fernández-Llatas, C., Bayo-Monton, J.L.: Synergy of information in multimodal IoT systems–discovering the impact of daily behaviour routines on physical activity level. arXiv preprint arXiv:2403.14707 (2024)
26. Shirali, M., Ahmadi, Z., Fernández-Llatas, C., Bayo Montón, J., Di Federico, G.: An interactive error-correcting approach for IoT-sourced event logs. ACM Trans. Internet Things (2024)

27. Shirali, M., Bayo-Monton, J.L., Fernandez-Llatas, C., Ghassemian, M., Traver Salcedo, V.: Design and evaluation of a solo-resident smart home testbed for mobility pattern monitoring and behavioural assessment. Sensors **20**(24) (2020)
28. Stikic, M., Huynh, T., Van Laerhoven, K., Schiele, B.: ADL recognition based on the combination of RFID and accelerometer sensing. In: 2008 Second International Conference on Pervasive Computing Technologies for Healthcare, pp. 258–263. IEEE (2008)
29. Ullah, I., Youn, H.Y.: Intelligent data fusion for smart Iot environment: a survey. Wireless Pers. Commun. **114**(1), 409–430 (2020)
30. Van Der Aalst, W.M., Dustdar, S.: Process mining put into context. IEEE Internet Comput. **16**(1), 82–86 (2012)
31. Yeshchenko, A., Mendling, J.: A survey of approaches for event sequence analysis and visualization. Inf. Syst. **120**, 102283 (2024). https://doi.org/10.1016/j.is.2023.102283

MDE and LCNC Tools in the Generation of User Interfaces for Different Contexts of Use: A Systematic Literature Review

Susel María Matos Claro[1,2(✉)], Jenny Ruiz de la Peña[2], Estefanía Serral Assension[3], and Monique Snoeck[1]

[1] KU Leuven, Naamsestraat 69, 3000 Leuven, Belgium
{suselmaria.matosclaros,monique.snoeck}@kuleuven.be
[2] University of Holguin, 80100 Holguin, Cuba
jruizp@uho.edu.cu
[3] KU Leuven, Warmoesberg 26, 1000 Brussel, Belgium
estefania.serralasensio@kuleuven.be

Abstract. The development of effective User Interfaces (UIs) is of crucial importance in software engineering, as they facilitate seamless communication between humans and computers. A well-designed UI that is intuitive and easy to use ensures a better user experience and optimises the perception of software. However, the current landscape of UI development is characterised by a wide range of contexts, spanning diverse platforms, user profiles, environments and application domains. This diversity presents a significant challenge, as it increases the complexity and time-consuming nature of UI development. Model-Driven Engineering (MDE) has been used to accelerate the software development process, as well as Low-Code/No-Code (LCNC) tools, which allow developing software without coding, making it accessible to non-experts. To investigate the latest results in the generation of UIs for different contexts of use using MDE or LCNC tools, a systematic literature review (SLR) was conducted. This review analyses the strengths and limitations of the existing approaches and identifies research gaps that have not been fully addressed in the existing literature. These gaps may serve as a foundation for new research initiatives that advance the state of the art in UI development for different contexts of use.

Keywords: Systematic Literature Review · User Interfaces · Model-Driven Engineering · Low-Code/No-Code · Context of Use

1 Introduction

The User Interface (UI) is the most significant point of interaction between the user and the software. Consequently, it has the capacity to influence the user's overall perception of the system, either positively or negatively. The development and maintenance of UIs is an intricate process that requires time, resources and effort. Research has indicated that the development of UIs consumes approximately 45% of the development time, 50% of the implementation time, and 37% of the maintenance time [1].

Published by Springer Nature Switzerland AG 2026
H.-G. Fill et al. (Eds.): PoEM 2025, LNBIP 570, pp. 227–244, 2026.
https://doi.org/10.1007/978-3-032-12063-2_15

In the current landscape, software and UIs are no longer limited to a single environment. As software becomes increasingly embedded in everyday life, ensuring its universal accessibility has become imperative. Software industry is expected to adopt inclusive practices with the goal of eliminating all forms of discrimination, exclusion, and inequality. This requires considering, from the earliest stages of software development, diverse contexts of use, consisting "of the users, tasks and equipment (hardware, software and materials), and the physical and social environments in which a product is used" [2]. As a result, the design and implementation of UIs capable of adapting to multiple contexts of use has become more demanding in terms of resources and time [3, 4].

In the past two decades, Model-Driven Engineering (MDE) has gained relevance in the software industry. MDE focuses on creating and exploiting models, which are abstract representations of the system, to automate code generation, configurations, and other artifacts, reducing manual effort and improving consistency and productivity [5]. MDE helps accelerate the software development cycle by operating at higher levels of abstraction through those models, which can be automatically transformed into other models and, finally, into functional code [6, 7]. In the MDE perspective, the models can capture key information about the UIs characteristics, behaviour, layouts. This can, reduce the inherent complexity and decrease the effort needed to develop them [8].

Low-code/No-code (LCNC) tools enable the creation of applications through graphical UIs, drag-and-drop components, and configuration-based logic, minimizing the need for traditional hand-coding. While some make use of models, they eliminate the use of transformations to intermediate models typical for MDE tools. These tools empower non-technical users to build functional applications reducing dependency on professional programmers. The main characteristic of these tools, which have been a principal factor in their popularity, is the rapid creation, deployment and release of new versions of the created application [9–11].

Considerable time and resources are dedicated to the development of UIs. It is therefore beneficial for companies, developers and users to adopt MDE or LCNC in order to accelerate the software development cycle. Furthermore, they can be used to develop UIs for different contexts of use in a shorter time with less effort. Additionally, the use of models enables the maintenance of UI key information and the preferences of the users. This, in turn, facilitates the development of more flexible, usable and accessible UIs that are compatible with a range of environments, platforms and user profiles.

Recently, Abrahão et al. [12] proposed a conceptual framework for model-based intelligent UI adaptation that identifies challenges and future directions. Amongst the challenges to be addressed by the modelling community, they suggest more research on user models, and specifically addressing the integration of the user model with other models (e.g. user interface model, context model) in order to ensure the traceability and consistency of these models during the adaptation process.

This study provides a structured and comprehensive overview of recent approaches in MDE and LCNC for UI generation across different contexts of use. Unlike previous reviews, this work identifies the lack of comprehensive tools that address all three context dimensions (user, platform, and environment) and highlights the need for inclusive, adaptable solutions for users with diverse capabilities. The goal is to address this challenge and progress from model-based to model-driven engineering of UI.

To identify key results in the field of MDE tools and methods or LCNC tools that allow to generate UIs for different contexts of use, we conducted a Systematic Literature Review (SLR) based on Kitchenham et al.'s guidelines [13]. The novelty of our study lies in bridging fragmented perspectives by offering the first systematic review that jointly considers MDE and LCNC approaches while explicitly incorporating all three context dimensions.

This paper is structured as follows: Sect. 2 explores other SLRs and studies that summarise important results, as well as limitations and remaining gaps; Sect. 3 describes the method used to conduct the SLR; Sect. 4 analyses the results and offers answers to the research questions; Sect. 5 provides a discussion and Sect. 6 formulates conclusions and challenges to be addressed by further work.

2 Related Work

This section provides an overview of existing SLRs and comparative studies focused on UI generation, particularly within MDE approaches or LCNC environments. The goal is to identify common trends, tools, and research gaps to inform future developments. In [14] the authors conducted an SLR about mobile UI development techniques to explore the main approaches for this type of UIs. They analysed 30 research studies published between 2014 and 2018 and identified 16 techniques and 12 tools. They concluded that MobiGUITAR and MDA SMARTAPP were the best tools for mobile UIs development. Qt framework, Human Machine Interface framework, AdYou framework, Usability Heuristics and UI Design patterns were identified as the best techniques as they meet a greater number of the criteria they set.

The most frequently used algorithms for developing adaptative web interfaces is investigated in [15] through an SLR. After three stages of reducing the scope, they analysed 10 studies and concluded that Machine Learning (ML) techniques are the most popular to develop adaptative UI for web platforms, both to improve the performance of some task or to improve user experience.

In [16] a systematic mapping study is carried out, reviewing 110 research studies published between 2004 and 2020 to identify limitations in Model Driven UI Development (MDUID). The authors acknowledge the absence of empirical evidence to assess the real impact of MDUID-based approaches on the software development process and on the software product. This limitation is further emphasised by the fact that only 4.4% of the papers include application in an industrial environment.

An SLR to understand the state of the art on Model-driven UI engineering was conducted in [17]. The objective was to understand the application of MDE in the construction and maintenance of UI, and to examine the research conducted in the field. The authors selected 51 research studies executed between 2005 and 2022. One of the conclusions of the study is that, besides the significant number of solutions identified, the majority of studies have concentrated on design time models. Consequently, a significant research challenge is to delve into the use of runtime models to promote the UI's autonomous adaptation. The authors have expressed concern regarding the large number of studies that have not been empirically evaluated.

The research presented in [10] conducted an SLR regarding the adoption of LCNC technologies in citizen development (CD) for digital transformation, and to understand the benefits and challenges of this utilization. The authors identified 40 studies published between 2017 and 2023. They concluded that the adoption of LCNC platforms enables the design and development of simple and usable mobile applications, but that it also faces some challenges such as low scalability and poor supportive infrastructure.

A SLR to understand the challenges of designing UIs for elderly people was conducted in [18]. The authors observe in their review that in all applications domains, the elderly users have vastly different requirement than young users. They also say that solutions that meet those requirements require some level of human-centred design. A notable observation is the lack of solutions addressing cognitive issues in the domain of mobile UIs. They conclude that, giving the small amount of work dedicated to them, older user could benefit from emerging literature and approaches specifically to address higher levels of usability for them.

A notable gap in the extant SLR and related work analysed is the absence of empirical evidence to substantiate the tangible impact of model-driven approaches in multiplatform and usable software production in industry. It is also crucial to acknowledge the growing popularity of LCNC tools in contemporary industrial contexts. It is recognised that the success of these visual environments is highly dependent on the proficiency and expertise of the developers and users involved.

In light of the significance of this domain of study, there is a notable absence of SLRs that provide a comprehensive overview of the current state of the field with regards to multiple contexts of use, including varied environments, user profiles, application domains, and platforms. There are, for this topic, significant aspects that require a novel literature study. The most significant aspect is the recent advances in the use of MDE techniques and LCNC tools for developing UIs in different contexts of use.

To fill the gap left by these prior reviews, our study provides an integrated comparison of methods, scope, and findings across different strands of research. Whereas some reviews concentrate on mobile UIs [14], others highlight adaptive web interfaces [15] or examine model-driven approaches at a general level [16, 17]. Unlike these fragmented perspectives, our review systematically combines MDE and LCNC approaches, while explicitly analysing three dimensions of context (user, platform, environment). This comparative lens enables a more holistic understanding of the strengths, limitations, and remaining gaps across the state of the art.

The investigation of the existing relevant research in this area and the gaps that still remain, constitutes the primary motivation for this research. A further aspect that merits consideration is the identification of studies that specifically address —beside the development for different contexts in terms of environments, platforms and application domains— end users' disabilities. The main research question of this paper is therefore: "What are the needs that are not yet satisfied by the current tools and methods for the generation of UIs for different contexts of use?". In this work, contexts of use refer to the combination of three key dimensions: the characteristics of the user (e.g., age, abilities, preferences), the platform (e.g., mobile, desktop, web), and the environment (e.g., lighting, location, device constraints). Addressing all three dimensions is essential to support inclusive and adaptable UIs: only those solutions addressing these three aspects simultaneously can be classified as truly supporting different contexts of use.

3 Methods

As proposed by Kitchenham et al. [13], the primary considerations before performing a SLR are the objective and the necessity. The primary motivation for this research is to address the incomplete discussion of model-driven approaches for the development of UIs for different contexts by existing SLRs. This section will explain the process of planning and conducting the review.

3.1 Planning the Review

In order to initiate the SLR, it is imperative to define the Research Questions (RQ) that will guide the entire review process. This SLR was conducted to answer the following specific RQ:

RQ1: What are, according to the literature, the main strengths and limitations of MDE approaches for automatic UI generation for different contexts of use?
RQ2: What are, according to the literature, the main strengths and limitations of LCNC platforms for automatic UI generation for different contexts of use?

For searching scientific papers systematically, we used the Scopus database, which contains >90 million records [19] and contains most well-known databases such as IEEE, ACM, and Web of Science. In addition, it has been recognised in methodological literature as a robust source for systematic reviews in software engineering. While the exclusive use of Scopus may limit the inclusion of some relevant papers, its breadth and multidisciplinary coverage ensure that the majority of influential publications in this domain are captured [20]. The keywords and search string were based on the research questions. A manual search was conducted to find keywords related to the research questions and to determine the most appropriate search terms.

Table 1 shows the keywords used and the final search string.

The results obtained from the automatic search in Scopus were evaluated by the researchers based on the title, keywords and abstract. The inclusion criteria focused on studies addressing the automatic generation of UI through MDE or LCNC approaches. Semi-automated approaches were excluded to focus strictly on fully automated solutions

Table 1. Keywords and Search String

Concept	Synonyms or Acronyms
Model-Driven (Include Model-Driven Engineering, Model-Driven Architecture, Model-Driven Development, Model-Driven User Interfaces Development)	Model Driven, Model-Driven
Model-Driven Engineering	MDE
Model-Driven Architecture	MDA
Model-Driven Development	MDD
Model-Driven User Interfaces Development	MDUID
Low-code	Low code, Low-code
No-code	No code, No-code
User interface	User interface, UI
Search String	(TITLE-ABS-KEY ("Model Driven") OR TITLE-ABS-KEY ("Model-Driven") OR TITLE-ABS-KEY ("MDE") OR TITLE-ABS-KEY ("MDA") OR TITLE-ABS-KEY ("MDD") OR TITLE-ABS-KEY ("MDUID") OR TITLE-ABS-KEY ("No code") OR TITLE-ABS-KEY ("No-code") OR TITLE-ABS-KEY ("Low code") OR TITLE-ABS-KEY ("Low-code") AND TITLE-ABS-KEY ("User Interface") OR TITLE-ABS-KEY ("UI"))

that align with the goal of systematic UI generation. To identify which papers are directly related with the area of our research, criteria of inclusion and exclusion were established as follows:

Inclusion criteria: a paper is included if one of the following criteria is satisfied.

- IC1: Research that presents a SLR about automatic generation of UIs.
- IC2: Research that identifies and presents gaps and limitations in the existing UI generation methods and tools.
- IC3: Research that describes a method or tool for the generation of UIs through MDE for different contexts of use.
- IC4: Research that describes a method for the generation of UIs using a LCNC tool or proposing a new LCNC tool for different contexts of use.

Exclusion criteria: a paper is excluded if one of the following criteria is satisfied.

- EC1: Research neither in English nor Spanish

- EC2: Research explaining methods or tools at an early stage of development (idea papers, not implemented research).
- EC3: Research explaining methods or tools using MDE tools unrelated to UIs (Backend part, database, etc.).
- EC4: Research focused only on manual UI design or semi-automatic development or generation.
- EC5: Conference reviews.
- EC6: Paper unavailable online.
- EC7: Short research (less than 5 pages) or lacking or sufficient details, methodology or results.
- EC8: Research that targets very specific contexts of use (e.g. aeronautics, medical, electricity, security systems, construction…) and are not generalizable.

To obtain better results when analysing and standardising the collection of articles selected, it was necessary to develop a data extraction strategy. This data extraction aspects are based on the conceptual reference framework proposed by Abrahão et al. in [12], from which we extracted a list of conceptual properties for UI adaptation a full blown approach would need to address (See Table 2).

Table 2. Data extraction aspects based on the conceptual reference framework proposed in [12]

Conceptual Properties for UI Adaptation	
Who	*Adaptation responsibility* (Who initiate/adapt?)
What	*Adaptation target* (What is being adapted in the UI?)
	UI Type (What type of UI is targeting?)
	UI Modality (How many modalities are incorporated into the UI adaptation?)
	Context coverage (Which part of the context model (User/Environment/Platform) is exploited for the UI adaptation?)
Why	*Adaptation rationale* (Why is adaptation performed?)
Where	*Adaptation location* (Where does adaptation take place?)
	Scopus level (In which level the adaptation occurs?)
	UI abstraction level (In which abstraction level the adaptation occurs?)
When	*Adaptation type* (When does adaptation occurs?)
How	*Adaptation Method* (How is adaptation achieved?)
	Automation level (Which level of UI adaptation is automated?)
	Tool support (What is the automation level provided by the UI adaptation manager?)
Other aspects	*User involvement* (Can user participate in or control adaptation decisions?)

(continued)

Table 2. (*continued*)

Conceptual Properties for UI Adaptation	
Who	*Adaptation responsibility* (Who initiate/adapt?)
	Evaluation (How is adaptation effectiveness evaluated?)
	Challenges addressed (What adoption challenges are targeted?)
	Open issues (What open challenges remains?)

3.2 Conducting the Review

After establishing the reviewing protocol, the next step is to perform the review. The article selection process aligns with the PRISMA 2020 framework [21]. Figure 1 shows the PRISMA flow diagram, providing a structured overview of records identified, screened, and included in the study.

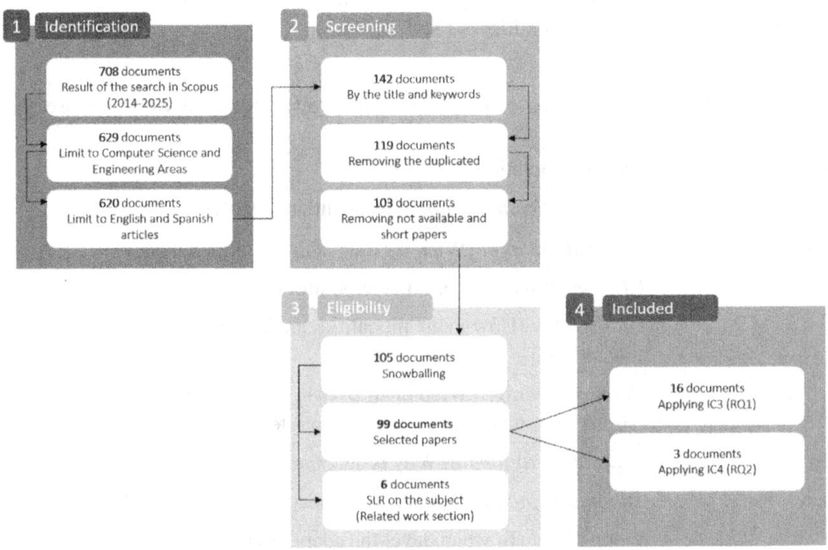

Fig. 1. Steps and activities in the reviewing process

The initial step involved conducting an automatic search in the Scopus database using the search string specified in Table 1. This resulted in the identification of 708 articles published between 2014 and April 2025, of which 629 in Computer Science and Engineering. Next, EC1 was applied, excluding articles written in languages other than English or Spanish, resulting in a collection of 620 documents.

A thorough analysis of the title, abstract, and keywords of each study was conducted, leading to the identification of 142 documents deemed relevant for further consideration. Removing the duplicated articles, as well as the short and not available papers, we obtained 103 documents about the generation of UIs. Two additional relevant papers were added after snowballing. This resulted in the 6 SLRs (IC1) already discussed in Sect. 2, and 99 papers about the generation of UIs. Given the specific focus on solutions for developing UIs for different contexts of use, the 99 selected papers were classified according to the target platform. As illustrated in Fig. 2, only a modest number of 19 papers address three different platforms (mobile, desktop and web applications).

While some solutions target two platforms (such as web and mobile, or desktop and web), we argue that true platform diversity requires support for at least three distinct modalities—desktop, web, and mobile—each of which entails unique technical, ergonomic, and interaction challenges. For instance, desktop applications often support mouse and keyboard inputs, whereas mobile UIs rely on touch gestures and limited screen real estate. Thus, full coverage of platform diversity requires adapting UIs to accommodate all three platforms. The 19 papers were further divided along IC3 and IC4, resulting in eventually 16 papers discussing MDE approaches and 3 presenting a LCNC approach. To address the RQs, the rest of the paper will focus on these 19 papers.

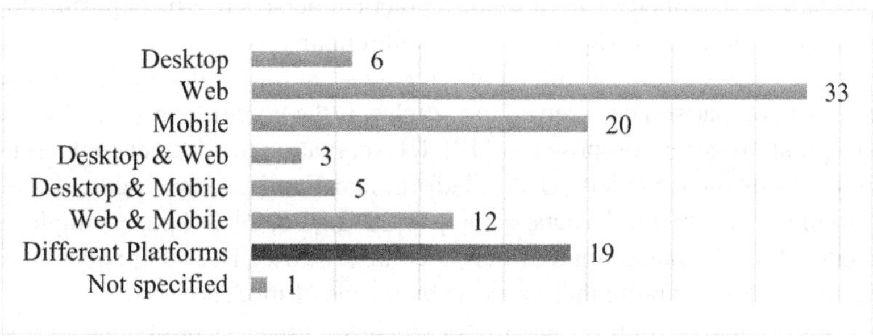

Fig. 2. Classification of the selected paper according to the target platform

4 Results

RQ1: What are, according to the literature, the main strengths and limitations of MDE approaches for automatic UI generation for different contexts of use?

Figure 3 shows the distribution of the 16 MDE publications per year. The graph reveals that the annual publication rate is approximately two or three per year, with zero publication in the last two year, thereby reinforcing the claim that this field remains underexplored.

For a better understanding of the MDE related publications, their content was analysed along the dimensions of Table 2. An extract of some of the principal properties is shown in Table 3. The dimensions offer a direct insight into the functional scope, technical approach and practical validation of each proposal. The complete extracted data is available in an online appendix[1]. The *adaptation target* reveal which part of the UI element are affected, reflecting the depth of adaptation. The *context coverage* reflects the

[1] The appendix is available here.

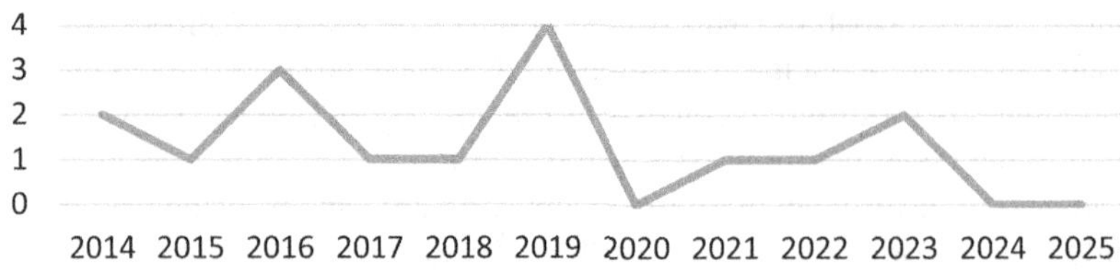

Fig. 3. Distribution of the 16 MDE publications across years.

ability to address different context of use. The *adaptation method* indicates the underlying mechanism, which is key to understand the level of complexity and reusability of the approach. *UI adaptation level* captures how early or late in the design process the adaptation occurs, relevant for integration with MDE workflows. The *adaptation location* further clarifies the system's responsiveness and flexibility. *Automation level* and *tool support* indicate the maturity and readiness for real-world deployment. Meanwhile, *evaluation* and *open issues* provide a practical perspective by exposing how each solution was validated and what limitations still remains.

Given the focus of our research on different context of use, one of the most relevant aspects of the comparison between all the articles, is the *context coverage*. According to the Conceptual Properties proposed by [12], UI Adaptation to different contexts requires a combination of three models: User, Platform and Environment. Figure 4 shows the models implemented by the 16 papers. Only 5 [22, 24, 26, 29, 34] papers implement the three models for UI Adaptation to different context of use. The other papers have only one or two, or do not capture these aspects by means of models.

Most of the analysed proposals do not reach the Final UI in the abstraction level. This indicate that the transformations are often incomplete, requiring additional steps to produce fully functional UIs. The limited presence of the Final UI models reflects a gap in end-to-end automation.

Automation level and *tool support* are crucial factors for real-world adoption of the approaches. *Automation level* is measured on a 1 – 10 scale, where 1 indicates fully manual adaptation and 10 denotes full automation with no human intervention. *Tool support* is assessed on a 0 – 2 scale; 0 means no tool support is provided, 1 indicates partial support and 2 corresponds to full tool availability. Figure 5 include a combined graphic of the two properties of the 16 selected studies.

Among the analysed studies, the works [6] and [33] stand out for achieving the highest scores in both *automation level* (level 9 out of 10) and *tool support* (level 2): both approaches provide highly automated adaptation processes with minimal manual intervention and are supported by mature platforms or tools. Scalability is the most often mentioned open challenged, followed by evaluation.

Another significant aspect (not reflected in the data extraction) is how much has been done to close the development gap between developing for the average users and for people with special needs or elderly people, who are not considered so often. From the 16 analysed papers related to MDE techniques, only 3 [26, 29, 34] of them are addressing those special type of users.

Table 3. Extract from the data collection from the 16 MDE papers

	Adaptation target	*Context Coverage*	*Adaptation method*	*UI abstraction level*	*Adaptation location*	*Automa-tion level*	*Tool Support*	*Evaluation*	*Open issues*
[22]	Content, Presentation, Structure, Navigation, Behaviour	User, Platform, Environment	Model-driven, Ontology-based	Abstract UI, Concrete UI	Client-side	Level 8	Level 2	Case study	Scalability, Evaluation
[23]	Presentation, Structure	User, Platform	Model-driven	Abstract UI, Concrete UI	Client-side	Level 7	Level 2	Case study	Scalability, Legacy integration
[24]	Content, Presentation, Structure	User, Platform, Environment	Model-driven, Role-based	Abstract UI, Concrete UI	Client-side	Level 8	Level 1	Case study	Extensibility, Tool support
[3]	Structure	Not specified	Model-driven	Abstract UI	Design-phase tool	Level 3	Level 1	Case study	Runtime integration
[4]	Structure, Behaviour	User, Environment	Model-driven	Abstract UI, Concrete UI	Client-side	Level 7	Level 2	Case study	Scalability, System integration
[25]	Structure, Behaviour	Platform	Model-driven	Concrete UI	Client-side	Level 7	Level 2	Case study	Scalability, System integration
[26]	Structure, Behaviour	User, Platform, Environment	Model-driven	Abstract UI, Concrete UI	Client-side	Level 7	Level 2	Empirical study	Scalability, Platform integration
[27]	Structure, Presentation	Not specified	Model-driven	Concrete UI, Final UI	Client-side	Level 6	Level 1	Example scenario	Scalability, Extensibility
[28]	Content, Structure, Behaviour	User, Environment	Model-driven, Rule-based	Abstract UI, Concrete UI	Client-side	Level 8	Level 2	Case study	UX, Evaluation
[29]	Presentation, Behaviour	User, Platform, Environment	Model-driven, Rule-based	Concrete UI, Final UI	Client-side	Level 7	Level 0	User study	Privacy, UX improvements, Evaluation
[6]	Presentation, Structure	Platform	Model-driven (parametric transfor-mations)	Abstract UI model, Concrete UI, Final UI	Design-time	Level 9	Level 2	Case study, usability test	User experience, scalability
[30]	Presentation, Structure	Platform, Environment	Model-driven (UsiXML-based)	Abstract UI, Concrete UI (UsiXML)	Design-time	Level 8	Level 1	Case example (prototype demonstra tion)	Real-time adaptation, dynamic context
[31]	Not especified	User, Environment	Model-based	Abstract UI, Concrete UI	Not especified	Level 6	Level 0	No	Conceptual Work
[32]	Presentation, Structure	Platform	Model transfor-mation rules	Abstract UI, Concrete UI	Design-time	Level 8	Level 2	Case study (multi-device scenario)	Real-time adaptation, rule generality
[33]	Presentation, Content	User, Platform, Domain	Ontology-based generation	Abstract UI, Concrete UI	Design-time	Level 9	Level 2	Prototype (ontology-based generator)	Scalability, dynamic context
[34]	Structure, Presentation, Behaviour	User, Platform, Environment	Rule-based integration	Task, Abstract UI, Concrete UI	Design-time, Runtime	Level 8	Level 2	Case study (users with disabilities)	Rule conflict resolution, flexibility

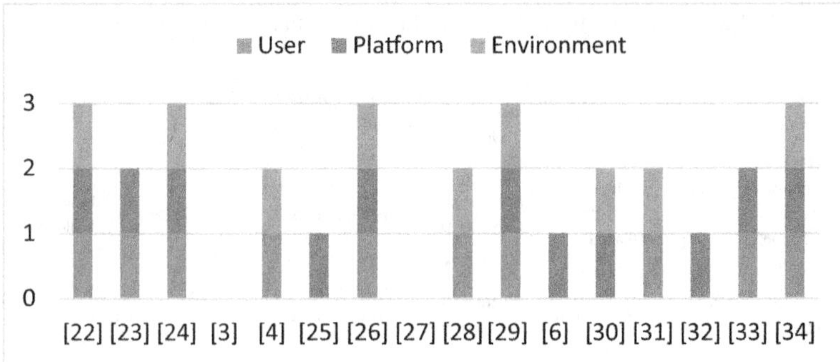

Fig. 4. Context Coverage of the 16 MDE papers

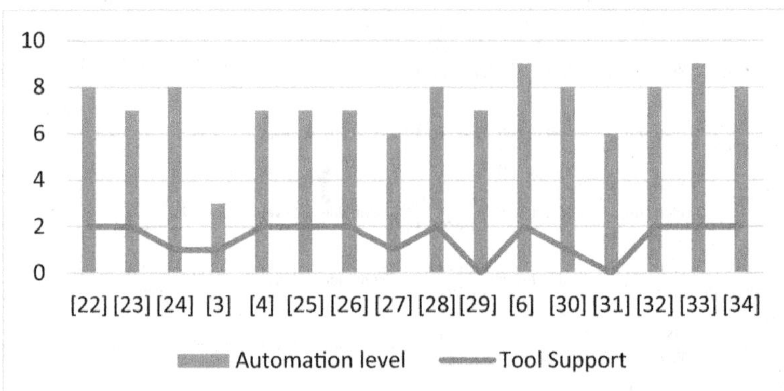

Fig. 5. Automation level & Tool support of the 16 MDE papers

RQ2: What are, according to the literature, the main strengths and limitations of LCNC platforms for automatic UI generation for different contexts of use?

To facilitate a more profound comprehension of the LCNC tools-related publications, we show the extracted data in an appendix[2] and provide an extract of the principal properties of each publication below (Table 4).

A review of the extensive literature reveals a paucity of comprehensive solutions for the parameters analysed. The analysed solutions are limited exclusively to the platform dimension. None of those approaches incorporate user or environment models to the adaptation process. This narrow context coverage implies a reduced capability for personalization and adaptability in real-world scenarios. The approaches under scrutiny are not freely accessible and do not offer the possibility of accessible designs for people with disabilities. Furthermore, the learning curve associated with these tools is typically steep, which can present a significant challenge for individuals lacking expertise.

[2] The appendix is available here.

Table 4. Extract from the data collection from the 3 LCNC papers

	Adaptation target	*Context Coverage*	*Adaptation method*	*UI abstraction level*	*Adaptation location*	*Automation level*	*Tool Support*	*Evaluation*	*Open issues*
[35]	Structure, Behaviour	Platform	Low-code Model Coordination	Abstract UI, Final UI	Design-time	Level 6	Level 2	Case study (collaboration scenario)	Semantic alignment, traceability
[36]	Structure, Content	Platform	Low-code Platform Experimentation	Concrete UI, Final UI	Design-time	Level 5	Level 2	Empirical study with practitioners	Scalability, long-term reuse
[37]	Structure, Presentation	Platform	Template-based generation	Template-based	Design-time	Level 9	Level 2	Use case demonstration	Expressiveness, template evolution

5 Discussion

In today's context, the generation of UIs for different contexts of use with MDE or LCNC tools face significant challenges and aspects that remain unaddressed. This SLR revealed several needs that should be addressed by future research. While numerous solutions exist within the domain of MDE-based UI generation, only a limited number of these address diverse contexts of use, encompassing, users, platforms and environments. This is a significant gap that we believe could be targeted in future research. An additional specific aspect that is insufficiently addressed in the literature is the consideration of diverse user types in terms of age, (dis)abilities, experience and preferences. A solution to this problem would be to find a way to include a more diversified set of users, which could improve the user experience, accessibility and satisfaction with the UIs and software.

The models used for generating UIs tend to lack consideration of crucial aspects concerning the design and position of elements and components. Besides the fact that only 5 publications address the 3 dimensions of context defined by Abrahão et al. in [12], these models also miss important design elements, such as font type, alignment, colour, and visual hierarchy needed to go from an abstract to a final UI. This limitation poses a significant challenge in achieving a UI that is flexible, intuitive, and easily navigable. It is therefore vital that solutions in this field take into consideration UI design aspects crucial for addressing diversity in usability. Furthermore, a significant number of studies lack empirical or practical testing. Moreover, some studies do not specify the programming language in which the UI is generated, or whether the proposed tool or method is free accessible.

A key observation is the variation in adaptation targets, with most approaches focusing on structural and presentational aspects of the UI, while relatively few of them address content-aware adaptation. Regarding adaptation location, most solutions operate at design time, limiting their flexibility to respond dynamically to changing context conditions. In terms of automation level and tool support, only a few studies demonstrate the highest maturity, offering fully supported tools and high degree of automation. In contrast, some studies lack tool implementation or rely on partially automated, designer-driven processes, reducing their practical applicability. The open issues common to several studies, such as the need for scalability, dynamic adaptation and expressiveness of modelling, remain critical challenges for advancing this research field.

It is widely acknowledged that LCNC tools facilitate the development of fully functional, multiplatform applications by individuals with limited to no experience in software development. Also in this domain, the literature has highlighted certain drawbacks associated with these tools, that are also confirmed by personal experience with these tools. A significant dependency on the platform is an inherent feature of LCNC tools, and any alterations or issues with the platform can have a substantial impact on the software developed with it. When considering the framework suggested by Abrahão et al. [12], a notable drawback is the lack of use of explicit models for context, which makes a systematic approach to context adaptation quite difficult. Furthermore, the use of LCNC tools often comes with limitations in terms of the control over the source code of the developed applications, as most of these tools are commercial platforms that may require payment for their use or to unlock key features. A further salient issue is the learning curve inherent to these tools, which is often steep for unexperienced users.

From a practical perspective, the findings of this review underline significant implications for industry. The lack of empirical validation restricts the adoption of many MDE solutions, while the platform-dependence of LCNC tools pose challenges for practitioners. These gaps affect scalability, accessibility, and long-term maintainability of UI solutions. By identifying these issues, our review provides a roadmap for practitioners to anticipate risks and for tool developers to prioritise improvements.

Performing a SLR is not exempt of threats. The selection of digital libraries and the construction of search strings can affect the results obtained, necessitating meticulous planning to ensure optimal outcomes. For the purposes of this research, the Scopus database was selected on the basis of its extensive database of records covering content of many other databases. However, it is important to note that conducting the search exclusively in Scopus may limit the validity of results obtained. To enhance the rigor of this study in the future, we propose the incorporation of the search in additional databases, such as IEEE, ACM and Web of Science. The construction of the search string was undertaken with consideration of all factors deemed pertinent. However, it should be noted that this does not provide an assurance that all relevant studies in the field have been included in the results. Grey literature (e.g., technical reports, theses) was not included, following common SLR practices to ensure quality and replicability.

Snowballing is a common step in conducting an SLR that helps to overcome the limitations of search strings and databases. For this research, we performed this step, but we only found two relevant works [18, 34]. When reviewing the work referenced in the 19 papers analysed, some papers were out of scope in terms of date (before 2014) and the others were already included in our selected papers. These results seem to suggest that the original search was of decent quality. Nevertheless, deeper snowballing could be performed in further improvements of this study.

Another potential threat to validity is the set of inclusion and exclusion criteria that has been defined. Specifically, IC3 and IC4 focused on the development of UIs for different contexts of use. It is imperative to acknowledge that studies addressing fewer than three target platforms have been excluded. This may be a limitation for the inclusion of articles with perspective to address different contexts in the future.

6 Conclusion and Research Challenges

The UI is a fundamental component of a software system, responsible for facilitating effective communication between the user and the system. As discussed above, a significant challenge and gap observed in the literature pertains to the paucity of solutions that address diverse contexts of use. A preponderance of MDE studies confines their scope to a single platform.

The analysis reveals significant variability in how adaptation is conceptualized, implemented and supported across different proposals. While there is clear progress in automation and tool maturity in some works, many approaches still exhibit limitations in flexibility, context-awareness and empirical validation. Furthermore, we notice a lack of attention to the needs of users. Indeed, only a small number of studies take into account senior or disabled people. The use of models allows to keep information about user preferences, thereby facilitating the creation of more accessible and flexible UIs. Finally, there is a lack of thorough validation and the use of proprietary and closed-source technology hamper the uptake of proposed solutions. All this presents significant gaps and challenges that researchers and developers may address in future work.

The LCNC tools have the potential to be a significant advancement in the development of multiplatform UIs. However, they have significant disadvantages related mainly to the access to source code, platform dependency, the commercial nature of many of them, and the steep learning curve for inexperienced users. Moreover, the lack of openness and the lack of integration of user and environment models, makes it difficult to incorporate support for various kinds of disabilities. In summary, the main research challenge that remains to be addressed is the creation tools that allow generating code for multiple contexts of use and also allow incorporating support for users with special needs, while providing full transparency on the code generation process and the generated code.

It is evident that none of the 19 papers reviewed in this research fully comply with the aspects analysed. This finding underscores the persistent absence of comprehensive solutions for the development of UIs that are suitable for different contexts of use, and that take into account the needs of special groups of users (such as people with disabilities or senior people). Future work should focus on bringing gaps between model-based reasoning and runtime adaptability, enhancing semantic interoperability across adaptation methods.

Looking forward, we identify several promising directions for research. First, bridging the gap between model-based reasoning and runtime adaptability remains a crucial challenge, particularly for dynamic and context-aware environments. Second, there is a need for tools that natively integrate accessibility features, supporting diverse user groups such as the elderly and people with disabilities. Third, advancing open-source and transparent platforms could reduce dependency on proprietary LCNC solutions and foster wider adoption. By addressing these directions, future research can contribute to more inclusive, flexible, and sustainable UI generation across multiple contexts of use with all dimensions (user, platform and environment). Future research should be validated in collaboration with industry, for instance by exploring integration with LCNC platforms such as Mendix or Microsoft PowerApps.

References

1. Paternò, F.: Concepts and design space for a better understanding of multi-device user interfaces. Univ. Access Inf. Soc. **19**, 409–432 (2020)
2. ISO 9241–210 Ergonomics of human-system interaction — Part 210: Human-centred design for interactive systems (2019). www.iso.org
3. Lumertz, P.R., Ribeiro, L., Duarte, L.M.: User interfaces metamodel based on graphs. J. Vis. Lang. Comput. **32**, 1–34 (2016)
4. Jaouadi, I., Ben Djemaa, R., Ben-Abdallah, H.: A model-driven development approach for context-aware systems. Softw. Syst. Model **17**(4), 1169–1195 (2018). https://doi.org/10.1007/s10270-016-0550-0
5. Brambilla, M., Cabot, J., Wimmer, M.: Model-Driven Software Engineering in Practice, 2nd ed. (2017)
6. Bouraoui, A., Gharbi, I.: Model driven engineering of accessible and multi-platform graphical user interfaces by parameterized model transformations. Sci. Comput. Program. **172**, 63–101 (2019)
7. Whittle, J., Hutchinson, J., Rouncefield, M.: The state of practice in model-driven engineering. IEEE Softw. **31**(3), 79–85 (2013)
8. Aquino, N.M., Cernuzzi, L.C., Pastor, O.: Applying transformation templates to diversify user interfaces generated by model-driven engineering (2018)
9. Rymer, J.R.: The forrester wave: low-code platforms for business developers (2019)
10. Ajimati, M.O., Carroll, N., Maher, M.: Adoption of low-code and no-code development: a systematic literature review and future research agenda. J. Syst. Software **222** (2025)
11. Hagel, N., Hili, N., Schwab, D.: Turning low-code development platforms into true no-code with LLMs. In: Proceedings: MODELS 2024 - ACM/IEEE 27th International Conference on Model Driven Engineering Languages and Systems: Companion Proceedings, pp. 876–885 (2024)
12. Abrahão, S., Insfran, E., Sluÿters, A., Vanderdonckt, J.: Model-based intelligent user interface adaptation: challenges and future directions. Softw. Syst. Model. **20**(5), 1335–1349 (2021)
13. Kitchenham, B., Charters, S.M.: Guidelines for performing systematic literature reviews in software engineering (2007). https://www.researchgate.net/publication/302924724
14. Qasim, I., Azam, F., Anwar, M.W., Tufail, H., Qasim, T.: Mobile user interface development techniques: a systematic literature review. In: 2018 IEEE 9th Annual Information Technology, Electronics and Mobile Communication Conference, IEMCON 2018, pp. 1029–1034 (2018)
15. Da Silva, M.R., Leite, L.L., Garcia Costa Dos Santos, G.L.: Algorithms for the development of adaptive web interfaces: a systematic literature review. In: 2022 17th Latin American Conference on Learning Technologies, LACLO 2022, Institute of Electrical and Electronics Engineers Inc. (2022)
16. Mejias, J.C., Silega, N., Noguera, M., Rogozov, Y.I., Lapshin, V.S.: Model-driven user interface development: a systematic mapping. In: Communications in Computer and Information Science, pp. 114–129. Springer Science and Business Media Deutschland GmbH (2022). https://doi.org/10.1007/978-3-031-24709-5_9
17. Erazo-Garzón, L., Suquisupa, S., Bermeo, A., Cedillo, P.: Model-driven engineering applied to user interfaces. A systematic literature review. In Communications in Computer and Information Science, pp. 575–591. Springer Science and Business Media Deutschland GmbH (2023). https://doi.org/10.1007/978-3-031-24985-3_42
18. Dodd, C., Athauda, R., Adam, M.: Designing user interfaces for the elderly: a systematic literature review review. https://aisel.aisnet.org/acis2017/61
19. Deeva, G., Bogdanova, D., Serral, E., Snoeck, M., De Weerdt, J.: A review of automated feedback systems for learners: classification framework, challenges and opportunities. Comput. Educ. **162** (2021)

20. Mongeon, P., Paul-Hus, A.: The journal coverage of web of science and scopus: a comparative analysis
21. Page, M.J., et al.: The PRISMA 2020 statement: an updated guideline for reporting systematic reviews (2021)
22. Zouhaier, L., Hlaoui, Y.B., Ben Ayed, L.J.: Generating accessible multimodal user interfaces using MDA-based adaptation approach. In: Proceedings - International Computer Software and Applications Conference, pp. 535–540. IEEE Computer Society (2014). https://doi.org/10.1109/COMPSAC.2014.76
23. Yigitbas, E., Fischer, H., Sauer, S.: Model-based user interface development for adaptive self-service systems (2014)
24. Akiki, P.A., Bandara, A.K., Yu, Y.: Engineering adaptive model-driven user interfaces. IEEE Trans. Software Eng. **42**(12), 1118–1147 (2016)
25. Gotti, S., Mbarki, S., Gotti, Z., Laaz, N.: A model driven approach for multi-platform execution of interactive UIS designed with IFML. Int. J. Comput. **18**(3), 293–306 (2019)
26. Bendaly Hlaoui, Y., Zouhaier, L., Ben Ayed, L.: Model driven approach for adapting user interfaces to the context of accessibility: case of visually impaired users. J. Multimodal User Interfaces **13**(4), 293–320 (2019). https://doi.org/10.1007/s12193-018-0277-z
27. Sajji, A., Rhazali, Y., Hadi, Y.: An approach to automate generation of graphical user interfaces through IFML. In: Procedia Computer Science, pp. 621–626. Elsevier B.V. (2022). https://doi.org/10.1016/j.procs.2022.03.081
28. Zouhaier, L., BenDalyHlaoui, Y., Ben Ayed, L.: Adaptive user interface based on accessibility context. Multimed Tools Appl. **82**(23), 35621–35650 (2023). https://doi.org/10.1007/s11042-023-14390-5
29. Wickramathilaka, S., Mueller, I.: Addressing age-related accessibility needs of senior users through model-driven engineering. In: Proceedings - 2023 IEEE/ACM 16th International Conference on Cooperative and Human Aspects of Software Engineering, CHASE 2023, pp. 121–126 (2023)
30. Tanaka, S., Iwata, H., Shirogane, J., Fukazawa, Y.: Development support of user interfaces adaptive to use environment. In: ACM International Conference Proceeding Series, pp. 223–228 (2019)
31. Taktak, H., Moussa, F.: Context-aware servUI: a conceptual method for user interfaces and associated services generation. In: Proceedings of IEEE/ACS International Conference on Computer Systems and Applications, AICCSA, pp. 856–862. IEEE Computer Society (2017)
32. Raneburger, D., Kaindl, H., Popp, R.: Model transformation rules for customization of multi-device graphical user interfaces. In: EICS 2015 - Proceedings of the 2015 ACM SIGCHI Symposium on Engineering Interactive Computing Systems, pp. 100–109 (2015). https://doi.org/10.1145/2774225.2774839
33. Braham, A., Khemaja, M., Buendía, F., Gargouri, F.: User interface adaptation through ontology models and code generation. In: Communications in Computer and Information Science, pp. 225–236. Springer Science and Business Media Deutschland GmbH (2021). https://doi.org/10.1007/978-3-030-92325-9_17
34. Miñón, R., Paternò, F., Arrue, M., Abascal, J.: Integrating adaptation rules for people with special needs in model-based UI development process. Univ. Access Inf. Soc. **15**(1), 153–168 (2016)
35. Pacheco, J., Garbatov, S., Goulao, M.: Improving collaboration efficiency between UX/UI designers and developers in a low-code platform. In: Companion Proceedings - 24th International Conference on Model-Driven Engineering Languages and Systems, MODELS-C 2021, pp. 138–147. Institute of Electrical and Electronics Engineers Inc. (2021)

36. Gottschalk, S., Bhat, R., Weidmann, N., Kirchhoff, J., Engels, G.: Low-code experimentation on software products. In: Proceedings - ACM/IEEE 25th International Conference on Model Driven Engineering Languages and Systems, MODELS 2022: Companion Proceedings, pp. 798–807 (2022)
37. Lourenço, H., Ferreira, C., Costa Seco, J., Parreira, J.: OSTRICH: a rich template language for low-code development (extended version). Softw. Syst. Model **22**(5), 1645–1663 (2023)

ContextER: An Entropy-Based Contextualized Process Discovery Approach to Balance Interpretability and Complexity

Zahra Ahmadi(✉), Jochen De Weerdt, and Estefanía Serral Assension

Research Centre for Information Systems Engineering (LIRIS), KU Leuven, Warmoesberg 26, 1000 Brussels, Belgium
{zahra.ahmadi,jochen.deweerdt, estefania.serralasensio}@kuleuven.be

Abstract. Process Mining (PM) is a technique with several applications, including process discovery, which involves extracting process models from event logs that reflect how processes are actually executed. However, the resulting models are often difficult to interpret, not only due to the complexity and variability of real-world processes but also because the event logs lack sufficient information about the process. Context variables in event logs, such as resource or location, can be used to enrich the process by contextualization, making it more understandable. Selecting the appropriate level of contextual detail remains a significant challenge, as excessive contextualization can lead to complex models, while insufficient detail can obscure important insights into the process. This paper addresses this gap by proposing an entropy-based approach for context-aware process discovery, called **Context**ualization using **E**ntropic **R**elevance (ContextER). The approach utilizes the Entropic Relevance (ER) metric to evaluate and propose contextualization that balances informativeness and complexity automatically. By evaluating the model ER, we can identify the models that optimize interpretability without hiding essential information. We demonstrate the effectiveness of the approach through a real-world case study, showing that it leads to more comprehensible and insightful process models.

Keywords: Process Mining · Contextualization · Entropy-Based · Model Interpretability · Entropic Relevance

1 Introduction

Process Mining (PM) is a data-driven discipline that derives process models from event logs, providing insights into how processes are executed and supporting tasks such as discovery, conformance checking, and performance analysis. While PM offers powerful tools for discovering and improving processes, the high variability and complexity of real-world scenarios can result in overly

H.-G. Fill et al. (Eds.): PoEM 2025, LNBIP 570, pp. 245–259, 2026.
https://doi.org/10.1007/978-3-032-12063-2_16

intricate models that are difficult to interpret and analyze. To enhance model interpretability, contextualization in PM has been proposed [12]. This involves incorporating additional information from context variables, such as resources or case attributes, that influence process behavior [6]. One promising method is "Activity Specialization Hierarchies", which hierarchically refines specialized activity labels based on context variables in the event log, creating context-aware process models [1]. Consider a service request process that includes the generic activity *Handle request*. The execution of this activity may vary significantly depending on contextual variables such as the *request type*, *priority level* or *client type*. For instance, *Handle request* may be completed quickly if the request is high-priority or submitted by a VIP client, whereas standard requests might require additional follow-up steps. Specializing the activity according to these contextual variables can lead to more informative discovered process models.

However, determining the optimal level of activity specialization presents a significant challenge. Although deeper specialization levels can provide more meaningful and detailed representations of the process, they may also increase model complexity and reduce interpretability. Therefore, selecting the appropriate level of specialization is crucial to striking the right balance between complexity and interpretability, ensuring that models remain insightful and suitable for effective analysis. In practice, this trade-off becomes even more challenging when multiple contextual variables are involved, as the number of possible specialization combinations increases rapidly.

The specialization approach proposed in [1] relies on expert knowledge to determine appropriate levels of activity refinement based on contextual variables. While expert-driven guidance can yield valuable results, the process is often time-consuming, not easily scalable, and influenced by individual expert perspectives and domain-specific assumptions. This lack of automation limits the approach's applicability in large or evolving process environments. Automating the level selection step is therefore essential to ensure scalability and consistency across diverse and dynamic processes.

To address this gap, we propose an automated entropy-based approach for determining the most suitable level of activity specialization, **Context**ualization using **E**ntropic **R**elevance (ContextER) approach. Our goal is to generate models with lower overall ER, which tend to exhibit more structured and interpretable behavior. By systematically evaluating all specialization levels defined by experts, ContextER identifies those that offer the best trade-off between complexity and interpretability by suggesting a model which is not more complex but provides essential information about the process. It can support more scalable and consistent contextualization. We use an entropy measure to support this selection process, Entropic Relevance (ER), which quantifies the unpredictability of trace behavior. We evaluate this approach using a real-world case study, which focuses on analyzing bees' behavior. Through this case study, we show how the proposed approach produces more interpretable and informative models by identifying specialization levels that minimize ER.

The remainder of this paper is structured as follows: Sect. 2 reviews related work. Section 3 reviews ER measure. Section 4 details the proposed approach. The case study, along with its evaluation and results, is presented in Sect. 5. Key discussion points are explored in Sect. 6, and conclusions are drawn in Sect. 7.

2 Related Work

Understanding and managing complexity is a significant challenge in PM, as it directly impacts the quality and interpretability of the discovered models. This section reviews related work in two key areas: (1) the complexity of process models, and (2) the use of entropy as a complexity measure.

2.1 Complexity of Process Models

Recent research has focused on both the structural complexity of process models and behavioral complexity present in event logs. Several studies have examined how this model complexity affects comprehensibility and practical usability. In this context, the relationship between log complexity and model quality has been studied using graph-based complexity measures, including a proposal for an entropy-based metric that uses structural variability [4]. Other work has introduced gateway complexity indicators to assess their influence on model understandability and modifiability, given the critical role of gateways in ensuring correctness [11]. An alternative approach builds on control structures and workflow patterns to define a complexity metric that offers greater granularity and responsiveness to structural changes compared to traditional measures [13]. Furthermore, structural properties have also been linked to the likelihood of formal errors, identifying early warning indicators for modeling flaws [8].

A systematic review of graph-based metrics recommends using measures such as restrictiveness, cyclomatic number, and tree count to capture structural intricacies in business process models [7]. Among the various complexity metrics, we chose entropy due to its ability to capture behavioral variability in a quantifiable and scalable way. It measures uncertainty in execution paths or transition patterns, suitable for analyzing event logs and discovered models. This makes entropy a powerful metric for our work, especially in the context of selecting activity specializations that balance complexity with interpretability.

2.2 Entropy in PM

Entropy has gained increasing attention in PM to quantify uncertainty, behavioral variability, and conformance checking between process models and event logs. It has been applied to measure structural complexity and behavioral unpredictability in processes and enables the evaluation of how diverse the observed executions are, how deterministic a process is, and how well a model reflects the actual behavior recorded in event logs.

Recent work has used entropy-based methods for conformance checking. For instance, entropy metrics have been employed to evaluate precision and recall by comparing observed and modeled behavior using stochastic or deterministic representations [9,10]. Additionally, entropy has also been applied to measure variability in traces and transitions to guide modeling decisions [5]. A particularly relevant application is the use of entropy for evaluating transition patterns in directly-follows graphs (DFGs), capturing the complexity of control flow in discovered models. Moreover, other approaches apply entropy at the trace level, using measures such as Entropic Relevance to assess the average unpredictability of traces based on transition probabilities [3]. These metrics provide scalable and quantitative insights into process models.

This paper uses an entropy metric not only to evaluate process models but also to guide the selection of activity specializations that optimize interpretability. It serves as a direct means of assessing interpretability, where a lower value indicates more structured and comprehensible models. Furthermore, because this is a numeric metric, it enables the evaluation of alternative specialized models, allowing us to systematically identify those that best balance detail and simplicity. The entropy-based measures used in our approach are introduced in detail in Sect. 3.

3 Preliminaries

This section defines the entropy-based metric known as Entropic Relevance (ER), along with its biased version, which is used in our approach.

ER measures the unpredictability of trace behavior by analyzing transition likelihoods across the entire log [3]. It is based on the Minimum Description Length principle and evaluates how well the observed traces can be encoded using transition probabilities. A lower ER score shows more regular, easily understood behavior, while a higher score suggests higher variability or complexity in the model. This makes ER a suitable metric for comparing different levels of activity specialization as it shows how specialization has an impact on behavioral clarity. It is calculated by following steps in this paper.

Step 1: Extract unique traces. First, all distinct trace variants which represent unique sequences of activities from start to end are identified from the event log. Then their frequencies are calculated to count the occurrences for each variant.

Step 2: Extract transitions and count frequencies. For each directly-follows pair $s \rightarrow n$ in a trace, the total number of occurrences across all traces is calculated. Each pair represent a transition from activity s to activity n, and frequencies are based on total occurrences in the event log, not per individual trace.

Step 3: Compute transition probabilities. For each extracted transition between two activities (nodes), the transition probability is calculated using the following formula:

$$P_{s\to n} = \frac{\text{Frequency of } (s \to n)}{\sum_{\text{all transitions on s}} \text{Frequencies}} \tag{1}$$

This probability reflects the likelihood of moving from activity s to activity n, normalized by the total number of transitions originating from s.

Step 4: Compute probability of each trace. To calculate the probability of each trace, the transition probabilities of all directly-follows pairs within the trace are multiplied:

$$P_{\text{trace}} = \prod P_{s\to n} \tag{2}$$

Step 5: Bias correction (Optional). To remove structural bias introduced by the Directly-Follows Graph (DFG), a bias correction is applied by comparing each trace's actual probability to its theoretical maximum. This ensures that the resulting value reflects behavioral uncertainty independent of the DFG structure. Let P_{real} be the actual probability of a trace, and P_{max} the maximal achievable probability. The bias-corrected probability is then calculated as:

$$P_{\text{bias}} = \frac{P_{\text{real}}}{P_{\text{max}}} \tag{3}$$

Step 6: Compute total entropic relevance. For each trace, the original (or bias-corrected) probability is used to compute its contribution to the entropic relevance. This is done by applying the following formula:

$$ER_{\text{sum}} = \sum_{i=1}^{N} (-\log_2 P_{\text{trace}_i} \times f_i) \tag{4}$$

where P_{trace_i} is the probability of the ith trace, f_i is its frequency, and N is the number of distinct traces.

Step 7: Normalize entropic relevance. The final ER is calculated by:

$$ER = \frac{ER_{\text{sum}}}{\text{Total number of traces}} \tag{5}$$

The resulting ER score reflects the average unpredictability of behavior across all traces. Note that with the bias correction, we get the Bias-corrected Entropic Relevance (Bias-corrected ER), which allows comparison across models with different control-flow structures and levels of specialization.

4 ContextER: Entropy-Based Contextualized Process Discovery

This section introduces our entropy-based approach to propose optimal process models using contextualized activity specialization. We begin with an illustrative example that demonstrates how the ER metric behaves under different model configurations, followed by a formal description of the approach.

4.1 Illustrative Example: Measuring Model Complexity Using ER

Consider an event log with 210 cases and five activities A, B, C, D and E. The corresponding baseline process model is shown in Fig. 1a. Suppose activity C is an important activity in the process and is selected for specialization. This activity has an impact on the execution of the process, affecting the sequence of subsequent activities, and its contextualization can reveal variations that are hidden in the baseline model. Using a contextual variable from the event log, C is specialized into two activities: C-x and C-y, where x and y are the contextual variable values that differentiate the execution paths of activity C.

To analyze the impact of using ER for a specialized model, we construct five alternative process models (Fig. 1b to Fig. 1f). Each model reflects a different configuration of transitions and frequencies related to C-x and C-y:

- **Fig. 1b**: Perfect model shows transition from C-x to D and from C-y to E.
- **Fig. 1c**: Transitions from C-x to E and C-y to D are introduced.
- **Fig. 1d**: Uneven transitions by adding paths from A to C-y and from B to C-x.
- **Fig. 1e**: Balanced transition frequencies across C-x and C-y.
- **Fig. 1f**: An unequal distribution of frequencies between C-x and C-y.

By computing the Bias-corrected ER metric of these process models, we can see the impact of using ER in specialization. The values for each model are shown in Table 1. The baseline model (a) has a value of 2.0. This value reflects the presence of multiple possible transitions in the model, which introduces variability and unpredictability in the behavior. Model (b) is the perfect model with zero Bias-corrected ER, meaning every activity always leads to exactly one next step, which is perfectly predictable. The model (c) has the second lowest value compared to the other models, indicating that this model would reach a better trade-off between process simplicity and contextual informativeness than using the general activity C. Also, model (d) has a lower value in comparison to model (a). It indicates multiple possible transitions between activities; the process model is more variable and less predictable. The structure of these models is easier to understand, which aligns with the goal of using specialization to isolate clearer paths and reduce control flow noise.

In contrast, if the specialization would derive the balanced model (model (e)) or the unequally splitter (model (f)), this would increase complexity and uncertainty in the process structure in comparison to other specialized models, as reflected by a higher value. These results emphasize the impact of transition balance and frequency distribution on process predictability. The models show that poor specialization choices can reintroduce noise or complexity and reduce the intended benefit of the specialization.

4.2 Contextualization Using Entropic Relevance

The ContextER approach consists of three steps, which are shown in Fig. 2. To apply this approach, an event log is required for specialization, with a hierarchy

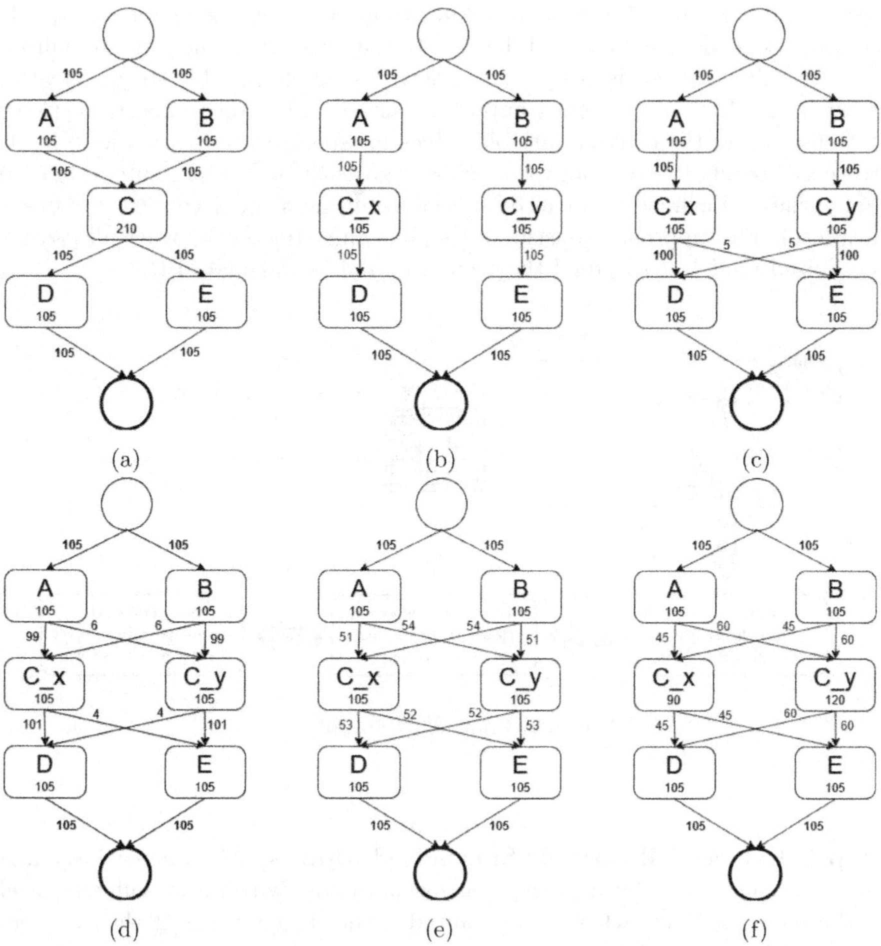

Fig. 1. Baseline model and different transitions for specialized model

Table 1. Extracted Bias-corrected ER values for different process models shown in Fig. 1. The table compares the Bias-corrected ER across five variations of the base process model.

Process model	Bias-corrected ER
a. Baseline model	2.0
b. Perfect model	**0**
c. Model with transitions	**1.2762**
d. Uneven transitions model	1.5495
e. Balanced transition model	2.9993
f. Model with unequal distribution	1.9852

tree that is constructed using expert knowledge based on analysis goals [2]. The hierarchy tree defines how high-level activities can be refined or specialized, into more detailed versions based on relevant context variables (e.g., resource, location, ...). It shows the most important activities based on expert knowledge to focus on and the context variable values for specialization. Each level in the tree corresponds to one context variable, and each node represents a value of that variable. Each activity can be specialized using a single context variable at each level. This approach consists of the following steps: 1) Extract all possible specialized models, 2) Extend the event log, and 3) Calculate ER.

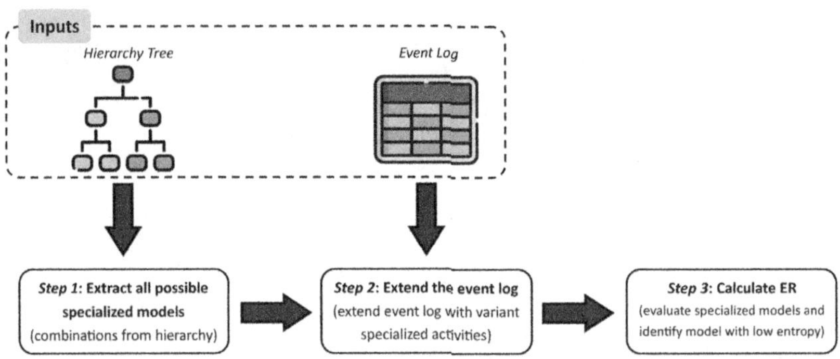

Fig. 2. ContextER approach

Step 1: Extract All Possible Specialized Models. All possible specialized models are extracted by replacing the specialized activities from different levels of the hierarchy tree, where a specialized model is a version of the base process model and specific activities are replaced by their more detailed variants according to the hierarchy tree. For instance, activity *Register* may have one specialized level, while activity *Handle request* can be specialized across two levels. This allows for constructing various combinations of specialized models: (1) *Register* specialized in level 1 and *Handle request* remains high-level, (2) *Handle request* specialized in level 1 and *Register* remains high-level, (3) *Handle request* specialized in level 2 and *Register* remains high-level, (4) *Register* and *Handle request* both specialized in level 1, (5) *Register* specialized in level 1 and *Handle request* specialized in level 2. A valid combination follows the pattern $Activity1 - LevelX$, $Activity1 - LevelX - Activity2 - LevelY$, ... which contains activity(ies) expanded by including multiple context values.

Step 2: Extend the Event Log. Extending the event log based on these combinations of specialized models to reflect activity specializations, i.e., by adding columns to the event log, events in the log are relabeled to include context-specific activity names. For each combination, it iterates over the activity column in the event log and constructs a specialized activity value column. The result is an extended event log where each row contains multiple versions of the specialized activity column, reflecting different hierarchical perspectives of specialization. These labels are created by combining hierarchical attributes from the original log based on predefined combinations. For example, the extended event log has the following columns: *case id*, *activity*, *timestamps*, *Register-Level1*, *Handle request-Level1*, *Handle request-Level2*, *Register-Level1-Handle request-Level1*, *Register-Level1-Handle request-Level2*, which the *Register-Level1-Handle request-Level1* column has all values of the activity column where *Register* and *Handle request* activities are specialized in Level 1 of the hierarchy tree. The detailed procedure of Steps 1 and 2 is described in Algorithm 1.

Algorithm 1. Extend Event Log with Contextualized Activity Labels

```
Require: event_log, specialized_activities: mapping from activity → list of
    (level_name, context_variable)
Ensure: extended_event_log with additional columns
                                                  ▷ Step 1: Generate candidates
candidates ← GenerateAllSpecializationCombinations(HIERARCHY_TREE)(
    )                                             ▷ Step 2: Extend event log
for all event ∈ event_log do
    for each specialization_combination in candidates do
        column_name ← ∅
        activity ← event[activity]
        extended_attributes ← empty dictionary
        extended_value ← ∅
        for all (specialized_activity, levels) ∈ specialized_activities do
            if activity ≠ specialized_activity then
                extended_value ← activity
            else
                column_name ← column_name + specialized_activity + "-" +
levels
                context_column_name ← specialized_activity + "-" + levels
                extended_value ← extended_value + activity +
event[context_column_name]
            end if
        end for
    end for
    extended_attributes[column_name] ← extended_value
    Add event + extended_attributes to extended_event_log
end for
    return extended_event_log
```

Step 3: Calculate ER. In the final step of our approach, we compute the ER of each extracted process model. For each specialized column generated in step 2, we derive a corresponding process model. Then the ER for each of these models is calculated to assess their relative complexity. Among all the models, the one with the lowest ER value is proposed as the most interpretable and less complex model. This step of the approach is formalized in Algorithm 2.

Algorithm 2. Select Optimal Specialization Level Using ER

Require: *extended_event_log*
Ensure: *optimal_specialization*

```
best_ER ← ∞
best_specialization ← ∅
for each specialized_column in extended_event_log do
    log_specialized ← extended_event_log.caseid, extended_event_log.timestamp, extended_event_log.combination_column
    ER ← ComputeER(log_specialized)
    if ER < best_ER then
        best_ER ← ER
        best_specialization ← specialization
    end if
end for
return best_specialization
```

5 Evaluation

To evaluate the ContextER approach, we conducted a real-world case study. Due to confidentiality agreements, the dataset used in this case study cannot be made publicly available.

5.1 Case Study

The case study investigates the behavior of bee colonies using Internet of Things (IoT) technology. During foraging, bees visit flowers for varying durations, which correspond to different types of activities. These activities were categorized based on the duration of flower visits into four types: *Probing*, *Eating*, *Resting*, and *Sleeping*. *Foraging* behavior was influenced by various factors, including bee health, flower color, nectar content (treated or untreated), distance from the hive, and environmental conditions.

Data was collected through four controlled experiments: two involving healthy bees and two involving sick bees. Each experiment was carried out in a pair of identical greenhouse tents. Each tent contained one colony with approximately 30 worker bees, one queen, and eight robotic flowers. The robotic flowers have either untreated sugar water or nectar simulating natural nectar medicine compounds. They also recorded the frequency and duration of flower visits. The analysis focused on colony-level behavior rather than individual bees.

Each colony was treated as a separate case. The Fig. 3 shows the process model, in which no activity has been specialized. It represents the behavior of the process in its most general form, without considering any contextual variable or hierarchical structure.

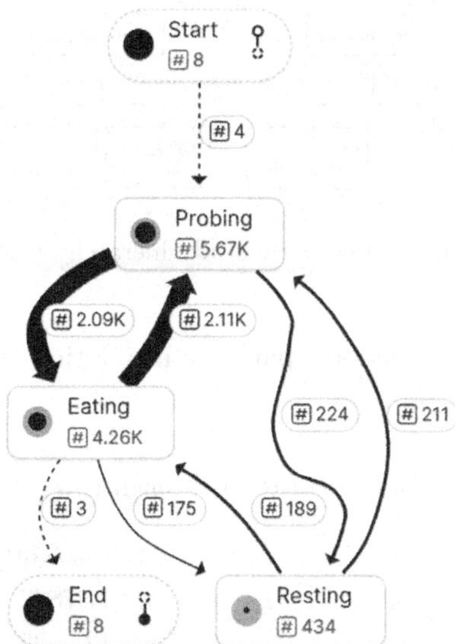

Fig. 3. The process model of the case study

Figure 4 shows the expert-defined activity hierarchy used in the analysis. It includes two levels of granularity for the *Eating* and *Probing* activities, providing a more detailed understanding of bee behavior. At the first level, the activities are categorized based on the health status of the bees, distinguishing between healthy and sick individuals. At the second level, the hierarchy refines activity labels according to the type of flower content, which contains regular sugar water or medicine. By analyzing these two levels together, we want to uncover patterns in how healthy and sick bees interact with different flower types.

5.2 Results

We evaluate the approach on the case study to show its applicability and usage on real event data. Table 2 presents the values of different specialized models in terms of Bias-corrected ER. The results of the Bias-corrected ER metric, which emphasizes behavioral interpretability, identify Eating-Level-1-Probing-Level-1 as the most comprehensible model with the lowest value of 5.8436. Eating-Level-2-Probing-Level-2, despite its higher structural value, achieves a lower Bias-corrected ER (8.1729) than both the Baseline model and Level 1 specialized models. From the expert perspective, this model is considered the most

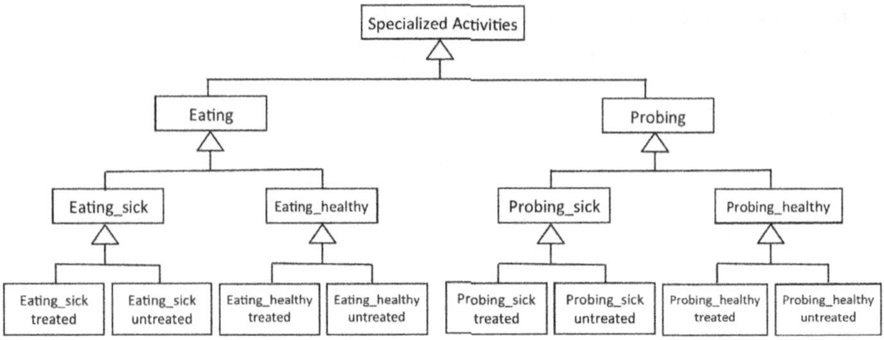

Fig. 4. Bees case study hierarchy tree

insightful, as it reveals behavioral patterns in relation to both the bees' health and flower content.

Table 2. Bias-corrected ER for discovered models

Model	Bias-corrected ER
Baseline Model	17.7822
Eating_Level_1	12.54055
Eating_Level_2	14.0704
Probing_Level_1	13.2993
Probing_Level_2	13.8471
Eating_Level_1_Probing_Level_1	**5.8436**
Eating_Level_1_Probing_Level_2	6.3914
Eating_Level_2_Probing_Level_1	7.3735
Eating_Level_2_Probing_Level_2	8.1729

Figure 5 shows the specialized process model in level 1 by distinguishing between healthy and sick behavior which adds more behavioral detail and lowest Bias-corrected ER value. Furthermore, Fig. 6 shows the extracted process model at Level 2, which was identified as the best model based on expert evaluation. This model increases granularity based on health and treatment effects. However, as specialization increases, the process model becomes more complex and less interpretable.

6 Discussion

This paper proposed an entropy-based metric to support an automated approach for proposing optimal process models through activity specialization based

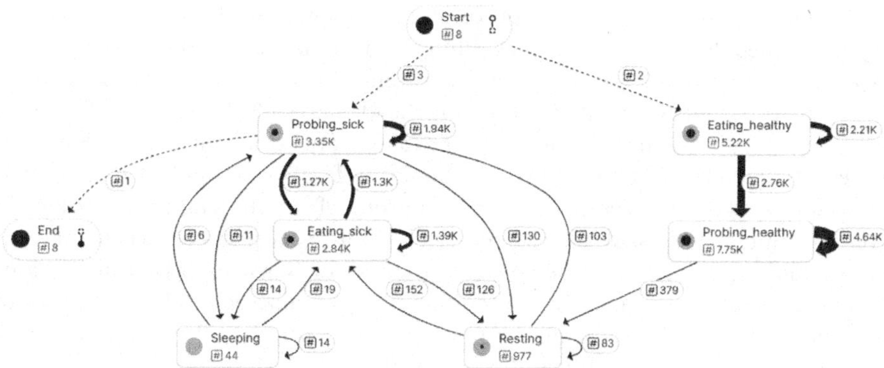

Fig. 5. The best specialized model based on the Bias-corrected ER metric

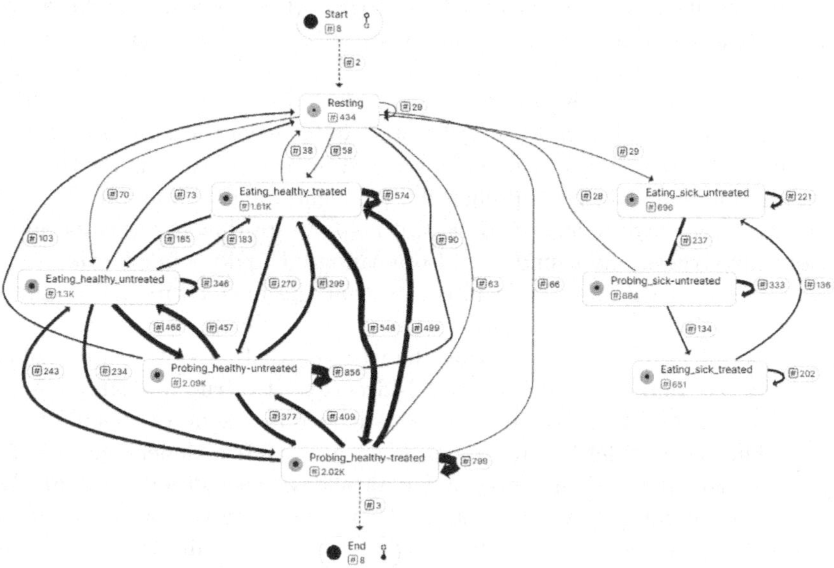

Fig. 6. The most effective specialized model, according to expert knowledge

on contextual information in the event log. By incorporating expert knowledge into a hierarchical representation of contextual information, the approach enables context-aware specialization, resulting in process models that are richer in behavioral insights. This automation reduces the need for manual trial-and-error, enhances scalability across applications, and provides adaptability for use with diverse different datasets. The results show how this approach can assist experts in identifying models that are either overly complex or particularly valuable for analysis.

Despite the advantages, the approach has certain limitations. Its reliance on expert-defined hierarchy trees may limit applicability in domains where such expertise is unavailable. In addition, the combination of possible specializations can lead to significant computational overhead, particularly when dealing with event logs that involve many activities or many contextual variables. Therefore, as recommended in [2], the approach should preferably be applied to a limited set of specialized activities and a restricted group of variables and values to avoid overly complex models. While ER effectively captures aspects of structural complexity and uncertainty, it does not fully account for other important dimensions of model quality, such as fitness, precision, or generalization. The usefulness of the approach also depends on the quality of the contextual variables; poorly chosen or noisy context can lead to less meaningful models.

To address these challenges, future work should explore more balanced evaluation frameworks that combine ER with additional process model quality metrics, such as fitness and precision. In the case of numerical contextual variables, the categorization used to construct the hierarchical tree can be tuned and integrated into the optimization process. This would allow the discovery of context specializations that are not only expert-informed but also data-driven. Furthermore, it is important to consider other entropy metrics, use simple metric weighting and investigate which entropy-based measures best align with human understanding and model comprehensibility. Identifying the most interpretable and informative entropy formulations will help ensure that the selected models are not only structurally sound but also meaningful to domain experts.

The results of the case study illustrate that the model with the lowest ER is not necessarily the most insightful from a domain perspective. It clarifies the approach's role as a way of narrowing the vast space of possible contextual specializations. By ranking candidate models according to structural simplicity, the approach ensures that experts are not overwhelmed by the number of alternative models. The best model is multidimensional and context-dependent. Analysts may prefer a model with higher ER if it provides richer detail or aligns more closely with specific process analysis goals. In this way, the proposed method guides to highlight candidates, while preserving the flexibility for expert judgment to determine the most appropriate balance between complexity and understandability. Therefore, we want to consider other complexity metrics in future work to further strengthen the automatic selection process.

7 Conclusion

In this paper, we addressed the challenge of selecting optimal activity specializations in context-aware PM. While contextualization through activity hierarchies can improve the interpretability of process models, excessive specialization may increase model complexity and reduce comprehensibility. To balance this, we introduced an entropy-based approach that systematically evaluates all possible specializations using ER. By selecting the model with the lowest ER, the ContextER identifies the most informative and less complex representation of the process. The proposed approach was validated using a real-world case study, demonstrating its effectiveness in producing clearer and more meaningful process models. These results suggest that ER can serve as a reliable metric for guiding specialization decisions in PM. More evaluation on diverse datasets will also help generalize the findings and improve the practical utility of the approach.

Acknowledgments. This research was supported by the Flemish fund for scientific research (FWO) with grant number G0B6922N.

References

1. Ahmadi, Z., De Weerdt, J., Serral Asensio, E.: A novel contextualization method for process discovery using activity specialization hierarchies. In: International Conference on Business Process Modeling, Development and Support, pp. 143–155. Springer (2024)
2. Ahmadi, Z., De Weerdt, J., Serral Asensio, E.: Context-driven process discovery: enhancing process flow interpretability with contextualized activity hierarchies: Z. ahmadi et al. Software and Systems Modeling, pp. 1–20 (2025)
3. Alkhammash, H., Polyvyanyy, A., Moffat, A., García-Bañuelos, L.: Entropic relevance: a mechanism for measuring stochastic process models discovered from event data. Inf. Syst. **107**, 101922 (2022)
4. Augusto, A., Mendling, J., Vidgof, M., Wurm, B.: The connection between process complexity of event sequences and models discovered by process mining. Inf. Sci. **598**, 196–215 (2022)
5. Back, C.O., Debois, S., Slaats, T.: Entropy as a measure of log variability. J. Data Semantics **8**, 129–156 (2019)
6. Koschmider, A., Mannhardt, F., Heuser, T.: On the contextualization of event-activity mappings. In: BPM 2018, Sydney, NSW, Australia, September 9-14, 2018, Revised Papers 16, pp. 445–457. Springer (2019)
7. Latva-Koivisto, A.M.: Finding a complexity measure for business process models (2001)
8. Mendling, J., Neumann, G., Van Der Aalst, W.: Understanding the occurrence of errors in process models based on metrics. In: OTM Confederated International Conferences" On the Move to Meaningful Internet Systems", pp. 113–130. Springer (2007)
9. Polyvyanyy, A., et al.: Entropia: a family of entropy-based conformance checking measures for process mining. arXiv preprint arXiv:2008.09558 (2020)
10. Polyvyanyy, A., Solti, A., Weidlich, M., Ciccio, C.D., Mendling, J.: Monotone precision and recall measures for comparing executions and specifications of dynamic systems. ACM Trans. Softw. Eng. Methodol. (TOSEM) **29**(3), 1–41 (2020)
11. Sánchez-González, L., García, F., Ruiz, F., Mendling, J.: Quality indicators for business process models from a gateway complexity perspective. Inf. Softw. Technol. **54**(11), 1159–1174 (2012)
12. Van Der Aalst, W.M., Dustdar, S.: Process mining put into context. IEEE Internet Comput. **16**(1), 82–86 (2012)
13. Yaqin, M.A., Sarno, R., Rochimah, S.: Measuring scalable business process model complexity based on basic control structure. Int. J. Intell. Eng. Syst. **13**(6), 52–65 (2020)

Intelligent and Secure Digital Transformation

Privacy-Preserving Computing in the Music Industry

Yulu Wang(✉), Charlotte van de Velde, Sabine Oechsner, and Jaap Gordijn(✉)

Vrije Universiteit Amsterdam, Amsterdam, The Netherlands
{y.wang4,s.a.oechsner,j.gordijn}@vu.nl, c.s.d.vander.velden@student.vu.nl

Abstract. Digital Business Ecosystems (DBEs) increasingly rely on the sharing of sensitive data between stakeholders to foster collaboration. However, to restrict access to this data, traditional security mechanisms are often not sufficient. This paper investigates one such case, part of the Horizon Europe MUSIC360 project, where policymakers want to know the economic value of music at the industry level. We propose a solution design approach that systematically links scenario-specific requirements to technical features of Privacy-Preserving Computation (PPC). A proof-of-concept experiment using the Prio+ protocol demonstrates the usability of our approach by showing that the selected implementation meets both the functional and security requirements.

Keywords: secure multi-party computation · privacy-preserving computation · music industry · requirement-solution matching

1 Introduction

A digital business ecosystem (DBE) is a system of economic actors that depend on each other for their economic well-being and survival [15]. Over the years, DBEs have become complex and decentralized, where numerous stakeholders exchange things of economic value, and to do so, share and transfer data. Data sharing, especially in the case of valuable or privacy-sensitive data, comes with the requirement to restrict access to data to selected parties [11]. Often, data can be protected by traditional security practices, like various ways of access control. However, there exist use cases where these well-known solutions are not sufficient. One of these cases is discussed in the paper, namely the need to calculate the average revenue of a set of companies, without disclosing the revenue of each company to the party(ies) that calculate(s) the average revenue.

In the Horizon Europe MUSIC360 project, we aim to understand the value of music. For example, an EU policymaker wants to know the average revenue of all EU rightholders (performers, lyricists, and composers) by genre. The MUSIC360 platform collects this data across Europe and stores it in a decentralized way, controlled by the data owner or their representative. The platform is designed such that stakeholders keep control of their own data and decide if and how to disclose their revenue information. Rightholders are willing to help answer

H.-G. Fill et al. (Eds.): PoEM 2025, LNBIP 570, pp. 263–280, 2026.
https://doi.org/10.1007/978-3-032-12063-2_17

policymakers' questions but, for privacy reasons, they do not want to share the individual revenue data. Also, there is no trusted third party who can collect all rightholders' revenue data, calculate the average, and share it with policymakers.

Such use cases can be solved by advanced privacy-preserving computation (PPC) techniques, such as Secure Multi Party Computing (SMPC), Homomorphic Encryption (HE), or Differential Privacy (DP). However, PPC is highly technical and requires a thorough understanding of cryptography and mathematics. What is lacking is a comprehensive approach to guide the selection and integration of these technologies for concrete use cases, which can be applied by practitioners. In contrast, existing PPC research focuses on the techniques themselves or narrow application domains at best, leaving practitioners without actionable guidance. A systematic approach to evaluating PPC techniques for DBEs is absent, complicating decisions for industry professionals. Also, PPC technologies such as secure multi-party computation (SMPC) are often costly and complex. This raises another core question: under what security requirement scenarios is their use truly justified? To answer this, our work also integrates a DBE security requirement-driven view into the solution design procedure.

Our research question, therefore is: *'How to systematically derive relevant security solutions to satisfy complex security requirements in DBEs, e.g., while keeping in control of own valuable data, even if that data is needed by others, e.g., to compute other data?'*. This paper addresses this question by an early-stage solution design procedure, and a decision-making framework that identifies hard-to-solve security scenarios and bridges technical PPC features with real-world requirements, validated through a case study in the music industry.

This paper is structured as follows. Section 2 summarizes relevant related work. Our research approach is outlined in Sect. 3. We propose a solution design procedure to deal with complex security requirements (Sect. 4), and show how that works out in a concrete case in the EU music industry (Sect. 5). In Sect. 6 we discuss the reflections. Section 7 presents conclusions.

2 Related Work

Suppose participants in a DBE need to perform operations such as computing the average of revenue data of all parties while ensuring that individual data remains confidential [31,36]. Without a trusted third party, such scenarios cannot be handled by traditional security methods. However, privacy-preserving computation (PPC) techniques can address this challenge.

PPC techniques commonly include (1) Secure Multi-Party Computation (SMPC), (2) Homomorphic Encryption (HE), and (3) Differential Privacy (DP). SMPC enables secure collaborative computation without exposing individual inputs, starting from Yao's garbled circuits [43] and its generalizations [25], with further developments combining secret sharing, zero-knowledge proofs, and HE [23,45]. HE supports operations on encrypted data and ensures that decrypted results match those in plaintext, but its high computational cost limits scalability [2,18]. DP protects privacy by adding noise to statistical outputs [10], and is often used alongside SMPC or HE. While effective for large-scale data analysis, DP involves a trade-off between utility and privacy guarantees.

Although prior work has compared these techniques in depth from a technical perspective [4,7,12,22], to the best of our knowledge, there remains a lack of systematic methods to help practitioners select appropriate PPC techniques based on specific DBE scenarios and security requirements. A well-structured mapping or decision-making framework is needed to support practitioners, particularly non-experts–in designing effective and practical PPC-based solutions.

3 Research Approach

We answer our research question (RQ) by Design Science Research (DSR) [16], and more specifically, a Technical Action Research (TAR) approach [41].
RQ*: How to systematically derive relevant security solutions to satisfy complex security requirements in DBEs, e.g. while keeping in control of own valuable data, even if that data is needed by others, e.g. to compute other data?*

We conduct our work with practitioners who (re)design and (re)develop the MUSIC360 platform to better understand the value of music. These practitioners are experts on intellectual property clearing, including the supporting processes. They are not knowledgeable on cryptography. The simplified engineering cycle that we will follow is described below and shown in Fig. 1.

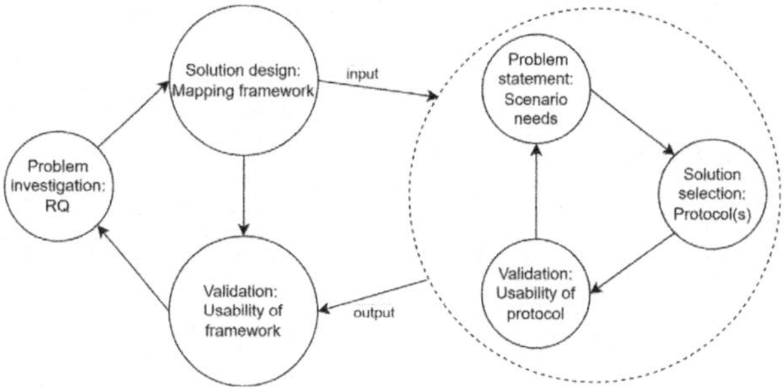

Fig. 1. Research design cycle

The left part of Fig. 1 shows the engineering cycle for the solution design process, meaning the cycle will be repeated several times. This paper reports on one such cycle. The research question comes from problem investigation and a literature review about security needs and privacy-preserving computation (PPC). The 'solution design: mapping framework' describes how to justify advanced PPC technologies in a specific DBE, identify the related security problem, and scenarios, and choose the best PPC technology. The key question is whether this procedure is useful. One way to assess usefulness is to check if the suggested PPC techniques at least meet the requirements. There are other criteria as well, but this paper focuses on verifying if the selected PPC techniques satisfy the stated security requirements. This is not straightforward, since most PPC techniques are still in early development and lack many practical use cases. Therefore, for the selected PPC technique, we use a prototyping approach to develop a Minimum Viable Product (MVP) to show whether the technique meets the requirements. We consider this as a partial validation of the whole procedure.

The right part of Fig. 1 presents how a specific DBE, here MUSIC360, will be explored. The steps are: (1) describing the problem statement, scenarios, and requirements, (2) selecting technical PPC solutions & protocols for the identified security and functional requirements via the proposed decision-making framework, and (3) validating whether the used protocols satisfy the requirements.

4 Solution Design: Mapping Framework

4.1 Solution Design Procedure

Figure 2 presents the solution design procedure to be executed, cf. the BPMN modeling language [40]. We explain the procedure below:

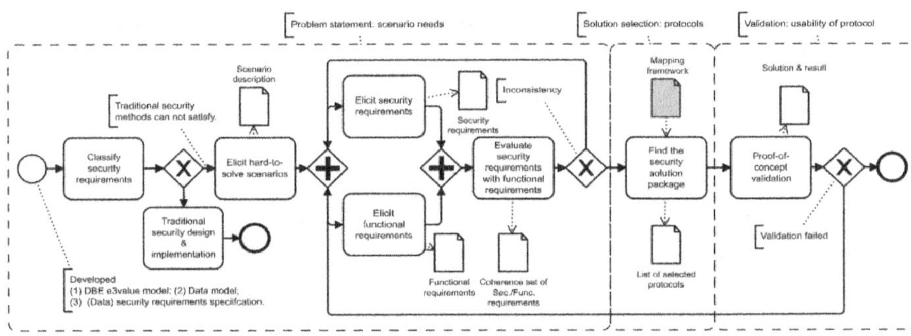

Fig. 2. Solution design procedure

Problem Statement: Scenario Needs. The solution design procedure starts with requirements elicitation. For DBEs, we develop a value-oriented model of the DBE at hand, cf. the e^3*value* modeling language [15]. We do so because e^3*value* shows the valuable objects that the actors in the ecosystem exchange with each other, which may subject to attack. Therefore, it is important to know these objects. From a security point of view, it is important to know the data objects associated with e^3*value* objects, because it is likely that these data objects are under attack too. And these data objects may be privacy sensitive, which results in an additional attack vector. Therefore, we also develop a UML class model to represent the structure of the data. Finally, we elicit security requirements directly related to the data in a series of workshops. These three requirement elicitation steps are reported in [37] in detail, but are not discussed in this paper due to lack of space. Based on these artefacts, we: (1) introduce an assessment step to cluster security requirements and identify hard-to-solve security scenarios. Security requirements that can easily be solved with standard security technology, such as access controls, are taken out of the process and addressed in their own right. This is outside the scope of this paper. This step acknowledges that not all requirements can be addressed by traditional security methods. It helps us to justify the necessity of applying expensive and complex PPC technologies in DBEs; (2) elicit these specific security scenarios with their functional and security requirements. These are analyzed for coherence and consistency, resulting in a final set of requirements, usually after a few iterations.

Solution Selection: Protocol(s). We then select the PPC techniques for implementing these security scenarios, using our decision-making framework (marked blue): consisting of *feature* extraction of known PPC techniques and *requirement factors*. Ideally, there would be a mapping from requirements factors onto PPC features beforehand. This mapping should be created by PPC experts, can be reused, and given the state-of-the-art of PPC techniques, should be updated regularly. In this paper, we perform the mapping ourselves.

Validation: Usability of Protocol. A proof-of-concept prototype implementation of the target scenario through the selected PPC technique(s) will be conducted for validation in terms of requirement satisfaction.

We emphasize that this paper is the first iteration to conduct the whole procedure of the proposed research design cycle in Fig. 1 and the solution design procedure in Fig. 2. More engineering cycle iterations will be required to arrive at a more comprehensive and mature framework. In the following subsections, we explain some of the core steps illustrated in Fig. 2.

4.2 Security Requirement Analysis for DBE

DBE-Specific Security Frames and Requirement Types. In DBEs, security requirements vary widely in complexity and urgency. Most of these requirements can be addressed by well-known technology. But sometimes there are hard-to-satisfy requirements. Below, we identify a number of these requirement types, as security problem frames, loosely based on the idea of problem framing [17]. Our problem frames serve not as an exhaustive list of all security concerns, but as a perspective for identifying when DBE-specific demand crosses the threshold into the domain of PPC technologies, and thus can be seen as a theory of complex security problems. Below are six representative security frames **[Sec-frame]** and their related requirement types **[RQTs]** observed in our case and validated through prior DBE literature [21,23,31,35].

1. **[Sec-frame 1] Secure multi-party data collaboration**
   - **[RQT1]** Confidential multi-stakeholder computation: Stakeholders can engage in joint computations without disclosing raw input values to each other, preserving the confidentiality of sensitive data.

- **[RQT2]** Trust-limited collaboration: The computation framework must avoid reliance on centralized or trusted third parties, ensuring decentralized execution without exposing data.
- **[RQT3]** Decentralized data ownership: The security design must ensure that data can only be included in computations when explicitly authorized by each independent stakeholder, reinforcing legal compliance.

2. **[Sec-frame 2] Privacy-preserving aggregation and results**
   - **[RQT4]** Protection against aggregation leakage: When publishing aggregate statistics, the security design must ensure that individual contributions cannot be inferred, even with auxiliary external knowledge.
   - **[RQT5]** Controlled exposure of computation results: Published results must be processed to prevent reverse-engineering of private inputs.
3. **[Sec-frame 3] Encrypted data processing**
   - **[RQT6]** Computation on processed inputs: The security design must support secure computation over processed (e.g., secret-shared, encrypted) data during processing, ensuring data protected end-to-end.
   - **[RQT7]** Persistent encryption across lifecycle: Sensitive data must remain encrypted during storage, transit, and use, avoiding plaintext exposure.
4. **[Sec-frame 4] Collusion-resistant computation**
   - **[RQT8]** Collusion-resistant protocol design: The security design must prevent coalitions of dishonest participants from inferring private data or manipulating computation outcomes.
   - **[RQT9]** Resilience to insider threats: Computation must remain secure even when some participants are compromised or act maliciously, without degrading global guarantees.
5. **[Sec-frame 5] Verifiability without disclosure**
   - **[RQT10]** Input/result verifiability without data disclosure: Security design should provide verification for the precise of computation results without gaining access to intermediate states or private inputs.
6. **[Sec-frame 6] Dynamic and resource-constrained security**
   - **[RQT11]** Resource-constrained environments: The security design must remain functional on devices or infrastructures with limited resources, using lightweight cryptographic techniques where necessary.
   - **[RQT12]** Compliance with evolving policies: The security design must adapt to varying or evolving privacy regulations across areas.

Assessing when PPC Application is Justified. The security frames and security requirements types above often appear in interdependent forms. For example, [RQT1] - Confidential multi-stakeholder computation coupled with the [RQT2] - Trust-limited collaboration makes PPC not only beneficial but necessary. When one or more of these compound conditions are observed, conventional methods such as Role Based Access Controls (RBACs), encrypted data-at-rest, or trusted logging infrastructures are insufficient. Our solution design procedure starts from leveraging this logic to assess when and why PPC (particularly SMPC) should be considered during security design. In general, the emergence of these independent/compound requirement types forms the decision boundary that justifies the adoption of advanced privacy-preserving computation.

4.3 Decision-Making Framework

We construct the decision-making framework (marked blue in Fig. 2) by two main components: (1) Security frames **[Sec-frame]** and their related requirement types **[RQTs]**, which can be linked to scenario-specific requirements items for reasoning; (2) PPC techniques features, which we explain below.

Features of PPC Techniques. Different PPC techniques have different sets of features that characterize the technique at hand. Understanding these features that characterize PPC techniques is important to match security requirements with the appropriate technique(s).

1. **The supposed *[TSM]* threat and security model:** One feature is the threats-and-security model, which defines adversary behavior during attacks. **Honest** parties follow the protocol and only access their own inputs and outputs. In contrast, **adversaries** attempt to break security or correctness, such as manipulating computation results [38]. They are typically classified as follows [1,45]: (1) **Semi-honest**: follow the protocol but try to infer additional information; (2) **Malicious**: behave arbitrarily to compromise security; (3) **Covert**: may misbehave if they believe they won't be caught.
2. **The *[CM]* computing model:** The computing model describes how PPC techniques perform secure computations, including task transformation, encryption methods, and security assumptions [27,30,34,39,44]. Different approaches offer trade-offs in computational and communication cost, and support different operations. **(1) HE-based** approaches enable computation on encrypted data with strong security, but incur high computational overhead, suitable for low-interaction settings [14,33]. **(2) SS-based** methods efficiently support linear operations using additive secret sharing, but require frequent communication [3,8,9,32]. **(3) OT-based** techniques balance communication and computation, ideal for secure lookups or key exchange, but less efficient for arithmetic operations [6,28]. **(4) GC-based** methods use constant communication rounds and suit boolean logic, but demand heavy pre-processing and bandwidth [13,26]. [13,26].
3. **The *[DM]* deployment model:** This defines how SMPC protocols are implemented, including participant roles and communication setup [1]. (1) **Server-side**: Data is distributed among multiple non-colluding servers for computation in a way that conceals the data from each server individually. This approach is efficient but still relies on trusting that the servers do not collude. (2) **Peer-to-peer**: Participants compute directly, reducing trust but increasing cost. (3) **Server-aided**: A hybrid model where some nodes are controlled by data providers, and others are external servers that help particularly heavy parts of the computation.
4. **The *[SF]* supported function:** The technical basis of different PPC techniques determines the scope of functions and the number of participants they can efficiently support. Any function that can be represented by a circuit can be computed in a privacy-preserving way. The efficiency of computing

different classes of functions, for example in terms of computation or communication cost, depends on the technique.

5 Case Study: MUSIC360

The Horizon Europe MUSIC360 ecosystem[1] is an innovative digital business ecosystem that aims to provide insights into the value of music for creatives (performers and authors), venues (restaurants, shops, offices), and policymakers (EU officials, national authorities, and lobbyists). The MUSIC360 ecosystem collects data about the value of music. One type of data collected is the economic impact of music, such as the increase in revenue for a venue that plays music. Venues like shops and bars play music to improve customer well-being, build their brand identity, and ultimately boost their revenue.

In the following, we use a scenario from the MUSIC360 DBE—'Average increased revenue'— to show one iteration of the security solution design and validation. In particular, we execute the right part of Fig. 1, which is further detailed in Fig. 2. The decision-making framework in Sect. 4.3 is the input for this case study.

5.1 Problem Statement

We present how we identify a specific hard-to-solve security scenario in MUSIC360 and state the problem by detailed scenario-specific requirements.

Identify and Elicit Specific Security Scenarios. Following our procedure as illustrated in Fig. 2, we start from the MUSIC360 e^3*value* model, UML data model (based on [24]) and (data) security requirements specifications resulting from a series of workshop sessions. During lack of space, this step is not presented here. During these sessions, we have identified a number of hard-to-solve security requirements, one of them the secure calculation of the average increased revenue, further referred to as 'Average increased revenue'.

Scenario Description: 'Average Increased Revenue'. In the MUSIC360 DBE, a policymaker would like to know the average increase in revenue of venues (located in a specific region) as a result of playing music in these venues. In order to use music, venues have to pay a fee to Collective Management Organizations (CMOs). Every country has at least one CMO, but usually there are more of them, each representing different kinds of rightholders and intellectual property rights. CMOs have a mandate to collect fees for their rights-holders. Revenue data of venues is confidential information, as it is competitive and sensitive. E.g. if the CMOs can obtain the precise revenue increase number associated with music played at each venue separately, they may consider adjusting the venue's licensing fee accordingly. This could have a negative impact on venues. Therefore, only the venue itself should have access to its respective revenue increase.

Scenario Requirements. For the scenario 'Average revenue of venues', the following requirements are identified:

[1] https://music-360.eu/.

Functional: A party (e.g., policymakers) wants to know the influence (in terms of average revenue increase for venues) of playing music at a number of venues:

1. The ability for venues to provide their data to compute the average revenue for a set of venues. **[RQT1]**
2. The ability to compute average over the input parties' data.**[RQT1, RQT2]**
3. The computation should be performed within an acceptable amount of time (seconds preferred, minutes acceptable, hours not). **[RQT11]**
4. The underlying PPC protocol used for the computations should be open source for the feasibility of the proof-of-concept experiment.
5. Complex privacy computational burdens should not be placed on venues due to typically limited computational resources. **[RQT11]**

Security: The average should be calculated without disclosing the individual revenue data from venues, which can be detailed as follows:

1. Policymakers as result receivers should only have *READ* access to the final result. Venues that did provide input data should only have *READ* access to the final result and *all access* to their own input data. **[RQT5, RQT10]**
2. *Venues* deliver their input without disclosing their full and readable input to a party. Parties interested in the *result* of the calculation obtain the calculated average result without obtaining the individual result or each party. This implies that no single party knows the input of the individual venue, except the venue itself, and also no single party knows the result, except the receivers (the policymaker and possibly venues). **[RQT1, RQT2, RQT4]**
3. Individual revenue values of venues must remain confidential and should not be inferable from the final output or any intermediate data. **[RQT4, RQT5]**
4. The solution must be resilient to collusion, e.g., a coalition of venues and CMOs should not be able to reconstruct venue-specific data. **[RQT8,RQT9]**
5. The technology should include mechanisms to prevent malicious inputs to guarantee the correctness and effectiveness of the result, such as zero or extreme outliers that could distort the average, without requiring disclosure of actual input values. **[RQT10]**
6. There is no trusted third party who can do the calculation on behalf of the party interested in the result. **[RQT2]**

In summary, this security scenario needs to introduce the advanced PPC technologies as it involves multiple RQTs we identified.

5.2 Solution Selection

Involved Parties. We distinguish *input* parties, *computation* parties and *result* parties. Figure 3 shows how the MUSIC360 parties play their role. (1) Venues as input parties: Each venue keeps its own increased revenue data (secret). (2) Servers as computation parties: Servers receive and process the parts of the revenue data without being able to reconstruct individual revenues. (3) Policymakers as result parties: Policymakers want to get the average revenue increase.

Using the Decision-Making Framework. We apply the decision-making framework (in Sec.4.3) to the security scenario 'Average increased revenue' analysis results. We linked the requirement types **[RQTs]** to the evaluated refined scenario-specific factors (by combining strong-related scenario requirement items) and mapped them to certain key PPC technology features via reasoning.

1. **Scenario factor: Required calculation type & function.**
   - *Requirement:* Type: sum (addition), mean (division). Function:$R_m = \frac{\sum(R_i)}{n}$, $(R_i = R_i\_before - R_i\_after)^2$.
   - *Reasoning:* Protocols supporting linear computation, especially an efficient addition operation, is needed.
   - *Related PPC feature:* **[SF]**: linear, addition.
2. **Scenario factor: Data ownership & confidentiality in multi-party nature [RQT1, RQT2, RQT3, RQT4, RQT5].**
   - *Requirement:* Venues must retain their revenue data ownership and ensure this confidential data will not be disclosed among computations, holds the fact that a TTP is not available.
   - *Reasoning:* Secret-sharing-based SMPC ensures raw data are never reconstructed. Data is split into shares distributed across multiple servers, where no single server (or minority coalition) can infer private values.
   - *Related PPC feature:* **[CM]**: secret-sharing-based.
3. **Scenario factor: [S] Collusion resistance [RQT8, RQT9].**
   - *Requirement:* The main collusion risk exists between servers or venues and needs to be prevented.
   - *Reasoning:*(1) Contracts between venues and CMOs help prevent dishonest behavior like faking data, so a semi-honest adversary model is appropriate. (2) The main risk is others inferring individual revenue, not active attacks. Secret sharing reduces this risk by splitting the data. (3) Using server-side SMPC separates venues from the servers doing the computation, which helps reduce chances of collusion.
   - *Related PPC feature:* **[TSM]**: at least semi-honest; **[CM]**: secret-sharing-based; **[DM]** Deployment model: server-side.
4. **Scenario factor: Resource-constrained [RQT11].**
   - *Requirement:* Venues may lack computational resources to perform intensive cryptographic operations and communications locally.
   - *Reasoning:* (1) Server-side SMPC shifts the computation to dedicated servers, avoiding peer-to-peer coordination. This lowers load on venues and allows more participants. (2) We choose semi-honest over malicious ones to avoid the high cost of frequent computation and communication.
   - *Related PPC feature:* **[DM]**: server-side; **[TSM]**: semi-honest.

[2] R_i_before: The revenue in a fixed period when not playing any music; R_i_after: The revenue in a fixed period while playing music;R_i: Each venue i has confidential increased revenue data; R_m: Average (mean) of increased revenue.

5. **Scenario factor: Efficiency/effectiveness in computation task [RQT10].**
   - *Requirement*: The computation should be performed within an acceptable amount of time (minutes is ok, hours not). Mechanisms to prevent malicious inputs to guarantee the correctness and effectiveness of the result without requiring disclosure of actual input values.
   - *Reasoning*: (1) Secret-sharing protocols outperform boolean-centric alternatives (e.g., GC) on most linear operations. (2) Server-side deployment usually minimizes latency for large-scale deployments.
   - *Related PPC feature:*: **[DM]**: server-side; **[CM]**: secret-sharing-based.

In summary, our solution selection will be protocols supporting linear or addition operations, having a server-side deployment, using a secret-sharing-based approach, and under a semi-honest adversarial model.

Protocol Selection. The protocol selection is based on the scenario-specific technology feature preferences we reasoned from the mapping process. As the first attempt, due to the time limit and page limit, we evaluate six protocols that are from active open-source projects or have been widely discussed in the PPC community. Table 1 below shows how well these popular protocols meet these technical features and corresponding requirements. EasySMPC [42] and Prio+ [3] match well with the SMPC features identified in our mapping. Their open-source nature is also a plus. However, practical use depends on how easy they are to deploy and operate. EasySMPC uses email for communication, which may raise security concerns and reduce reliability. Its data input method (CSV files) works for small, structured data but is too heavy for our needs. Prio+ is more suitable for a proof-of-concept. It allows scenario-specific settings, supports basic validation, and meets all our requirements. Therefore, we chose Prio+ as the security solution for the "average increased revenue" scenario.

Table 1. The degree of satisfaction of different protocols for scenario-specific technical feature preferences

SMPC technology	SMPC technology feature preferences			
	[SF] linear, addition	**[TSM]** semi-honest	**[DM]** server-side	**[CM]** secret sharing
Prio+ [3]	•	•	•	•
Overdrive [20]	•	○	•	○
FRESCO (BGW) [5]	•	•	○	•
Mascot [19]	•	○	○	○
Whisper [29]	•	○	•	•
EasySMPC [42]	•	•	•	•

5.3 Validation: Usability of Protocol

To evaluate the applicability and usability of SMPC protocols selected according to our proposed decision-making framework, we conducted a proof-of-concept experiment utilizing the selected protocol prototype [3]: *Prio+*. This section outlines the protocol execution procedure, presents the experimental test results, clarifies the usability, and offers reflections from the perspective of this first attempt.

Protocol Execution Procedure. Based on the above analysis, we listed relative results as below: (1) the selected PPC protocol: *Prio+*; (2) the required calculation formula: $R_m = \frac{\sum(R_i)}{n}$ $(R_i = R_i\_before - R_i\_after)$; (3) the involved parties: input parties (venues), computation parties (CMOs), output parties (policymakers). All involved participants should acknowledge the specific computation task and the procedure of the security scenario, 'Average increased revenue'. The conceptual security model by the SMPC protocol for this scenario is shown in Fig. 3. We explain it as below:

1. *Input submission:* Each venue i submits its confidential revenue R_i as input client. We assume honest submissions due to the semi-honest security model.
2. *Data validation: Prio+* checks that inputs are valid (e.g., non-negative, reasonable) using share conversion.
3. *Computation factor generation & aggregation:* Each venue splits its data into secret shares and sends them to the aggregators.
4. *Computation execution:* The computing servers perform secure computations on the received shares following the protocol.
5. *Reconstruction & output:* The final sum is sent to policymakers and reconstructed locally. Aggregators don't learn individual inputs or results unless they collude. To compute the average, *Prio+* allows revealing the number of participants.

Experiment Setting and Result. Our basic container deployment using the *Prio+* protocol via Docker is conducted through simulating two server instances and multiple clients (operates in a cluster of individual clients). We used the supported function: INT_SUM. We tried different values in two parameters: (1) max_bits (data size can be input): $2^{12}/2^{16}$; (2) num_inputs (number of venues): 10/100/1000. These two parameter settings are related to the actual scenario nature. We look into two variables - total sent bits and total time - under the different settings of the two parameters we mentioned before. These two variables can help to measure whether the basic execution (time, data volume) of the selected protocol is within an acceptable range in terms of the requirements.

Validation Discussion. The Prio+ [3] protocol was selected as a promising security solution to satisfy the scenario's needs. Its technology features align well with all the security and functional requirements (see Sect. 5.2) and meet practical constraints. We demonstrate part of (due to page limit) the matching

[3] https://github.com/KuraTheDog/Prio-plus.

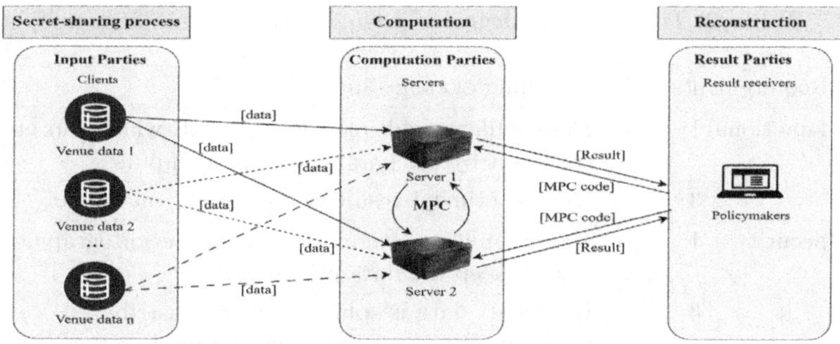

Fig. 3. SMPC model for scenario 'Average increased revenue': [data] and [result] are secret shares divided by SMPC protocol. Different line styles are used solely for visual clarity, without implying any semantic distinction.

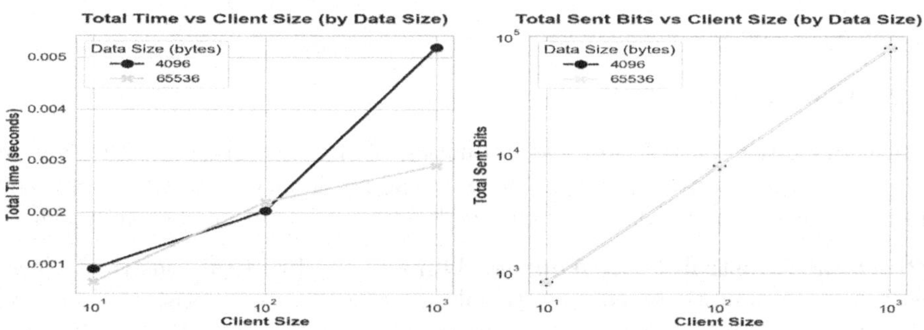

Fig. 4. Experimental results obtained using the different parameter settings

in Table 2. The experiment results suggest the usability of the selected protocol in this specific 'Average increased revenue' scenario.

6 Discussion

6.1 Usability of Solution Design: Mapping Framework

The reasonable result in this proof-of-concept experiment shows the feasibility and usability of our proposed design procedure and framework in finding an appropriate SMPC technology for a specific scenario. By analysing its execution, we derive critical insights into how technical features and scenario-specific requirements interact, and how these interactions can guide future experiments and framework development. The scenario 'Average revenue of venues' serves as a case study to refine our procedure and inform the design of a more comprehensive and rigorous decision-making framework.

Table 2. The matching degree of *Prio+* to scenario requirements

Requirements	Index	Matching evidence in *Prio+*
Functional	1	*Prio+* allows multiple clients' input, which can be easily set by the parameter: 'num_inputs'.
	3	Our experiment result in Fig. 4 confirmed this.
Security	1	*Prio+* built on 'secret-sharing' as a cryptographic tool to keep the data private.
	3	In *Prio+*, data is split into shares distributed across multiple servers, where no single server (or minority coalition) can infer private values.
	5	*Prio+* enables the input verification using share conversion to make sure the provided revenue increase data are within acceptable bounds.

6.2 Reflections

Throughout the construction and evaluation of the early-stage solution design process and decision-making framework in the music DBE context, several key insights have emerged that highlight the limitations of our current approach.

Practical Constraints as Another Dimension. Practical constraints (e.g., cost, trust assumptions, computational resources) have a decisive impact on the PPC deployment strategy. In real-world use cases like MUSIC360, some participants cannot afford high-latency or high-overhead protocols. Our framework allows trade-offs between security and performance, but does not yet formally model or quantify these trade-offs. We suggest incorporating a resource-evaluation layer that measures protocol feasibility in constrained environments.

Priority Weighting Between Factors/Features. The use of scenario factors (e.g., 'resource-constrained', 'collusion-resistant') allows qualitative prioritization. However, these mappings are currently performed manually. The framework lacks formal weighting mechanisms to balance competing requirements (e.g., performance vs. cost). A possible extension is to support multi-criteria decision analysis (MCDA) for feature ranking and protocol scoring.

Gaps in Scenario-to-Requirement Mapping. Although our framework maps functional and security requirements to scenario-specific factors, our experiment exposed cases where requirement types (RQTs) were underspecified or unmapped: (1) The scenario factor "required computation type" was difficult to trace to a specific RQT. This weakens traceability and hinders automatic reasoning. (2) The scenario mandated open-source protocol availability, yet this constraint was not represented in the framework. This suggests the need to add realistic, non-functional requirement types such as transparency or maintainability. These gaps indicate that the current framework may benefit from a non-functional requirement module for context-specific factors.

Deployment Complexity as an Overlooked Metric. Our experience shows that while many PPC protocols align well with security and functional requirements in theory, deployment complexity often becomes the real challenge in practice. Even relatively practical options like Prio+ demand container orchestration and manual client-server coordination if needed. This indicates that deployment feasibility is multifaceted, involving aspects such as technical setup burden, integration cost, tooling maturity, and operational risk. We believe that future versions of the framework should include a Deployment Complexity Evaluation (DCE) component to ensure protocol selection is guided not only by security alignment, but also by practical feasibility, especially in resource-constrained DBEs where technical capacity is limited.

Need for Broader Types of RQTs. The current list of 12 RQTs (grouped under six security frames) was sufficient for the "average increased revenue" scenario. However, more complex scenarios in DBEs may have more security concerns. The MUSIC360 project itself includes other data flows (e.g., artist metadata, cross-country licensing) that raise such concerns. This suggests that our framework needs a broader and evolving taxonomy of requirement types, which can ideally be expanded with new domain contexts.

7 Conclusion

This study highlights the feasibility of privacy-preserving computation technologies, especially secure multi-party computation as a security solution for several hard-to-solve requirement types in DBEs. By analyzing the MUSIC360 case, we show how to find suitable PPC technologies for specific security scenarios to achieve secure aggregation of sensitive data (e.g., venue revenue) while meeting security and functional requirements and practical constraints. The proposed decision-making framework successfully links scenario-specific requirements factors (e.g., computation type, anti-collusion, resource constraints) with the technical features of PPC (e.g., secret sharing and semi-honest adversarial model). Experimental verification confirms the usability of the highly satisfied protocols found according to the decision-making framework in specific DBE security scenarios. This research emphasizes that SMPC's strength lies in its ability to keep privacy in a limited mutual trust environment without sacrificing data utility. It is a critical advantage for DBEs where stakeholders must collaborate without exposing proprietary information. By combining the theoretical capabilities of PPC with the real-world DBE needs, this work advances the application of PPC techniques in multi-party settings. It provides practitioners with a foundational approach to systematically evaluate and implement SMPC.

Acknowledgements. Funded by the European Union under project no. 101094872. Views and opinions expressed are however those of the author(s) only and do not necessarily reflect those of the European Union. Neither the European Union nor the granting authority can be held responsible for them.

References

1. Ieee recommended practice for secure multi-party computation: IEEE Std **2842–2021**, 1–30 (2021)
2. Acar, A., et al.: A survey on homomorphic encryption schemes: theory and implementation. ACM Comput. Surv. **51**(4), 1–35 (2018)
3. Addanki, S., et al.: Prio+: privacy preserving aggregate statistics via Boolean shares. In: International Conference on Security and Cryptography for Networks, pp. 516–539. Springer (2022)
4. Almagrabi, A.O., et al.: A classification-based privacy-preserving decision-making for secure data sharing in internet of things assisted applications. Digital Commun. Netw. **8**(4), 436–445 (2022)
5. Amini, R., et al.: Fresco: a framework for spacecraft systems autonomy. In: 2021 IEEE Aerospace Conference, pp. 1–18. IEEE (2021)
6. Asharov, G., et al.: More efficient oblivious transfer extensions. J. Cryptology **30**, 805–858 (2017)
7. Boulemtafes, A., et al.: A review of privacy-preserving techniques for deep learning. Neurocomputing **384**, 21–45 (2020)
8. Corrigan-Gibbs, H., et al.: Prio: private, robust, and scalable computation of aggregate statistics. In: 14th USENIX Symposium on Networked Systems Design and Implementation, pp. 259–282 (2017)
9. Cramer, R., Damgård, I., Maurer, U.: General secure multi-party computation from any linear secret-sharing scheme. In: Preneel, B. (ed.) EUROCRYPT 2000. LNCS, vol. 1807, pp. 316–334. Springer, Heidelberg (2000). https://doi.org/10.1007/3-540-45539-6_22
10. Dwork, C.: Differential privacy. In: Bugliesi, M., Preneel, B., Sassone, V., Wegener, I. (eds.) ICALP 2006. LNCS, vol. 4052, pp. 1–12. Springer, Heidelberg (2006). https://doi.org/10.1007/11787006_1
11. Fabian, B., et al.: A comparison of security requirements engineering methods. Requirements Eng. **15**, 7–40 (2010)
12. Feng, J., et al.: Privacy-preserving computation in cyber-physical-social systems: a survey of the state-of-the-art and perspectives. Inf. Sci. **527**, 341–355 (2020)
13. Gascón, A., et al.: Privacy-preserving distributed linear regression on high-dimensional data. Cryptology ePrint Archive (2016)
14. Gentry, C.: Fully homomorphic encryption using ideal lattices. In: Proceedings of the forty-first annual ACM Symposium on Theory of Computing, pp. 169–178 (2009)
15. Gordijn, J., et al.: E3value User Guide - Designing Your Ecosystem in a Digital World. The Value Engineers, 1st edn. (2021)
16. Hevner, A.R., et al.: Design science in information systems research. MIS Q. **28**(1), 75–105 (2004)
17. Jackson, M.: Problem frames: analyzing and structuring software development problems. Addison-Wesley Longman Publishing Co., Inc, USA (2000)
18. Jin, W., et al.: Fedml-he: An efficient homomorphic-encryption-based privacy-preserving federated learning system. arXiv preprint arXiv:2303.10837 (2023)
19. Keller, M., et al.: Mascot: faster malicious arithmetic secure computation with oblivious transfer. In: Proceedings of the 2016 ACM SIGSAC Conference on CCS, pp. 830–842 (2016)
20. Keller, M., Pastro, V., Rotaru, D.: Overdrive: making SPDZ great again. In: Nielsen, J.B., Rijmen, V. (eds.) EUROCRYPT 2018. LNCS, vol. 10822, pp. 158–189. Springer, Cham (2018). https://doi.org/10.1007/978-3-319-78372-7_6

21. Lenkenhoff, K., et al.: Key challenges of digital business ecosystem development and how to cope with them. Procedia Cirp **73**, 167–172 (2018)
22. Lindell, Y.: Secure multiparty computation for privacy preserving data mining. In: Encyclopedia of Data Warehousing and Mining, pp. 1005–1009. IGI global (2005)
23. Lindell, Y.: Secure multiparty computation. Commun. ACM **64**(1), 86–96 (2020)
24. McLaren, A., et al.: Value-based security requirements in a highly decentralized digital ecosystem: the music360 case. In: Hacks, S., Roelens, B. (eds.) PoEM 2024, pp. 1–15. CEUR Workshop Proceedings, CEUR-WS (2024)
25. Micali, S., et al.: How to play any mental game. In: Proceedings of the Nineteenth ACM Symposium on Theory of Computing, STOC, pp. 218–229. ACM New York (1987)
26. Mohassel, P., et al.: Fast and secure three-party computation: the garbled circuit approach. In: Proceedings of the 22nd ACM SIGSAC Conf. on CCS, pp. 591–602 (2015)
27. Mohassel, P., et al.: Aby3: A mixed protocol framework for machine learning. In: Proceedings of the 2018 ACM SIGSAC Conf. on CCS, pp. 35–52 (2018)
28. Naor, M., et al.: Efficient oblivious transfer protocol. In: SODA, pp. 448–457 (2001)
29. Rathee, M., et al.: Private analytics via streaming, sketching, and silently verifiable proofs. In: 2024 IEEE Symposium on SP, pp. 3072–3090. IEEE (2024)
30. Riazi, M., et al.: A hybrid secure computation framework for machine learning applications. In: Proceedings of the ACM Asia Conference on CCS (2017)
31. Senyo, P.K., et al.: Digital business ecosystem: literature review and a framework for future research. Int. J. Inform. Manage. **47**, 52–64 (2019)
32. Shamir, A.: How to share a secret. Commun. ACM 612–613 (1979)
33. Smart, N.P., Vercauteren, F.: Fully homomorphic encryption with relatively small key and ciphertext sizes. In: Nguyen, P.Q., Pointcheval, D. (eds.) PKC 2010. LNCS, vol. 6056, pp. 420–443. Springer, Heidelberg (2010). https://doi.org/10.1007/978-3-642-13013-7_25
34. Song, L., et al.: Sok: Training machine learning models over multiple sources with privacy preservation. arXiv preprint arXiv:2012.03386 (2020)
35. Susanto, H., et al.: Digital ecosystem security issues for organizations and governments: Digital ethics and privacy. In: Web 2.0 and Cloud Technologies for Implementing Connected Government, pp. 204–228. IGI Global (2021)
36. Suuronen, S., et al.: A systematic literature review for digital business ecosystems in the manufacturing industry: prerequisites, challenges, and benefits. CIRP J. Manufact. Sci. Technol. **37**, 414–426 (2022)
37. Wang, Y., et al.: An exercise in concurrent software engineering: The music360 digital ecosystem. In: Proceedings of the IEEE Conference on Business Informatics. CBI 2025. IEEE (2025)
38. Wang, Z., et al.: Information-theoretic secure multi-party computation with collusion deterrence. IEEE Trans. Inf. Forensics Secur. **12**(4), 980–995 (2016)
39. WeiLi, H., et al.: Secure multi-party learning: From secure computation to secure learning. Chinese J. Comput. **46**(7), 1494–1512 (2023)
40. White, S.A., et al.: BPMN modeling and reference guide: understanding and using BPMN. Future Strategies Inc. (2008)
41. Wieringa, R., Moralı, A.: Technical action research as a validation method in information systems design science. In: Peffers, K., Rothenberger, M., Kuechler, B. (eds.) DESRIST 2012. LNCS, vol. 7286, pp. 220–238. Springer, Heidelberg (2012). https://doi.org/10.1007/978-3-642-29863-9_17
42. Wirth, F.N., et al.: Easysmpc: a simple but powerful no-code tool for practical secure multiparty computation. BMC Bioinform. **23**(1), 531 (2022)

43. Yao, A.C.C.: How to generate and exchange secrets. In: 27th Annual Symposium on Foundations of Computer Science, pp. 162–167. IEEE (1986)
44. Zhang, Q., et al.: Privacy-preserving deep learning based on multiparty secure computation: a survey. IEEE IOT J. **8**(13), 10412–10429 (2021)
45. Zhao, C., et al.: Secure multi-party computation: theory, practice and applications. Inf. Sci. **476**, 357–372 (2019)

Towards Architectural Coordination of Digital Twin Development in Urban Planning

Marianne Schnellmann[1](✉), Marija Bjeković[2], Henderik A. Proper[1], and Jean-Sébastien Sottet[2]

[1] TU Wien, Vienna, Austria
marianne.schnellmann@tuwien.ac.at
[2] LIST, Esch-sur-Alzette, Luxembourg

Abstract. Digital Twins (DTs) carry the promise of improved decision-making about, as well as monitoring and understanding of, the twinned entity. This makes them an attractive instrument to support the, often complex and multi-faceted, decision-making processes germane to urban planning. DTs require considerable technological investments, as they tend to be data-hungry and computing-intensive. Business-wise, such investments are only meaningful if they really add value to the intended decision-making processes. However, most current DT development approaches primarily focus on the technological potential of DTs within the limited scope of isolated business scenarios, and rarely address trade-offs between costs and benefits towards the business case, let alone the broader implications for IT/IS portfolio management. These broader considerations are crucial in urban planning contexts, which typically involve a broad ecosystem of parties, complex decision-making challenges, and pre-existing technological landscapes. Drawing on the discipline of Enterprise Architecture Management (EAM), this paper argues that *architectural coordination* of DT development initiatives would enable more effective valorisation of DTs potential, and more effective management of DT-related technology within a broader technological landscape. To this end, the paper discusses the vision for and an initial sketch of a specialisation of EAM for DT development.

Keywords: Enterprise Architecture · Architectural Coordination · Digital Twins for Urban Planning · Local Digital Twin

1 Introduction

The concept of Digital Twin (DT) was coined by the National Aeronautics and Space Administration (NASA) [2] in the context of digitally mirroring and predicting the behaviour of spacecraft during space missions[1]. The original definition of DT conceived it as providing a virtual model of a *physical entity*, designed

[1] More specifically, "*The idea of a "digital twin" was born at NASA in the 1960s as a "living model" of the Apollo mission*" [2].

Published by Springer Nature Switzerland AG 2026
H.-G. Fill et al. (Eds.): PoEM 2025, LNBIP 570, pp. 281–297, 2026.
https://doi.org/10.1007/978-3-032-12063-2_18

to collect, transmit, and analyse real-time data, facilitating a bi-directional relationship [18] between the virtual model and its counterpart, to offer real-time monitoring, simulation, and optimisation functions [11] regarding the twinned entity. These *DT functions* are generally enabled by collecting large amounts of data, which are combined with digital models, symbolic and sub-symbolic AI, as well as different optimisation, simulation, and visualisation techniques.

The emergence of industry 4.0 [17] resulted in the exploration of the DT concept in other areas[2], such as e.g. infrastructure, vehicles, environment, and buildings. This also resulted in broadening the scope of entities to be twinned well beyond *physical entities*, to include even complex socio-technical systems (STS) such as in urban planning [31], business processes, and enterprises [22]. In these domains, the capability of DT to analyse large amounts of data, draw insights and visualise them in 2D/3D space adapted to non-technical stakeholders, offers an interesting potential for DTs to *better inform decision-making* pertaining to a twinned entity, allowing to even *actuate* these decisions. In the context of urban planning, DTs are advocated as a particularly promising technology to assist urban planners and policy makers [9,38]. The urban environments in which we live and work involve an increasingly complex web of social, ethical, economic, and ecological needs. Planning these environments involves decision-making processes regarding design and development of land use, planning construction projects, mobility and transportation network management, energy use and production, water and waste management, etc. Nowadays, such decisions face the urgency of balancing the mentioned needs across different systems to leave sustainable and resilient urban environments for future generations. Therefore, making well-informed decisions with high confidence in estimated consequences becomes vital.

Although not specific to urban planning, the major challenge with DTs lies in demonstrating the business value of DTs, which justifies the required technological investments. Twinning requires investments for Internet of Things (IoT) equipment, as well as for serious computing power [46] to store, manipulate and visualise large quantities of data. The efforts of twinning in urban planning settings are typically realised in an ad-hoc manner, focusing on the technological potential of DTs within the scope of an isolated scenario [19]. Insufficient integration of domain knowledge and processes [26] limits the added value of thus developed DT services to the business. Furthermore, due to pre-existing organisational silos, it is not uncommon to observe parallel DT initiatives within the boundaries of a single organisation, which only exacerbates technological fragmentation and functional silos. To fully harness the potential of twinning, a significant change is needed in not only digital capability of organisations involved, but also at operational and strategic levels, governance of technology and data (eco)systems [19,31], as well as decision-making culture of urban planning. Within the information systems (IS) field, the discipline of Enterprise Architecture Management (EAM) is positioned [23,36] as enabling informed decision-making in managing and coordinating structural planning challenges

---

[2] https://awortmann.github.io/research/digital-twins/.

in enterprises and in their portfolio of ISs. EAM provides structured approaches for *architectural coordination* [36], in particular to (1) align technological, information, and organisational architectures towards strategic objectives [39], (2) specify and restrict the design space of solutions towards strategic business needs [10], (3) enable informed decision-making [23,24] regarding the impact of, and roadmaps for, transformation initiatives, (4) coordinate among relevant stakeholders and ensure the overall coherence and alignment of business initiatives [35,36], and (5) govern (digital) transformation programs and projects to ensure their delivery and overall coherence [23,36].

In this paper, we argue that challenges underlying the development and evolution of DTs need to be considered in a broader context, i.e. involving a structured approach of alignment and coordination, such as the ones established by EAM. In this context, and in line with [5], we argue that DTs should not be treated as a monolithic notion, but rather as a paradigm of functions/services provided to 'the business' based on a sophisticated combination of emerging and advanced technologies. As such, DTs can be seen as fundamentally a class of advanced (active) ISs, and treated as an integral part of larger IT/IS portfolio. This makes it more natural to see investments in DTs as being part of a broader portfolio of data collection and processing, embedded in the wider organisational strategy, from which to consider a more (economically and organisationally) sustainable development of DT services. In our view, existing EAM approaches could be (en)able(d) to manage and coordinate the development of (portfolios of) DTs. While we expect to be able to use existing EAM frameworks and associated modelling languages for the development of DTs as a starting point, we do expect a need for specialisations and even extensions to deal with the challenges of DT development in general and of urban planning in particular.

This vision paper provides a first sketch of the ingredients needed for the above-mentioned specialisation/extension. As such, we position this paper at the start of the design science research cycle [51], or in terms of van Aken and Nagel [1], at the *fuzzy front end* of design science, where we are still exploring the specific needs and requirements for a design artifact (i.e. an EAM framework to support the development of DTs in an urban planning context).

The remainder of this paper is structured as follows. Section 2 explores some of the key planning challenges regarding DTs for urban planning. Subsequently, Sect. 3 highlights the value of adopting a broader EAM perspective to effectively address these challenges in terms of *architectural coordination*. To have a better overall understanding of the design trade-offs and possible synergies in a broader IT-landscape context, Sect. 4 explores some of the key functions involved in a DT. This is followed in Sect. 5 by an initial sketch of an EAM framework for DT development in an urban planning context. Finally, Sect. 6 discusses our next steps and concludes the paper.

2 Urban Planning and the Role of Digital Twins

Urban planning (UP) is the process of directing the use and development of land, urban environment, and its infrastructure, the related ecosystem, and human services, to promote sustainable growth, high quality of life, efficient service delivery, and responsible use of natural resources [4]. This involves the coordinated planning of physical structures (e.g. buildings, streets, neighbourhoods), infrastructure systems (e.g. transport, water supply, communication), ecosystem services (e.g. energy, water, food, air quality), human services (e.g. education, healthcare, culture), and administrative functions (e.g. regulatory compliance, public service provision, policy development). The overarching goal of UP is to create resilient, inclusive, and sustainable urban environments that are both liveable and attractive [14]. Nowadays, these environments are made up of an ever more intricate combination of human, physical, and IT-based components. Those "*technological components and social arrangements are so intertwined that their design requires the joint optimisation of technological and social variables*" [3].

With the growing complexity and interconnectedness of systems within UP, comes a growing pressure to ensure planning decisions are well-informed, taking global impacts across different systems into account. This requires delicate trade-offs across a range of relevant needs (sustainability, cost optimisation, safety, social needs, etc.) and stakeholders' concerns. In this context, DTs are seen as a promising technology because of their ability to process large amounts of data, combine the resulting insights with background knowledge, while also allowing for the simulation and visualisation of the effects of different scenarios [38][3]. However, the rate at which decision-makers adopt this technology is still relatively low, due to factors ranging from financial to human ones [33]. DTs still struggle to demonstrate their added value to decision-making: the efforts of twinning are typically realised in an ad-hoc manner, with overly techno-centric focus and a reduced scope and understanding of the requirements of decision-making processes [19]. At the same time, critical reflection on how DTs contribute to broader policy goals and integrated urban solutions remains limited [30]. Next to not enabling to fully materialise the potential of DT technology, this situation induces significant costs and long-term challenges to DTs' socio-economical sustainability [41]. Based on [41] and a selective literature search that does not claim to be complete, we discuss some of these challenges below.

DTs as Isolated Monolithic Systems – DTs are often introduced within narrow case-specific problems without embedding them in a broader socio-technical and governance context [19]. This risks to induce or exacerbate architectural inconsistencies, redundancy, scalability, and maintenance issues [19]. In a UP context, another crucial factor to consider is how DTs constructed with this approach would evolve in light of continuously changing policy requirements.

From a technological perspective, DTs involve different IT components and functions, including sensors and actuators, external data sources, the integration and further processing of data, as well as advanced simulation and user interfacing. Such components and function, may not only be beneficial towards

[3] In this context, Local Digital Twin (LDT) as a notion is coined by [27] as being "*virtual city replicas that make it easier for anyone to visually understand the complex real-time interrelation between different urban factors such as traffic, noise, and environment*".

a specific DT, but also used by other DT initiatives within organisation [19,40], and even other ISs within the broader IT/IS landscape [41].

Furthermore, while a monolithic DT platform may appear technically compelling, the realistic integration of such a system into existing urban governance structures is far from guaranteed, as current institutional arrangements and decision-making processes are often not aligned with centralised, data-driven models. Additionally, a centralised 'single source of truth' DT platform also brings about the risk of (and resistance towards) power centralisation, reduced transparency, or dependency on proprietary technologies [31].

The Lack of User Engagement and Domain Expertise Integration – Applications of DTs in UP are still limited to basic functions such as static data visualisation and near real-time monitoring [37], with their marginal integration into actual decision-making processes. One key obstacle lies in the inherent technical complexity of DTs, which can alienate decision-makers who may lack the required technical background [33]. Without a clear understanding of DT functions and benefits, the perceived complexity of the technology can hinder user engagement and limit DTs' practical application in policy and planning processes. Furthermore, the opaque or 'black-box' nature of predictive algorithms and AI/ML components tends to raise concerns among domain professionals, thereby reducing their willingness to rely on outputs like simulation results for critical decisions [8].

Nonetheless, the involvement of domain experts and other stakeholders throughout the DT lifecycle is crucial, not only to align DT services with decision-making needs but also to embed domain expertise and help establish transparency and trust. As a consequence, DT development approaches cannot remain techno-centric, but need to use a more participatory approach.

Avoiding Fragmented Data Ecosystems – DTs are inherently data-intensive systems. While sensor networks and other data acquisition technologies enable the continuous collection and monitoring of system behaviour, the mere accumulation of data does not automatically translate into value. On the contrary, the integration of large volumes of data – often collected at varying temporal resolutions, in heterogeneous formats, and across multiple levels of abstraction – can significantly exacerbate existing issues of fragmentation within data landscapes [8,26]. This highlights the critical importance of robust data management strategies and the development of well-defined data semantics as foundational elements of effective DT implementation. Next, due to their reliance on high-quality and timely data, DTs require dependable and secure data access, an objective that presents a range of technical challenges, e.g. interoperability, data quality assurance, and cybersecurity. Beyond these technical dimensions, the socio-technical context of DTs in urban planning contexts [9] brings about the intricate questions of data governance. In such cases, the challenges of data access are often shaped less by technical limitations and more by institutional concerns such as data ownership, competitive sensitivities, and the willingness (or reluctance) of actors to share data across organisational boundaries [32,47].

Managing the Necessity and Costs of Organisational Maturation – A purely techno-centric perspective fails to account for the individual (e.g. upskilling) and organisational (e.g. inter-institutional collaboration) learning processes and their associated costs, which are essential for the effective adoption and integration of DTs into policy-making structures and workflows. Also important is the consideration of skills and capability gaps, as input for educational outcomes, to enable a more meaningful digitalization as part of smart urban development [19,31]. The resulting costs, both financial and social, of such *organisational maturation*, are often implicitly expected to be borne by the intended users, including local authorities, institutions, and urban residents. In contrast, we argue that these learning requirements should be systematically embedded into the design and implementation of DTs.

3 Architectural Coordination for DT Development

The previously discussed challenges provide a broad range of concerns towards socio-economically sustainable development and evolution of DTs. As mentioned in the introduction, within the IS field, the discipline of EAM is positioned to meet these challenges by providing a means for *architectural coordination* of DT development. In this section, we discuss what we see as being the key needs for such architectural coordination for DT development in an UP context.

The Need for a Modular Perspective on DTs – In line with the challenge to avoid *DTs as isolated monolithic systems*, and as argued by e.g. [5], to cost-effectively and sustainably realise the potential of DTs, they should be regarded not as a monolithic, stand-alone technology, but rather as a modular assembly of functions/services provided to 'the business', having potentially different levels of service and complementing traditional IS functions. In other words, DTs can be regarded as a special kind of (active) IS, and be managed as an integral part of the IT/IS landscape. The details and implications of such conception of DTs are further elaborated on in Sect. 4. Just as modern information system architectures are expected to be integrated, modular, and interoperable, DTs should also be conceived as components within the broader IT/IS landscape [25]. Furthermore, their development and evolution should be managed against this background and be subject to architectural coordination.

The Need for a Holistic Perspective – Next to the need for a more modular view on DTs, their planning, design, and evolution of DTs should be managed with a comprehensive understanding of the data, technological, business and institutional landscape of the twinned entity. This would not only be beneficial to anticipate integration challenges, but also to identify valuable additional data sources (including historical data from traditional ISs/databases), and certainly aid in managing the challenge of *fragmented data ecosystems*. It is evident that such a holistic perspective also allows for better coordination among parallel DT initiatives within the same technological landscape, avoiding further silo formation and preserving its coherence. This also counts for 'business-IT alignment' concerns in this context: the holistic perspective allows to better relate decision-making requirements to DT services, and establish their business value more clearly. In the UP context, it is important to also take into account diverse cross-functional and/or cross-cutting opportunities in case of complex decisions, where DT services can be particularly valuable. Taking a more holistic perspective on an enterprise within its ecosystem, is a natural part of most EAM approaches, and certainly requires architectural coordination among the relevant stakeholders involved to also ensure *coherence* within the IS/IT landscape in relation to the business activities [35].

The Need for Stakeholder Engagement – Next to taking a holistic approach, it is crucial to ensure the engagement of different stakeholders all along the DT lifecycle process to translate holistic models into a coherent approach [29,35], also ensuring the involvement of 'the right' stakeholders [50]. The challenge of ensuring *lack of user engagement and domain expertise integration* stresses this need even more.

The Need for a Strategic Outlook – The considerable investments in DT technology and the needed organisational maturation can only be justified from a strategic perspective. Required investment should be planned incrementally, in stages, and in line with the expected business value of DTs, to better manage the involved risks [19]. A long-term, i.e. strategic, vision on digital capability also facilitates the effective governance, through establishing roadmaps and translating them into DT developments which can be monitored accordingly. From this perspective, it becomes evident that sustainable development of DTs demands change which resides in the governance space rather than technological space alone. DTs are not about introducing IoT, AI/ML and using their insights for quick gains in isolated domain challenges, they are about creating significant shift in how data, technology and infrastructure are harnessed to anticipate/emerge the business need, and turn it into value [20] while ensuring strategic alignment.

As EAM approaches generally make a clear link to the enterprise's strategy level, architectural coordination can be used to ensure DT developments are embedded in a broader strategic outlook, thus also aiding towards the challenge to leverage synergies from *DTs as isolated monolithic systems*, avoid *fragmented data ecosystems*, and manage *necessity and costs of organisational maturation.*

4 Key Digital Twin Functions

This section elaborates on our conception of DT as a modular assembly of functions/services provided to 'the business' with differing service levels. This conception partially blurs the lines between traditional IS and DTs, suggesting to regard DTs as a class of highly advanced and possibly (re)active IS, whose functions complement the ones of traditional ISs.

At the very core of a DT, we identify two **overarching functions**, namely to (1) ***inform*** users to support them in e.g. decision-making, monitoring, and learning tasks in relation to the twinned entity, e.g. by way of simulation and visualization techniques, and possibly, (2) allow users to ***control***[4] the twinned

[4] Taken in a broad sense, including *influencing*, *changing*, *nudging*, etc.

entity by immediate **actuation**(s), or deferred ones in terms of e.g. trigger rules. The functions that sit 'behind' these are illustrated in Fig. 1, in terms of ***sensing***, ***acting***, ***triggering***, ***deriving*** and ***interacting*** (all marked with a cog-wheel). In the remainder of this section, we will have a closer look at their differing service levels and involved cost/benefit trade-offs.

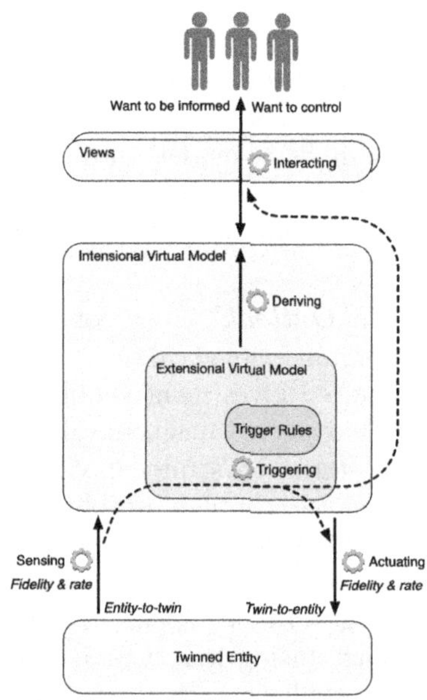

Fig. 1. Overview of key digital twin functions

These functions are enabled by what Jones et al. [18] refers to as the *virtual model* of the twinned entity. The relationship between the virtual model and the entity is bi-directional: by ***sensing***, changes in the twinned entity should result in an update of the virtual model, while changes in the virtual model should result in the ***actuating*** of changes in/of the twinned entity.

The ***sensing*** function should be seen in a broad sense, as ranging from capturing human based observations, inclusion of existing models pertaining to the twinned entity, via inputs of existing data sets, to real-time IoT-sensor based data collecting. Needless to say that behind the term ***sensing*** a world of data integration and harmonisation [42] is 'hidden'.

Both ***sensing*** and ***actuating*** functions may come with requirements regarding *twinning fidelity* and *twinning rate* [18], where *twinning fidelity* refers to the level of correspondence (at a given moment in time) between the virtual model and the twinned entity, while the *twinning rate* refers to the frequency at which the two are kept in sync.

DTs are often divided [21], into those that provide only a *digital model*, or a *digital shadow*, or actually a *'true' digital twin*. In terms of Fig. 1, the distinction is that a DT qua *digital model* has a very low twinning rate on the entity-to-twin side, and basically none on the twin-to-entity side. A DT qua *digital shadow* adds a stronger (IT-enabled) twinning rate on the entity-to-twin side, but has no ambitions regarding the twin-to-entity side. A *'true' digital twin* adds a stronger (again IT-enabled) twinning rate on the twin-to-entity side on top of the latter. Specific choices and requirements on the twinning fidelity and twinning rate will have a significant impact on the architecture of a DT, the insights it may offer to its users, as well as the associated potential costs involved, thus leading to an important cost/benefit trade-off.

The *virtual model* at the core of a DT does share fundamental similarities with the underlying database of (computerised) information system [16], as it essentially constitutes a model of the domain it represents, capturing its state and, often, its historical evolution. However, what distinguishes contemporary DTs from traditional ISs is the integration with IoT devices for ***sensing/actuating*** the twinned entity, as well as an AI-enabled a real-time ***derivation*** function (monitoring, simulation, optimisation) and potentially even combined with automated ***triggering*** of ***actuation***. By incorporating advanced data-fuelled, real-time, and AI-powered functions, DTs go beyond traditional ISs, which serve as a mere repository of the factual data. Another advanced function of DTs, setting them further apart from traditional ISs, is the ability to use the virtual model as a base for a wide range of (what-if) analyses regarding the twinned entity. Such analyses may pertain to the present 'state of affairs' of the twinned entity, as well as its expected/predicted 'states of affairs'.

From a more fundamental perspective, it is relevant to draw a parallel between what Ullman [48] defined as the so-called *extensional database*, being the data that is stored as tuples in a database, and the *intensional database*, involving the extensional data, as well as all data that can be derived from the former data using derivation rules. In the context of DT's virtual model, we argue that, architecturally, one should make a distinction between (1) the *extensional virtual model* corresponding to what is known about the twinned entity (in relation to the chosen level of fidelity) that cannot be derived from other elements in the model, and (2) the *intensional virtual model* pertaining to all things that can (potentially!) be *derived* from the extensional model using any form of analytics (including the use of symbolic and sub-symbolic AI, and/or simulations). The ***deriving*** function in Fig. 1, therefore, refers to the function (e.g. involving symbolic or sub-symbolic AI, optimization techniques, etc.) needed to actually derive relevant parts of the intensional model. Needless to say, that this function potentially requires significant computational power, likely to induce significant costs, resulting in another important cost/benefit trade-off consideration.

A *'true' digital twin* is likely to include a function to, based on sub-symbolic or symbolic *action rules*, pro-actively *trigger* actions when data stream from the twinned entity (and its environment) give rise to do so. The resulting action may involve the ***triggering*** of actuations towards the twinned entity, or notifications towards users (the dashed flow in Fig. 1). Again, a function with its own cost/benefit trade-off.

To enable users of a DT to be ***informed*** about the twinned entity and/or to ***control*** the twinned entity (via DT), they need to ***interact*** with the virtual model. This interaction is typically centred on the use of (focussed) *views* on the virtual model, while making use of advanced user interfaces, involving e.g. 3D rendering, animations, as well as augmented, or virtual, reality based interaction. Needless to say, that such advanced interfacing comes with its own costs-benefit trade-offs.

While each of the DT functions comes with cost-benefit ratios, each of them also comes with opportunities for synergy. Some examples include:

- *Sensing & actuating* – Existing, to be collected, or externally purchased, data collections/streams may be used to feed multiple ISs. The data communication, integration, cleaning, and harmonisation infrastructures needed for both sensing and actuating can potentially be shared among multiple ISs. Additional sources of domain knowledge (e.g. enterprise models, information models, domain ontologies, etc.) can also be utilized as inputs for the virtual model, and/or used to better contextualize other 'raw' data sources [26] from e.g. IoT sensors.
- *Deriving & triggering* – Rulesets, trained neural networks, etc., are likely to be specific to a single DT. However, the 'engines' (rule engines, simulation engines, etc.) these run on, and associated computing infrastructures, can be used as shared infrastructures among ISs – in general, not just DTs – within, and beyond, an enterprise.
- *Interacting* – Again, the views used for the interaction are likely to be DT specific. However, the underlying rendering engines, can be used across different DTs and possibly even ISs in general.

Having a more component-based view on DTs is also supported by recent efforts such as [25], which explore the embedding of DTs into comprehensive digital infrastructures. Aligning with the approach proposed by [40], such a component-based view also enables a progressive development path for DTs: starting from conventional decision-support systems and incrementally enriching them with additional data sources, more sophisticated virtual models, and advanced simulation and optimisation capabilities, thus ultimately evolving toward comprehensive DT-enabled decision-making environments tailored to specific domains and policy challenges. The suggested progressive development path for DTs has to, in our view, be motivated by clear business requirements and priorities, derived from a clear strategic outlook on the digital transformation of the UP (eco)system as a whole.

5 Towards an EAM Framework for DT Development

In Sect. 3, we discussed the need for architectural coordination of DT development for STS in general, and UP in particular. While for this purpose, existing EAM related frameworks and modelling languages could be a starting point, we expect there to be a need for specialisations, and even extensions, specific to the challenges outlined in Sect. 2. In this section, we explore key ingredients for such a specialised EAM framework. Based on e.g. [23,44], the framework should cover at least the following key ingredients:

- a description of the *processes* needed to do architectural coordination, as well as the *roles* (e.g. stakeholders, architects, developers) to be involved,
- an integrated *content framework*, and associated *modelling language(s)*, defining the topics, aspects and concerns, to be addressed,
- *reference models* of the application context (i.c. urban planning), as well as DT related function,
- *architectural roadmaps* for (de-)growing DT function, and
- situation-specific *guidelines and heuristics* for the application of the framework.

In shaping such a framework, we intend to apply the following **key principles**:

- ***Digital twin(ing) as a collection of functional components*** - This principle is a direct consequence of the challenge to avoid *DTs as isolated monolithic systems* (Sect. 2) and the *need for a modular perspective on DTs* (Sect. 3 and Sect. 4). Doing so also requires the *need for a holistic perspective*, in particular a comprehensive understanding of the data, technological, and institutional landscape of the twinned entity. It also requires a *need for a strategic outlook*, when e.g. taking decisions regarding infrastructural investments, to ensure *no regret* decisions.
- ***Embedded in a broader socio-technical ecosystem*** - This principle primarily addresses the challenges of avoiding *fragmented data ecosystems* and ensuring *necessity and costs of organisational maturation*, while answering the *need for a holistic perspective* as well as the *need for stakeholder engagement*. The core of the principles lies in a correct understanding the fabric of (data) ecosystems surrounding a (planned/existing) DT, and goals, interests and concerns of the involved stakeholders [32,47].
- ***Thriving information & control market*** - This principle primarily targets the challenge to manage the *necessity and costs of organisational maturation* as well as the information economical considerations behind the challenge to avoid a *fragmented data ecosystems*. Ultimately, the business case for any DT needs to be based on the added value it provides towards its users. Key in this is to consider a DT from the perspective of an *information & control market*, where demand for information and control (the top of Fig. 1) meets the available services from DTs[5]. Just as an actual marketplace may involve some pro-active marketing, the *information and control* market of DTs can also involve some marketing. For instance, in an UP context, one could imagine to provide insight (to the users) not only of the presently available information (and controls), but also create awareness of the *potential*

[5] This is actually a generalisation of the *information market* [6,7] in an information retrieval sense, as well as (since the heart of a DT is formed by its *virtual model*) an operationalisation of the RoME (Return on Modelling Effort) concept [12,34].

for access to more relevant information and control options. Even more, this could lead to pro-active investments in DT related infrastructures, based on expected needs.

- ***Integrated in a broader dynamic capability*** - This principle addresses the general need to anchor the management of DT development within the broader context of organisational development and change, and more specifically digital transformation [49]. EAM is proven as a valuable instrument to govern such changes, offering its long-term holistic view of the organising logics of processes, systems, and technology [39], enabling decision-making on organisation's projects such that it actually builds capabilities[6] and is not only impacted by immediate needs. For DT projects in UP, this embeddedness in the broader context through architectural coordination will grow in importance as this novel technology gets increasingly explored in UP. Ultimately, it will become crucial to have DTs firmly embedded in the broader *dynamic capability* [43].
- ***Customer engagement*** - The previous principle positions the users of DTs as essentially being 'customers'. This principle makes it explicit that these 'customers' should be deeply engaged in the decision-making and development (priorities) of the DTs. This primarily addresses the challenge to avoid a *lack of user engagement and domain expertise integration* towards the development of the (future) DT. This also entails enabling them to learn about the opportunities (and limitations) of DTs and their development.

The (key) consequences of the above principles towards the design and development of (components of) an envisaged specialised EAM are discussed below.

Processes and Roles – The *embedded in a broader socio-technical ecosystem* and *customer engagement* principles will lead to a stronger focus on the identification of the relevant stakeholders, as well as a need to actually engage them in the architectural decision making process. Starting points for an elaboration of existing EAM approaches can be found in e.g. [29,35].

Furthermore, as a result of the *necessity and costs of organisational maturation*, it will also be necessary to increase the general awareness of the involved stakeholders regarding the use, threats, and opportunities of DTs. In line with the *thriving & control market* principle, the latter will also need to involve the creation of awareness of the (potential) users of DTs of the information, and control, they may potentially have access to, by way of the DTs.

Content Framework and Modelling Languages – Typically, EAM (content) modelling frameworks [44,45,52] cover the essential requirements for design of the enterprise in terms of multiple layers. Typically, involving *business* (ideally both in terms of strategic (e.g. objectives, capabilities, resources) and operational perspectives (e.g. services, processes, functions, roles)), *information* (e.g. information objects, services) [52], *IS/applications* (e.g. application services, functions, components, data) and *physical/infrastructure* layers (e.g. servers, network

[6] For managing and developing DTs in a technology agnostic way, Digital Twin Consortium's *Capabilities Periodic Table* offers some guideline.

connections, operating systems), as well as their mutual dependencies. To cover the specifics of DTs development and management, it is expected that a typical EA modelling framework would need to be expanded at least at the level of:

- *Ecosystem perspective* – The *embedded in a broader socio-technical ecosystem* principle will require models that capture the ecosystem of the planned DTs, in terms of the involved socio-cyber-physical actors and their potential role (e.g. user, supplier of data, etc.).
  Especially for the potential users, it will be important to also quantify (or at least qualify) the added value of the DT towards their tasks. Starting points could, e.g. be existing work on the economics of DTs [46], as well as work on dimensions to define the value of data [13] (data *in use* actually), or more fundamentally, the economics of/behind decision-making [28].
- *Information perspective* – At this level, as with other information services [52] in the IS landscape, it will be important to characterise the added information value DT provides towards decision-making. However, for DTs, there is the additional concerns to be covered, namely the data and model harmonisation concerns, both in terms of technical aspects (towards specific systems/platforms [42]), as well as in terms of link toward decision-making contexts, i.e. clear business case of DT. In line with the *thriving & control market* principle, it will be necessary to explicitly capture the decision-making and monitoring processes, and the potential added value which the DTs may provide to this. We hypothesise also that this information 'world' will have the crucial role in the extended framework, also as a strategy to avoid fragmentation of data.
- *Physical/infrastructure perspective* – For the purpose of architectural coordination between different DTs/ISs, we anticipate that characterisation of IoT sensors/actuators, their locations and objects, gathered 'raw' data, frequencies of their collection would at least be relevant to capture.

Reference Models – We foresee the development of a reference models for urban planning covering topics such as: (1) what urban planning 'is about', i.e. the 'subject of planning', (2) the typical roles/actors related to urban planning, (3) the associated decision-making processes and topics, (4) the potential added value of a DT towards the these decision-making processes, as well as (5) the skills needed regarding the use and development of DTs.

Architectural Roadmaps – In line with work as, e.g. reported in [40] regarding an agile way to 'grow' digital twins, architectural roadmaps can be defined. Such roadmaps would capture possible strategies to gradually grow (and de-grow) DT functions, based on the needs of their users (in relation to the added value to them), and embedded in the larger data ecosystem. Such roadmaps also need to cater for the optimisation of synergies in the IS/IT landscape, as well as *no regret* investments in infrastructure.

Guidelines and Heuristics – Depending on the specific UP context (large city, country, etc.), the more specific social and geographic setting, the maturity level of the organisations involved, etc., one may expect the need for situation [15] specific adjustments and priorities to the generic parts of the framework.

6 Conclusion

In this *vision* paper, we have argued that the development, deployment, and evolution of DTs should be subject of *architectural coordination* within the broader frame of EAM. This proposition comes hand in hand with the elaborated proposition to consider DTs not as monolithic systems, but as a modular assembly of components/services that can be combined and integrated with existing information (systems) architectures. As such, DTs can be considered as fundamentally special kinds of ISs, integrated into a broader (inter-organisational) IT/IS landscape, and their development and evolution managed against this background. The paper discussed different elements and dimensions regarding how such a broader perspective lays ground for a more socio-economically sustainable twinning, in particular in the urban planning context.

The reported results are positioned (in terms of van Aken and Nagel [1]) at the fuzzy front end of the design science research cycle [51]: the specific requirements for a design artifact, namely an EAM framework for DT development in an urban planning context are explored, as discussed in Sect. 5. The next steps of this research include: (1) further refinement of requirements for the framework, through combining the results of our ongoing structured literature review and observations from existing DT projects in UP setting (e.g. the Interreg project Twin4Resilience[7], and (2) the development and validation of the framework. The use cases will support the research process throughout different stages: in terms of refining requirements, or validating the framework or its components. Notwithstanding the generality ambition, the applicability of the targeted framework is, at this point of our research, consciously limited to UP, as the existing and planned use cases originate in this domain.

Acknowledgements. This research was supported in part by the Interreg NWE project Twin4Resilience (https://t4r.nweurope.eu/

References

1. van Aken, J.E., Nagel, A.P.: Organising and Managing the Fuzzy Front End of New Product Development, ECIS Working Paper Series, vol. 04.12. Technische Universiteit Eindhoven (2004)
2. Allen, B.D.: Digital twins and living models at NASA. In: Digital Twin Summit (2021)
3. Bauer, J.M., Herder, P.M.: Designing socio-technical systems. In: Meijers, A. (ed.) Philosophy of Technology and Engineering Sciences, Handbook of the Philosophy of Science. North-Holland (2009)

[7] https://t4r.nweurope.eu.

4. Bibri, S.E., Krogstie, J.: Smart sustainable cities of the future: an extensive interdisciplinary literature review. Sustain. Cities Soc. **31** (2017)
5. Bolton, A., et al.: Gemini principles. Centre for Digital Built Britain (2018)
6. van Bommel, P., van Gils, B., Proper, H.A., van Vliet, M., van der Weide, T.P.: The information market: its basic concepts and its challenges. In: Ngu, A.H.H., Kitsuregawa, M., Neuhold, E.J., Chung, J.-Y., Sheng, Q.Z. (eds.) WISE 2005. LNCS, vol. 3806, pp. 577–583. Springer, Heidelberg (2005). https://doi.org/10.1007/11581062_50
7. van Bommel, P., van Gils, B., Proper, H.A., van Vliet, M., van der Weide, T.P.: Value and the information market. Data Knowl. Eng. **61**(1) (2007)
8. Bukhsh, Z.A., Stipanovic, I.: Predictive maintenance for infrastructure asset management. IT Prof. **22**(5), 40–45 (2020)
9. Ferré-Bigorra, J., Casals, M., Gangolells, M.: The adoption of urban digital twins. Cities **131** (2022)
10. Greefhorst, D., Proper, H.A.: Architecture Principles – The Cornerstones of Enterprise Architecture, TEES, vol. 4. Springer, Heidelberg (2011)
11. Grieves, M., Vickers, J.: Digital twin: mitigating unpredictable, undesirable emergent behavior in complex systems. In: Kahlen, F.-J., Flumerfelt, S., Alves, A. (eds.) Transdisciplinary Perspectives on Complex Systems, pp. 85–113. Springer, Cham (2017). https://doi.org/10.1007/978-3-319-38756-7_4
12. Guizzardi, G., Proper, H.A.: On understanding the value of domain modeling. In: Guizzardi, G., Prince Sales, T., Griffo, C., Fumagalli, M. (eds.) Proceedings of the International Workshop on Value Modelling and Business Ontologies Bolzano, Italy, 4–5 March 2021. CEUR Workshop Proceedings, vol. 2835. CEUR-WS.org (2021)
13. Hafner, M., Mira da Silva, M., Proper, H.A.: Towards a reference ontology for a data valuation business capability. Enterp. Inf. Syst. **18**(7) (2024)
14. Haghani, M., et al.: The landscape and evolution of urban planning science. Cities **136** (2023)
15. Henderson-Sellers, B., Ralyté, J., Ågerfalk, P.J., Rossi, M.: Final summary and future work. In: Situational Method Engineering, pp. 273–274. Springer, Heidelberg (2014). https://doi.org/10.1007/978-3-642-41467-1_11
16. ISO/IEC JTC 1/SC 32 Technical Committee on Data management and interchange: Information Processing Systems – Concepts and Terminology for the Conceptual Schema and the Information Base. Technical Report. ISO/TR 9007:1987, ISO (1987)
17. Javaid, M., Haleem, A., Suman, R.: Digital twin applications toward industry 4.0: a review. Cogn. Rob. **3** (2023)
18. Jones, D., Snider, C., Nassehi, A., Yon, J., Hicks, B.: Characterising the digital twin: a systematic literature review. CIRP J. Manuf. Sci. Technol. **29** (2020)
19. Kawas, D., Conolly, T.: Digital Twin Business Maturity Model. Technical report, Digital Twin Consortium (2024). https://www.digitaltwinconsortium.org/publications/digital-twin-business-maturity-model/
20. Korhonen, J.J.: Degrees of change in enterprises. In: Architectural Coordination of Enterprise Transformation. TEES, pp. 57–70. Springer, Cham (2017). https://doi.org/10.1007/978-3-319-69584-6_6
21. Kritzinger, W., Karner, M., Traar, G., Henjes, J., Sihn, W.: Digital twin in manufacturing: a categorical literature review and classification. IFAC-PapersOnLine **51**(11) (2018)
22. Kulkarni, V., Reddy, S., Clark, T., Proper, H.A.: The AI-Enabled Enterprise. TEES, Springer, Heidelberg (2024). https://doi.org/10.1007/978-3-031-29053-4

23. Op 't Land, M., Proper, H.A., Waage, M., Cloo, J., Steghuis, C.: Enterprise Architecture – Creating Value by Informed Governance. TEES. Springer, Heidelberg (2009). https://doi.org/10.1007/978-3-540-85232-2
24. Lankhorst, M., et al.: Enterprise Architecture at Work: Modeling, Communication and Analysis. TEES, 4th edn. Springer, Heidelberg (2017). https://doi.org/10.1007/978-3-662-53933-0
25. Lick, J., et al.: Digital factory twin: a practioner-driven approach for integrated planning of the enterprise architecture. Procedia CIRP **128** (2024)
26. Mattioli, J., Robic, P.O., Jesson, E.: Information Quality: the cornerstone for AI-based Industry 4.0. Procedia Computer Science **201** (2022)
27. McAleer, S.R., McAleer, M., Kogut, P.: Forging the future of responsive cities through local digital twins. In: ERCIM News (2021)
28. McNamara, J.R.: The economics of decision making in the new manufacturing firm. Manag. Decis. Econ. **13**(4) (1992)
29. Nakakawa, A., van Bommel, P., Proper, H.A., Mulder, H.B.F.: A situational method for creating shared understanding on requirements for an enterprise architecture. Int. J. Cooper. Inf. Syst. **27**(4) (2018)
30. Nochta, T., Wan, L., Schooling, J., Lemanski, C., Parlikad, A., Jin, Y.: Digitalisation for smarter cities: moving from a static to a dynamic view. Proc. Inst. Civil Eng. - Smart Infrastruct. Constr. **171**(4) (2018)
31. Nochta, T., Wan, L., Schooling, J.M., Parlikad, A.K.: A socio-technical perspective on urban analytics: the case of city-scale digital twins. J. Urban Technol. **28**(1–2) (2021)
32. Oliveira, M.I.S., Lóscio, B.F.: What is a data ecosystem? In: Janssen, M., Chun, S.A., Weerakkody, V. (eds.) Proceedings of the 19th Annual International Conference on Digital Government Research: Governance in the Data Age, DG.O 2018, Delft, The Netherlands, 30 May–01 June 2018, dg.o '18. Association for Computing Machinery (2018)
33. Opoku, D.G.J., Perera, S., Osei-Kyei, R., Rashidi, M., Bamdad, K., Famakinwa, T.: Barriers to the adoption of digital twin in the construction industry: a literature review. Informatics **10**(1) (2023)
34. Proper, H.A., Guizzardi, G.: Modeling for enterprises; let's go to RoME ViA RiME. In: Clark, T., Zschaler, S., Barn, B., Sandkuhl, K. (eds.) Proceedings of the Forum at Practice of Enterprise Modeling 2022 (PoEM-Forum 2022) co-located with PoEM 2022, London, United Kingdom, 23–25 November 2022, CEUR Workshop Proceedings, vol. 3327. CEUR-WS.org (2023)
35. Proper, H.A., Wagter, R., Bekel, J.: On enterprise coherence governance with GEA: a 15-year co-evolution of practice and theory. Softw. Syst. Model. **22**(2) (2023)
36. Proper, H.A., Aier, S., Winter, R.: Conclusion and reflections. In: Architectural Coordination of Enterprise Transformation. TEES, pp. 293–304. Springer, Cham (2017). https://doi.org/10.1007/978-3-319-69584-6_26
37. Qi, Q., et al.: Enabling technologies tools for digital twin. J. Manuf. Syst. **58** (2021)
38. Raes, L., Ruston McAleer, S., Croket, I., Kogut, P., Brynskov, M., Lefever, S.: Decide Better: Open and Interoperable Local Digital Twins. Springer, Heidelberg (2025)
39. Ross, J.W., Weill, P., Robertson, D.: Enterprise architecture as strategy: Creating a foundation for business execution. Harvard Business Press (2006)
40. van Schalkwyk, P., Isaacs, D.: Achieving scale through composable and lean digital twins. In: Crespi, N., Drobot, A.T., Minerva, R. (eds.) The Digital Twin. Springer, Heidelberg (2023). https://doi.org/10.1007/978-3-031-21343-4_6

41. Schnellmann, M., Bjeković, M., Proper, H.A., Sottet, J.S.: Towards architectural coordination for digital twins. In: Pufahl, L., Rehse, J.R. (eds.) Proceedings of the 15th International Workshop on Enterprise Modeling and Information Systems Architectures, EMISA 2025, Heilbronn, Germany, 14–16 May 2025, LNI, vol. P-362. Gesellschaft für Informatik (2025)
42. Sottet, J.S., Pruski, C.: Data and model harmonization research challenges in a nation wide digital twin. Systems **11**(2) (2023)
43. Teece, D.J., Pisano, G., Shuen, A.: Dynamic capabilities and strategic management. Strat. Manag. J. **18**(7) (1997)
44. The Open Group: TOGAF Version 9.1. TOGAF Series, Van Haren, Zaltbommel, The Netherlands, 1st edn. (2011)
45. The Open Group: ArchiMate 3.2 Specification. Van Haren, The Netherlands (2024)
46. Thomas, D.: Economics of digital twins: Costs, benefits, and economic decision making. Advanced Manufacturing Series AMS 100-61, National Institute of Standards and Technology (2024)
47. Turki, S., Martin, S., Renault, S.: How open data ecosystems are stimulated? In: Proceedings of the Internationl Conference on Electronic Governance and Open Society: Challenges in Eurasia (2017)
48. Ullman, J.D.: Principles of Database and Knowledge-Base Systems, Volume I, Principles of computer science series, vol. 14. Computer Science Press (1988)
49. Verhoef, P.C., et al.: Digital transformation: a multidisciplinary reflection and research agenda. J. Bus. Res. **122** (2021)
50. Wagter, R., Proper, H.A.: Enterprise coherence governance: involving the right stakeholders. In: Architectural Coordination of Enterprise Transformation. TEES, pp. 99–110. Springer, Cham (2017). https://doi.org/10.1007/978-3-319-69584-6_10
51. Wieringa, R.J.: Statistical difference-making experiments. In: Design Science Methodology for Information Systems and Software Engineering, pp. 295–317. Springer, Heidelberg (2014). https://doi.org/10.1007/978-3-662-43839-8_20
52. van't Wout, J., Waage, M., Hartman, H., Stahlecker, M., Hofman, A.: The Integrated Architecture Framework Explained: Why, What, How. Springer, Heidelberg (2010). https://doi.org/10.1007/978-3-642-11518-9

Formal Security Proof Assurance in Architecture Design for IT/OT Convergence

Massimiliano Masi[1], Giovanni Paolo Sellitto[2], Helder Aranha[3], and Tanja Pavleska[4(✉)]

[1] Autostrade Per L'Italia SpA, Via Bergamini 50, 00118 Rome, Italy
mmasi@autostrade.it
[2] Rome, Italy
[3] Lisbon, Portugal
[4] Jozef Stefan Institute, Jamova 39, 1000 Ljubljana, Slovenia
atanja@e5.ijs.si

Abstract. Cybersecurity in OT environments is challenging, due to persistent threats and legacy systems using outdated protocols. Formal methods can verify protocol correctness, but their assumptions often fail to appear in system design. We propose a methodology that maps protocol specifications to architectural assets and simulates attacker behavior to test these assumptions. Applying our approach to a real OT use case shows how evolving infrastructure can break initial assumptions and create new risks. Simulations reveal attacker paths and support targeted mitigations, aligning formal verification with real-world resilience through an iterative process.

Keywords: formal methods · cybersecurity · protocol specifications · model-driven architecture · IT/OT Convergence

1 Introduction

The introduction of an Information Technology (IT) infrastructure to support Operational Technology (OT), a process known as *IT/OT Convergence*, exposes the previously isolated legacy systems to modern cyber-threats [9], expanding the attack surface.

In an OT environment, availability is of paramount importance and cybersecurity protocols and countermeasures must be carefully designed to ensure that it is preserved, since OT environments often rely on legacy systems, typically certified for long-term use and not easy to take offline. Standards such

G. P. Sellitto and H. Aranha—Independent Scholar.

Published by Springer Nature Switzerland AG 2026
H.-G. Fill et al. (Eds.): PoEM 2025, LNBIP 570, pp. 298–307, 2026.
https://doi.org/10.1007/978-3-032-12063-2_19

as the ISA/IEC 62443 family reflect this difference, inverting the confidentiality/Integrity/Availability (CIA) triad to Availability/Integrity/Confidentiality (AIC).

Model-Driven Design (MDD) is often employed to manage the complexity of introducing new features or system modifications in OT environments [3]. Models enable use of mathematically rigorous techniques to assess the impact of changes before their deployment.

Logic-based reasoning allows to prove security properties under various assumptions. A critical challenge is to ensure that these assumptions are present in the implementation or explicitly carried over into it. The transition from formal proof to real-world implementation hinges on the alignment between formal assumptions and how they are implemented in the architecture.

Existing tools analyze security at the architectural level [7,13], but we lack a systematic mechanism to map formal assumptions to system components. Likewise, protocol-level verification tools rarely address enforcing these assumptions in architecture. This paper fills the gap with a framework that translates formal protocol models into architectural components, enabling simulations to test assumptions and strengthen system resilience.

2 Background and Related Work

Formal methods are rigorous techniques for verifying system properties in a *specification language* grounded in *process algebra* and formal logic [12]. These specifications are analyzed by *model checkers*, which explore all possible system behaviors to determine if said properties hold. Since full verification is often computationally intractable [10], such methods rely on simplifying *assumptions*. This underlies the motivation for our work: assumptions made during modeling must be enforced architecturally to maintain the proof's validity. For example, if a protocol's security proof assumes confidentiality of a cryptographic key, the architecture must guarantee it through mechanisms like Hardware Security Modules (HSMs) or Trusted Platform Modules (TPMs).

From a **cybersecurity perspective**, formal methods also model adversaries, such as in the Dolev-Yao (DY) model [2], where an attacker has full control of the network and can read, inject, and modify messages. This aligns with the "assume breach" principle of modern frameworks like Zero Trust Network Architecture (ZTNA) [11]. In this setting, the attacker operates over protocol *traces* - symbolic representations of message exchanges - gaining knowledge and possibly breaking confidentiality or authentication guarantees if assumptions are violated.

Several studies call for the need for integrated strategies to manage security risks across complex IT/OT systems. While some focus on enforcement of security assumptions through formal verification [4], others explore automated risk management tailored to IT/OT convergence [14]. Iterative refinement methods, such as access control and privacy enforcement [8] or SySML-based validation [1] also support early integration of security requirements. Further, [6] integrates standardized methodologies (IEC 42010) to align architecture with security expectations. Despite these efforts, most approaches either focus on formal modeling or architectural design, rarely addressing how assumptions from formal verification translate into system architecture. Availability - a critical requirement in OT - is often overlooked. Moreover, most solutions remain IT-centric, limiting their applicability to hybrid and legacy-constrained environments.

To fill this gap, we propose a methodology tailored to IT/OT environments, that bridges formal security protocol verification and architecture-level threat simulation. By mapping elements from formal models into architectural components, we enable simulations that test whether architectural assets uphold the assumptions. This supports iterative threat modeling and the application of targeted mitigations, reinforcing security and availability in IT/OT convergence.

In our work, **architecture models** are structured system representations developed via architectural frameworks. These include *views* defined by stakeholder-specific *viewpoints*, supporting analysis of system-level properties.[1] Given the non-negotiable requirement of availability, it becomes crucial that formally verified protocols are also enforceable in practice. This raised the challenge of *translating process algebra semantics into concrete architectural elements.* The next section introduces a systematic approach to map formal protocol elements (and their assumptions) into architectural models suitable for threat analysis and mitigation planning, addressing this problem.

3 Methodology

The proposed methodology relies on two complementary technologies: a verification tool to formally analyze security protocol correctness against stated goals (Tamarin), and an architectural modeling framework to evaluate security in deployment contexts (Meta-Attack Language).

Tamarin. The Tamarin prover[2] is a symbolic modeling and analysis tool for formal verification of security protocols, which enables the formal specification of protocol behavior, the modeling of adversaries, particularly the DY attacker model, and the expression of desired security properties. The specification language is based on the widely used *Alice-Bob* notation, where a message (m) exchange from Alice (A) to Bob (B) (denoted as $A \rightarrow B : m$) is modeled in Tamarin as a state transition characterized by the *Fact* m. The DY attacker can observe, block, alter, or inject transmitted and received messages (`Out` and `In` Facts, respectively). Architects cannot foresee all vulnerabilities or attacker strategies, but Tamarin enables rigorous exploration of security guarantees under adversarial conditions. Beyond verifying protocol correctness, we use it to inform architectural design by highlighting critical assumptions that must be upheld to ensure system security and availability.

[1] https://www.opengroup.org/architecture/togaf7-doc/arch/.
[2] Available at https://tamarin-prover.com.

MAL-LANG. The Meta Attack Language (MAL-LANG) [7,13] provides a powerful framework for modeling and simulating attacker behavior in relation to architectural assets. It enables the creation of Domain-Specific Languages (DSLs) tailored for specific stakeholder communities, as recommended by ISO/IEC 42010. In this work we utilize the coreLang DSL variant, which defines a rich set of architectural constructs: *host*, *network*, and *communnication channel*; those help verify whether the assumptions made during formal modeling are upheld in practice. An architecture built with these constructs can be "war-gamed" from the attacker's perspective by defining *objectives* - the compromising of critical assets that are meant to be protected.

Formally, the methodology unfolds in two main phases:

Security Protocol Modeling : The process input is a security protocol defined in Alice-Bob notation. This is then translated into Tamarin specifications, where each state transition is encoded as a Tamarin rule, and each business requirement (such as availability and integrity) is represented as a lemma - a formal property to be verified. A verification loop follows, involving: identification of assumptions–model checking–iterative refinement of the model. This cycle continues until all lemmas are successfully proven, ensuring that the protocol behaves according to the requirements under the given assumptions.

Architecture and Threat modeling : Once the protocol is formally proved to comply with business requirements, it is mapped onto a coreLang-based architectural model using MAL. Here, protocol participants are transformed into architectural assets as defined by MAL's coreLang DSL, such as: *ComputeResources*, *DataResources*, *IAM* components, *Networking* elements, *User*, and *Vulnerabilities*.[3] Given the DY attacker model, the network is assumed to be compromised by default. The mapping is then performed as follows:

- Each protocol participant becomes an *Application* running on *Hardware* $\in$ *ComputeResource*.
- Each *ComputeResource* is assigned hardware or software *Vulnerabilitie(s)*.
- Each *Hardware* component is associated with a *PhysicalZone*, representing location and access conditions.
- Each state transition from the original protocol becomes a *ConnectionRule*, modeling communication between participants.
- Each message exchange is translated into a *DataResource*, capturing the flow and sensitivity of data.

Additionally, business requirements and legal constraints are captured in the *Scenario file* (the configuration input to the simulation engine) as *Rewards*, representing the value or impact an attacker gains upon compromising specific assets. Rewards guide the simulation engine to prioritize attack paths toward high-value targets. These mappings represent the transformation from

[3] For a complete list of classes, please refer to: https://github.com/mal-lang.

an algebra-based formal model into an attacker-aware architectural model and are the cornerstone of our methodology.

4 An OT Use Case

To demonstrate the practical application of our methodology, we present a simplified, but real-world OT use case. The source code containing the simulations performed in this use case is available on GitHub.[4]

We consider a scenario in which a *Control Room Operator* issues a command to *actuate a Pump* via a *SCADA* system. The control message *Activate Pump* is recorded and forwarded through a *PLC Interface* to the Pump *PLC* actuator. Communication follows a typical OT protocol, such as Modbus/S, which uses TLS-encrypted frames to ensure confidentiality and authenticity. A key risk-point is the *PLC Interface* particularly as it becomes cloud-exposed resulting from IT/OT convergence. A core requirement is to ensure that the PLC Interface can verify the authenticity of incoming messages, i.e., that they originate from a trusted source.

Formal Model Analysis. Tamarin is fed the security protocol encoded in Alice-Bob notation, treating each message exchange as a state transition:

$$A \rightarrow B : \texttt{'actuate\_60'} \qquad B \rightarrow A : \texttt{'ok'}$$

The model consists of three rules related with the state transitions:

- `SCADA_sends_message`: The SCADA (A) sends an actuation command (`Out` Fact) to the PLC (B). A fresh `nonce` is generated to correlate the message trace, and the Fact `Start()` is triggered to indicate start of protocol execution;
- `PLC_receives_and_responds`: A message (`In` Fact) is received by the PLC. This triggers the Fact `PLCReceives()` and emits the `'ok'` message (`Out` Fact);
- `SCADA_receives_ok`: The SCADA receives the PLC response (`In` Fact), triggering the `Finish()` Fact and marking successful protocol completion.

To verify the correctness of this protocol, two lemmas are defined:
1. Lemma `executable`:

$$\exists\ b, nonce1 : \texttt{Finish}(b, nonce1) \wedge \exists\ a : \texttt{PLCReceives}(a, b, nonce1)$$

asserts that there is at least one execution trace in which the protocol completes successfully, i.e.: the `Finish` event occurs, preceded by a corresponding `PLCReceives` event involving the same participants a, b and $nonce1$.

2. Lemma `authentic`:

$$\forall\ a, b, nonce1\ : \{\textit{trace exists with}\ \texttt{PLCReceives}(a, b, nonce1), \texttt{Start}(nonce1)\}$$
$$\nexists\ k1 : K(nonce1)$$

[4] https://github.com/mascanc/mal-tamarin-assumptions/.

aims to prove that no attacker can gain knowledge (K) of the nonce under any valid trace involving a *Start* and *PLCReceives* event. As the network is considered fully compromised (as per the DY model), this property does not hold: as shown in the Tamarin diagram in Fig. 1, a passive attacker observing the network can intercept and extract the nonce, which we use as a modeling proxy for the channel contents. This demonstrates that unless a secure channel is explicitly modeled, the attacker is assumed to have full visibility of messages in transit. We therefore protect both messages under the assumption of a secure communications channel provided with TLS, which must then be enforced both at the modeling and architectural levels. In *A*-*B* notation:

$$A \rightarrow B : \{'\texttt{actuate\_60}'\}_{TLS} \qquad B \rightarrow A : \{'\texttt{ok}'\}_{TLS}$$

Since a formally proven TLS 1.3 model already exists, we adopt it into Tamarin by replacing all `In` and `Out` Facts with `In_S` and `Out_S`, simulating authenticated and encrypted message exchanges [5]. This captures TLS main security properties without adding further complexity. It does not address replay attacks though, which must be mitigated separately.

We make these assumptions explicit in and from the model:

Assumption 1: *The communication channel between SCADA and the PLC Interface is secured using TLS, ensuring authentication of message origin and confidentiality of the data in transit.*

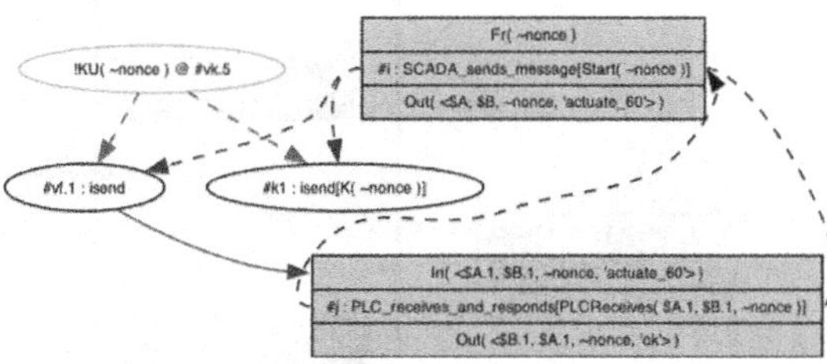

Fig. 1. Tamarin diagram of the failed proof

This leads to a broader infrastructural requirement as a second assumption.

Assumption 2: *A complete PKI is available, including a CA, an RA, a DNS, and NTP synchronization. These components are required to issue, validate and restore the certificates required to establish and maintain TLS connections.*

This simplification shifts enforcement to the architecture. Even if formal proofs hold, simulations are needed to verify that real-world conditions uphold assumptions and security guarantees. This leads to a third assumption.

Assumption 3: *The protocol participants (SCADA and PLC) must securely store the respective private keys and protect them from being compromised.*

Although Assumption 3 may seem obvious, our model makes it explicit: if the attacker learns of the key the lemma fails, as shown in the Tamarin trace. This turns key secrecy from a vague requirement into a provable assumption that must be enforced architecturally. With core assumptions defined, we can build an architectural model that implements the protocol and embeds the assumptions.

Architectural Modeling of the Protocol. We start by mapping the protocol's *process logic* from the formal model to a MAL/coreLang representation. Each protocol participant is modeled as an *Application*, executed via a *SysExecution* component on a *Hardware* platform. Communications between participants are captured through `NetworkExposure` over a `CompromisedNetwork`, following the DY attacker model. The *ActivatePump* message is represented as a bidirectional `ConnectionRule`, reflecting its flow and potential exposure. The MAL components above are outlined in blue in the general architecture depicted in Fig. 2, obtained with the `MAL-GUI` tool. The attacker is instantiated as a DY adversary, placed in a man-in-the-middle position to intercept and tamper with network traffic.

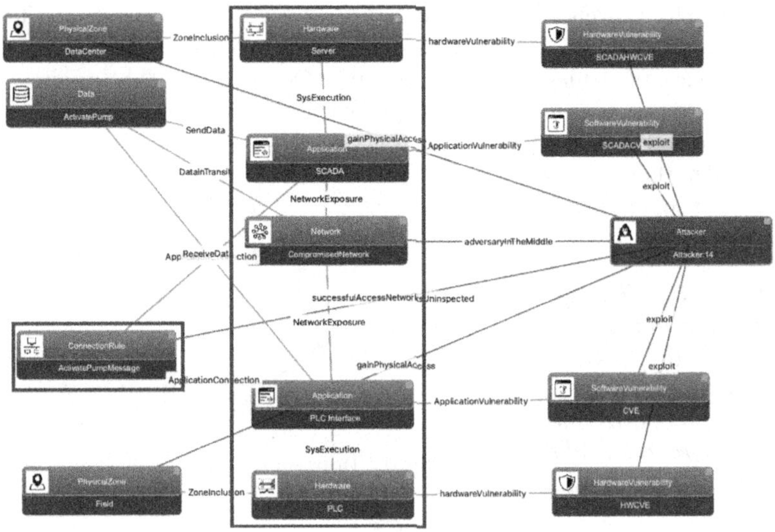

Fig. 2. Use case cybersecurity architecture view

For clarity, we assume Assumptions 1 and 2 are already provided in the environment. The focus of the architectural enforcement then shifts to Assumption 3, which requires implementation of mechanisms that guarantee the secrecy of private keys within the SCADA and PLC components. This sets the stage for applying risk-based mitigation to harden the architectural components responsible for key storage and protect against key extraction by a potential attacker.

Modeling Threats and Countermeasures. To enable a realistic simulation of adversarial behavior, the attack surface is extended as follows:

- For each *Application*, a corresponding SoftwareVulnerability may be exploited by the *Attacker*;

- For each *Hardware*, a HardwareVulnerability introduces potential physical or firmware-level exploits;
- Each *Hardware* element is placed within a `PhysicalZone`, which the attacker may attempt to breach (GetPhysicalAccess);
- For each `ConnectionRule`, the *Attacker* can successfully access the network.

This enables threat simulations on the extended model, showing how an attacker might progress through the system via lateral movements. The resulting architecture, reflecting these extended threat paths, is illustrated in Fig. 2.

We employ the tool `MAL-SIM` to execute the simulation. In this scenario, the attacker aims to: 1) Deny the execution of the `ActivatePump` command, and 2) Extract private keys from the `PLC`, by accessing its physical zone. This tests Assumption 3, which requires key secrecy. If the simulation shows that key extraction is feasible, the assumption fails. To mitigate this the architecture must enforce protections, such as equipping the PLC with tamper-resistant hardware (TPM or HSM) and adding unidirectional firewalls. Though such measures may incur high costs in large deployments, the simulation justifies them as necessary to uphold the security assumption. An example of mitigation is as follows.

Mitigation 1: *(For devices in the Field Physical Zone to support Assumption* 3) *Devices shall be equipped with anti-tampering protections and a TPM-like solution for secure key storage. Private keys must be provisioned and locked into the device during initial trusted boot by an authorized operator.*

The IT/OT Convergence. To demonstrate how the methodology supports evolving system architectures, we introduce a new business requirement: *Migrating the SCADA system to the cloud.* This shift exposes isolated OT components, particularly the *PLC Interface*, to new cloud-related risks.

As a result, the architecture is updated: the network is modeled as public, and SCADA is now cloud-hosted without physical protections. The revised model is depicted in Fig. 3.

While protections for the PLC remain intact, the simulation reveals that an attacker can now compromise the `ActivatePump` command by targeting the cloud-based SCADA. This breaks Assumption 3, prompting the need for:

Mitigation 2: *(For cloud-based components to support Assumption 3) Cloud-hosted systems shall use an HSM to securely manage and store private keys.*

This should ensure key confidentiality even in multi-tenant environments and restore compliance with the original formal model. The scenario also demonstrates the flexibility of the methodology, showing how business-driven changes can trigger architectural revisions and shift attacker paths in the threat model.

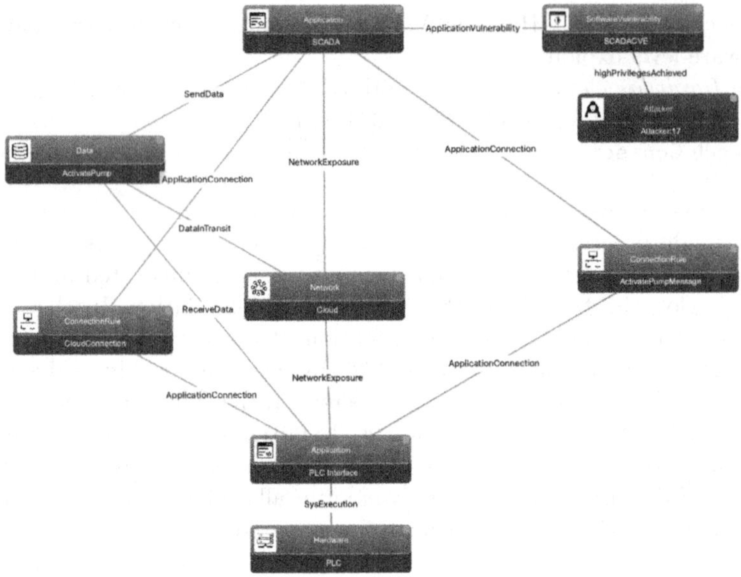

Fig. 3. Evolution: Cybersecurity architecture view with cloud-hosted SCADA

5 Conclusion

This paper presented a methodology linking protocol verification with architectural modeling to ensure formal assumptions hold in real-world OT systems. By mapping protocol elements to MAL `coreLang`, we enable simulation-based validation of protocol logic, assumptions, and requirements under attack scenarios. A real-world use case showed how evolving needs can break assumptions; our approach both detects such risks and guides targeted mitigations to preserve security and availability.

References

1. Amiri, A., Steindl, G., Hollerer, S.: Integrated safety and security by design in the it/ot convergence of industrial cyber-physical systems. In: IEEE 7th International Conference on Industrial Cyber-Physical Systems (2024)
2. Dolev, D., Yao, A.: On the security of public key protocols. IEEE Trans. Inf. Theory **29**(2), 198–208 (1983)
3. El Gaoual, Y., Hanine, M.: Critical overview of model driven engineering. In: Innovations in Smart Cities Applications, vol. 7, pp. 87–97. Springer, Cham (2024). https://doi.org/10.1007/978-3-031-54376-0_8
4. Hardin, D.S., Slind, K.L.: Formal synthesis of filter components for use in security-enhancing architectural transformations. In: 2021 IEEE Security and Privacy Workshops (SPW), pp. 111–120 (2021)
5. Hofmeier, X.: Formal analysis of web single-sign on protocols using Tamarin. Technical report, ETH-Zurich (2019)

6. Hosseini, A.M., Sauter, T., Kastner, W.: Integrating security into industrial control system architecture based on iec 42010. In: 2024 IEEE 29th International Conference on Emerging Technologies and Factory Automation (ETFA), pp. 1–8 (2024)
7. Johnson, P., Lagerström, R., Ekstedt, M.: A meta language for threat modeling and attack simulations. In: Proceedings of the 13th International Conference on Availability, Reliability and Security, ARES '18. Association for Computing Machinery, New York (2018)
8. Kammüller, F.: Combining secure system design with risk assessment for iot healthcare systems. In: 2019 IEEE International Conference on Pervasive Computing and Communications Workshops (PerCom Workshops), pp. 961–966 (2019)
9. Maleh, Y.: IT/OT convergence and cyber security. Comput. Fraud Secur. **2021**(12), 13–16 (2021)
10. Van Der Meyden, R., Patra, M.K.: Undecidable cases of model checking probabilistic temporal-epistemic logic. ACM Trans. Comput. Logic **21**(4), 1–26 (2020)
11. Rose, S., Borchert, O., Mitchell, S., Connelly, S.: Zero trust architecture, special publication (NIST SP). Technical report, National Institute of Standards and Technology (2020)
12. ter Beek, M.H.: Review on formal methods for software engineering: Languages, methods, application domains. Form. Asp. Comput. (2025)
13. Wideł, W., Hacks, S., Ekstedt, M., Johnson, P., Lagerström, R.: The meta attack language - a formal description. Comput. Secur. **130**, 103284 (2023)
14. Zahran, B., Hussaini, A., Ali-Gombe, A.: Security of it/ot convergence: design and implementation challenges (2023)

Author Index

Published by Springer Nature Switzerland AG 2026
H.-G. Fill et al. (Eds.): PoEM 2025, LNBIP 570, pp. 309–310, 2026.
https://doi.org/10.1007/978-3-032-12063-2

Made in the USA
Monee, IL
13 September 2026

62975221R00184